ELITES ON TRIAL

RESEARCH IN THE SOCIOLOGY OF ORGANIZATIONS

Series Editor: Michael Lounsbury

Recent Volumes:

Volume 30A:	Markets on Trial: The Economic Sociology of the US Financial Crisis: Part A
Volume 30B:	Markets on Trial: The Economic Sociology of the US Financial Crisis: Part B
Volume 31:	Categories in Markets: Origins and Evolution
Volume 32:	Philosophy and Organization Theory
Volume 33:	Communities and Organizations
Volume 34:	Rethinking Power in Organizations, Institutions, and Markets
Volume 35:	Reinventing Hierarchy and Bureaucracy – From the Bureau to Network Organizations
Volume 36:	The Garbage Can Model of Organizational Choice – Looking Forward at Forty
Volume 37:	Managing 'Human Resources' by Exploiting and Exploring People's Potentials
Volume 38:	Configurational Theory and Methods in Organizational Research
Volume 39A:	Institutional Logics in Action, Part A
Volume 39B:	Institutional Logics in Action, Part B
Volume 40:	Contemporary Perspectives on Organizational Social Networks
Volume 41:	Religion and Organization Theory
Volume 42:	Organizational Transformation and Scientific Change: The Impact of Institutional Restructuring on Universities and Intellectual Innovation

RESEARCH IN THE SOCIOLOGY OF ORGANIZATIONS
VOLUME 43

ELITES ON TRIAL

EDITED BY

GLENN MORGAN
Cardiff Business School, UK

PAUL HIRSCH
Northwestern University, USA

SIGRID QUACK
Universität Duisburg-Essen, Germany

United Kingdom – North America – Japan
India – Malaysia – China

Emerald Group Publishing Limited
Howard House, Wagon Lane, Bingley BD16 1WA, UK

First edition 2015

Copyright © 2015 Emerald Group Publishing Limited

Reprints and permissions service
Contact: permissions@emeraldinsight.com

No part of this book may be reproduced, stored in a retrieval system, transmitted in any form or by any means electronic, mechanical, photocopying, recording or otherwise without either the prior written permission of the publisher or a licence permitting restricted copying issued in the UK by The Copyright Licensing Agency and in the USA by The Copyright Clearance Center. Any opinions expressed in the chapters are those of the authors. Whilst Emerald makes every effort to ensure the quality and accuracy of its content, Emerald makes no representation implied or otherwise, as to the chapters' suitability and application and disclaims any warranties, express or implied, to their use.

British Library Cataloguing in Publication Data
A catalogue record for this book is available from the British Library

ISBN: 978-1-78441-680-5
ISSN: 0733-558X (Series)

ISOQAR certified Management System, awarded to Emerald for adherence to Environmental standard ISO 14001:2004.

Certificate Number 1985
ISO 14001

INVESTOR IN PEOPLE

CONTENTS

LIST OF CONTRIBUTORS	ix
ADVISORY BOARD	xiii

ELITES ON TRIAL: INTRODUCTION *Glenn Morgan, Paul Hirsch and Sigrid Quack*	1

THE NEW CONTEXT OF ELITES: NEO-LIBERALISM AND GLOBALIZATION

THE RISE OF THE 1%: AN ORGANIZATIONAL EXPLANATION *Jonathan Murphy and Hugh Willmott*	25
ELITES, VARIETIES OF CAPITALISM AND THE CRISIS OF NEO-LIBERALISM *Glenn Morgan*	55
THE COUNTER-CYCLICAL CHARACTER OF THE ELITE *Shamus Rahman Khan*	81

THE FIELD OF POWER: THE CHANGING NATURE OF ELITE NETWORKS

UNDERSTANDING THE CHANGING NATURE OF THE RELATIONSHIP BETWEEN THE STATE AND BUSINESS ELITES *Ali Ergur, Sibel Yamak and Mustafa Özbilgin*	107

IMPACTS OF GLOBALIZATION PROCESSES ON THE
SWISS NATIONAL BUSINESS ELITE COMMUNITY:
A DIACHRONIC ANALYSIS OF SWISS LARGE
CORPORATIONS (1980–2010)
Eric Davoine, Stéphanie Ginalski, André Mach and   *131*
Claudio Ravasi

THE EURO ZONE CORPORATE ELITE AT THE CLIFF
EDGE (2005–2008): A NEW APPROACH OF
TRANSNATIONAL INTERLOCKING
Antoine Vion, François-Xavier Dudouet and Eric Grémont   *165*

BUSINESS ELITES AND THE FIELD OF POWER IN
FRANCE
Mairi Maclean, Charles Harvey and Gerhard Kling   *189*

ELITES AND THE PROBLEM OF LEGITIMACY

THE DEMOCRATIC DILEMMA: ALIGNING FIELDS
OF ELITE INFLUENCE AND POLITICAL EQUALITY
Elisabeth Clemens   *223*

LEGITIMATION STRATEGIES OF CORPORATE
ELITES IN THE FIELD OF LABOR REGULATION:
CHANGING RESPONSES TO GLOBAL FRAMEWORK
AGREEMENTS
Markus Helfen, Elke Schüßler and Sebastian Botzem   *243*

ELITE DISCOURSE AND INSTITUTIONAL
INNOVATION: MAKING THE HYBRID HAPPEN IN
ENGLISH PUBLIC SERVICES
Mike Reed and Mike Wallace   *269*

ELITES AND THE POLITICS OF CRISIS

BUSINESS ELITES AND UNDEMOCRACY IN
BRITAIN: A WORK IN PROGRESS
Andrew Bowman, Julie Froud, Sukhdev Johal,   *305*
Michael Moran and Karel Williams

Contents vii

FROM DESIGNERS TO DOCTRINAIRES: STAFF
RESEARCH AND FISCAL POLICY CHANGE
AT THE IMF
    Cornel Ban *337*

FIGHTING THE FINANCIAL CRISIS: THE SOCIAL
CONSTRUCTION AND DECONSTRUCTION OF
THE FINANCIAL CRISIS IN DENMARK
    Peer Hull Kristensen *371*

FROM CLASSWIDE COHERENCE TO
COMPANY-FOCUSED MANAGEMENT AND
DIRECTOR ENGAGEMENT
    Michael Useem *399*

ABOUT THE AUTHORS *423*

LIST OF CONTRIBUTORS

Cornel Ban	Pardee School for Global Studies, Boston University, Boston, MA, USA
Sebastian Botzem	Institute for Intercultural and International Studies, University of Bremen, Bremen, Germany
Andrew Bowman	University of Manchester, Manchester, UK
Elisabeth Clemens	Department of Sociology, University of Chicago, Chicago, IL, USA
Eric Davoine	Department of Management, University of Fribourg, Fribourg, Switzerland
François-Xavier Dudouet	CNRS - University of Paris Dauphine, Paris, France
Ali Ergur	Sociology Department, Galatasaray University, Istanbul, Turkey
Julie Froud	Manchester Business School, University of Manchester, Manchester, UK
Stéphanie Ginalski	Institute of Economic and Social History, University of Lausanne, Lausanne, Switzerland
Eric Grémont	Political and Economic Structures of Capitalism Observatory (OPESC), Jouaignes, France
Charles Harvey	Newcastle University, Newcastle upon Tyne, UK
Markus Helfen	School of Business and Economics, Management Department, Freie Universität Berlin, Berlin, Germany

Paul Hirsch	Department of Management and Organization, Kellogg School of Management, Northwestern University, Evanston, IL, USA
Sukhdev Johal	School of Business and Management, Queen Mary University of London, London, UK
Shamus Rahman Khan	Department of Sociology, Columbia University, New York, NY, USA
Gerhard Kling	Department of Financial and Management Studies, School of Oriental and African Studies, University of London, London, UK
Peer Hull Kristensen	Department of Business and Politics, Copenhagen Business School, Frederiksberg, Denmark
André Mach	Institute of Political and International Studies, University of Lausanne, Lausanne, Switzerland
Mairi Maclean	Newcastle University Business School, Newcastle University, Newcastle upon Tyne, UK
Michael Moran	Manchester Business School, University of Manchester, Manchester, UK
Glenn Morgan	Cardiff Business School, Cardiff University, Cardiff, Wales, UK
Jonathan Murphy	Cardiff Business School, Cardiff University, Cardiff, Wales, UK
Mustafa Özbilgin	Brunel Business School, Brunel University, Uxbridge, London, UK
Sigrid Quack	Institut für Soziologie, Universität Duisburg-Essen, Duisburg, Germany
Claudio Ravasi	Department of Management, University of Fribourg, Fribourg, Switzerland

List of Contributors

Mike Reed	Cardiff Business School, Cardiff University, Cardiff, Wales, UK
Elke Schüßler	School of Business and Economics, Management Department, Freie Universität Berlin, Berlin, Germany
Michael Useem	Wharton School, University of Pennsylvania, Philadelphia, PA, USA
Antoine Vion	LEST-LabexMed, Aix-Marseille University, Aix-en-Provence Cedex, France
Mike Wallace	Cardiff Business School, Cardiff University, Cardiff, Wales, UK
Karel Williams	Manchester Business School, University of Manchester, Manchester, UK
Hugh Willmott	Cardiff Business School, Cardiff University, Cardiff, Wales, UK
Sibel Yamak	Management Department, Galatasaray University, Istanbul, Turkey

ADVISORY BOARD

SERIES EDITOR

Michael Lounsbury
Associate Dean of Research

Thornton A. Graham Chair
University of Alberta School of Business, Alberta, Canada

ADVISORY BOARD MEMBERS

Howard E. Aldrich
University of North Carolina, USA

Stephen R. Barley
Stanford University, USA

Nicole Biggart
University of California at Davis, USA

Elisabeth S. Clemens
University of Chicago, USA

Jeannette Colyvas
Northwestern University, USA

Barbara Czarniawska
Göteborg University, Sweden

Gerald F. Davis
University of Michigan, USA

Marie-Laure Djelic
ESSEC Business School, France

Frank R. Dobbin
Harvard University, USA

Royston Greenwood
University of Alberta, Canada

Mauro Guillen
The Wharton School, University of Pennsylvania, USA

Paul M. Hirsch
Northwestern University, USA

Brayden King
Northwestern University, USA

Renate Meyer
Vienna University of Economics and Business Administration, Austria

Mark Mizruchi
University of Michigan, USA

Walter W. Powell
Stanford University, USA

Hayagreeva Rao
Stanford University, USA

Marc Schneiberg
Reed College, USA

W. Richard Scott
Stanford University, USA

Haridimos Tsoukas
ALBA, Greece

ELITES ON TRIAL: INTRODUCTION

Glenn Morgan, Paul Hirsch and Sigrid Quack

In 2008, the world entered a new period of turmoil. Financial markets collapsed, banks and other financial institutions went into crisis as their balance sheets quickly moved into the red. As a result, credit dried up, consumption reduced and firms started to cut back and reduce investment in the light of uncertainty. Unemployment increased and welfare payments increased. States that had stepped in to support their banking system now faced a second challenge of how to fund growing expenditure at a time when tax revenues were declining with the fall in economic activity. A combination of borrowing from the financial markets and implementing austerity policies to cut state spending became the norm but it impacted differently in different countries and on different social groups. This book is concerned with what happens when elites are challenged by such a crisis; in our terms, elites are 'on trial', sometimes literally for the criminal part they played in the financial crisis by misleading and defrauding people and institutions but also metaphorically in the sense that they led societies to this crisis. They are thus on trial for their role in the past and in the crisis but they are also on trial in terms of what role they are playing in the aftermath. Can they reestablish their legitimacy or will they fail this trial and find themselves replaced by other groups with different objectives? In order to begin to answer these questions, we need approaches that are comparative across societies, historical across time and relational in the sense of focusing on the interaction between elites and other social groups. This

Elites on Trial
Research in the Sociology of Organizations, Volume 43, 1−21
Copyright © 2015 by Emerald Group Publishing Limited
All rights of reproduction in any form reserved
ISSN: 0733-558X/doi:10.1108/S0733-558X20150000043012

collection draws together a variety of approaches which helps us understand elites on trial.

Yet looking at the field of organization studies, it is a paradox that whilst the concept of power is ubiquitous, the term 'elite' to describe those who exercise power or who are gatekeepers to power resources has been generally overlooked. In the work of C. Wright Mills, however the two terms went together in the study of what he described as 'The Power Elite' (Mills, 1959). Mills, of course, wrote in a specific historical context seeking to understand the United States during the 1950s and the heyday of 'the military-industrial complex'. He sought to make the argument of a close personal connection between the leaders of US corporations, the government and the military. It was a power elite that was relatively small, identifiable at the level of individuals and national in nature, yet this elite was central in the design of institutions, industries and firms. What was crucial to Mills, however, was the way in which this power elite exercised influence over societies that were ostensibly democratic. For him, this influence was exercised in order to sustain the position of the elite even as the broader context changed. Therefore Mills' work suggests that the study of elites is essentially about politics and power and how elites sustain their influence in these circumstances (see the paper in this volume by Bowman et al. for a similar interpretation of Mills' legacy).

Economic and political challenges to the status quo arise from many sources and put elites 'on trial'. Therefore elites are continually engaged in repair and recuperation rather than just reproduction, and have to face the potentially uncertain outcomes of their actions. Repair and recuperation requires intervention directly or indirectly when key challenges emerge that could undermine elite projects. Such challenges can obviously come from social groups within the society that perceive they are losing out because of the existing system; such groups may be new powerful economic interests wanting to force themselves and their interests into the elite or they may be those who feel themselves dispossessed and disadvantaged by the power of the elites. These sorts of challenges to elites are endemic to the interaction between capitalism, markets and the process of creative destruction and crisis as described by Schumpeter on the one side and liberal democratic politics on the other side where ideas of citizenship can be drawn upon to challenge elite interests. Challenges can also come from shifts in the international economy or the international political system, from demographic changes, from new technologies, from the emergence of new sorts of markets (such as the rise of the financial markets) and new sorts of competitors. Social movements and opposition parties might also challenge elites because they consider their politics and policies, or institutional arrangements as inappropriate to changed circumstances. For example, the challenge of climate change has led to increasing efforts by elites to develop global agreements on greenhouse gas reductions using amongst other mechanisms the financial markets through carbon trading. At the 2009 UN-organized Climate Change Conference in Copenhagen, multiple demonstrations against this top-down process were staged including an alternative conference, Klimaforum09, which was attended by about 50,000 people. A People's Declaration was formulated before and during the People's Climate Summit calling for 'System change – not climate change'; meanwhile no agreement was concluded in the main conference. Grassroots transnational movements as well as local and national movements against climate change, against the impact of neo-liberalism and growing inequality, against the loss of indigenous land rights, etc., continue to arise, sometimes in novel and semi-utopian forms (see, e.g. the examples in Parker, Cheney, Fournier, & Land, 2014) and sometimes in loosely coordinated events and networks such as the World Social Forum.

Directly or indirectly, these changes can challenge elites, put them 'on trial' and force them to engage in finding ways to respond that maintain their position. Sustaining the position of the elite is unlikely to mean simple reproduction; instead it is likely to mean some changes for the elite itself, for example changes in its composition and recruitment through the incorporation of new groups that might otherwise become challengers, changes in its key legitimating ideologies and strategies in response to broader cultural trends (e.g. shifting from the defence of privilege to the defence of meritocracy where its cultural resources can be used to ensure it 'wins' the meritocratic race, see Khan, 2012), changes in its economic positioning (e.g. to respond to the growth of finance and within finance to the increased centrality of private organizations such as hedge funds and private equity partnerships). The ability of elites to manage these changes is facilitated by the control of elite groups over forms of capital which are mutable, that is can be exchanged or turned into other forms of capital such as cultural and symbolic capital as described by Bourdieu (2010). Judicious switching of resources at the appropriate time is one of the characteristics of elites; unlike the bulk of the population whose assets are limited and usually fixed, for example in terms of their skills or their economic capital (predominantly embedded into sunken assets such as a house or a pension pot), the assets of elites are much larger and much more flexible over the short, medium and long term. And yet the ways in which and the extent to which elites on trial will be able to reconvert their capital to maintain their influence is an empirically open, yet under-researched question, in particular with regard to the role of these forms of capitals as mediated through organizations.

From this perspective, therefore, the interest in elites is primarily longitudinal and dynamic, understanding their influence as societies struggle with internal and external challenges. Part of their influence is exercised by how they transmute and change themselves in response to struggles and uncertainties. We have to be careful therefore about identifying elites with a single group of individuals characterized by a particular social location and identity because these can change, not least because as Morgan emphasizes in his paper in the volume, elites are deeply embedded within particular forms of capitalism and therefore whilst elites across different countries may share certain goals the structures within which they exercise their influence can be fundamentally different. There is, therefore, a focus on the 'shape-shifting' quality of elites over time that has to be central to our analysis.

It is also evident that much of this shape-shifting lacks visibility most of the time. It occurs gradually, across a number of arenas (ideological change, positional change, organizational change, changes in the international order) until it starts to cohere in a new elite pattern. Is it 'designed' by the elite? It goes without saying that there are many groups intent on 'design'; such groups have varying relationships to elites but some of them can become central to elite reconstruction, as happened with the Mt Pelerin group and its role in pushing free market liberalism back into the centre of elite identity in the West and ejecting Keynsianism. However, as with any project of design, the multiple uncertainties that exist in contemporary societies and economies mean that there are many possibilities for institutional redesign projects to fail, some possibilities for them to be implemented in a compromised form but very few possibilities for them to be implemented outright without amendment.

What makes the present period particularly interesting, however, is that following 30 years of relative success in implementing neo-liberalism that led to much shape-shifting amongst elites (as described in many of the papers in this volume), a massive crisis at the centre of this system (i.e. in the United States and the developed economies and in the financial markets which were the engine of the system) revealed elites that were suddenly and almost overnight (during the frenzied days of the Lehman meltdown) at a loss as to how to respond (Engelen et al., 2012). Rarely before have the living standards of great swathes of the population in the developed economies fallen without this leading to a fundamental destabilization of democratic societies.

The 1930s was the last time this happened and world peace collapsed as democracy itself collapsed in some key countries under the strain of a large disaffected population of unemployed poor and desperate people, being replaced by vicious forms of dictatorship and ethnic populism. In the process, some parts of the old elites were destroyed in places like Germany and Japan and some of those elite groups which had struggled to power in the 1930s and were most directly responsible for the war were literally killed off. Nevertheless even in these circumstances of societal catastrophe, there were continuities; in Germany, some old Nazis and their allies came back relatively quickly and continued in positions of power up into the 1970s. Similar processes occurred in Japan. It seems characteristic at moments of 'trial' for elites that some individuals become scapegoated whilst others with some judicious 'shape-shifting' are able to eventually reestablish or reinvent themselves in the post-crisis period. In the Allied countries, old elites that had presided over the inter-war years and the depression were forced into new compromises both with labour and with new emerging meritocratic groups, a process that was knitted together in different societies through Keynsianism welfarism as a new legitimating ideology and set of practices that shaped firms, states and the international order.

By comparison the years since the Lehman's crash in 2008 have continued to reveal elites in crisis struggling to regain the initiative in an extraordinary period for democratic politics. After an initial period of moderate Keynesianism to reflate the economy led by the G20 meeting under Bush and Brown and later supported by Obama, the crisis mutated into a fiscal crisis of the state (at least for some members of the Eurozone and the United Kingdom) because of the borrowing necessitated to deal with the fall in tax revenue and the rise in welfare payments consequent on the crash. At this point, elites and political parties were able to revive some of the language of neo-liberalism since as financial markets responded to state debts by pushing interest rates higher for sovereign bonds, it became legitimate again to return to arguments about the need to cut back on state expenditure and welfare. As Blyth shows (2013), the discourse of austerity was used as a way of explaining the crisis that took the blame away from the financial markets and the wealthy and placed it instead on the state and on the recipients of welfare.

Austerity as a discourse and set of practices, however, had uncertain outcomes. Some academic economists such as Krugman, Reich Stiglitz and Blanchflower, etc., have continuously challenged the orthodoxy. Some governments were reluctant to fully subscribe, with the US maintaining a modestly Keynesian reflation as far as Obama could negotiate budgets through a resistant Congress and the Fed could use quantitative easing and low interest rates to encourage spending and investment. In some European countries, most notably Greece, elements of the politics of the 1930s have emerged complete with right wing populism and violence. In many countries, populist parties of the right have grown in significance, most obviously, in France with Le Pen's National Front but also in some of the Nordic countries, the United Kingdom and the Netherlands. As the 1930s showed, existing elites often try to use such parties whilst retaining control themselves. This can have dangerous consequences as the traditional right discovered in Germany where Nazism crushed the left but evolved in ways that the old German elites could not control.

By comparison in the current era, the challenge from the traditional social democratic left to the elites in the aftermath of the crisis has not been forthcoming. Only in France has a left-wing government explicitly resisted neo-liberal discourses but it has come under increasing pressure to modify its position as the economy has deteriorated and in March 2014, Hollande replaced his centrist Prime Minister, Jean-Marc Ayrault with the more right leaning Manuel Valls following defeat in local elections. Most social democratic parties have been almost as wedded to the austerity discourse as other parties (see, e.g., in this volume, Kristensen's discussion of the Danish experience of the crisis and its aftermath) though this has in turn opened up a space for newer left parties such as Die Linke in Germany, Syriza in Greece and the Red-Green Alliance in Denmark. In Europe, most governments (of the right or the left) have taken on austerity policies but as these have, contrary to the expectations of their supporters, failed to bring back growth, one can observe a gradual shift away from pure austerity to more differentiated approaches towards economic growth at the World Bank, IMF and EU (see e.g. the discussion by Ban in this volume on the IMF). Nevertheless in the aftermath of the crisis austerity's impact has been cuts to state services and reductions in real wages and employment conditions but at the same time an environment in which elite earnings and wealth have actually begun to power away again from the bulk of the population. Rewards for CEOs and for key actors in the financial sector have increased over the last few years even in a context of austerity and limited economic growth.

How do we understand these processes? This is fundamentally the subject of this book. It is not a general collection of papers on elites but rather a set of contributions which aim to illuminate through studying elites how we reached this moment of crisis, if and how elites have been challenged by the crisis and how elites are trying to manage their way out of it back to some sort of 'normal politics' in which they can 'get back to business' by adapting in various ways to changes and challenges in their environment.

The structure of the book reflects this concern bringing together these themes under the idea of 'elites on trial'. Elites are metaphorically on trial in a number of ways; for their role in the development of a neo-liberal regime which has resulted in fundamental changes in power and inequality; for their role in the financial crisis and in rebuilding the system post-2008. These 'trials' reflect how elites have contributed to and benefitted from the rise of neo-liberalism and globalization over the last three decades as well as the turmoil which has resulted from the financial crash. By providing a comparative and international perspective on these challenges, the volume in its four main sections contributes to placing the study of elites back into the arena of the sociology of organizations since it is through organizations in the public and private sectors that elites exercise their power and influence.

THE NEW CONTEXT OF ELITES: NEO-LIBERALISM AND GLOBALIZATION

The papers in this section explore the wider historical and geographical transformations in the global economy and how this impacts on processes of elite formation. An essential part of these changes concerns the growth of inequality that has occurred over the last 20 years. In his recent monumental book 'Capital', Piketty (2014) has marshaled a mass of evidence to reveal that since the end of the Keynesian era and the rise of neo-liberalism, there has been increasing inequality in many societies. On the one side, wages have been held down and squeezed over this period; the loss of manufacturing jobs to China and elsewhere in Asia has meant that in societies such as the United Kingdom and the United States, there has been a shift to service sector employment. Whilst there is a segment of this which is professional and well-paid there is an even larger segment where wages are low, hours of work variable (going down to zero hours contracts) and terms of employment and employment benefits limited. Trade unions are weak in the service sector outside state employment but even here privatization of state services has meant that wages have declined here as well. Murphy and Willmott's paper analyses these processes from an organizational point of view. In particular it emphasizes the significance of the change from large hierarchical firms to disaggregated global value chains.

Here their argument connects with that of others such as Davis (2009, 2013), and Davis and Cobb (2010) who argue that in the large firms, there tended to be a hierarchy of wages and salaries and this limited the extent of the divide between top and bottom. Once firms are able to outsource to cheap wage countries, their numbers employed shrink dramatically. Lead firms in global value chains place sustained pressure on their suppliers to keep wages down. At home they reward their chief executives more highly linking these rewards to share price. Rather than one single continuous hierarchy, there are now multiple hierarchies with more difference between top and bottom. The growth in inequality, Murphy and Willmott explain, is related to these changes in how firms are organized and this in turn relates to the ability of firms to shift production around the globe to find the cheapest production sites. They relate this to the rise of neo-liberal ideology and the discourse of shareholder value which they show derived from a small and uncertain start in the Keynesian era, later becoming a dominant perspective and in the process building new institutions and markets which gave firms and elites the opportunity to change the balance of power with labour and increase levels of inequality. This is the new context in which elites and inequality are constructed and explains in part the growing divide between the very rich and the rest — the rise of the 1%, Wall Street versus Main Street.

Morgan examines this changing context from a different perspective. Firstly he emphasizes that elites are part of particular forms of capitalism. This gives them distinctive characteristics because they are embedded in social institutions which are predominantly nationally bound. However, they all face similar tasks and problems in terms of legitimating their role and ideology, managing their recruitment, coordinating their activities and communicating to the rest of the population. Drawing on various cases, he shows how this means elites have different characteristics across countries. However, he also notes that there are not infrequently common challenges that arise externally to elites. One set of challenges arises from gradual changes in the nature of the international environment. He discusses how the gradual change from the Keynesian era to neo-liberalism changed the terrain on which elites were constructed and on which they worked. He emphasizes three general features of this new terrain — financialization, internationalization and privatization — and discusses how different national elites sought to respond, adapt and change to this different international environment.

Khan's paper concentrates on the United States and drawing on resources such as Piketty and Bourdieu also examines how the elite has responded to this new environment. He shows how the experience of the last 30 years has been different for the elite compared to the mass of the US population. For the elite, it has been a period of growing income and wealth with the possibility to achieve unimagined wealth in a number of ways ranging from technology start-ups, financial trading through to becoming CEO of a major corporation. By contrast, the mass of the population have seen their earnings stagnate and their debts increase as they struggle to maintain their standard of living. This creates two world views; for the elite, their success is predicated on their own efforts; they see themselves as winners of the meritocratic race and are unsympathetic to the 'losers'. They want to reduce state expenditure on welfare and force individuals to look after themselves and their families. By contrast, Khan argues, most Americans favour some sort of state intervention. For those with an historical memory, the period from the 1950s to the 1970s is seen by the elites as a period of stagnation which needed to be overcome even though for the bulk of the population it remains a sort of 'golden age' of jobs, rising real wages and employment security. For the elite, the current period is characterized by increasing individual opportunities. Drawing on his fascinating study of a high status private school in the United States, Khan shows how this has opened up to a variety of ethnic groups as well as to girls compared to 30 years ago. This opening up has happened through the use of scholarships which allow small numbers of pupils from poor backgrounds to access the elite. In the process, the school has increasingly shifted its official discourse and practice away from family connections, social contacts and a narrow WASP elite towards an emphasis on individual achievement and meritocracy. As Khan points out, however, the reality is that the great majority of pupils are still from the very wealthy. Thus the school's rhetoric of meritocracy conceals the continued influence of wealth. Khan sees this as characterising elite educational institutions more generally in the United States. They imbue their students with the social and cultural capital to succeed whilst obfuscating the role of economic capital as the continued basis for access to these institutions in the first place. Paradoxically, however, it is the elite which now stresses itself as open, not hide bound by traditional markers of distinction in Bourdieu's sense but 'omnicultural'. The future belongs to them because they are open, flexible, entrepreneurial, skilled, educated, cultured. By contrast, the poor are marked by narrowness of vision, lack of culture, parochialism, conservatism − a powerful combination of moral and cultural 'failings' that guarantees failure. Couple Khan's cultural analysis of education with Thelen's recent account of the weakness of the US skills and training system (Thelen, 2014) and a pessimistic picture of an increasingly divided society appears.

THE FIELD OF POWER: THE CHANGING NATURE OF ELITE NETWORKS

This section offers a different perspective on elites and how they have evolved in a number of countries under the impact of neo-liberal politics. The papers in this section mainly draw on data concerning members of the corporate elite defined in terms of directorships of large firms. They all identify a series of changes which have been emerging in these countries as a result of wider international challenges.

Ergur et al. provide a fascinating analysis of changes occurring amongst the Turkish elite. In recent decades, Turkey's economy has been growing significantly, sitting as it does at the intersection of Western Europe, Eastern Europe and the Middle East together with links through Turkic culture and the old Silk Road trading routes across Central Asia and into China which have re-emerged after the collapse of the Sociel Empire. The origins of Turkey as a nation-state go back to the First World War, the collapse of the Ottomans and the rise of Kemal Ataturk and secular Turkish nationalism. Under the Ottomans, business was subordinated to the state and Ataturk followed this model, essentially giving permission to certain business groups to develop but constraining the possibilities for other actors (similar to how the state in South Korea sponsored industry in its push for industrialization). These businesses were dependent on their tight connections to the state, benefitting in terms of protected markets, cheap capital and export credit guarantees. In order to mitigate risks, as they grew they diversified into a variety of very often different sorts of businesses which were held together at the centre by a small group of powerful individuals and families. However, during the 1980s, these conditions changed. Turkey sought to move more into the mainstream of the world economy and began to contemplate joining the European Union. It began to deregulate, encourage limited competition and allow the development of new firms. This particularly benefitted small- and medium-sized producers of textiles, shoes, carpets, etc. manufactured in cheaper labour areas in the middle of the country around the capital Ankara. The growth of these businesses shifted the gravity of economic power away somewhat from Istanbul and the old established business groups and towards new businesses which were more openly Islamic, less wedded to Ataturk's secularism and also less connected to the state, the military and the traditional political parties. Drawing on interviews of members of the main business groups in Turkey, the paper shows how these different elites reached various forms of accommodation with the state which was itself also changing and democratizing with the rise of Islamic parties, in particular the AKP (the Justice and Development Party) and its leader Recep Tayyip Erdogan, who, after a period as Prime Minister, became President of Turkey in 2014. The paper shows, however, that both the old and new elites are now more sceptical and distanced from the state but that as Turkey has opened up, it has become diverse, its elite less unitary than it once was and more divided by issues of Europe, religion, secularism and free markets.

The paper by Davoine et al. offers an account of the changing elite in Switzerland. This is another compelling example of how elites which are strongly embedded in a particular form of capitalism have found that changes in the international system have necessitated internal adaptations. Drawing on an analysis of directors of major Swiss companies between 1980 and 2010, the authors reveal a fundamental change. In the early period, the directors were overwhelmingly Swiss, with a common educational background mainly in Law from prestigious Swiss universities. This common background was reinforced by the Swiss militia system and the fact that directors were often part-time officers in the militias for many years. It was through schooling and the militias that these elite members became known to each other and learnt the same values and culture about how to run Swiss companies – with caution and secrecy! However as these firms sought to internationalize, they opened themselves up to new influences. International shareholders were not interested in maintenance of Swiss national identity or the survival of Swiss companies per se. They emphasized more performance and return to shareholders. The firms began to be more aggressive in terms of acquisitions and activities. Swiss banks in particular expanded overseas using their safe capital on risky endeavours in the financial markets and eventually proving amongst the biggest losers in the aftermath of 2008. Shareholders pressed the Swiss corporations to internationalize their management. As these international managers entered Switzerland, the significance of militia service decreased as did the effects of this common socialization. Swiss managers themselves no longer saw it as essential to their promotion. Nor did they start their careers with law degrees; instead they were increasingly attracted by Economics as a first degree followed by an MBA preferably in a school of international renown either in Switzerland itself (IMD) or abroad. As a result, the Swiss elite transmogrified; it became more international, more shareholder-friendly (which required more transparency) and more business- and economic-oriented. In the process, its interest in Switzerland as an entity declined, its focus now being more on the firms and businesses in which it was embedded (a process similar in nature if smaller in scale to that described for the United States by Mizruchi, 2013 and Useem in his paper in this volume). Whether this may explain some of the changes in Swiss politics towards more populist policies and away from engagement with the European Union is a question that arises from this analysis.

Dudouet et al. are interested in the degree to which the formation of the Eurozone has been accompanied by the development of Eurozone corporate elite. Drawing on an extensive dataset of directors who serve on companies listed in the main stock market indices of France, Germany, the Netherlands, Belgium and Italy in the period from 2005 to 2008, they examine the degree to which directors serve more than one board and if they do the degree to which their positions involve crossing borders and serving on the board of a major company in another European country. The paper draws attention to a number of features of these interlocks. Firstly transnational interlocks remain relatively low but secondly they do vary considerably. An important issue here is the degree of bilateral integration which is occurring between some countries within the Eurozone, for example France and Belgium, and the degree to which other countries, most notably, Italy are increasingly disconnected, whilst the two most powerful economies, France and Germany, are very weakly connected. This variability reflects a series of structural divides between big business in the Eurozone that makes it difficult for this group to act together at the European level as was revealed during the Eurozone crisis when the major actors were states and eventually the European Central Bank. Thus whilst trade integration within the Eurozone is high, at the level of the key decision-making arenas inside large companies integration is weak except in the exceptional case of France and Belgium and appears to be getting weaker as Italy becomes less connected to the others and links between France and German business which are already low seem to be falling further.

Maclean et al. focus specifically on the French elite and how it has been evolving. They emphasize in particular Bourdieu's construct of the *field of power* which has received relatively little attention in the discussion of elites and organizations despite its novelty and theoretical potential. For them, the *field of* power represents the point at which the careers of elite actors transcend organizational boundaries and become about connecting contests within the organization with broader struggles for power in society-at-large. To transcend their particular organizational field, dominant agents must achieve voice beyond the confines of organization and field. The Field of Power sets elite agents from different fields such as health, public administration, politics, intelligentsia, art and culture, law or the media against one another while at the same time providing the necessary structural conditions for them to collaborate through forming time-limited, issue-based coalitions of interests. Through these alliances and networks, elite agents seek to influence societal decision-making processes, resource flows, opinion formation and wider logics of action by strengthening commitment to particular projects or objectives. Drawing on an extensive dataset profiling the careers of members of the French business elite, the paper compares and contrasts those who enter the field of power with those who fail to qualify for membership, exploring why some succeed as 'hyper'-agents while others do not. The alliance of social origin and educational attainment, class and meritocracy, emerges as particularly compelling. The field of power is shown to be relatively variegated and fluid, connecting agents from different life worlds.

ELITES AND THE PROBLEM OF LEGITIMACY

This section explores how elites develop, draw on and seek to defend their legitimacy in the context of challenges from other actors. Clemens' paper takes a long historical perspective on this issue. For Clemens, as for many other authors in the book, there is a fundamental question about the tension between the maintenance of elite sources of advantages and democratic political commitments to equality. She argues that this dilemma has shaped the long-term institutional development of the American polity and the economy, as those with extra-political advantages have sought new forms of political influence that can co-exist with democracy. At times, this can involve subverting rules by using economic power to buy lobbyists, politicians and opinion-makers to ensure the interests of the elite are not threatened. However, Clemens concentrates her attention on another strategy which has been pursued by American business and this is where American elites have also worked at the margins of the formally democratic policy to construct fields of public action that are accepted as public, legitimate and admirable, but not strictly democratic. Corporate philanthropy has been central to these efforts. Organizations like the Community Chest can be understood as practical responses to the constraints of ideological commitments to political egalitarianism. Thus aspects of welfare provision are provided through the creation by business of these organizations. This can be legitimated in terms of private charity and individual responsibility and it keeps the state out, denying the legitimacy of the state to raise taxes from the rich to fund the poor. The rules for eligibility can be set by the private charity and can emphasize 'moral' qualities rather than rights of citizenship as the grounds for receiving help. This line of response to the democratic dilemma is 'constructive' in the non-normative sense that it produces new fields of social action and reconfigures institutional arrangements. By linking economic position to civic influence that is perceived as positive, organizations of this type translate economic power into elevated influence over public affairs through the constitution and stabilization of partially hybridized forms or fields which in turn weakens egalitarian efforts to use the state to redistribute from the rich to the poor.

Helfen et al. focus more directly in their paper on how corporate elites are responding to the challenge of being held responsible for issues of sustainability, including working conditions and workers' rights in global production networks. As an indicator of corporate legitimation strategies, they examine how companies respond to requests by labour representatives to sign Global Framework Agreements (GFAs). These agreements are intended to hold multinational corporations (MNCs) accountable for the implementation of core labour standards across their international operations. Helfen et al. use a field-level approach to the study of transnational struggles over labour regulation that recognizes the fluidity of elites in today's globalized, post-industrial society in which legitimate influence is the outcome of specific interaction patterns in complex webs of relationships. From their perspective, transnational regulatory fields are like other fields spaces of possibilities for both corporate elites and challenging actors. Within these spaces, opportunity structures are created and enacted dynamically in specific actor constellations and with regard to specific regulatory issues. Their findings suggest that while corporate elite's initial reaction to unions mobilizing for a GFA is typically rejection or defiance, they eventually feel compelled to enter negotiations when faced with continuous demands for such agreements. Out of the subsequent interactions, the authors see three different trajectories of legitimation strategies evolving: While many MNCs avoid responsibility altogether, others delegate and shift responsibility, and others again take responsibility for labour standards by signing a GFA. In sum, Helfen et al.'s study suggest that more attention should be paid to the variety in corporate elites' responses to union challenges, and to the sequences of interactions between elites and challenging groups which apart from institutional and contextual factors seem to shape the outcome of the process.

Reed and Wallace examine how elites in the English public service have adapted their legitimation strategies to fit in with the broad thrust of neoliberal policies towards state services, in terms of processes of privatization, contracting out and restructuring. They highlight the unintended consequences of this elite-driven programme of institutional reform arguing that it is realized in the emergence of hybridized regimes of 'polyarchic governance' and their dependence on the emergence of innovative discursive and organizational technologies. Within the latter, 'leaderism' is identified as a hegemonic 'discursive imaginary' that has the potential to connect selected marketization and market control elements of new public management (NPM), network governance, and visionary and shared leadership practices that 'make the hybrid happen' in public services reform. They argue therefore that old ideas of public service and professionalism are not simply replaced by markets, competition and entrepreneurialism as governments implement new strategies and structures. Rather they are combined with new discourses and practices in which senior managers in this reformed public services see themselves as 'leaders', managing processes of organizational change. A whole panoply of management development and training as well as careers has grown up in English public services around the idea of leadership, embodying a notion of dealing with internal and external pressures through providing a direction, a culture, a vision.

ELITES AND THE POLITICS OF CRISIS

This section examines particularly how elites have responded to the financial and economic crisis since 2008, drawing on a number of examples of countries and institutions. Bowman et al. focus on business elites in the United Kingdom and their relationship (or rather lack of relationship) with democracy, what they describe as 'undemocracy'.

They discuss what they describe as the undemocratic agenda setting of elites in Britain and how it has changed politics within a form of capitalism where much is left undisclosed in terms of mechanism and methods. Drawing on C. Wright Mills they ask the crucial question as whether British business elites have, through their relation with political elites, used their power to constrain democratic citizenship? Similar to Morgan's paper, they argue that the power of business elites is most likely conjuncturally specific and geographically bounded with distinct national differences. In the United Kingdom, the outcomes are often contingent and unstable as business elites try to manage democracy; this reflects how the composition and organization of business elites have changed through successive conjunctures, and in particular the growing financialization of the British business elite and what they describe as the 'defenestration' of the productionist elite from the 1980s onwards. They recommend that sectoral level studies can reveal how elites impact on businesses and institutions in ways which sidestep democratic agendas and instead replace them with a focus on profits and shareholder value (for further elaboration and more sectoral case studies, see Bowman et al., 2014). They provide a rich case study of the privatization of the railways in the United Kingdom and the way in which private actors organized to maximize their economic returns from the state whilst pushing back onto the state aspects of the railways business which required high investment but promised low returns (such as the rail infrastructure or some rail routes).

Ban's paper is a careful account of how elites in the IMF responded to the financial crisis. He notes how the more simplistic models of austerity espoused by national governments as well as some sections of the IMF were challenged within the organization. Soon after the Lehman crisis, the International Monetary Fund surprised its critics with a reconsideration of its research and advice on fiscal policy. The paper traces the influence that the Fund's senior management and research elite has had on the recalibration of the IMF's doctrine on fiscal policy. The findings suggest that overall there has been some selective incorporation of unorthodox ideas in the Fund's fiscal doctrine, while the strong thesis that austerity has expansionary effects has been rejected. Indeed, the Fund's new orthodoxy is concerned with the recessionary effects of fiscal consolidation and, more recently, endorses calls for a more progressive adjustment of the costs of fiscal sustainability. These changes notwithstanding, the IMF's adaptive incremental transformation on fiscal policy issues falls short of a paradigm shift and is best conceived of as an important recalibration of the pre-crisis status quo. Nevertheless it reveals the importance of not over-estimating elite ideological cohesion. In some ways, the argument reflects Khan's idea that the US elite is more open and omnicultural than it was and this provides new forms of flexibility, not only to draw in new members but also to be more intellectually open than might be expected. Where elites are myopic, unable to see beyond the confines of a narrow intellectual vision, they may make themselves vulnerable. By making themselves open (within very limited parameters, admittedly) to different views, they potentially offer new experimental ways out of crisis (see e.g. the role performed in the Bank of England and the UK financial sector more generally by critical inside commentators such as Andrew Haldane and Adair Turner as discussed in Erturk, Leaver, Froud, Moran, & Williams, 2012).

Kristensen's paper is concerned to show how the Danish political elite interpreted and responded to the consequences of the 2008 financial crisis for the Danish economy. In particular, the paper describes how this interpretive construction focused primarily on three features of the Danish context to the exclusion of other perspectives: the first was an emphasis on the problems of the financial sector, of interest rates and state finances; the second was that Danish productivity increases were falling behind other comparable countries and part of the solution required new strategies towards labour and unemployment benefits; the third was that the adverse effects of the crisis were causing an increase in government expenditure and a decline in government revenues which was rapidly becoming unsustainable. As a consequence, the Danish elite fell into the broader interpretation of the crisis embedded in the dominant view within the EU institutions as well as amongst the international financial institutions, that a period of austerity and fiscal consolidation was the required remedy, even though this was likely to be pro-cyclical in its effects. However, the paper shows that alternative data which is more reflective of Denmark's position in the global economy and the trajectory and form of its growth over the last decade reveals that the interpretation of the Danish elite has been too narrow and neglects the distinctive roots of Denmark's competitive strengths. Indeed, by responding in the way which they have, the Danish elite is in danger of undermining the very conditions of Denmark's competitiveness. It is an interesting case of an elite which by becoming increasingly tied into international policy-making discourses has lost touch with the specificities of its own national form of capitalism. As a result, the danger is that by pursuing an austerity agenda, it undermines what has made Denmark so successful over the last 20 years, a position reflected in its high ranking in most indices of national competitiveness.

In the final paper, Michael Useem reflects on the changes in the United States elite since he wrote his classic book on The Inner Circle (1986). He argues that the defining features of the American corporate apex have evolved in recent decades from a modest classwide coherence to a more dispersed amalgam of company-focused management and then to greater director engagement in company leadership. The rise of institutional investing had moved executives and directors to focus more on the specific interests of their own firms and less on their common concerns (see Mizruchi, 2013 for a similar argument). More recently, the nation's borders that have long defined its business elite have been giving way to an elite-ness transcending those boundaries. While the classwide sinews of the American business elite are diminishing within the United States, he argues that they have at the same time been strengthening with other national business elites to create a transnational informal network with a modicum of global coherence.

CONCLUSIONS

The papers in this book provide impetus for a renewal of elite research in the sociology of organizations. Through their combination of historical and comparative research, they start to open up the ways in which elites are constituted and recruited, how they exercise their influence and how they are able to legitimate this in an era of liberal democracy. They reveal how elites are deeply embedded in particular social formations but, as many of the papers show, the shift towards a neo-liberal policy paradigm in which finance and financial markets have become crucial has fundamentally altered the terrain on which elites act. The gravity of economic activity has shifted in many developed countries towards finance and this is reflected in where income and wealth can be most rapidly accumulated. In the United Kingdom, old and new elites congregate in the City of London, establishing new products, new markets and new types of firms; they have also found ways of turning these possibilities into new ways of rewarding themselves and stretching degrees of inequality even at a time of austerity and crisis. This reflects the need to focus our attention more on how different forms of organization impact on inequality as discussed for example by Murphy and Willmott in this volume (see also Davis & Cobb, 2010).

Whilst elites are becoming wealthier, however, the context in which this is occurring has become more problematic. Before 2008, it might have been easy to believe that financialization and neo-liberalism had found a way to ensure that most people had an improved standard of living. The key to this was easy credit, enabling even 'subprime' borrowers to buy their own homes. Wages might be stagnating but easy borrowing could fill the gap. In this environment, finance and rising incomes and wealth at the top end might seem justified and legitimate but the financial crisis showed that this was a temporary illusion. When the financial crisis exploded, it revealed a vast array of actions by the elites that had created a network of interrelated and codependent risks (Engelen et al., 2011). Risky loans to sub-prime borrowers had been securitized and then wrapped into complex derivative products which were sold to investors seeking high yield products. Banks leveraged themselves up so that they could engage in more of this business borrowing overnight in order to lend longer-term, an inherently risky venture. Speculators in hedge funds and elsewhere bought Credit default swaps as a bet on the direction in which the market would go over the short and medium term. Many of the participants in the market were borrowing too much without collateral, investing in instruments which were much riskier than they realized and failing to hedge against potential switches in the market. As the sub-prime mortgages went sour, returns to the securitized instruments started to dry up and leveraged banks suddenly found they were unable to renew their short-term borrowing whilst at the same time being unable to liquidate their long-term assets without taking massive losses. For a variety of reasons, Lehmans stood at the centre of this storm in September 2008 and even though many other financial institutions were similarly weak, it was Lehmans that was bankrupted whilst the others were rescued in various ways by their home states. Finance from the great saviour of the Western economies, the great benefactor of their populations, was suddenly stripped of its allure as states pumped huge sums into saving their banks. What sort of elites was had brought the global economy as well as the everyday life of societies to the brink of this collapse?

Whilst this debate led quickly to condemnation of the financial sector in many quarters and an effort to identify the specific ways in which collapse had occurred and regulation had been ineffective, the problem was that discussions about solutions rapidly became highly technical and bogged down in specialist committees in the US Congress, in Basle, in the European Union. The populist backlash against the elites was rarely mobilized in a coherent and effective way. On the contrary as state borrowing increased to deal with the crisis, what might have been a legitimation crisis for those elites which had been the main beneficiaries was turned into a crisis of state finances necessitating austerity measures that impacted predominantly on the growing section of the population dependent on the state for part of their income support. Whilst some members of the elite were offered up as sacrificial lambs to the altar of public opinion (for the extremity of their greed and their arrogance, e.g. Fred Goodwin in the United Kingdom, Dick Fuld in the United States), there was no wholesale 'defenestration' of this elite, to borrow the term of Bowman et al. in this volume. Indeed, even where outright fraud was concerned such as in the LIBOR markets, the US Justice Department followed by their counterparts in other countries increasingly moved away from trying to criminalize individuals and instead negotiated fines with companies that had were implicated in these activities (Taibbi, 2014). If elites were on trial, it was a trial from which as individuals they generally escaped relatively unscathed other than a few unlucky individuals who were made examples of. On the other hand, the prosecution and punishment of elite organizations (most notably in banking where heavy fines have been levied, e.g. in 2012 Barclays were fined £290m for LIBOR rate-fixing or in 2014 Goldman Sachs $1.2m settlement with the US housing regulator for the role it played in the sub-prime mortgage crisis) may indicate a deeper legitimation crisis on the organizational level. Nevertheless there is a deeper sense in which this trial is not over; the disillusion that emerged from the crisis, and the failure of the dominant political parties to offer much other than years more of austerity for the mass of the population whilst the rich grow richer, has led to dissatisfaction with conventional politics. In some countries, this has been directly responsible for violence and in many others it has contributed to the rise of new forms of authoritarian populism often directed at immigrants and ethnic groups. In other countries, like the United Kingdom, it fed into the debate on Scottish independence and what looks like the start of a process of prolonged constitutional uncertainty.

Can existing elites manage their way through these challenges and trials? How will they do so in the light of the challenges to their legitimacy that have emerged over the last few years? What will be the implications of these struggles for distributional inequalities, for welfare systems, for sectoral governance, for politics? To make progress on these issues, we need detailed studies of elites in their own national contexts, how they are interconnected across national boundaries and the degree to which global and transnational elites are being constituted in particular areas, how they are able to reconstitute and renew themselves in the *longue duree* but also in the short-term response to crises. We also need such studies to show how elites influence the structuration of sectors, firms and markets but it is increasingly important to recognize that many of these challenges are arising from shifts at the international level, in terms of the relations between different economies, the way in which capital flows across national boundaries and across different sectors. Part of the power of elites is the power to move assets and resources around and not be locked in to one time and place. Neo-liberalism and its accompanying globalization has made this easier, not just in the sense of enabling easier foreign direct investment or foreign portfolio investing but also in encouraging the growth of offshore (and onshore) tax havens. The studies in this book have revealed the range of interesting questions and debates which can emerge by bringing the concept of elites into our understanding of the contemporary era. We hope it will encourage those already working in this area as well as newcomers to these debates to take this seriously and renew the study of elites within the sociology of organizations.

REFERENCES

Blyth, M. (2013). *Austerity: The history of a dangerous idea*. Oxford: Oxford University Press.
Bourdieu, P. (2010). *Distinction*. London: Routledge.
Bowman, A., Erturk, I., Froud, J., Johal, S. V., Law, J., Leaver, A., ... Williams, K. (2014). *The end of the experiment?* Manchester: Manchester University Press.
Davis, G. F. (2009). *Managed by the markets: How finance re-shaped America*. Oxford: Oxford University Press.
Davis, G. F. (2013). After the corporation? *Politics and Society, 41*(2), 283−308.
Davis, G. F., & Cobb, J. A. (2010). Corporations and economic inequality around the world: The paradox of hierarchy. *Research in Organizational Behavior, 30*, 35−53.
Engelen, E., Erturk, I., Froud, J., Leaver, A., Johal, S., Moran, M., & Williams, K. (2012). Misrule of experts? The financial crisis as elite debacle. *Economy and Society, 41*(3), 360−382.
Engelen, E., Erturk, I., Froud, J., Leaver, A., Moran, M., & Williams, K. (2011). *After the great complacence: Financial crisis and the politics of reform*. Oxford: Oxford University Press.
Erturk, I., Leaver, A., Froud, J., Moran, M., & Williams, K. (2012). Haldane's gambit: Political arithmetic and/or a new metaphor. *Journal of Cultural Economy, 4*(4), 387−404.
Khan, S. R. (2012). *Privilege: The making of an adolescent elite at St Paul's school*. Princeton, NJ: Princeton University Press.
Mill, C. W. (1959). *The power elite*. Oxford: Oxford University Press.
Mizruchi, M. (2013). *The fracturing of the American corporate elite*. Cambridge, MA: Harvard University Press.
Parker, M., Cheney, G., Fournier, V., & Land, C. (Eds.). (2014). *The companion to alternative organization*. London: Routledge.
Piketty, T. (2014). *Capital in the twenty first century*. Cambridge, MA: Harvard University Press.
Taibbi, M. (2014). *The divide: American injustice in the age of the wealth gap*. New York, NY: Scribe Publications.
Thelen, K. (2014). *Varieties of liberalization and the new politics of social solidarity*. Cambridge: Cambridge University Press.
Useem, M. (1986). *The inner circle: Large corporations and the rise of business political activity in the US and UK*. Oxford: Oxford University Press.

THE NEW CONTEXT OF ELITES: NEO-LIBERALISM AND GLOBALIZATION

THE RISE OF THE 1%: AN ORGANIZATIONAL EXPLANATION

Jonathan Murphy and Hugh Willmott

ABSTRACT

The paper adopts an organizational perspective to explore the conditions of possibility of the recent re-emergence of overt class-based discourse on one hand, epitomized by the 'We are the 99%' movement, and the rise on the other hand of a populist, nativist and sometimes overtly fascist right. It is argued that these phenomena, reflecting the increasingly crisis-prone character of global capitalism, the growing gap between rich and poor and a generalized sense of insecurity, are rooted in the dismantling of socially embedded organizations through processes often described as 'financialization', driven by the taken-for-granted dominance of neoliberal ideology. The paper explores the rise to dominance of the neoliberal 'thought style' and its inherent logic in underpinning the dismantling and restructuring of capitalist organization. Its focus is upon transnational value chain capitalism which has rebalanced power relations in favour of a small elite that is able to operate and realize wealth in ways that defy and often succeed in escaping the regulation of nation states.

Keywords: Inequality; insecurity; financialization; transnational value chain capitalism

INTRODUCTION

This paper adopts an organizational perspective to address the re-emergence of overt class antagonisms. It is argued that corporate restructuring is central to the ascendency of the neoliberal model of capitalism and in turn to the destabilization of social order in the advanced capitalist countries. Social relations of production sedimented within relatively stable organizational systems are being supplanted by webs of contractual networks, in which economic relationships — and network membership — can be more rapidly reconfigured to reduce costs and circumvent subaltern resistance. The rise of networked economic processes has consolidated and strengthened the position of elites (the 1%), reflected in a dramatic widening of the gap in income, wealth and power between the 1% and the 99%. This has caused class differentials to sharpen, leading to rising dissatisfaction and diverse forms of resistance on the part of the 99%, ranging from leftist popular movements to rapidly growing nativist and neofascist parties.

There has been inadequate attention within organization scholarship to the relationships between the new organization of capitalism, and class and power relationships. The primary focus in mainstream organization studies is on mechanisms for mobilizing networks to increase profits, although much work within the field of critical organization studies has taken a cultural turn, in which considerations of power and identity are decoupled from political economy. However, an important contribution to understanding the dynamics of class and class conflict in neoliberal capitalism can be made by critical organization studies through reconnecting with issues of perennial concern to critical social science. Specifically, this paper considers the wider sociological implications of restructuring of corporations around short-term contractual networks. Our analysis underlines that organizations are intensely politico-economic arenas of action, and that the development of new, networked corporate forms is central to the evolution and also to the problematic reproduction of class domination in contemporary capitalism.

This chapter begins by tracing the renewed attention to economic inequality that has accompanied the extended international economic crisis. It briefly explores the outcome of the post-organizational economy in terms of growing inequality and particularly the accelerating enrichment of a small elite. It then goes on to examine how wealth is produced and accumulated within capitalism and the role of corporations in that process. It discusses recent changes in the organizing of economic activity and particularly the dismantling of the 'traditional' capitalist corporation and its replacement by the value chain/'nexus of contracts' approach, underpinned by the rise of a newly aggressive finance capitalism. In exploring the conditions of possibility for these changes, it traces the restructuring of economic relationships to the rise of neoliberalism, a creed that has become the dominant political economic thought style (Fleck, 1979) through its assiduous formation and development of an alliance between anti-socialist intellectuals and influential representatives of business interests. After outlining some of the key nodal points in economic organization that has been fashioned and captured by proponents of neoliberalism, it shows how an erosion of terms and conditions of employment has underpinned enhanced elite value extraction. The paper goes on to discuss how the expansion of socially disembedded, value chain capitalism has been facilitated by such mechanisms as transfer pricing and the mobilization of unpaid labour in the creation and branding of products. The paper concludes by summarizing the argument that the neoliberal project to reorganize capitalism by disembedding and dismantling organizations has reversed the immediate post-War trend of declining inequality, shifting power as well as wealth away from the '99%' and towards the '1%', destabilizing the international economy and precipitating the global economic crisis, and provoking re-emergent class antagonisms on the one hand and the scapegoating of vulnerable groups such as immigrants and visible minorities on the other.

Economic Crisis, Growing Inequality and the Re-Emergence of Class Conflict

The international economic crisis that began unfolding overtly in 2007 shows little sign of ending. The overall financial infrastructure of capitalism has been saved, or reprieved, through state bailouts financed through the subsequent imposition of major cutbacks in the social safety net and in state services in numerous countries, most harshly in the European periphery, as countries seek to repay international stabilization loans and respond to cutback-induced recession. Rather perversely, rather than tempering neoliberal policies, the crisis has invited their reaffirmation, resulting in a deepening and hastening of privatization and deregulation as well as a vicious circle of more punitive austerity measures in order to stabilize borrowing costs. By May 2012, 12 European economies were officially in recession (Rooney, 2012), and the Eurozone as a whole remained in recession through 2013.

In this context, for the first time in a generation, radical public discourses have re-emerged. At first, these were often articulated through a familiar leftist discourse that challenged capitalism and its class inequalities. Then, in the latter months of 2011, more populist, elite-inflected slogans proclaiming that 'we are the 99%' were adopted in protests and occupations that spread rapidly around the globe. The self-serving '1%' wase held responsible for causing the crisis and then forcing the '99%' to shoulder the burden of austerity. Meanwhile, the '1%' remained at liberty to enjoy a gilded existence, assisted by the (captured) capitalist state's dilatory efforts to rein in untrammelled tax evasion and avoidance.

On the European periphery, Greece, for example, has faced the brunt of the neoliberal EU 'recovery plan', having been allowed to join the Eurozone and subsequently encouraged to ratchet up its debts in a reckless and possibly illegal manner, for which investment banks and advisors were very well rewarded. As we write (2014), Greece is widely reported to be in a state of social breakdown, with one citizen appealing to the International Criminal Court to intervene in what she describes as a genocide of the population mandated by 'the bond markets' and implemented by an unelected 'technocratic' government imposed on the country by the EU/IMF (Salemi, 2011)[1]. Across Europe, public responses to the pursuit and enforcement of neoliberal policies has centred on the differential treatment of the 1% and the 99%, as was the case with the British government's 2012 budget which reduced taxes for the top 1% while cutting senior citizens' tax allowances and imposing VAT on cheap hot food mainly consumed by working class Britons (Midgely, 2012). Activist groups' campaigns have focused particularly on examples of tax-avoiding corporate elite 'stars' such as Topshop's Sir Philip Green who was enlisted by the UK Conservative-Liberal coalition to advise on cutting government expenditures despite having notoriously deprived the state coffers of substantial revenues through aggressive 'tax efficiency' manoeuvres (Straw, 2010). Despite UK government claims of economic recovery, between 2013 and 2014 food bank usage in that country rose to record levels (Eaton, 2014).

In a sequence redolent of the 1930s, a second phase of citizen resistance has combined the same rejection of elite-imposed market globalization with a nativist and even fascist scapegoating of transnational migrants who, as a consequence, have become doubly victims; first, they have been forced to move from their homelands in search of economic survival, and then they are accused of being feckless welfare cheats, petty criminals and even jihadists (Rooduijn, 2014). European elections of 2014 resulted in breakthroughs for political movements of both far right and far left, ranging from the overtly neo-Nazi Golden Dawn in Greece, to the first place finish of the 'reformed' Holocaust deniers of the French Front National, to the emergence on the Left of Spain's 'indignados' from street movement to electoral force (Leonard, 2014).

Globally, there is a plethora of official data consistently supporting the 'We are the 99%' hypothesis of growing inequality. In the United States, the Congressional Budget Office, examining income trends for the top 1%, found that in 1980 they earned 9.1% of all income, while by 2006 this had risen to 18.8% of total earned income (CBO, 2009). Paul Krugman notes that 'Between 1979 and 2005 the inflation-adjusted, after-tax income of Americans in the middle of the income distribution rose 21 percent. The equivalent number for the richest 0.1 percent rose 400 percent' (Krugman, 2011). Similar trends exist in terms of accrued wealth; in 2010 the United States top one percent owned 40% of all wealth, up from 33% in 1985 (Wolff, 2010).

In the United Kingdom, the Gini coefficient of inequality – a measure comparing incomes at the top of the income distribution with those at the bottom – increased from 26 to 40 in the decade to 2009 (Monbiot, 2011). The income share taken by the top 1% doubled to 14.3% between 1970 and 2005 (OECD, 2011). Sikka (2012) reports that while the bottom half of employees earned 16% of GDP in 1977, this had declined to 10% by 2010, while in the same period the top 10% of earners had increased their share (including bonuses) from 10% to 16%; there had been a direct transfer of income share from the bottom to the top of the class ladder. The OECD also noted that during the past generation the United Kingdom has enjoyed progressively less social mobility and that the social benefits and tax systems have become less effective in redistributing income, not least because in the 30 years between 1981 and 1982 and 2011 and 2012, UK tax revenues as a proportion of GDP declined from 45.5% to 37.8%, reducing the state's ambitions and capacity to deliver equal opportunity (Sikka, 2012).

This phenomenon of a growing gap between elite and average salaries has also occurred within mainstream corporate life. CEO salaries have risen 10 times as fast as those of the workforce as a whole (Hayes & Schaefer, 2009), with in-company ratios of between 250 and 500 times average employee salary not uncommon (Faleye, Reis, & Venkateswaran, 2010). A survey of USA CEO salaries found that average CEO compensation rose by 27% in 2009 (the latest period for which data are available) outstripping share price increases by 10%, bringing into doubt the legitimating argument that elite salaries are tied to share performance (Rushe, 2011).

The growth in inequality has sufficiently captured public attention to result in a surprising 2014 bestseller, Thomas Piketty's dense treatise

Capital in the Twenty-First Century, whose meta-analysis of historical data on income and wealth concludes simply that a 'spectacular increase in inequality largely reflects an unprecedented explosion of very elevated incomes from labour, a veritable separation of the top managers of large firms from the rest of the population' (Piketty, 2014, p. 24). Somewhat overlooked in the debate over Piketty's findings about increasing inequality is his equally important conclusion that while Marx's absolute law of capitalist crisis is inappropriately deterministic (the system and its internal laws are not immutable), the sanguine belief of mainstream economists that the system is self-correcting is equally naïve. There is no reason why destabilizing tendencies associated with rapidly increasing inequality should naturally end. Without reform, Piketty argues, the inequality trend and its attendant deleterious social and economic effects are likely to continue or worsen.

Frank (2010) demonstrates that elite capture of societal resources extends beyond finance and includes key factors in generationally transmittable social capital (Bourdieu, 1987) so that, for example, access to elite education is highly correlated to income and social class (Perry & Francis, 2010; Sodha & Margo, 2010). Both Frank and Stiglitz (2011) conclude that large disparities in market power cause wider social changes that are generally deleterious. The wealthy have less need for collective service provision as they can buy services like education and health care privately. In turn, this leaches resources out of public systems so that education quality declines, and minor or preventable health conditions go untreated. Frank has focused particularly on the dynamic of 'stardom' which has become prevalent. Originating in entertainment fields such as sports and music, mass communications have opened a wide gulf between the incomes of those at the very top in comparison with those even marginally below them in 'marketability' (Appadurai, 1996; Crothers, 2010).

The exponential increase in rewards extracted by those at the very top of the income distribution impacts not only on the working and poorer classes but also on the erstwhile middle class, a group created by the complex embedded system of Fordist capitalism and the regulatory state (Ehrenreich & Ehrenreich, 1977). A stable middle class is widely viewed by (mainstream) development economists as a correlate of parliamentary democracy and strong economic performance (Easterly, 2001). Conversely, the disintegration of the middle class has been closely associated with the rise of fascism (Burris, 1986; Guerin, 1936; Lasswell, 1933; Reich, 1933). In the second decade of the 21st century, there are significant and disturbing parallels with the widespread questioning of the moral legitimacy of the social and economic order, and the rise of populist movements including those built through scapegoating of minorities that were manifest in the social dislocations of the 1930s.

From the Fordist Corporation to Financialized Network Capitalism

The post-war economy was built around the ideal type of the American corporation which internalized much if not all of a production process from product or service conceptualization through production to marketing (Aglietta, 1979; Amin, 1994). Mainstream organization studies has treated this entity as a given, and so has continued to focus on its design, management, and internal life (Daft, 2009; Mintzberg, 1979) as if the golden age, or golden dream, of the great American corporation in the 1950s continued undisturbed. Many proponents of critical organization studies have adopted a more sceptical standpoint but have generally retained the organization as a relevant unit of analysis (Hatch & Cunliffe, 2006).

Mainstream analysis is built around a kernel that embraces an industrial vision of capitalism and represents a functional response to the functional requirement to organize and co-ordinate processes as they become more complex and machinery- and technology-dependent. This thinking is epitomized in Taylorist production systems and their contemporary variants and refinements in which 'soft' systems (e.g. teamworking) are designed with the same mechanistic vision (Young, 1990). 'Scientific management' has delivered industrial productivity and has resulted in a large number of white collar staff responsible for administering its systems (Andrew, 1981), paralleled by a growth in the regulatory state bureaucracy. In this established narrative, organizational design is presented as a largely linear, staged process of growing internal complexity considered necessary in order to expand scale and scope of production, *largely within the vertically integrated organization*, identified as Chandler's (1977) 'visible hand'. Even mainstream iterations of post-Fordist organizational design, in which partnerships and joint ventures are acknowledged to be strategic approaches, emphasize the need for 'explicit collaboration mechanisms' (Anand & Daft, 2007, p. 342); in other words, the necessary re-construction of productive unity even within the 'virtual organization'.

Notably, classic theories of the multinational corporation emphasize a staged development in which the process of internationalization is driven by organizational heft, that is in turn built upon an entrenched managerial hierarchy and upon bureaucratic reproduction. The archetypal (multinational) corporation is presented as *internalizing* productive inputs that in a traditional liberal capitalist model would be sourced through the market (Hymer, 1970). In early transnational capitalism this approach enabled multinational corporations to operate in less developed environments where efficient markets did not exist (Murphy, 2008).

Any capitalist system is based upon the generation of profit (or in the Marxist version, of surplus value), the quest for which drives continuous innovation and enhanced productivity. The archetypal Fordist industrial corporation permitted the concentration, the standardization and the regulation of this process. However, this came at a price for elites (Mizruchi, 2013). Although the concentration of labour in one place permitted not only the measurement and predictability of labour input costs, it also made it possible for workers to organize together to increase their wages, leading to the creation of powerful industrial unions first in the United States and later elsewhere (Preis, 1972). It also resulted in the growth of a substantial managerial overhead in the form of a burgeoning cadre of managers and supervisors hired to operate the Fordist productive system and, increasingly, to administer the social contract benefits wrested from the corporation by organized labour. The management 'problem' inherent in Fordist production was captured by Berle and Means's (1935) classic description of a growing separation of ownership from control, in which company managers are seen as tending to usurp the leadership of shareholders as they organize and develop corporations in ways that enhance and secure the benefits and prospects of the managerial cadre. Berle and Means argue that because corporate managers' power and prestige is derived from the organization, they have a strong incentive to place organizational growth ahead of profitability. The common interest of managers and workers in the Fordist system, therefore, is in a social contract and form of governance which will enable the organization to grow, enhancing the powerful status of managers as the 'captains of industry', and assuring the relative prosperity and security of workers.

In the Anglo-American context, this contract came under pressure during the late 1960s and early 1970s as the Keynesian post-War settlement began to break down, economically and socially, under the weight of its own contradictions. Rising inflation, coupled with increased public expenditure, meant that investment and growth could not keep pace with the rising expectations of workers-as-consumers. State fiscal crisis was then precipitated by the 'oil shock' of the 1970s as soaring energy prices fuelled inflationary pressures, resulting in declining living standards for all but the most protected and well organized of employees. This fiscal crisis signalled the beginning of the demise of the Fordist social contract. It ushered in a new era of global business processes in which mass production is outsourced to locations with repressive labour relations (cf. China) and/or neo-feudal social and economic relationships (cf. India).

When addressing the post-1970s shift in corporate organization, we consider the value chain approach (Gereffi, 2005; Kaplinsky, 1985) to be particularly instructive. In value chain capitalism, strategic attention is placed not on the organization but on the process chain, a network of reconfigurable elements. In the loosened regulatory environment that was established during the 1980s as part of the neoliberal strategy to reverse declining profits and stimulate growth, there are multiple opportunities for value chain reconfiguration, a process that has been described evocatively as 'Lego capitalism' (Berger, 2006). By 1993, Fortune magazine attributed increased profits to corporate modularization (Tully & Welsh, 1993). What has been characterized as a disarticulation process permits the valuation and marketization of ever smaller chunks of the value chain. In turn, disarticulation facilitates outsourcing and also provides various other opportunities for elite enrichment, including the creation of legal firewalls and transfer pricing to secure greater profit realization in low tax jurisdictions (Prechel, 2000; Prechel & Harms, 2007). The phenomenon of disarticulation is associated with the break-up of large corporate entities into smaller units – units that are themselves regularly combined and restructured, traded between holding conglomerates that may have hundreds of small subsidiaries – what Ackroyd (2011) calls 'capital extensive firms' (CEFs), forming part of reconfigurable value-realizing networks. The management of subsidiaries by their holding company is typically hands-off, being primarily directed to meeting financial targets; in this sense 'financialization' represents and is part of a broader phenomenon than the growth of the financial sector of the economy (Krippner, 2005); it is an integral phenomenon of the ascendant neoliberal thought style (Murphy & Ackroyd, 2013). The post-organizational[2] approach treats each element of the value chain as an independently marketable commodity whose assets can either be sweated and sold on or stripped (and possibly rebuilt) for subsequent disposal. This financial(ized) conception of organizations as disarticulated modules in value chains configured by markets for use in value extracting processes is singularly different from the corporeal conception of organization presented in mainstream management texts.

Corporate structures are strongly influenced by state regulation; for example, New Deal era policymakers' understanding of the dangers of the holding company − subsidiary model resulted in legislation that, until repealed, effectively limited the spread of the model (Prechel, 2000). Management of today's holding companies is strategically focussed and elevated apart from management of the process subsidiaries. The holding companies can be structured in a number of different ways; they may be stock-market traded or private firms attracting pension fund, hedge fund and/or private equity investment or they may be owned directly by private investors (Metrick & Yasuda, 2010). The management strategy pursued by holding companies tends to converge with two key characteristics: substantial and growing rewards to executives and expert intermediaries and a recurrent reconfiguration and restructuring of business processes in search of quick profits (Folkman, Froud, Johal, & Williams, 2007). Holding company executives often have considerable shareholdings and are part of an international executive elite. Even large organizations that remain formally intact such as BT have effectively been disembowelled through the wholesale outsourcing of previously internalized functions (Colwill & Gray, 2007), while other former traditional giants have reinvented themselves to fit into the value chain model. IBM, for example, has become a specialist both in providing business process reengineering solutions (Miozzo & Grimshaw, 2011) and in delivering shared (outsourced) services.

These changes form part of the overall process of capitalist reinvention which is typically described in shorthand as financialization. While the term is widely used, there is no common understanding of its core meaning.[3] Here we deploy it to indicate how decisions about the application of industrial capital, as invested in processes which produce and distribute goods and services, has become increasingly geared to the short-term pursuit of shareholder value.

In most accounts of the 'new capitalism', the driving force for the emergence of these financialized models is assumed to be the financial sector itself. Particular attention is placed, for example, on changes in financial sector regulation in the United States − driven by financial sector lobbying − that provided much greater scope for development and marketing of financial instruments (Davis, 2009). The possibility for securitization is in turn often attributed to advances in IT which permit development of far more complex and sophisticated investment modelling than had previously been possible (Shiller, 2003). While these regulatory and technological changes provided the mechanisms whereby a shift towards financial or value chain capitalism could be implemented, *it is argued here that the conditions of possibility for this shift to the 'financialization' of corporations lie in the ascendance of the neoliberal thought style,* and its underpinning of a reinvigorated elite hegemony beginning in the 1970s (Gamble, 2009), that enabled, and indeed invited, the financial sector to become dominant. It is to the rise of neoliberalism that we now turn.

Neoliberalism and the Conditions of Possibility for Value Chain Capitalism

Within any sphere or field of thought, certain ways of viewing the world tend to predominate only to be replaced by other, similarly predominant perspectives. There have been various attempts to explain the process whereby different structuring world views arise and are then replaced. One of the more flexible approaches is the 'thought style' typology conceived by Ludwik Fleck, a Polish mid-20th century biologist who noted that a number of competing broad understandings of the nature of disease structured the way groups of scientists adhering to these competing viewpoints went about creating tests for its presence. The predominance of one perspective over another was not necessarily reflective of the merits of the perspective but was dependent instead on the power, prestige, resources and effective organization of the nuclei of scientists ('thought collectives') adhering to the different 'thought styles'. In other words, the merit attributed to ideas was contingent upon a number of broadly 'political' considerations. From Fleck's perspective, the development of scientific approaches is linked both to power (pre-existing resources) and the assiduousness with which certain thought collectives advocate their approach. Douglas (1986) developed and refined Fleck's ideas by specifying the ways in which thought styles structure thinking about its sphere of interest. Specifically, Douglas underlined how thought styles not only frame the way issues are addressed but also close off alternative and incompatible perspectives. In this light, the emergence of value chain capitalism, and the consequent rebalancing of power and resources towards the elite, can be viewed as an outcome of the establishment of a neoliberal hegemony or thought style that is itself responsive to historical circumstances (Douglas, 1986; Fleck, 1935), echoing Weber's notion of an elective affinity of material and ideal interests.

From the 1940s a small group of economists, including prospective luminaries such as Hayek, von Mises and Milton Friedman, gathered in the Mont Pelerin Society (MPS) (Mirowski & Plehwe, 2009) and in a small number of other think tanks and associations. Supporters of MPS successfully organized the capture of a number of prestigious university economics departments from erstwhile Keynesian domination in America and beyond (van Horn, 2009). By the late 1970s the International Monetary Fund and the World Bank had also come under neoliberal domination, as evidenced in an about-turn in economic development orthodoxy (Kapur, 2000). The subsequent rise of neoliberalism is often presented, particularly by its advocates, as the victory of a disinterested intellectual movement over its adversaries. However, from an early stage, the neoliberal movement was deeply intertwined with business interests that were attracted by the material benefits as well as the ideological confirmation which implementation of the MPS doctrine promised to provide. Financial support was provided directly by politically active businesspeople and indirectly through right-wing foundations established to promote business interests; this occurred on both sides of the Atlantic (Cockett, 1995; Phillips-Fein, 2009).

Neoliberal intellectuals promoted the idea of 'free markets' as an integral part of a philosophic defence against 'the road to serfdom' (Hayek, 2001), but its business supporters welcomed neoliberalism for its potential to restore and extend the power and wealth of established elites in the face of a perceived socialist threat. This can be seen in the MPS debate on monopoly (Van Horn, 2009, 2011) where neoliberals within MPS marginalized classical, old-school liberals such as Jacob Viner, who advocated the break-up of monopolies in order to permit the operation of competitive markets. From the early days of their movement, or thought collective, the neoliberals were conscious advocates of a general right-wing *political* agenda in which the discipline of 'free' markets is *selectively* applied to transform workers into individualized producers and consumers, resulting in a concentration of power in the hands of business elites (Van Horn, 2011). This agenda was reflected both by changing attitudes towards regulation depending on whether it was assessed to facilitate stable profit realization (Prechal & Harms, 2007), and in support by prominent members of MPS for brutal dictatorships such as that of Pinochet in Chile when they were perceived to be pursuing business-friendly policies (Valdes, 1995).

Emergent neoliberalism was remarkable for the breadth of its interests. Quite deliberately, the MPS from its earliest days organized groups and workshops on issues as diverse as macroeconomics, the power of unions, international development, the structure of global governance institutions, etc. Action on these wide-ranging preoccupations added up to a multifaceted assault on the Keynesian class compromise that had underpinned the New Deal in the United States, and subsequently the Bretton Woods system which was established to manage global capitalism after World War II (Helleiner, 1996, p. 3). The various strands of neoliberal initiatives and their interconnections are important in understanding the logic and dynamics of neoliberalized global capitalism (Morgan, 2014; Seabrooke & Wigan, 2014). We will briefly explore six core elements — what Grinspun and Kreklewich (1994) describe as the necessary 'conditioning framework' — of the neoliberal agenda which, we argue, interacted to make value chain capitalism possible; free trade, privatization, marketization, deregulation, restructuring the legal framework of economic relationships and reinventing international development.

A key formal element of the neoliberal agenda is the implementation of *free trade arrangements* at the national, bilateral, regional and global levels (Krueger, 1985). Notwithstanding the impact of free trade on overall national economic performance, it intensifies competition by exposing production processes to international cost comparison. This permits imports from low-wage economies, undercutting prices in developed countries with the (largely invisible) impact of undermining the bargaining power of workers while enhancing the capacity of those in work to consume. Free trade agreements also typically entail limits of the scope of state action, for example, to maintain state-run health care and education systems or to maintain national control of resources like water (Barlow & Clarke, 2002). Free trade is a prerequisite for the creation of transnational business processes and for the operation of value chain capitalism. Notably, the accession of countries such as China to the WTO facilitates FDI and the integration of their citizens' low-wage labour into the global economy.

Privatization of state services is another central element of neoliberalism. While it originated as a response to perceived inefficiencies in state-run productive enterprises, it now extends into the heartland of state services including prisons (Dolovich, 2007) and even waging war (Singer, 2003). Privatization is integrated into the infrastructure of international law, whether through trade agreements as noted above, in the conditionalities of international financial institution support — such as the 'best practice' guidelines of institutions like the OECD,[4] or in accession requirements for transnational projects such as the European Union (Zile & Steinbuka, 2001). Countries bankrupted by the scale of the global economic crisis made possible by neoliberalism which sanctified unchecked financialization are, ironically, required, as a condition of financial support, to engage in further privatizations and other neoliberal restructuring (Gabor, 2010). In most dramatic form, this medicine has been applied in Greece as well as several other Eurozone countries, leading to further economic damage and serious social unrest (Wolff, 2011). Restrictions on state-operated organizations strengthen the neoliberal corporate norm, and privatization typically weakens trade unions and worker protections in general. Frequently, privatized services are disassembled in a series of value chain processes, some of which can be outsourced, including offshore. For example, when British Rail was privatized it was broken up into a variety of processes as well as geographic service companies, with ticket booking and customer enquiries offshored to India (Nadeem, 2009).

Marketization — closely linked to privatization — is typically defined as the introduction of market incentives in public services. Neoliberals such as the Chicago School economist Friedman (1997) urged the introduction of education vouchers, thereby allowing parents of children in State schools to 'choose' their children's school. Marketization changes the nature of the citizen's relationship to the state into one of individualized consumer. The introduction of substantial fees for university education, for example, instrumentalizes learning as a monetary investment that is calculated to reap a financial reward later (Latimer et al., 2011), rather than a social good. Teachers and professors are expected to facilitate students gaining their diplomas and are disciplined through 'measurement by results'. Marketization tends to de-professionalize and potentially proletarianize these employees as their scope for self-regulation, and exercise of discretion, is circumscribed and harnessed to metrics imposed by an elite managerial cadre. Market discipline has of course long been a management tool in the private sector, involving the routinization of tasks, permitting outsourcing and/or deskilling and thereby curtailing labour costs (Braverman, 1974). Public sector marketization expands the opportunities for value chain capitalism and limits or precludes the possibility for alternative models of economic organization.

Financial deregulation, another key demand of neoliberals, underpins the logic of value chain capitalism. Deregulation, combined with currency convertibility and internationally enforceable property rights, permits speedy cross-border capital flows. It thus facilitates rapid reconfiguration of value chains, with operations shifted seamlessly from location to location. Deregulation also simplifies securitization, severing dependence on internal capital reserves, and again permitting business processes to be re-engineered and sold on. Financial deregulation enables elites to easily evade labour rent-seeking efforts by reorganizing the productive process to bypass real and potential resistance points (Soederberg, 2011).

Another important strand of neoliberal activism involves *restructuring legal relationships* to fit neoliberal ideological precepts. In early neoliberalism, two aspects were particularly emphasized: limitation of the freedom of action of trade unions (Hayek, 2001) and definition of property rights to exclude collective initiatives (Alchian & Demsetz, 1973). The objective in both areas was not only to simply facilitate capitalist economic activity but also to change the ways in which people conceptualized the world around them. The naturalization of individualized economic relationships (as opposed to collective or class relationships) and the aspiration to home ownership (as opposed to social rights to secure and affordable living space) invite acceptance of the neoliberal world view as a whole. Most recently, neoliberal legislative reform campaigns have resulted in the construction of a corporate legal personality that grants quasi-human rights to the corporation (such as the right to engage in politics) and also insulates corporate executives from legal and moral responsibility for corporate actions (Veldman, 2011).

Concerning trade unions, Hayek emphasized the need to end what he considered harmful 'collusive' relationships between employers and unions (Richardson, 1993), where both sides aimed to balance their differing interests (in the vein of the so-called 'German model'). Neoliberal thinking influenced governments to 'take on' unions in set-piece disputes, particularly in the Anglo-American context, such as in the Reagan administration's 1981 conflict with air traffic controllers (Farber & Western, 2002), and the Thatcher government's mid-1980s dispute with the National Union of Mineworkers (Towers, 1989). The defeat of trade unions in these disputes decisively recast common understanding regarding the nature of labour relations along neoliberal lines, entrenching another key aspect of the neoliberal thought style in politico-economic thinking. In the European context, unions have tended rather to be co-opted into permitting outsourcing and offshoring in return for job and social protection guarantees, although this negotiation is again structured by the constructed 'inevitability' of neoliberal globalization. The defeat, or co-optation, of unions has been critical as they potentially presented a serious barrier to outsourcing and the creation of global value chains.

Similarly, in relation to home ownership, the UK Thatcher government's 'right to buy' policy, providing tenants of government housing ('council houses') with a legal right to purchase their homes at preferential rates, was a highly effective tool in cementing and universalizing attitudes towards home ownership and, more generally, class orientation (Jacobs, Kemeny, & Manzi, 2003). The expanded marketization of the real estate sector also provided expansive opportunities for financialization and securitization. Indeed, it was the extension of real estate markets into the highly speculative field of mortgages designed expressly to attract the poor and insolvent – particularly in the United States and United Kingdom – which, as a consequence of securitization, massively inflated the unsustainable bubble that ultimately exploded into the sub-prime crisis and set off the global recession (Roubini, 2008; Willmott, 2011). More generally, a consequence of unleashing the neoliberal thought style has been an expansion, concentration and deregulation of financial institutions, and especially the banking and insurance sectors. Their core business is debt and its insurance, and their exponential growth since the late 1980s reflects the explosion of indebtedness by individuals and states as well as the high leveraging of assets by corporations.

Finally, neoliberals placed considerable emphasis on *restructuring the international political economy*, particularly through domination of the International Monetary Fund, World Bank and WTO, as well as regional development banks and institutions such as the OECD. During the 1980s, several leading neoliberals secured senior management positions in the IMF and World Bank, and set about reshaping the theory and practice of international development. Developing countries were no longer encouraged to pursue national industrialization policies but would rather be expected to seek export markets for their (mainly primary) goods. They were also required to shrink the size of their state administration and reduce investment in higher education (Murphy, 2008; Plehwe, 2009). These policies were enforced through 'policy conditionality', a new international development funding modality that was rapidly adopted as an international norm by most bilateral and multilateral international development organizations. Policy conditionality tied provision of aid to adoption of a broad range of neoliberal policies (Cooke, 2004; Mosley, Harrigan, & Toye, 1995). This renegotiation of development paradigms has been a more important feature of the neoliberal project than is generally acknowledged. Neoliberal policies have permitted the integration of third world workers into the bottom rung of the global labour force, creating the final, crucial condition for the full implementation of value chain capitalism. This has resulted in a strong downward pressure on wages worldwide (see discussion of global labour arbitrage below). For advocates of neoliberalism, the integration of developing economies, even those nominally under 'Communist' governments such as China and Vietnam, into a global neoliberal economic system has the welcome effect of reducing or even eliminating the risk of alternative economic and social paradigms being embraced. As the neoliberal thought style comes to dominate the field, its general acceptance effectively precludes consideration of alternatives (Douglas, 1986), at least until

The Rise of the 1%: An Organizational Explanation 41

the point at which its contradictions can no longer be contained (e.g. the need for huge state bailouts to avert financial meltdown).

While neoliberalism can be considered in terms of its constituent aspects, as explored above, it would be a mistake to regard it as a complex networked programme of conspiratorially planned actions. The core principles of neoliberalism are simple, even if advocates and opponents alike might quibble over their wording. Harvey (2005, p. 2) defines it as the belief that 'human well-being can best be advanced by liberating individual entrepreneurial freedoms and skills within an institutional framework characterized by strong private property rights, free markets and free trade'. In established capitalist economies, or in other contexts where people aspire to what these economies deliver, this conception of the key to well-being has an appeal that is largely blind to its politico-economic implications and contradictions. The neoliberal thought style is concentrated initially in the economic field, but its logic reaches into deeper attitudes and perspective on politics and society. The thought style provides a 'conditioning framework' as discussed above, that shapes and animates actors' attitudes and actions in their domains of interest and intervention. Moreover, the thought style notion provides a structuring explanation for elite conduct that offers an alternative to critical scholars' attribution of self-interested and systemically perilous behaviour to individual executives' personal wickedness (Perrow, 2010). In each of the six key targets of neoliberalism explored above, the neoliberal thought style promotes organizational restructuring which extends from a 'free trade' reorientation of economic activity vis a vis export markets, to the sphere of family life where freedom and autonomy is instantiated in the privatization of housing. We next turn to the interactions between the neoliberal thought style, organization and the reinforcement of elite domination.

Organizing Exploitation: Elite Domination, Value Extraction and Tax Avoidance

The supplanting of institutionalized, Fordist relationships by reconfigurable value chain processes, we have argued, is manifest in a cascade of impacts on the organization of the economy as well as on relationships between different economic actors (Davis, 2009; Lounsbury & Hirsch, 2010). The eclipse of the integrated, Fordist corporation, as well as the dismantling of the integrated state, have further skewed power relations within economy and society in favour of elites as the resources mobilized by oppositional forces have been destroyed or outlawed and forms of critique have been recuperated (Boltanski & Chiapello, 2005).

We now explore more directly how the disembedding and disarticulation of organizations operates to the benefit of the 1%, as we contend that a primary impact of the neoliberal thought style has been to change how surpluses are allocated by reinventing the system of production and distribution, extracting it from its institutionalization in the vertically integrated organization. By relying more heavily upon markets within and between organizations, the mutuality that existed within the institutionalised corporation has been eroded, thereby permitting enhanced profits that, further, are increasingly exempt from socialized tax obligations.

In the neoliberal mythology of free market capitalism, contractual relationships are always between equals. However, by breaking down value processes into ever smaller chunks that can be performed by production units located anywhere in the world, and in the context of the free international movement of capital, goods and services, those controlling the strategic configuration of value chains are able to maximize *their* share of overall income to the detriment of others who are squeezed by the threats posed by capital mobility. Costs are incurred in low-wage economies and revenues are realized in high priced markets. This advantage, which is enjoyed disproportionately by elites, leads to growing income and wealth disparity. It also produces increased instability in the economy. In the context of wholesale outsourcing of production, income declines in the high-wage economies where, historically, the engine of growth has been fuelled. For several years, declining income was concealed, or offset, by exponential growth in personal credit, a bubble whose bursting triggered the current global crisis but also, with few exceptions, perversely consolidated the dominance of financial institutions in relation to nation states. This dominance of financial institutions and the associated continuation of financialization is evident in the simultaneous bail-out of banks, the squeeze on public services in order to pay for the bailouts and the reliance on credit to compensate for the absence, or falling value, of wages.

It is often argued by mainstream economists and organization scholars that outsourcing simply reflects the creative destruction inherent within capitalism as economic functions are carried out in the location of maximum economic efficiency. In this perspective, it is anticipated that manufacturing jobs in the West will be replaced by higher value employment, for example, in design and innovation. It is imagined that the world can profitably be divided between, 'Those who grow; those who make; those who create; those who coordinate' (Czinkota & Ronkainen, 2005, p. 117). When some areas of the West lose jobs, such as America's Rust Belt or Britain's West Midlands, other areas gain, like Silicon Valley or London's City. This win-win account obscures the potential for elite extraction of additional value through the dynamics of global value chains. Stephen Roach, Morgan Stanley chief economist, noted as early as 2004 that, 'Wage rates in China and India range from 10% to 25% of those for comparable-quality workers in the United States and the rest of the developed world. Consequently, offshore outsourcing that extracts product and/or services from relatively low-wage workers in the developing world has become an increasingly urgent survival tactic for companies in the developed economies' (Roach, 2004).

Smith (2008, 2011) extends this argument in a more critically radical direction, noting that although an increasingly large proportion of consumer goods are produced in developing countries, only a small proportion of the overall value of the goods is realized in those countries. There are numerous accounts of different finished goods that are largely produced by developing country labour but the bulk of their value is realised in developed countries, of which the iconic Apple Corp. products are probably the best known example (Xing & Detert, 2011). Kraemer, Linden, and Dedrick (2011) calculate that only around 2% of the cost of the iPad and iPhone actually contributes to China's GDP: 'Much of the value in high-end products is captured at the beginning and end of the process, by the brand and the distributors and retailers' (Barboza, 2010). Similar calculations for products such as shoes manufactured in Central America reveal a similar picture of a miniscule proportion of product value remaining in countries such as the Dominican Republic (Smith, 2011). Despite modestly rising wages in China and other developing countries, these remain many multiples below Western levels – the *purchasing power* of Chinese workers' salaries in 2010 was only 6% of that of US workers with the nominal income even smaller as a proportion (De Regil, 2010). Chinese workers provide their labour in conditions of repressed free speech, restrictions on physical movement and absence of free trade unions (Pun & Smith, 2007) – undermining the credibility of the neoliberal argument that their incorporation in the global economy reflects 'efficiency' rather than simple exploitation. Similarly, in India, the major service outsourcing location, global economic integration occurs in a society still widely structured according to feudal social relationships, so that the labour released to function in global enclaves is underpinned by a caste-oppressed underclass of support workers (Murphy, 2010). Again, the neoliberal argument of a global 'free' labour market is not well grounded.

Global labour arbitrage substantially increases the surplus value that accrues to elites controlling transnational value chains. A key feature of value chain capitalism is also, however, the increasing proportion of value assigned to intangibles such as branding and other 'intellectual property'. Lego capitalism's value chain disarticulation has resulted in a relative decline in the status of the physical production process — which, as we have noted, can be reconfigured largely at will — and a substantially increased share of value captured in the branding process (Willmott, 2010). This phenomenon is significant not only because it provides a vehicle for further strategic elite value capture but also because of the intangible nature of intellectual property whose value can therefore be realised anywhere. Although under Fordist capitalism the corporation had little choice but to realize its profits in production and/or sales locations, brand property can be vested in offshore corporations in tax havens, and increasingly in pseudo-havens such as the Irish Republic with very low corporation tax rates (Desai, Foley, & Hines, 2006). Just as outsourcing under Lego capitalism undercuts workers' bargaining power, so states' bargaining power is undermined by the ability of holding corporations to re-assign value realization locations at will and thus realize profits in the most advantageous location, leading to the transfer of tax burden from corporate to individual tax and state financing crises (Avi-Yonah, 2000). Declining state revenues and consequent budget deficits increase pressures, and amplify calls, to reduce state administration costs, driving a vicious circle of privatization and outsourcing, thereby more deeply embedding value chain capitalism and the neoliberal thought style into the heart of state decision-making.

The developments discussed above indicate how corporate restructuring operates to shift wealth from its producers to corporate investors. This wealth is then retained, rather than redistributed, through the use of tax havens by major corporations and members of the global elite to shield their wealth from taxation and public scrutiny. Such havens have been used for the past 100 years but their importance in the global economy has grown exponentially since the 1970s. They have been associated with rapid movements of capital and with global financial instability (Larudee, 2009). Ninety-eight of the 'blue chip' FTSE 100 companies have tax haven subsidiaries, with many having several hundred (ActionAid, 2011). It is well known that corporations involved in major fraud scandals have made extensive use of tax havens — such as Enron (Larudee, 2009), WorldCom (Sikka, 2010), Stanford Financial Corporation (Dhesi, 2010) and Madoff Investment Securities (Palan, Murphy, & Chavagneux, 2010). However, their use is by no means restricted to 'rogue capitalism'. For example,

GlaxoSmithKline has used tax havens to reduce tax exposure on drugs going off-patent during the 2000s. The three major banana suppliers Dole, Chiquita and Fresh Del Monte minimized global taxation through distribution via a Bermuda-registered subsidiary, and Honda made use of tax holidays offered by the Chinese government to attempt to reduce its tax exposure in higher rate jurisdictions (Sikka & Willmott, 2010). Aggressive use of tax havens has become the norm and is used widely by the iconic giants of contemporary international capitalism such as Google, Amazon and Starbucks (de Graaf, 2013).

The use of tax havens has been driven by the activities of major consulting/audit/accounting companies that design tax avoidance vehicles, frequently making use of offshore financial centres and in particular transfer pricing, described euphemistically by KPMG as 'Tax Efficient Supply Chain Management' (Sikka & Hampton, 2005). Tax havens are also associated with innovative corporate structuring such as 'cell companies' that isolate liability in a plethora of 'cells' within an overall ownership umbrella (Sharman, 2006). The tax and liability avoidance mechanisms developed in tax havens are also available within developed country jurisdictions (Sharman, 2011). It can also be seen how this 'cell' approach to tax minimization dovetails with the structure of value chain capitalism in which holding companies control hundreds of units or cells.

Notwithstanding the substantial leakage of potential tax revenues — already estimated 10 years ago by the UK-based Tax Justice Network at $255 billion on the $11.5 trillion-plus of assets held in offshore financial corporations (TJN, 2005) — and the parlous state of state finances globally, the UK government in its 2011 budget introduced a special tax rate of 5.75% instead of the then standard rate of 23%, for companies running their internal banking through a tax haven subsidiary. This move, apparently driven by a desire to attract more corporate headquarters to the City, is indicative of the impact of tax havens in encouraging legitimate states to bid down their tax rates for both corporations and wealthy elites, and also the complicity of governments with elites using globalization to evade taxation.

CONCLUSION

Proceeding through three stages of analysis, the first part of this paper explored the evidence regarding a growing gap between a small elite and mass of the population. There has been a demonstrable, substantial shift in income and wealth towards the '1%' — a shorthand for a small elite that has benefited disproportionately from the new global economy. Shifts in the global economy were then linked to the emergence and eventual domination of the neoliberal 'thought style' built through the assiduous advocacy of its adherents. A central focus of the neoliberal programme was the dismantling of institutionalized organizations, including the traditional corporation, where stubborn residues of extra-market relationships of mutuality are embedded. Key arenas of neoliberal interventions — the promotion of free trade, privatization, marketization and deregulation, restructuring the legal frameworks governing economic relationships and redefining the international development agenda — were then examined. The redefinition of international development to emphasize integration into global production processes was crucial in order to draw new actors into the lower reaches of an emergent global value chain economy. The stretching of value networks across national boundaries in a loosened regulatory environment has provided opportunities for global labour arbitrage — driving labour costs down by incorporating new and vulnerable sectors into a globalized workforce — and the use of offshore havens where the elite can maximize their wealth largely free of scrutiny, regulation or taxation. These phenomena account for the shifting balance in wealth and power in favour of the 1%.

The organizational transformations and power rebalancing entailed in value chain capitalism have received inadequate attention within both organization studies and political economy. For organization studies, this weakness in tracing and understanding broad transformations in organizational structuring and their connection with wider political economy is an inevitable outcome of the narrow internal focus of most scholarship in the field, even of the critical variety (Morgan, Froud, Quack, & Schneiberg, 2011). Although most theories of organizational change acknowledge the existence of an 'external environment' that has some impact on organizations (Kezar, 2011), the role of politics and power in structuring that 'environment', to which corporate elites directly or indirectly contribute (e.g. through the Mont Pelerin Society and the neoliberal movement as a whole), is generally marginalized, perhaps because many contributions to this field take the focus of organization studies to be the de-politicized 'organization' abstracted from its politico-economic conditions of possibility and reproduction. Yet, as we have shown, the impact on organizations of the ascendency of neoliberal thought style has been extensive and pervasive and has led to thoroughgoing transformations in their forms and processes.

Organization of any kind embodies and sediments dominant ideology and power relationships. However the market-based contractual relationships that are at the core of the neoliberal thought style release elites from the social contracts inherent in socially and geographically embedded institutionalized organizations, providing unimpeded control of the (re)configuration of transnational value chains. The thought style also provides a moral justification and policy rationale for elites to relentlessly advance ever more comprehensive neoliberal restructuring of economic and social relationships. The neoliberal ideology or thought style facilitates the empowerment and enrichment of the elite through the systematic disavowal and dismantling of relationships of mutuality. Within a weak regulatory environment, itself conditioned by the hegemony of the neoliberal thought style, alternative, subaltern strategies are systematically disavowed and undermined. To be clear, we are not arguing that work organization(s) are reducible to a conveyor belt for class relationships; they are also a locus for the enactment of broader social relationships and frictions, and impacted by the configuration of forces and dominant ideologies. However, conflict over power and resources between competing class interests is a central and enduring theme in the politics of organization and so must become a key preoccupation of the study of organization(s) when such study is located within the field of critical social science.

NOTES

1. The United Nations independent expert on foreign debt and human rights, Cephas Lumina, has warned that, "the austerity measures and structural reforms proposed to solve Greece's debt crisis may result in violations of the basic human rights of the country's people" (UN, 2011).

2. Post-organizational as viewed in mainstream organization studies terms; in which the organization is invested with quasi-corporeal qualities (Cornelissen, 2005).

3. Financialization refers to at least three interconnected and interdependent phenomena. The first is the tendency for the financial industry to assume an ever greater influence in economic policy-making (Phillips, 2006, 2008). The second is the emergence of marketized finance as the primary source of corporate investment, in place of accumulated capital (Hudson, 2010). Finally, financialization is used to refer to the tendency for the financial industry and its instruments (such as real estate) to represent an ever greater share of economic activity in comparison with productive industries such as manufacturing (Crotty, 2009).

4. See OECD Global Network on Privatisation and Corporate Governance of State-Owned Enterprises, available at http://www.oecd.org/document/56/0,3746,en_2649_34847_40097080_1_1_1_1,00.html

REFERENCES

Ackroyd, S. (2011). The post-war organization of large British firms. In S. Clegg, M. Harris, & H. Hopfi (Eds.), *Managing modernity* (pp. 176–202). Oxford: OUP.
ActionAid. (2011). *Addicted to tax havens: The secret life of the FTSE 100*. London: ActionAid. Retrieved from http://www.actionaid.org.uk/doc_lib/addicted_to_tax_havens.pdf
Aglietta, M. (1979). *A theory of capitalist regulation: The US experience*. London: Verso.
Alchian, A. A., & Demsetz, H. (1973). The property right paradigm. *The Journal of Economic History, 33,* 16–27.
Amin, A. (Ed.). (1994). *Post-fordism: A reader*. Oxford: Blackwell.
Anand, N., & Daft, R. (2007). What is the right organization design? *Organizational Dynamics, 36,* 329–344.
Andrew, E. (Ed.). (1981). *Closing the iron cage: The scientific management of work and leisure*. Montreal: Black Rose.
Appadurai, A. (1996). Disjuncture and difference in the global cultural economy. In *Modernity at large: Cultural dimensions of globalization* (pp. 27–47). Minneapolis, MN: University of Minnesota Press.
Avi-Yonah, R. (2000). Globalization, tax competition, and the fiscal crisis of the welfare state. *Harvard Law Review, 113,* 1573–1676.
Barboza, D. (2010). *Supply chain for iphone highlights costs in China*. NY Times. Retrieved from http://www.nytimes.com/2010/07/06/technology/06iphone.html. Accessed on July 5.
Barlow, M., & Clarke, T. (2002). *Blue gold: The fight to stop the corporate theft of the world's water*. New York, NY: New Press.
Berger, S. (2006). *How we compete*. London: Doubleday.
Berle, A. A., Jr., & Means, G. C. (1935). *The modern corporation and private property*. New York, NY: Macmillan.
Boltanski, L., & Chiapello, E. (2005). The new spirit of capitalism. *International Journal of Politics, Culture, and Society, 18,* 161–188.
Bourdieu, P. (1987). What makes a social class. *Berkeley Journal of Sociology, 32,* 1–18.
Braverman, H. (1974). *Labor and monopoly capital*. New York, NY: Free Press.
Burris, V. (1986). The discovery of the new middle class. *Theory and Society, 15,* 317–349.
CBO (Congressional Budget Office). (2009). *Historical effective federal tax rates, 1979 to 2006*. Washington: CBO. Retrieved from http://www.cbo.gov/ftpdocs/100xx/doc10068/effective_tax_rates_2006.pdf
Chandler, A. (1977). *The visible hand: The managerial revolution in American business*. Cambridge, MA: Harvard University Press.
Cockett, R. (1995). *Thinking the unthinkable: Think-tanks and the economic counter-revolution*. London: HarperCollins.
Colwill, C., & Gray, A. (2007). Creating an effective security risk model for outsourcing decisions. *BT Technology Journal, 25,* 79–87.
Cooke, B. (2004). Managing of the (third) world. *Organization, 11,* 603–629.
Cornelissen, J. P. (2005). Beyond compare: Metaphor in organization theory. *Academy of Management Review, 30,* 751–764.
Crothers, L. (2010). *Globalization and American popular culture*. Lanham, MD: Rowman & Littlefield.

Crotty, J. (2009). Structural causes of the global financial crisis: A critical assessment of the 'new financial architecture'. *Cambridge Journal of Economics, 33*, 563–580.

Czinkota, M., & Ronkainen, I. (2005). A forecast of globalization, international business and trade. *Journal of World Business, 40*, 111–123.

Daft, R. (2009). *Organization theory and design*. Mason, OH: Southwestern.

Davis, G. F. (2009). *Managed by the markets: How finance re-shaped America*. Oxford: Oxford University Press.

de Graaf, A. (2013). International tax policy needed to counterbalance the 'excessive' behaviour of multinationals. *EC Tax Review, 22*, 106–110.

De Regil, A. (2010). *A comparative approximation into China's living-wage gap*. Moorpark, CA: Jus Semper Global Alliance. Retrieved from http://www.jussemper.org/Resources/Economic%20Data/Resources/China_LW_gap.pdf

Desai, M. A., Foley, C. F., & Hines, J. R., Jr. (2006). The demand for taxhaven operations. *Journal of Public Economics, 90*, 513–531.

Dhesi, N. (2010). The conman and the sheriff: SEC jurisdiction and the role of offshore financial centers in modern securities fraud. *Texas Law Review, 88*, 1345–1380.

Dolovich, S. (2007). How privatization thinks. UCLA School of Law Public Law & Legal Theory Research Paper No. 07-07.

Douglas, M. (1986). *How institutions think*. London: Routledge.

Easterly, W. (2001). The middle class consensus and economic development. *Journal of Economic Growth, 6*, 317–335.

Eaton, G. (2014). *Food bank use rises to record level of more than 900,000*. New Statesman. Retrieved from http://www.newstatesman.com/politics/2014/04/food-bank-use-rises-record-level-more-900000. Accessed on April 16.

Ehrenreich, J., & Ehrenreich, B. (1977). The professional-managerial class. *Radical America, 11*, 7–31.

Faleye, O., Reis, E., & Venkateswaran, A. (2010). *The effect of executive-employee pay disparity on labor productivity*, European Financial Management Association Annual Meeting, Aarhus, June 23–26, Retrieved from http://www.efmaefm.org/0EFMAMEETINGS/EFMA%20ANNUAL%20MEETINGS/2010-Aarhus/EFMA2010_0438_fullpaper.pdf

Farber, H. S., & Western, B. (2002). Ronald reagan and the politics of declining union organization. *British Journal of Industrial Relations, 40*, 385–401.

Fleck, L. (1979/1935). *Genesis and development of a scientific fact*. Chicago: University of Chicago Press.

Folkman, P., Froud, J., Johal, S., & Williams, K. (2007). Working for themselves? Capital market intermediaries and present day capitalism. *Business History, 49*, 552–572.

Frank, R. (2010). *The winner takes all society*. London: Random House.

Friedman, M. (1997). Public schools: Make them private. *Education Economics, 5*, 341–345.

Gabor, D. (2010). The IMF and its new economics of crisis. *Development and Change, 41*, 805–830.

Gamble, A. (2009). *The spectre at the feast: Capitalist crisis and the politics of recession*. London: Palgrave Macmillan.

Gereffi, G. (2005). *The new offshoring of jobs and global development*. Geneva: ILO.

Grinspun, R., & Kreklewich, R. (1994). Consolidating neoliberal reforms: "Free Trade" as a conditioning framework. *Studies in Political Economy, 43*, 33–61.

Guerin, D. (1936). *Fascisme et grand capital, Italie-Allemagne*, Paris, Editions de la Révolution prolétarienne.
Harvey, D. (2005). *A brief history of neoliberalism*. Oxford: Oxford University Press.
Hatch, M. J., & Cunliffe, A. (2006). *Organization theory: Modern, symbolic, and postmodern perspectives*. Oxford: Oxford University Press.
Hayek, F. (2001). *The road to serfdom*. London: Routledge.
Hayes, R. M., & Schaefer, S. (2009). CEO pay and the lake wobegon effect. *Journal of Financial Economics*, *94*, 280–290.
Helleiner, E. (1996). *States and the re-emergence of global finance: From bretton woods to the 1990s*. Ithaca, NY: Cornell University Press.
Hudson, M. (2010). *The transition from industrial capitalism to a financialized bubble economy*. Levy Institute Working Paper No. 627. University of Missouri-Kansas City.
Hymer, S. (1970). The efficiency (contradictions) of MNCs. *American Economic Review*, *60*, 441–448.
Jacobs, K., Kemeny, J., & Manzi, T. (2003). Privileged or exploited council tenants? The discursive change in conservative housing policy from 1972 to 1980. *Policy & Politics*, *31*, 307–320.
Kaplinsky, R. (1985). Electronics based automation technologies and the onset of systemofacture: Implications for third world industrialisation. *World Development*, *13*, 423–440.
Kapur, D. (2000). Who gets to run the world? *Foreign Policy*, *121*(November/December), 44–50.
Kezar, A. (2011). *Understanding and facilitating organizational change in the 21st century: Recent research and conceptualizations*. San Francisco, CA: Wiley (Kindle edition).
Kraemer, K. L., Linden, G., & Dedrick, J. (2011). *Capturing value in global networks: Apple's ipad and iphone*. University of California Irvine Working Paper. Retrieved from http://pcic.merage.uci.edu/papers/2011/Value_iPad_iPhone.pdf
Krippner, G. R. (2005). The financialization of the American economy. *Socio-Economic Review*, *3*, 173–208.
Krueger, A. (1985). Importance of general policies to promote economic growth. *World Economy*, *8*, 93–108.
Krugman, P. (2011). "We are the 99.9%". New York Times. Retrieved from http://www.nytimes.com/2011/11/25/opinion/we-are-the-99-9.html. Accessed on November 24.
Larudee, M. (2009). Sources of polarization of income and wealth: Offshore financial centers. *Review of Radical Political Economics*, *41*, 343–351.
Lasswell, H. D. (1933). The psychology of hitlerism. *The Political Quarterly*, *4*, 373–384.
Latimer, C., Collier, C., Shah, J., Burrows, K., Woodcraft, M., & Fitzpatrick, S. (2011). Creative subversions: A politics beyond representation in the UK. *Qui Parle*, *20*, 271–278.
Leonard, M. (2014). *Rage against the machine*. New Statesman. Retrieved from http://www.newstatesman.com/politics/2014/06/rage-against-machine-rise-anti-politics-across-europe. Accessed on May 28.
Lounsbury, M., & Hirsch, P. (Eds.). (2010). *Markets on trial*. Bradford: Emerald.
Metrick, A., & Yasuda, A. (2010). The economics of private equity funds. *Review of Financial Studies*, *23*, 2303–2341.
Midgley, C. (2012). Just don't call them the pasty party. *The Times*, March 29.
Mintzberg, H. (1979). *The structuring of organizations*. New York, NY: Prentice-Hall.

Miozzo, M., & Grimshaw, D. (2011). Capabilities of large services outsourcing firms: The "outsourcing plus staff transfer model" in EDS and IBM. *Industrial and Corporate Change, 20*, 909–940.

Mirowski, P., & Plehwe, D. (Eds.). (2009). *The road from mont pèlerin: The making of the neoliberal thought collective.* Cambridge, MA: Harvard University Press.

Mizruchi, M. (2013). *The fracturing of the American corporate elite.* Cambridge, MA: Harvard University Press.

Monbiot, G. (2011). The 1% are the very best destroyers of wealth the world has ever seen. Guardian. Retrieved from http://www.guardian.co.uk/commentisfree/2011/nov/07/one-per-cent-wealth-destroyers/. Accessed on November 7.

Morgan, G. (2014). Financialization and the multinational corporation. *Transfer: European Review of Labour and Research, 20*, 183–197.

Morgan, G., Froud, J., Quack, S., & Schneiberg, M. (2011). Capitalism in crisis: Organizational perspectives. *Organization, 18*, 147–152.

Mosley, P., Harrigan, J., & Toye, J. F. J. (1995). *Aid and power: The world bank and policy-based lending* (Vol. 1). London: Routledge.

Murphy, J. (2008). *The world bank and global managerialism.* London: Routledge.

Murphy, J. (2010). A toxic mix? Comparative efficiency and the privatization of sanitation services in India. *Public Administration and Development, 30*, 124–135.

Murphy, J., & Ackroyd, S. (2013). Transnational corporations, socio-economic change and recurrent crisis. *Critical perspectives on international business, 9*, 336–357.

Nadeem, S. (2009). Macaulay's (cyber) children: The cultural politics of outsourcing in India. *Cultural Sociology, 3*, 102–122.

OECD. (2011). *Divided we stand: Why inequality keeps rising.* Paris: OECD Publishing.

Palan, R., Murphy, R., & Chavagneux, C. (2010). *Tax havens: How globalization really works.* Ithaca, NY: Cornell University Press.

Perrow, C. (2010). The meltdown was not an accident. In M. Lounsbury & P. Hirsch (Eds.), *Markets on trial: The Economic Sociology of the U.S. Financial Crisis: Part A* (Vol. 30, pp. 309–330). Research in the Sociology of Organizations. Bingley, UK: Emerald Group Publishing Limited.

Perry, E., & Francis, B. (2010). *The social class gap for educational achievement.* Retrieved from http://www.thersa.org/__data/assets/pdf_file/0019/367003/RSA-Social-Justice-paper.pdf

Phillips, K. (2006). *American theocracy: The peril and politics of radical religion, oil, and borrowed money in the 21st century.* London: Penguin.

Phillips, K. (2008). *Bad money, reckless finance.* New York, NY: Viking.

Phillips-Fein, K. (2009). *Invisible hands: The businessmen's crusade against the new deal.* New York, NY: Norton.

Piketty, T. (2014). *Capital in the twenty-first century.* Cambridge, MA: Harvard University Press.

Plehwe, D. (2009). The origins of the neoliberal economic development discourse. In P. Mirowski & D. Plehwe (Eds.), *The road from mont pèlerin: The making of the neoliberal thought collective* (pp. 238–279). Cambridge, MA: Harvard University Press.

Prechel, H. (2000). *Big business and the state: Historical transitions and corporate transformations, 1880s–1990s.* Albany: SUNY Press.

Prechel, H., & Harms, J. B. (2007). Politics and neoliberalism: Theory and ideology. *Research in Political Sociology, 16*, 3–17.

Preis, A. (1972). *Labor's giant step: The first twenty years of the CIO: 1936–55*. New York, NY: Pathfinder Press.
Pun, N., & Smith, C. (2007). Putting transnational labour process in its place: The dormitory labour regime in post-socialist China. *Work, Employment and Society, 21*, 27–45.
Reich, W. (1933). *The mass psychology of fascism*. London: Farrar, Straus and Giroux.
Richardson, R. (1993). *Hayek on trade unions: Social philosopher or propagandist?* Centre for Economic Performance Working Paper 178. London School of Economics and Political Science, London.
Roach, S. (2004). *How global labour arbitrage will shape the world economy*. Global agenda, Magazine of the World Forum Economic Annual Meeting 2004. Retrieved from http://ecocritique.free.fr/roachglo.pdf
Rooduijn, M. (2014). Vox populismus: A populist radical right attitude among the public? *Nations and Nationalism, 20*, 80–92.
Rooney, B. (2012). *Europe's next recession risk: Germany*. Fortune. Retrieved from http://money.cnn.com/2012/05/02/markets/germany-recession/index.htm. Accessed on May 2.
Roubini, N. (2008). *The rising risk of a systemic financial meltdown: The twelve steps to financial disaster*. RGE monitor. Retrieved from http://www.quartetfest.ca/documents/30239/12_steps_NR.pdf. Accessed on February 8.
Rushe, D. (2011). *Revealed: Huge increase in executive pay for America's top bosses*. Guardian. Retrieved from http://www.guardian.co.uk/business/2011/dec/14/executive-pay-increase-america-ceos. Accessed on December 14.
Salemi, C. (2011). *Information and evidence pertinent to serious breach of the rome statute of the International Criminal Court (ICC) by political and state leadership of Greece*. Retrieved from http://www.scribd.com/fullscreen/83515418
Seabrooke, L., & Wigan, D. (2014). Global wealth chains in the international political economy. *Review of International Political Economy, 21*, 257–263.
Sharman, J. C. (2006). *Havens in a storm: The struggle for global tax regulation*. Ithaca, NY: Cornell University Press.
Sharman, J. C. (2011). *The money laundry*. Ithaca, NY: Cornell University Press.
Shiller, R. (2003). *The new financial order: Risk in the twenty-first century*. Princeton, NJ: Princeton University Press.
Sikka, P. (2010). Smoke and mirrors: Corporate social responsibility and tax avoidance. *Accounting Forum, 34*, 153–168.
Sikka, P. (2012). *Squeezing ordinary people's finances always leads to disaster*. Guardian. Retrieved from http://www.guardian.co.uk/commentisfree/2012/apr/23/squeezing-ordinary-people-finances/. Accessed on April 23.
Sikka, P., & Hampton, M. P. (2005). The role of accountancy firms in tax avoidance: Some evidence and issues. *Accounting Forum, 29*, 325–343.
Sikka, P., & Willmott, H. (2010). *The dark side of transfer pricing: Its role in tax avoidance and wealth retentiveness*. Essex Business School Working Paper 2010/1. Retrieved from http://www.essex.ac.uk/ebs/research/working_papers/WP2010-1%20-%20PSikka%20Transfer%20Pricing%20Paper.pdf
Singer, P. (2003). War, profits, and the vacuum of law: Privatized military firms and international law. *Columbia Journal of Transnational Law, 42*, 521–549.
Smith, J. (2008). Offshoring, outsourcing & the 'Global Labour Arbitrage'. Paper presented to IIPPE 2008 – Procida, Italy, 9–11 September.

Smith, J. (2011). *Imperialism and the law of value*. Global discourse, 2. Retrieved from http://globaldiscourse.files.wordpress.com/2011/05/john-smith.pdf

Sodha, S., & Margo, J. (2010). *A generation of disengaged children is waiting in the wings ...* London: DEMOS.

Soederberg, S. (2011). Cannibalistic capitalism: The paradoxes of neoliberal pension securitization. *Socialist Register, 2011*, 224–241.

Stiglitz, J. (2011). *Of the 1% by the 1% for the 1%*. Vanity Fair. Retrieved from http://www.vanityfair.com/society/features/2011/05/top-one-percent-201105?currentPage=1. Accessed on May.

Straw, W. (2010). *Philip green is an odd choice for efficiency tsar*. The Guardian. Retrieved from http://www.theguardian.com/commentisfree/2010/aug/13/philip-green-eficiency-savings. Accessed on August 13.

TJN (Tax Justice Network). (2005). *The price of offshore*. Retrieved from http://www.taxjustice.net/cms/upload/pdf/Briefing_Paper_-_The_Price_of_Offshore_14_MAR_2005.pdf

Towers, B. (1989). Running the gauntlet: British trade unions under thatcher, 1979–1988. *Industrial and Labor Relations Review, 42*, 163–188.

Tully, S., & Welsh, T. (1993). The modular corporation. *Fortune*, February 8, pp. 52–55.

Valdes, J. (1995). *Pinochet's economists: The Chicago school in Chile*. Cambridge: Cambridge University Press.

Van Horn, R. (2009). Reinventing monopoly and corporations: The roots of Chicago law and economics. In P. Mirowski & D. Plehwe (Eds.), *The road from mont pèlerin: The making of the neoliberal thought collective* (pp. 204–237). Cambridge: Harvard University Press.

Van Horn, R. (2011). Chicago's shifting position on concentrations of business power. *Seattle University Law Review, 34*, 1527–1544.

Veldman, J. (2011). Governance Inc. *Business Ethics: A European Review, 20*, 292–303.

Willmott, H. (2010). Creating 'value' beyond the point of production: Branding, financialization and market capitalization. *Organization, 17*, 517–542.

Willmott, H. (2011). Making sense of the financial meltdown. *Organization, 18*, 239–260.

Wolff, E. N. (2010). *Recent trends in household wealth in the United States: Rising debt and the middle-class squeeze – an update to 2007*. Levy Economics Institute of Bard College Working Paper No. 589. Retrieved from http://www.levyinstitute.org/pubs/wp_589.pdf

Wolff, R. D. (2011). *From economic to social crisis: Deficits, debt, and a little class history*. Monthly Review. July 22. Retrieved from http://mrzine.monthlyreview.org/2011/wolff220711.html

Xing, Y., & Detert, N. (2011). *How the iPhone widens the United States trade deficit with the people's republic of China*. Asian Development Bank Institute Working Paper Series No. 257, Retrieved from http://www.adbi.org/files/2010.12.14.wp257.iphone.widens.us.trade.deficit.prc.pdf

Young, R. (1990). Scientism in the history of management theory. *Science as Culture, 1*(8), 118–143.

Zile, R., & Steinbuka, I. (2001). Latvia on the way to the European Union. *Finance and Development, 38*(2), 30–33.

ELITES, VARIETIES OF CAPITALISM AND THE CRISIS OF NEO-LIBERALISM

Glenn Morgan

ABSTRACT

The paper argues that the form, structure and ideologies of elites are embedded in particular forms of capitalism. Whilst elites in these different societies are engaged in a common task of ensuring that their position is sustained and protected in the light of economic and political uncertainties, the way in which they are able to do this is shaped by the particular forms of legitimation, coordination and cohesion that are embedded in particular institutional trajectories, path dependencies and complementarities. However, the paper emphasizes that these institutional structures are dependent on particular international economic orders and when these change either over the short or the long term, elites often find themselves struggling to maintain their position without significant changes. The paper examines firstly how the long-term change from Keynesianism to neo-liberalism in the international economic order led to changes in the terrain on which elites in different countries formed and exercised power and secondly how the immediate and drastic short-term changes in the global economy arising from the financial crisis has impacted on elites.

Keywords: Elites; varieties of capitalism; legitimation; global economic order

INTRODUCTION

With some recent notable exceptions (Maclean, Harvey, & Chia, 2010; Reed, 2012; Zald & Lounsbury, 2010) researchers in the field of organization studies have tended to steer clear of discussion of elites over recent decades. By comparison, the issue of elites drawing on C. Wright Mills' Power elite (Mills, 1999) was a central debate in organization studies during the 1970s and 1980s since researchers were concerned with the nature of the groups that ruled the dominant hierarchies in society via their positions in large organizations such as corporations and state bureaucracies. Investigating the connections between these actors within and across organizations and their impact on societies was central to such classic empirical studies in the United States as Useem's 'The Inner Circle' and the analyses in Mintz and Mizruchi (Mintz, 1987; Mizruchi, 1982; Useem, 1984) and the Neo-Weberian approaches of authors such as Clegg (Clegg, 1989; Clegg & Dunkerley, 1980) and Scott (Scott, 1997; Stokman, Ziegler, & Scott, 1985). During the 1990s, however, these studies tended to become submerged as a sub-category of the discussion of power and whilst there is no doubt that the two have traditionally been integrally connected, subsequent discussions of power have become much more variegated and in some versions, antithetical to the concept of 'elite', for example, in most readings of Foucault's theory of power (Clegg, Courpasson, & Phillips, 2006). This is reflected in Zald and Lounsbury's opening statement that 'since the mid-20th century, organizational theorists have increasingly distanced themselves from the study of core societal power centres' (Zald & Lounsbury, 2010, p. 963). In part, this neglect is because what were seen as the centres of power in the period of the 1950s through to the late 1970s, particularly the large private corporations and public bureaucracies, have arguably diminished in their role and significance from the 1990s onwards. The shareholder value revolution seems to have rendered top corporate managers as simply transmitters of the pressures of financial markets, and their time and inclination for other broader social activities have been curtailed

(Mizruchi, 2013 see also Useem, 2015). Instead they are focused on increasing the value of company shares, sometimes by divestments or share buy-back that are in effect forms of shrinkage of the company. Some authors argue that the era of the large corporation is passing as firms become disaggregated along their supply chain and their core activities shrink in order to meet shareholders' expectations (Davis, 2009, 2013). Disaggregation potentially creates smaller firms acting as contractors to lead firms which are themselves hollowed out, consisting as in the case of companies such as Nike, mainly of design and marketing and consequently employing directly many fewer people than when these activities took place inside the integrated Chandlerian corporation. Power now resides in the financial markets and even here, although there are large corporate actors that are central to these processes, there are also small, less visible but increasingly influential actors such as hedge funds that drive market movements. The development of financialization has served to put the Chandlerian corporation of the mid-20th century which was the centrepiece of the work of Useem, Mizruchi and Mintz, into its place (Froud, Johal, Leaver, & Williams, 2006; van der Zwan, 2014). Therefore, the idea of an economic elite identifiable primarily through its occupancy of top positions in the largest private sector firms and public bureaucracies as Mills suggested needs rethinking.

Such a rethinking also needs to take into account the way in which state bureaucracies have been shrunk as activities have been privatized and outsourced, a process which has seen an increasing interconnectedness between private sector elites and public sector elites that intermediate between the privatizing state and the companies which take on this work (Crouch, 2013). The structural separation between the state elite and the economic elite that existed for Mills and needed to be bridged by various activities and organizations is no longer so obvious. State activities have been marketized; private sector firms and their senior managers are inside the state shaping privatization and marketization policies and structures. State officials and politicians are increasingly involved in a revolving door system, moving in and out of private sector and the state apparatus in various ways. Furthermore, the state itself by reason of the increased role of borrowing from the financial markets in order to balance state finances is ever more tangled up with satisfying these markets. When the markets collapsed in 2008, states moved in to rescue and revive the financial markets, only to find themselves within a short period again at the mercy of those markets as the sovereign debt crisis arose particularly in the Eurozone. It does not therefore make sense simply to import Mills's categorizations into the current period. As Bowman, Froud, Johal, Moran, and Williams (2015) argue, the point, however, is not abandon the debate about elites and power in modern societies but to find ways to renew its relevance given these changes in social and economic structure.

In order to do this, this paper suggests that it would be useful to link these debates to the wider question of institutional change and crisis in contemporary societies that have been discussed under various headings such as Varieties of Capitalism (Hall & Soskice, 2001), national business systems (Morgan & Whitley, 2012; Whitley, 2007) and comparative historical institutionalism (Crouch, 2005; Streeck & Thelen, 2005). These studies have been concerned with issues such as how institutions are shaped and by whom, and in terms of the recent period, how change has emerged and with what consequences. But here too, it is noticeable that the concept of elites rarely emerges. From a theoretical perspective, this is understandable because institutionalism has sought to avoid explaining social structure by reference to economic concepts of 'interests', preferring to see institutions as shaping how interests are defined and constructed rather than vice versa. In doing so, the centrality of elite power tends to be downplayed in favour of analyses which draw on wider and more diffuse categories such as class and the state or in organizational terms, associations (of employers and employees). Explaining institutions, then, is less about showing how the interests of one particular group ('the elite') have become embedded in the taken-for-granted reality of a particular social context and more about explaining how various groups in society with different capacities and different powers find their actions shaped, constrained and directed by pre-existing path dependencies.

For example, recent research has sought to identify the origins of the differences between coordinated and liberal forms of capitalism (in the United States and Europe) by looking at the way in which different patterns of social class formation emerged in particular territorial entities during the transition from feudalism to capitalism. Their interaction over the 19th century produced political institutions which subsequently shaped and constrained the ways in which interests were articulated. They particularly influenced the degree to which social groups entered into alliances with each other or maintained conflictual, zero-sum types of politics. Where cross-class alliances emerged that enabled groups between capital and labour (such as agricultural interests or small independent crafts) to find representation in parliamentary structures through proportional representation, then at the political and the economic level, this led to negotiation and coordination becoming established modes of operating in society.

Coalition politics characterized by incremental policy adjustments were matched by industrial relations systems that were built on forms of cooperation at various levels. Where such intermediary groups were lacking in a strong autonomous identity, a process reinforced by majoritarian political systems, politics became more polarized between capital and labour and more subject to winner-takes-all and pendulum changes in policy. Industrial relations systems reflected this conflict. As these institutional mechanisms were reinforced by financial institutions, labour market regulations, skill and training mechanisms, the resulting institutional complementarities constrained elites as much as any other groups in society. Referring to Germany, Streeck introduced the idea of 'beneficial constraints', that is, that the different actors had become locked in to institutional constraints despite their preferences, but the outcome in this case was beneficial to all of them, if in different ways and to different degrees (Streeck, 1997). Where these institutions failed to appear and political representation was majoritarian, intermediate groups between labour and capital had less chance for independent representation and politics became more conflictual with the main divide between the party of capital aiming to oppose the party of working class collectivism by enforcing more market driven solutions to economic and political issues (Cusack, Iversen, & Soskice, 2007; Iversen & Soskice, 2006, 2009). In these arguments, elites are as constrained by the institutions as any other group even if their capabilities and capacities are generally more powerful.

More recent studies of institutional change have looked at how these institutional constraints may have weakened resulting in changing relations between these groups due to changing global market conditions, competition strategies, size, demography, firms and technologies, and how this in turn has led to incremental but qualitative institutional change (Streeck & Thelen, 2005; Thelen, 2014). Streeck's analysis of Germany sees these changes in terms of a fundamental reordering of the German political economy towards more liberalization and with it higher levels of inequality, reflecting a broader assertion of the power of capital over labour in the neo-liberal global world order (Streeck, 2008, 2011, 2014). Thelen together with the contributors in Schmidt and Thatcher sees more variation in the responses of coordinated societies whilst recognizing the importance of growing liberalization in Europe (see also Palier & Thelen, 2010; Schmidt & Thatcher, 2013; Thelen, 2014). Whilst other work has aimed to identify the types of actors and the sorts of manoeuvres which they undertake in order to change institutions (Mahoney & Thelen, 2009), this rarely makes reference to the concept of elites.

This lack of discussion of elites in institutional analysis fits strangely with the broader effort amongst critical commentators to understand the last 20 years of financialization, institutional change and the 2008 crisis and its aftermath where elite failure and elite malfeasance are seen as central issues. In the United States, the 1%/99% discourse has captured a broader sense that not only do elites lie behind the current crisis but they have managed to push the costs of the crisis on to 'Main Street', continuing to reward themselves extravagantly whilst the mass of the population is subject to increased uncertainty and austerity (see Murphy & Willmott, 2015). There has been an increased awareness of the growing extent of inequality over the last few decades and that this is particularly reflected in the rapidly growing incomes of the top earners in the economy and the wider impact of inequality (Dorling, 2014; Piketty, 2014; Therborn, 2014; Wilkinson & Pickett, 2010). The idea of an economic elite benefitting disproportionately from the economy and protecting themselves from criticism or falling living standards has become more salient to public discourse, particularly in the light of the austerity imposed after the financial crisis – an austerity that had major implications for most of the population but which seemed to make no difference to this elite's ability to continue to increase its income and wealth, even though their actions in the financial markets were central to causing the crisis (Blyth, 2013). In the Eurozone, EU policy elites and bankers (together with international organizations such as the IMF) are blamed for forcing austerity and cuts in state budgets at the expense of the broader populations, most obviously in Greece, Spain and Italy (Fazi, 2014; Lapavitsas, 2012). The tension between so-called technocratic elite solutions to economic problems implemented through the actions of Central Banks and Finance Ministries and the democratic decisions of the population at the ballot box, where extremist, nationalist and populist parties rejecting these solutions have found increasing support in national and European elections have heightened the sense of a divide between an elite and the mass of the population. If we want to explore institutional change, then it seems we need to reconsider how elites might fit in that account rather than avoid this vocabulary.

In academic terms, therefore, there is good reason for 'Remembering Elites' as a recent edited collection was entitled (Savage & Williams, 2008) if we are interested in institutional change and this would appear to be an important cross-over point where organization studies and comparative capitalisms research co-exist. This paper, therefore constitutes a preliminary effort to bring together the analysis of elites with the comparative capitalism perspective in the light of the recent and ongoing financial and economic crisis in the global economy. Its aim is to suggest a number of ways to make these links and illustrate them briefly by reference to recent research. In the first section, the concept of elites is discussed and how it could fit into the analysis of changing forms of capitalism. The paper then relates this concept to the idea of different varieties of capitalism and how therefore elites are differently constructed across distinct institutional terrains even though they face common problems and use similar techniques to resolve them. This leads into a discussion of how one of the main common problems which they face is fitting into the broader international economic order. As this order changes through war or economic restructuring and crisis, the broader terrain for elites also changes. The paper follows this up by discussing how the long-term change from Keynesianism to neo-liberalism in the world order had specific effects on the terrain of elites in different forms of capitalism. Because there were these different forms, elites had different ways to manage these changes. As a result elite formations changed in the period leading up the financial crash; this crash, however, created new urgent challenges for elites as they struggled to stabilize the international environment and their national institutional order. The paper argues that it is only by linking elite challenges and processes at both the national and the international level to the path-dependent trajectories of different forms of capitalism that it becomes possible to identify both capacities and the limitations of elite action in institutional reproduction and change.

THE CONCEPT OF ELITES

The emphasis is placed in this paper on the role of elites in guiding and shaping institutional change and responses to crises through their positioning and ability to act at key junctures to stabilize or adapt societal challenges. In this respect, it follows authors such as Zald and Lounsbury, for example, who refer to 'command posts' as 'traditional centres of societal power that regulate, oversee and aim to maintain social order in society and economy, both at regional, nation-state and inter-state levels' (2010, p. 964). As Reed states, 'even the most well-integrated and stabilized domination structures will inevitably be subject to destabilizing shocks and ruptures that begin to unstitch the very fabric of organizational coordination and control through which they are authorized' (Reed, 2012, pp. 212–213). If elites ignore these emerging problems, they may find their conditions of reproduction undermined or worse still, that they are replaced by others. As the actors with the strongest material interest in the maintenance of the status quo, elites are unlikely to step away from these challenges. Whether they have the ability to meet them and if so what this means in terms of their overall legitimacy and the distributional systems which they defend is an open question.

Reed argues that these command situations 'are linked to one another through demographic processes of interaction and circulation', becoming institutionalized forms of power embedded in organizational infrastructures that make elites 'less dependent ... on coercive powers to maintain their hegemonic positions within prevailing domination structures' (Reed, 2012, pp. 212–213). One of the key issues here is that described by Boltanski in his discussion of the dominant class where he states that 'to make the idea of a dominant class meaningful, it is necessary to invoke the existence of specific links between the actors who in different ways and to various degrees ensure the maintenance of the established order (and benefit from it, albeit unequally) and this without necessarily assuming the existence of explicit cooperation between them, still less a complicity realized in secret in the manner of a conspiracy' (Boltanski, 2011). In the discussion which follows, we treat elites as variable in their scale, power and structure but retain the term 'elite' as a useful way to conceptualize the role of powerful actors in trying to maintain the social and economic order in their own interests.

The idea that institutional arrangements in capitalism are inherently uncertain, unpredictable and precarious (see e.g. Morgan & Whitley, 2012) is now common in analyses of comparative capitalism. Institutions are 'efforts' at stabilising relationships between conflicting parties (most obviously capital and labour in its various forms). Patterns of institutions emerge that are pragmatic adjustments to the current context. As that context changes, which it invariably will given the uncertainty and dynamism of capitalist competition, not to mention other political and social challenges which can arise, then the centrality, significance and role of particular institutional arrangements may decline and potential forms of change emerge; for example, as discussed in Streeck and Thelen (2005) and Mahoney and Thelen (2009). From this perspective, we can look at institutions as the outcomes of power distribution contests and as a result, having the potential to be questioned and changed as power distributions alter — for whatever reason. From this perspective, elites constitute those groups whose aim is broadly speaking to protect their existing position in society by accruing sufficient power over decisions and over social mechanisms that they are able to make the institutional system reproduce itself (and its distributional effects) even when it faces internal and external challenges.

If we insert this within the VOC/comparative capitalisms framework, then we can identify a common set of challenge and tasks faced by, as well as instruments, tactics and strategies used by, elites in order to stabilize the institutions which support capitalism in general. However, there is also considerable variety (deriving from path dependent processes which shape particular forms of capitalism) in terms of how any particular elite is constituted (its recruitment, composition, positioning, discursive strategies) and how this shapes its use of particular strategies etc. This variety derives from the path-dependent processes which shape particular forms or varieties of capitalism. In the following section of the paper, this interaction between *capitalism* and *capitalisms* (Morgan & Whitley, 2012) is discussed.

ELITES, CAPITALISM AND CAPITALISMS

What constitutes an elite/the elite(s) in one form of capitalism is likely to be distinctive but there are certain common elements that define their challenges.

The first commonality is the issue of legitimacy. Elites in democratic societies aim to have a level of legitimacy in the eyes of the wider population so that their policies and solutions to problems are acceptable. Legitimacy does not have to imply normative commitment; it can also signal a pragmatic adjustment to the status quo (Suchman, 1995; Suddaby & Greenwood, 2005). Elite legitimacy strategies and discourses are shaped by the variety of capitalism in which they exist. For example, we can hypothesize that in societies dominated by strong states, elites act through the state and legitimate their efforts in nationalistic terms. In societies characterized by social partnership arrangements, where goals of social justice are high, then the discourse and practice of elite institution and organization building reflects this expectation. In more market dominated societies, elites may be expected to manage markets so they work efficiently in the expectation that this will bring benefits to the broader population. Sustaining the legitimacy to act in these ways is placed under strain when external circumstances change; for example, a global financial crisis. Each elite faces a different legitimacy crisis at the national level for the simple reason that the basis of its legitimacy has been constructed differently.

Secondly, however, legitimacy needs to be supplemented by the capacity to coordinate across the elite. As 'field' type analysis points out, there are a variety of discourses, actors, institutions and practices within a modern capitalist economy. There is a problem, therefore, of how to coordinate key actors. The concept of 'key actors' of course is not theoretically or empirically neutral. The centrality of an actor depends on a time and a setting even in terms of the focus on the reproduction of a particular form of capitalism. Elite studies generally have identified a number of features that facilitate coordinative capacity. One of the oldest has been the idea of shared social background, supplemented by a shared social milieu in which actors from different 'fields', for example, finance, law, the civil service, politics, industry, mix together and establish shared understandings outside of formal roles and responsibilities. A second has been the existence of formal organizations that act to bring together members of the elite where they can openly discuss and resolve current problems in the management of capitalism. A third is to emphasize the process of recruitment into the elite and the notion that only a certain set of proven characteristics (in Bourdieu's terms, forms of social and cultural capital as well as financial capital) enables entry into the elite.

Each of these processes is structured by the particular form of capitalism in which the elite is embedded. In some societies, elite secondary and tertiary educational institutions with highly selective entry policies that combine wealth and cultural capital act both as a funnel into the elite and as a means of generating a common perspective (Khan, 2010, 2012); see also Bourdieu's studies of France (Bourdieu, 1998, 2013). In other societies where education is less hierarchically stratified, this 'distinction' may be less central to elite membership; instead, access to formal organizations, firstly through achievements within the firm or the profession and secondly through the recognition of relevant skills by being called on to participate in collective agencies of the elite such as employers' associations and industry groups or through interlocking directorships which bring individuals contacts across companies.

Thirdly and related to this is the degree of cohesion of the elite actors. Issues of cohesion can be affected by the degree to which the state system is centralized, the degree and ways in which political, social and economic power is integrated and the degree of interdependency and interaction across different institutional spheres. Overall the degree of competition between elites or within elites has frequently been identified as key to the amount of change which occurs within a system. Mahoney and Thelen's distinction between different types of institutional change agents and power coalitions (insurrectionists, parasitic symbionts, subversives and opportunists) can be integrated into this analysis of competition between and within the elite – with a key issue being the degree to which these conflicts have the potential to spill over into the wider society and create legitimacy and capacity breakdowns which heighten crises and increase the uncertainty of outcomes (Mahoney & Thelen, 2009).

Schmidt (2008, 2010) has taken a different approach to this issue distinguishing between two forms of coordination. The first is the coordinative discourse of policy construction amongst elite policy actors; to what degree is the elite centralized, sharing norms and values, engaged in continued interaction? Or is it alternatively geographically dispersed, seldom interacting, split through different religions, norms etc.? Highly centralized societies such as the United Kingdom and France fall into the first category whilst Germany and the United States are more federal. Small societies, which have been of such interest to political scientists provide another context in which coordinative discourses may be strong due to the concentration of key institutions and actors in a limited geographical and social space (Campbell & Hall, 2009; Katzenstein, 1985; Ornston, 2012) The second aspect of coordination which Schmidt identifies is the communicative capacity of the elite in relation to the mass of the population. Are there intensive means of communication and negotiation with the broader population of civil society, involving the creation of commitment on the part of these actors to elite solutions? Or are the means of communication attenuated and limited so that the elite feels ready and able to act on its own without much recourse to the rest of the population? This in turn relates to what Mahoney and Thelen (2009) describe as 'veto points'; where there are few veto points, the elite may feel it can act alone as the public is either disinterested or disengaged. For example, in the United States and the United Kingdom, financial deregulation and financial innovation during the 2000s was an elite project with little resistance or debate from elsewhere.

Drawing on Boltanski and Thevenot's terms, it is possible to ask how do elites construct systems of legitimation in particular forms of capitalism so that these systems fit with the path-dependent processes of those different societies? Once these systems are constructed, how do elites ensure they have the cohesion and coordinative capacities to pass the tests by which these systems of legitimation encourage the population more broadly to judge them? What happens if they do not pass those tests (Boltanski & Thevenot, 2006)?

ELITES AND THE CONTEXT OF *CAPITALISM*

At this stage, it is necessary to return to the idea of *capitalism* as opposed to *capitalisms* (see the discussion in Morgan & Whitley, 2012). Thus far, the idea of elites and path dependency has been conceptualized within a state-centric or national model. In his approach, for example, Reed is notably state-centric. He is explicit about the centrality of the state, quoting Mann to the effect that 'only the state has this centralized-territorial spatial form and a monopoly of institutionalized violence' (quoted in Reed, 2012, p. 208). This is reflected in each of the case studies which he discusses which are concerned with elite dynamics in specific societies. Although this is not made explicit, elite power is seen as primarily constructed within the state and capable of analysis without reference to the wider international economic and political context. This accords well with much comparative capitalisms research where the nation-state is also the main focus of analysis for reasons very similar to those described by Reed in terms of the nation-state remaining the central most powerful organizing principle of politics and economics in the contemporary era.

However, the greatest challenges to elites and their ability to reproduce or adapt national capitalisms have emerged when the international regime supporting a particular stage of capitalism has broken down or undergone fundamental restructuring. It is impossible to ignore *capitalism's* impact on *capitalisms*. Recent authors have suggested the need to bring back the concept of capitalism, to take it seriously (in the singular as opposed to 'national capitalisms' in the plural) seriously (Streeck, 2011) and to embed the analysis of particular comparative capitalisms into an analysis of the broader international regime in which they are embedded (Morgan & Whitley, 2012). Elites which are primarily constituted through path-dependent processes of social formation at the national level are nevertheless managing in this wider international context which may facilitate the status quo or undermine it in various ways.

How might this international context change and impact on national elites? Two sorts of changes can be considered. The first is rapid collapse of the international system because of war or economic crisis. The second is a more long-term restructuring of the underlying relations of the global economy. Both of these have an impact on national elites.

With regard to the first set of processes which concern a rapid collapse of the global order because of war or the outbreak of severe economic depression, these are capable of undermining national institutional settlements and creating a major crisis of reproduction. At this stage, elites which had been 'passing' the legitimation test begin to face major new challenges. Adjustment now is a more complex task for the national elite. They may be blamed for the external crisis or they may claim they are a victim of it — two views of Britain's role in the financial crisis of 2008 reflecting how the Labour government after claiming credit for the growth in the period up to 2008, quickly blamed the 'global' context for that collapse. These moments of crisis are times when resources are severely depleting so distributional questions which elites generally try to downplay are also likely to come more to the surface. The degree and nature of this depletion, for example, in economic terms, varies across different forms of capitalism as the Eurozone crisis showed; it had relatively little impact on Germany where minor adjustments were made to employment and welfare as part of an ongoing series of reforms but it had a massive impact on Greece, exacerbating social tensions in that country. Whilst distributional issues are becoming more complex in Germany with growing inequality, these changes were not driven by the Euro crisis but a more longer term restructuring of the German economy (Palier & Thelen, 2010; Streeck, 2008; Thelen, 2014). The fragile institutional order of Greece was put under severe pressure and its traditional elites which had run the country since it joined the EU found it difficult to stay in control at the electoral level, having lost control of the economy to the financial markets, the IMF and the EU. Left and right wing parties rejecting the old models garnered considerable support and the eventual outcome of these processes in terms of elite preservation is still unclear (Fazi, 2014; Lapavitsas, 2012). The paper returns to this theme later.

First, however, it is necessary to examine more deeply the second process in which developments in the capitalist economy reshape the terrain in which national forms of capitalism exist and through which elites have sustained themselves. This is a process which has occurred a number of times over the last three centuries as particular patterns of accumulation associated with distinctive states and forms of capital have been superseded by new patterns, new state hegemons and new rules of the international order (see e.g. the approaches in Aglietta, 2000; Arrighi, 1994, 2007; Boyer & Saillard, 2001). The following section, however, concentrates on the change from a Keynesian 'embedded liberalism' world order (Ruggie, 1982) to a neo-liberal world order. How has this process reshaped the terrain for elites inside national forms of capitalism?

THE ESTABLISHMENT OF THE NEO-LIBERAL WORLD ORDER

The process whereby the neo-liberal order displaced Keynesianism has been analyzed in many places and will not be repeated here (Harvey, 2005; see also Murphy & Willmott, 2015). Peck's description with its emphasis on particular local adaptations and resistances provides a suitable framework for present purposes. He talks about

> A story of the never-inevitable ascendancy of neo-liberal*ization*, as an open-ended contradictory process of politically assisted market rule. This is no bloodless, semi-automatic process but the work of situated social actors ... it is a [process] of repeated prosaic and often botched efforts to fix markets, to build quasi-markets and to repair market failures. (Peck, 2011)

It is obvious that in the early stages of this process, these ideas flowed predominantly through the United States though as Peck makes clear, the intellectual origins of the neo-liberal order were also European, through the influence of Hayek and the Vienna school articulated through the Mont Pelerin society with its European origins and its linkages into the Chicago School (Mirowski, 2013). Many of these individuals took on the role of public intellectuals and advisers to presidents and prime ministers from the 1970s onwards, reshaping ways of thinking about economic policy that influenced the United States and the United Kingdom. Through the influence which these countries – most particularly the United States – had in international institutions, they became the basis of the Washington Consensus. Even international institutions that might have been seen as potential bulwarks against this process, such as the EU, for various reasons espoused the neo-liberal message (Abdelal, Blyth, & Parsons, 2010). Reinforcing this process was the role of the US economics profession and its influence globally on how economic policy should evolve as well as the role of US lawyers and policy makers in international institutions (Dezalay & Garth, 2002; Fourcade, 2009) and in the justification of the deregulation of financial markets and the development of new modes of managing risk (Mackenzie, 2008a, 2008b; Mackenzie & Millo, 2003). Deregulation, privatization of state services and supporting the development of open financial markets constituted the key features of these debates.

The neo-liberal process of deregulation had three main implications for the broader global political economy that affected national capitalisms in path-dependent but consequential ways in terms of restructuring the terrain on which elites were reproduced within national settings.

Firstly, neo-liberalism in principle freed financial markets from the constraints which Keynesianism had very deliberately placed on them. Capital was able to flow freely across borders searching out profitable opportunities for investment in new markets, both in portfolio investments (stocks and bonds) and in foreign direct investment (through mergers and acquisitions as well as the establishment of new plants). Currencies were floating and interest rates moving variably across currencies. The amount of goods traded across borders grew and surplus and debtor countries had fewer mechanisms for adjusting their position. This in turn created a huge financial business in terms of sovereign bonds as one group of countries had to borrow whilst another group of countries had to find places to invest. Funds flowed into countries characterized by low savings rates and high consumption as banks borrowed so they could lend to their personal customers who in turn entered into debt to buy large items such as houses and cars. The financial sector grew spectacularly after this shift to neo-liberalism developing new products, opening up new markets, finding new ways to avoid tax, etc. A plethora of smaller institutions exemplified by hedge funds and private equity partnerships emerged, as well as lawyers, tax advisers, consultants, etc. Hedge funds and private equity funds gained access to huge amounts of capital with which they were able to move markets, threaten the existence of large corporations and make massive profits often in tax-lite shelters. The big bulge banking institutions became larger than ever; they employed more people than ever before in their front and back offices, their trading rooms, their M+A corporate finance departments, their broking and institutional investment arms. Most crucially from the point of view of this paper, as finance and financial markets grew, they exerted greater direct and indirect influence over governments to keep deregulating. The taxes they paid (mainly on payroll rather than on profits where tax avoidance was rife) and the employment they provided as well as the services they delivered which made the population dependent on them (for money transmission, for mortgages, for credit cards, for loans, for pensions, for savings etc.) made governments highly unwilling to challenge or control what was going on. What these large financial institutions also did and what was less clear until 2007–2008 was that they shifted the downside risk of their collapse onto governments; they became in the famous phrase 'too big to fail'. They could take on more and more risk, which enhanced the earnings of the bank, its shareholders, its senior executives and its traders so long as things kept moving; in the event that the bubble burst, the losses would be taken by governments and their populations because the alternative was to create such massive uncertainty as to threaten the whole system (Engelen et al., 2011). The collapse of Lehmans gave a brief moment of insight into how quickly the whole system could unravel and was rapidly followed by government guarantees to other banks for fear that anything else would cause chaos.

Whilst not all societies became as dominated by the financial sector as the United States and the United Kingdom, nevertheless, the great power of finance in the period from the 1990s through to 2007–2008 developing from this process of deregulation fundamentally changed the terrain for elites in particular national contexts. At a simple level, the question of how policy affected finance, how different interests in an economy should be balanced, what institutions needed to be reformed now had to be factored in to national elite decisions in a way which Keynesianism had striven to avoid by controlling and downgrading finance, keeping it small, keeping it 'in its box' because of the long history of booms and busts that seemed to be associated with the freeing of finance from state control (Kindleberger & Aliber, 2011; Reinhart & Rogoff, 2009).

The second main change that emerged from deregulation was in the changing nature of firms. Financialization and the shareholder value revolution which grew out of financial deregulation and increasing global flows of capital pushed firms in many countries towards strategies based purely on maximizing short-term shareholder returns (Davis, 2009). This in turn encouraged the search to shift capital and production around the globe to take advantage of differences in the price of labour and other factors of production and to open up new markets. This fundamentally changed how firms interacted with their local contexts. Options now opened up in terms of the degree to which managerial elites wished to maintain the social pacts that characterized the Keynesian era or alternatively wished to take advantage of new opportunities in shifting production to new sites where labour costs were lower This is clearly a complex process and as the continued industrial competitiveness of Germany, the Nordic countries, Japan and France and the United States to a degree demonstrate this is not simply a one-directional and permanent shift. Nevertheless, it has a number of potential effects on elite formations. It offers a partial disengagement of firms from national contexts to which elites need to adjust. One process of adjustment undertaken by states is by developing policies to keep these ties strong (e.g. by adapting to demands for liberalization, labour market reform, tax reform, reform of the public sector, thereby opening up different sorts of markets to home-based firms that are no longer finding mass manufacturing employment a viable option in the developed world when labour is so much cheaper elsewhere). Thus by acquiescing to the neo-liberal agenda and expanding the opportunities in the non-traded service sector, some recompense is achieved for the loss of jobs elsewhere though these jobs are very different with low wages, more temporary and part-time employment, less employment rights etc. (Thelen, 2014; Wren, 2013).

Another form of adjustment is a shift in the composition of the elite itself to become more international, in terms of experience and orientation. As firms and markets internationalize, elites begin also to develop more international connections. Multinationals may no longer fill their headquarters with local managers but start to recruit internationally, thereby disabling social ties in the home country; see for example, the study in this volume on Switzerland by Davoine, Ginalski, Mach, and Ravasi (2015). Another indicator of this is the degree to which elites now combine study in their home country with study overseas, which may in turn impact on policies about how the corporation will be run (Morgan & Quack, 2005; Silver, 2007). The growth of international interlocks amongst directors in large firms (see Vion, Dudouet, & Grémont, 2015) also indicates the growing relevance of international connections as does the growth of lobbying in international organizations such as the EU. Finally, researchers have identified the development of transnational communities drawn from elite groups in societies and constituting an international grouping around particular institutions and policy areas; for example, central banking, the IMF, the WTO and emerging issue areas (Djelic & Quack, 2010; Murphy, 2007; Seabrooke, 2012, 2014; Seabrooke & Tsingou, 2014; Weaver, 2008). The speed and manner in which this 'new breed of international experts' (Zald & Lounsbury, 2010, p. 967) is emerging from different national elites is clearly path-dependent, related both to linkages in earlier periods as well as the development of firms, financial markets and regulatory patterns more recently.

The third main change is in relation to the state. As numerous authors have shown, the introduction of privatization and deregulation into the state sector fundamentally changes the relationship between the state and civil society as well as the role of state elites. In particular, the state becomes increasingly an open site for corporations as more and more of its roles become subjected to marketization and competition (Crouch, 2013; Meek, 2014). As Crouch shows, this stretches across the whole gamut of activities that were previously considered the prerogative of the state in many countries — such as education, health, utilities, regulatory bodies, advice to ministers etc. This goes alongside a change in the nature of the civil service that is left. Civil servants in turn become less representatives of some common national interests (however defined and however distorted by class interests and class background) and more and more entrepreneurs, market actors within the confines of the state (Du Gay, 2010).

In summary, neo-liberalism changes the terrain on which national elites act. It turns it into a more financialized, more international, less state-centric environment. It offers the possibility of access into a growing international elite as well as the ability to trade in elite status in one context for elite status in another (see e.g. the career of an individual like Leo Apotheker who led the German company SAP for a number of years, was made a member of the Legion D'Honneur in France in recognition of his business leadership and was appointed CEO and President of Hewlett-Packard in 2010, only to resign less than a year later as HP's share price fell by over 40%[1]). Neo-liberalism does not impact uniformly on societies or the elites within them; instead it creates a different global environment and elites can respond to this in a variety of ways.

IMPACTS ON LOCAL ELITES

If the terrain potentially changes in this way, what happens in particular national contexts? There have been numerous studies of the broad impact of neo-liberalism on specific societies (Blyth, 2013). Many of these show the complex way in which ideas, practices, rules are resisted, hybridized, implemented in various ways etc. These studies show the importance of path dependency effects though they have focused less on how these changes affect the nature and reproduction of national elites.

In this respect, it is possible to suggest a number of issues which might emerge. It is likely that the elites which were dominant under conditions of Keynesianism will have to adapt or change depending on the degree to which they were already financialized and/or internationalized. To what degree are elites in particular contexts capable of achieving this and in what ways? For example, in France, it might be argued that the old elite, characterized as the grandes ecoles elite that dominated senior positions in the state, industry, finance and the civil service have not actually changed much. Recruitment into the elites remains much the same, the interaction amongst the elites remains much the same with individuals moving easily and comfortably between the various sectors, and the challenge to the power of these elites remains limited to sporadic outbursts of civil discontent (Maclean et al., 2010; see also Maclean, Harvey, & Kling, 2015). The French elite sustained itself by directing the changing of institutions (and to a degree ideologies) towards more financialization in a relatively orderly and limited way (Huault & Richard, 2012) rather than being forced to do so by the financial markets or outside interference – though it could be said that the current Eurozone crisis leaves the outcome still somewhat uncertain.

By contrast, elites in Britain may be seen to have changed more, becoming more international, more highly rewarded, more based around finance and the City of London and more committed to open deregulated markets than was the case in the 1970s. Power has shifted more completely in the UK case towards finance than it has in France, even though it is certainly true that the influence of finance has expanded there. The role of new entrants such as international management consultancies or US health care firms has gone much further in the United Kingdom than in France, changing the nature of state provision. Finance which always had a powerful position in the United Kingdom expanded that power as a result of neo-liberalism but in the process of doing so, the elite became both more international but also more dispersed – in hedge funds, private equity, accountancy, law firms as well as in the large financial institutions as well as more distant from old forms of control and regulation (Augar, 2006, 2008, 2009; Engelen et al., 2011).

These changes impact on coordinative capacities and communicative discourses. Elites in most developed countries have had to make room for finance and for representatives of international firms and international capital. In some countries, new elites emerged on the basis of these changes, integrating themselves with pre-existing elites through a mixture of corruption, political financing and joining the social calendar of the old elites (see e.g. Ireland and the rise of super-wealthy property developers using banking and political connections to develop their business (Donovan & Murphy, 2013; O'Toole, 2009; Riain, 2013) or in Iceland, with the rise of new banking empires and the combination of international property developers and retail chains which borrowed from these banks (Boyes, 2010, Wade & Sigurgeirsdottir, 2010, 2012). Societies like Ireland and Iceland, as well as many of the Eastern European economies were fundamentally changed by the rise of financialization, the flow of easy borrowings and how this funnelled in to old elites, new elites and political parties.

Even where these developments were more in accord with existing institutional arrangements, changes occurred. For example, it is clear that the internationalization of the City of London from the mid-1980s changed the terrain on which the Governor of the Bank of England had previously been able to coordinate and control bankers through the simple mechanism, supposedly, of 'raising the eyebrows' as a symbol of warning about bad or inappropriate behaviour (Moran, 2003). On the other hand, in the United Kingdom, there was a strong effort to communicate to the population that financialization and privatization were in their interests because they enabled house purchase and consumption etc. (Langley, 2008). Financialization dug deeper into the UK society than had been the case before (Engelen et al., 2011; Froud et al., 2006; Martin, 2002).

Understanding the nature of these path-dependent trajectories, the impact which they had on the institutions and organizations through which the elite exercised influence in the local context is clearly a task for the comparative study of elites. Similar processes of the shift to a neo-liberal order impacted differentially across the world, reshaping the social structure of different forms of capitalism. The degree of this reshaping was highly variable; in some contexts, existing elites resisted or tried to follow a path of minimal adaptation whilst in others the dynamics of the global economy effectively pushed old elites aside replacing them with new actors drawing primarily on financial expertise and power, supported by their ability to connect with powerful overseas institutions (banks, lawyers, accountants as well as multinational manufacturing companies) eager to enter new markets. This new environment in some cases allowed existing elites to continue on in their old ways because now they could borrow to expand the economy; banks could lend to personal customers who could at last buy a house or trade up with a seeming profit as the house price boom increased. The world of easy lending allowed many elites to continue as before except that now they could also benefit from this financialization of their economy. For the 2000s up to the financial crash, there seemed to have been a relatively smooth adjustment made by different elites to this new world. But what would happen to the different elites when this financial system collapsed?

CONCLUSIONS: THE FINANCIAL CRASH AND ELITE LEGITIMATION

The financial crisis and its aftermath has created a new set of complexities for a variety of reasons. Most obviously, the crisis has confronted national elites with varying forms of delegitimation that have led in many contexts to changes of government and in nearly all contexts to policies of austerity. Managing national forms of capitalism through periods of swingeing austerity is a massive challenge for elites that has not been attempted since the inter-war years an example which offers little in the way of reassurance. Secondly, the system of international elite coordination which appeared to be working so smoothly in the period of neo-liberal hegemony is under severe strain because of the continued power of financial markets to disrupt any plans which are laid by politicians and the severe pressure on national elites not to agree to any international measures that may impact negatively on local interests. Thirdly, it seems that resistance and challenge to the system, whilst it remains confused and disparate, has a global dimension itself.

It is in this phase that the design of new institutions and organizations to resolve the crisis has become most problematic. As many authors have pointed out, as the financial crisis evolved into a sovereign debt crisis particularly within the Eurozone but also in countries outside it which had borrowed heavily in order to stabilize their economies and reduce the impact of the crisis. The character of the crisis was shifted towards a fiscal crisis of state spending in which elites drew on traditional discourses of austerity to legitimate their actions (Blyth, 2013; Lapavitsas, 2012). The banking crisis which lay behind this fiscal crisis was pushed back into the realms of the specialists and the financial institutions themselves to come up with technical solutions to issues such as reserve ratios, leverage ratios, capital adequacy, structural separation between forms of banking, tighter regulation of product development particularly for retail markets and the general operation of the financial markets (Engelen et al., 2011; Lapavitsas, 2014; Morgan, 2012). In some countries such as the United Kingdom, this coupled with deft scapegoating of welfare recipients by the Coalition government and certain high-profile figures in the banking sector whose extravagance and greed was accompanied by incompetence and shady dealings was sufficient to sidestep more complex issues of responsibility for the crash. The fact that the Labour opposition had presided over this period of financialization and therefore found it hard to develop an alternative position on the crisis per se only served to reinforce the elite strategy. Other countries particularly in Southern Europe found it more difficult to respond as unemployment increased and the welfare system was slashed but eventually in each country a rejuggling of old alliances and new movements led to a temporary stabilization of the situation, helped by the actions of the European Central Bank to reduce some of the hard edges of Eurozone imposed austerity (Woll, 2014).

The post financial crisis period reveals yet again the need to understand the path-dependent trajectory of elites in particular forms of capitalism, the way in which they responded to the changing terrain of the global political economy and what this meant for both their structuration in the period leading up to the financial crash and their capacity to respond to that crisis. Only by drawing all these elements together can we expect to develop a full understanding of elites in the current situation.

This paper has made the case for the comparative studies of elites within a broadened institutional framework that takes seriously national path dependencies but also changing international regimes. Drawing on a range of recent research, it argues that elites are socially embedded within particular varieties of capitalism. This embedding shapes their capacities for coordination and action when it comes to managing the process of reproduction and crisis. These management processes require a focus on coordinative mechanisms, on legitimacy and tests of legitimacy and on communicative discourses. The degree to which elites constitute highly coordinated and integrated groups of actors is an empirical question that can only be properly understood by comparative studies at particular historical points. Part of any such study has to also include the international level, what sort of accumulation regime exists at a particular phase of capitalism, to use the terminology of Regulation Theory (Aglietta, 2000; Boyer & Saillard, 2001) and how is it controlled and managed? What are the international elites that come to the fore at different phases of capitalism and how do these relate to national elites? In conclusion, the empirical study of elites will be furthered by the growth of comparative studies that pay attention to processes of institutional change and reproduction within particular varieties of capitalism. Placing this in the broader context of developments in the political economy of capitalism enables us to see more clearly the challenges faced by elites in the current crisis and suggests some of the reasons why elites in certain countries have been destroyed whilst others have been strengthened. In this way, studies of organizations, institutions and varieties of capitalism can be drawn together through a focus on elites that offers substantial challenges for further research.

NOTE

1. Thanks to Antoine Vion and Francois-Xavier Dudouet for this reference.

REFERENCES

Abdelal, R., Blyth, M., & Parsons, C. (2010). *Constructing the international economy*. Ithaca, NY: Cornell University Press.

Aglietta, M. (2000). *A theory of capitalist regulation*. London: Verso.
Arrighi, G. (1994). *The long twentieth century: Money, power, and the origins of our times*. London: Verso.
Arrighi, G. (2007). *Adam Smith in Beijing*. London: Verso Books.
Augar, P. (2006). *The greed merchants*. London: Penguin UK.
Augar, P. (2008). *The death of gentlemanly capitalism: The rise and fall of London's investment banks*. London: Penguin.
Augar, P. (2009). *Chasing alpha*. London: Random House.
Blyth, M. (2013). *Austerity*. Oxford: Oxford University Press.
Boltanski, L. (2011). *On critique*. Cambridge: Polity.
Boltanski, L., & Thevenot, L. (2006). *On justification*. Princeton, NJ: Princeton University Press.
Bourdieu, P. (1998). *The state nobility*. Stanford: Stanford University Press.
Bourdieu, P. (2013). *Distinction*. London: Routledge.
Bowman, A., Froud, J., Johal, S., Moran, M., & Williams, K. (2015). Business elites and undemocracy in Britain: A work in progress. In G. Morgan, S. Quack, & P. Hirsch (Eds.), *Elites on trial* (Vol. 43). Research in the Sociology of Organizations. Bingley, UK: Emerald Group Publishing Limited.
Boyer, R., & Saillard, Y. (2001). *Regulation theory: The state of the art*. London: Routledge.
Boyes, R. (2010). *Meltdown Iceland*. London: Bloomsbury.
Campbell, J. L., & Hall, J. A. (2009). National identity and the political economy of small states. *Review of International Political Economy, 16*(4), 547–572.
Clegg, S. R. (1989). *Frameworks of power*. London: Sage.
Clegg, S. R., Courpasson, D., & Phillips, N. (2006). *Power and organizations*. New York, NY: Pine Forge Press.
Clegg, S. R., & Dunkerley, D. (1980). *Organization, class and control*. London: Routledge.
Crouch, C. (2005). *Capitalist diversity and change: Recombinant governance and institutional entrepreneurs*. Oxford: Oxford University Press.
Crouch, C. (2013). *Making capitalism fit for society*. Cambridge: Polity.
Cusack, T. R., Iversen, T., & Soskice, D. (2007). Economic interests and the origins of electoral systems. *American Political Science Review, 101*(03), 373–391.
Davis, G. F. (2009). *Managed by the markets: How finance re-shaped America*. Oxford: Oxford University Press.
Davis, G. F. (2013). After the corporation. *Politics & Society, 41*(2), 283–308.
Davoine, E., Ginalski, S., Mach, A., & Ravasi, C. (2015). Impacts of globalization processes on the Swiss National Business Elite Community: A diachronic analysis of Swiss Large Corporations (1980–2010). In G. Morgan, S. Quack, & P. Hirsch (Eds.), *Elites on trial* (Vol. 43). Research in the Sociology of Organizations. Bingley, UK: Emerald Group Publishing Limited.
Dezalay, Y., & Garth, B. G. (2002). *Global prescriptions: The production, exportation, and importation of a new legal orthodoxy*. Ann Arbor, MI: University of Michigan Press.
Djelic, M.-L., & Quack, S. (2010). *Transnational communities*. Cambridge: Cambridge University Press.
Donovan, D., & Murphy, A. E. (2013). *The fall of the Celtic Tiger*. Oxford: Oxford University Press.
Dorling, D. (2014). *Inequality and the 1%*. London: Verso.
Du Gay, P. (2010). Without regard to persons: Problems of involvement and attachment in 'Post-bureaucratic' public management. In S. Clegg, M. Harris, & H. Höpfl (Eds.). *Managing modernity: The end of bureaucracy?* (pp. 11–29). Oxford: Oxford University Press.

Engelen, E., Erturk, I., Froud, J., Johal, S., Leaver, A., & Moran, M. et al. (2011). *After the great complacence: Financial crisis and the politics of reform*. Oxford: Oxford University Press.

Fazi, T. (2014). *The battle for Europe*. London: Pluto Press.

Fourcade, M. (2009). *Economists and societies*. Princeton, NJ: Princeton University Press.

Froud, J., Johal, S., Leaver, A., & Williams, K. (2006). *Financialization and strategy*. London: Routledge.

Hall, P. A., & Soskice, D. W. (2001). *Varieties of capitalism: The institutional foundations of comparative advantage*. Oxford: Oxford University Press.

Harvey, D. (2005). *A brief history of neoliberalism*. Oxford: Oxford University Press.

Huault, I., & Richard, C. (Eds.). (2012). *Finance: The discreet regulator: How financial activities shape and transform the world*. London: Palgrave Macmillan.

Iversen, T., & Soskice, D. (2006). Electoral institutions and the politics of coalitions: Why some democracies redistribute more than others. *American Political Science Review*, *100*(02), 165–181.

Iversen, T., & Soskice, D. (2009). Distribution and redistribution: The shadow of the nineteenth century. *World Politics*, *61*(03), 438–486.

Katzenstein, P. J. (1985). *Small states in world markets*. Ithaca, NY: Cornell University Press.

Khan, S. R. (2010). *Privilege*. Princeton, NJ: Princeton University Press.

Khan, S. R. (2012). The sociology of elites. *Annual Review of Sociology*, *38*(1), 361–377.

Kindleberger, C. P., & Aliber, R. Z. (2011). *Manias, panics and crashes: A history of financial crises* (6th ed.). London: Palgrave Macmillan.

Langley, P. (2008). *The everyday life of global finance: Saving and borrowing in Anglo-America*. Oxford: Oxford University Press.

Lapavitsas, C. (2012). *Crisis in the Eurozone*. London: Verso Books.

Lapavitsas, C. (2014). *Profiting without producing*. London: Verso Books.

Mackenzie, D. (2008a). *An engine, not a camera*. Cambridge, MA: MIT Press.

Mackenzie, D. (2008b). *Material markets: How economic agents are constructed*. Oxford: Oxford University Press.

Mackenzie, D., & Millo, Y. (2003). Constructing a market, performing theory: The historical sociology of a financial derivatives exchange. *American Journal of Sociology*, *109*(1), 107–145.

Maclean, M., Harvey, C., & Chia, R. (2010). Dominant corporate agents and the power elite in France and Britain. *Organization studies*, *31*(3), 327–348.

Maclean, M., Harvey, C., & Kling, G. (2015). Business elites and the field of power in France. In G. Morgan, S. Quack, & P. Hirsch (Eds.), *Elites on trial* (Vol. 43). Research in the Sociology of Organizations. Bingley, UK: Emerald Group Publishing Limited.

Mahoney, J., & Thelen, K. (2009). *Explaining institutional change*. Cambridge: Cambridge University Press.

Martin, R. (2002). *Financialization of daily life*. Philadelphia, PA: Temple University Press.

Meek, J. (2014). *Private Island*. London: Verso.

Mills, C. W. (1999). *The power elite*. Oxford: Oxford University Press.

Mintz, B. A. (1987). *The power structure of American business*. Chicago, IL: University of Chicago Press.

Mirowski, P. (2013). *Never let a serious crisis go to waste: How neoliberalism survived the crisis*. London: Verso Books.

Mizruchi, M. S. (1982). *The American corporate network, 1904–1974*. London: Sage.

Mizruchi, M. S. (2013). *The fracturing of the American corporate elite*. Cambridge, MA: Harvard University Press.
Moran, M. (2003). *The British regulatory state: High modernism and hyper-innovation*. Oxford: Oxford University Press.
Morgan, G. (2012). Reforming OTC markets. *European Business Organization Law Review, 13*, 391–412.
Morgan, G., & Quack, S. (2005). Institutional legacies and firm dynamics: The growth and internationalization of UK and German law firms. *Organization studies, 26*(12), 1765–1785.
Morgan, G., & Whitley, R. (2012). *Capitalisms and capitalism in the twenty-first century*. Oxford: Oxford University Press.
Murphy, J. (2007). *The world bank and global managerialism*. London: Routledge.
Murphy, J. & Willmott, H. (2015). The rise of the 1%: an organizational explanation. In G. Morgan, S. Quack, & P. Hirsch (Eds.), *Elites on trial* (Vol. 43). Research in the Sociology of Organizations. Bingley, UK: Emerald Group Publishing Limited.
Ornston, D. (2012). *When small states make big leaps*. Ithaca, NY: Cornell University Press.
O'Toole, F. (2009). *Ship of fools: How stupidity and corruption sank the Celtic Tiger*. London: Faber and Faber.
Palier, B., & Thelen, K. (2010). Institutionalizing dualism: Complementarities and change in France and Germany. *Politics & Society, 38*(1), 119–148.
Peck, J. (2011). *Constructions of neoliberal reason*. Oxford: Oxford University Press.
Piketty, T. (2014). *Capital in the twenty-first century*. Cambridge, MA: Harvard University Press.
Reed, M. I. (2012). Masters of the universe: Power and elites in organization studies. *Organization Studies, 33*(2), 203–221.
Reinhart, C. M., & Rogoff, K. (2009). *This time is different*. Princeton, NJ: Princeton University Press.
Riain, S. Ó. (2013). The crisis of financialisation in Ireland. *The Economic and Social Review, 43*(4, Winter), 497–533.
Ruggie, J. G. (1982). International regimes, transactions, and change: Embedded liberalism in the postwar economic order. *International Organization, 36*(2), 379–415.
Savage, M., & Williams, K. (2008). *Remembering elites*. Oxford: Wiley-Blackwell.
Schmidt, V. A. (2008). Discursive institutionalism: The explanatory power of ideas and discourse. *Annual Review of Political Science, 11*, 303–326.
Schmidt, V. A. (2010). Reconciling ideas and institutions through discursive institutionalism. In D. Béland, & R. H. Cox (Eds.), *Ideas and politics in social science research*. Oxford: Oxford University Press.
Schmidt, V. A., & Thatcher, M. (2013). *Resilient liberalism in Europe's political economy*. Cambridge: Cambridge University Press.
Scott, J. (1997). *Corporate business and capitalist classes*. Oxford: Oxford University Press.
Seabrooke, L. (2012). Pragmatic numbers: The IMF, financial reform, and policy learning in least likely environments. *Journal of International Relations and Development, 15*(4), 486–505.
Seabrooke, L. (2014). Epistemic arbitrage: Transnational professional knowledge in action. *Journal of Professions and Organization, 1*(1), 49–64.
Seabrooke, L., & Tsingou, E. (2014). Distinctions, affiliations, and professional knowledge in financial reform expert groups. *Journal of European public policy, 29*(3), 389–407.

Silver, C. (2007). Local matters: Internationalizing strategies for U.S. law firms. *Indiana Journal of Global Legal Studies*, *14*(1), 67–93.
Stokman, F. N., Ziegler, R., & Scott, J. (1985). *Networks of corporate power: A comparative analysis of ten countries*. Cambridge, MA: Polity Press.
Streeck, W. (1997). Beneficial constraints: On the economic limits of rational voluntarism. In J. R. Hollingsworth & R. Boyer (Eds.), *Contemporary capitalism: The embeddedness of institutions* (pp. 197–219). Cambridge: Cambridge University Press.
Streeck, W. (2008). *Re-forming capitalism: Institutional change in the German political economy*. Oxford: Oxford University Press.
Streeck, W. (2011). Taking capitalism seriously: Towards an institutionalist approach to contemporary political economy. *Socio-Economic Review*, *9*(1), 137–167.
Streeck, W. (2014). *Buying time*. London: Verso.
Streeck, W., & Thelen, K. A. (2005). *Beyond continuity*. Oxford: Oxford University Press.
Suchman, M. C. (1995). Managing legitimacy; strategic and institutional approaches. *Academy of Management Review*, *20*(3), 571–610.
Suddaby, R., & Greenwood, R. (2005). Rhetorical strategies of legitimacy. *Administrative Science Quarterly*, *50*(1), 35–67.
Thelen, K. (2014). *Varieties of liberalization and the new politics of social solidarity*. Cambridge: Cambridge University Press.
Therborn, G. (2014). *The killing fields of inequality*. Cambridge, MA: Polity.
Useem, M. (1984). *The inner circle*. Oxford: Oxford University Press.
Useem, M. (2015). From classwide coherence to company-focused management and director engagement. In G. Morgan, S. Quack, & P. Hirsch (Eds.), *Elites on trial* (Vol. 43). Research in the Sociology of Organizations. Bingley, UK: Emerald Group Publishing Limited.
van der Zwan, N. (2014). Making sense of financialization. *Socio-Economic Review*, *12*(1), 99–129.
Vion, A., Dudouet, F.-X., & Grémont, E. (2015). Euro Zone corporate elites at the cliff edge (2005-2008): a new approach of transnational interlocking. In G. Morgan, S. Quack, & P. Hirsch (Eds.), *Elites on trial* (Vol. 43). Research in the Sociology of Organizations. Bingley, UK: Emerald Group Publishing Limited.
Wade, R. H., & Sigurgeirsdottir, S. (2010). Lessons from Iceland. *New Left Review*, *65*, 5–29.
Wade, R. H., & Sigurgeirsdottir, S. (2012). Iceland's rise, fall, stabilisation and beyond. *Cambridge Journal of Economics*, *36*(1), 127–144.
Weaver, C. (2008). *Hypocrisy trap*. Princeton, NJ: Princeton University Press.
Whitley, R. (2007). *Business systems and organizational capabilities*. Oxford: Oxford University Press.
Wilkinson, R., & Pickett, K. (2010). *The spirit level: Why equality is better for everyone*. London: Penguin.
Woll, C. (2014). *The power of inaction*. Ithaca, NY: Cornell University Press.
Wren, A. (2013). *The political economy of the service transition*. Oxford: Oxford University Press.
Zald, M. N., & Lounsbury, M. (2010). The wizards of oz: Towards an institutional approach to elites, expertise and command posts. *Organization studies*, *31*(7), 963–996.

THE COUNTER-CYCLICAL CHARACTER OF THE ELITE

Shamus Rahman Khan

ABSTRACT

This paper begins by outlining the basic attitudinal differences between the elite and the rest of society. Understanding these divergent views does not require resorting to arguments that reply upon error, ignorance, manipulation, or differences in individual character. Instead, both elites and others are correct in their understanding of these processes because they overgeneralize from their own experience. The major proposition of this paper is that if we compare the economic conditions of the average American and to that of the elite, we find that they are, in important ways, the inverse of one another. During times when Americans as a whole were experiencing economic advancement and mobility, elites were comparatively stagnant. And today, as most Americans are locked in place, elites observe tremendous mobility. The counter-cyclical character of the elite has important implications for our understanding of elite culture, and elite response to inequality and redistribution.

Keywords: Elites; economic trends; mobility; inequality

INTRODUCTION

Why do elites[1] see the world differently than the rest of the society? Behind this simple question lies an empirical claim — that they do in fact see the world differently — which I will establish, at least in relationship to the divergent political attitudes of elites compared to the rest of society. Also implicit is the suggestion that this difference makes a difference; I will argue that it does. In this paper, I make two arguments: (1) elites seek to enact policies that often misunderstand the condition of the mass of society and (2) we need not rely upon explanations of manipulation or oppression to make sense of why they do so. The implications for these arguments are important particularly under conditions where elite political power is considerable and elites are disproportionately able to enact their views. Understanding why elites get mass society wrong may help us see how they might instead get it right. But before moving to such speculation, I ask why the difference in world views in the first place?

One explanation for divergent elite and mass views of the world is that dominated groups suffer from error or ignorance, and/or dominant groups construct ideologies to oppress or manipulate them. Working class voters don't understand their interests (Frank, 2004, but see Gelman, Park, Shor, Bafumi, & Cortina, 2008), and in a hegemonic haze act and believe things they should not. In the extreme version of this point of view, elites use "ideology" to manipulate masses. Giovanni Sartori famously argued, "ideologies are the crucial lever at the disposal of elites for obtaining political mobilization and for maximizing the possibilities of mass manipulation" (1969, p. 411). There may well be something to this approach, yet it borders on conspiracy theory, giving extreme agency, coherence, and power to elites and turning the rest into dim-witted lemmings.

Another explanation for why elites and others have different world views is that they are different kinds of people. Call this what you want — perhaps selection on the basis of preferences or human capital. This explanation tends to focus on the individual-level characteristics of elites in order to explain their social position. When exploring those in advantaged positions, this seems like a good enough strategy. We see this approach both within our own scholarship but also throughout the popular press on elites (which is far more voluminous[2]). Yet we might do well to remind ourselves that we were exploring those in disadvantaged positions, we would call such an approach — explaining social positions by the attributes of those within those positions — something quite different: the fundamental attribution error. And for good reason, there are not only logical concerns with explaining social positions by the attributes of those occupying such positions but there are also empirical ones. For the attribute that seems to explain most of the variance between the rich and rest is not actually a property of rich individuals. Instead, it is a relationship. That is to say that rich people tend to have had rich (or at least richer) parents.

This points to the strength of a third approach to understanding elites. And that is to understand the social worlds within which they are embedded. This is hardly a profound or radical stance; indeed, we might go so far as to call it pedestrian or mundane. But it is an important one if we are to explain the basic puzzle without resorting to explanations that suggest that actors are puppets or their masters, or that individual attributes are the engines of all outcomes. My approach, then, is to explore the social world that elites inhabit – its history, dynamics, and basic character – and use the difference between that world and the world of the rest of society to explain divergent world views.

This paper has three basic sections. First, drawing upon some recent work in political science, I briefly establish some of the attitudinal differences between the elite and the rest of society. The evidence here is hardly extensive. But it shows that on important issues – particularly around those of redistribution and support for government insurance programs – elites and the rest view the role of the state quite differently.

Second, I argue that we can explain such differences without resorting to arguments that reply upon error, ignorance, manipulation, or differences in individual character. Instead, drawing upon recent work of economists that focuses on questions of inequality and mobility, I suggest that both elites and others are correct in their understanding of these processes but curiously their understandings are different. There are two reasons. "Their worlds" are different. Particularly in the American context that I will draw upon, the social isolation/segregation of elites from the rest of society means that the worlds they experience (and draw their conclusions from) are not the same worlds. But the more important underlying mechanism is not just that the worlds are different because in one world people have lots of resources and in the other they have few. Instead, I propose that these different worlds actually have different economic dynamics. The major proposition of this paper is that if we take the economic conditions of the average American and compare it with that of the elite, we observe something as interesting as it is important: they are, in important ways, the inverse of one another. During times when Americans as a whole were experiencing economic advancement and mobility, elites were comparatively stagnant. And today, as most Americans are locked in place, elites observe tremendous mobility. Just as different sectors of the economy experience different dynamics (American finance has boomed as other sectors have declined, see Lin & Tomaskovic-Devey, 2013; Tomaskovic-Devey & Lin, 2011), so too do social classes. As such, groups can be correct in understanding *their world* while misunderstanding *the world* more generally. Scholars have a term for this: availability bias, which is the tendency to generalize based on nearby information. Such overgeneralization plagues most humans. And it becomes particular acute under two conditions: when nearby information is significantly different from other information and related, when such experiential bases of information are particularly concentrated across lines of difference (in short, when you have what we might call segregation).

The third part of this paper draws upon some of my own sociological work (Khan, 2011; Khan & Jerolmack, 2013), to outline the cultural dynamics of the elite understanding of the world, with particular attention to our contemporary period. That is, having provided an earlier explanation for why it is that elites view the world as increasingly meritocratic even though mobility is locked in place, I draw out some of the implications for this upon elite identities (Khan, 2012b).

How Do the Rich View the World Compared to Others?

Studies of elite attitudes are both difficult to interpret and rare. The interpretive problem is partially tied to the concern that expressed attitudes might not relate to revealed preferences (Jerolmack & Khan, forthcoming). The issue of rarity is one of both numbers and access: on large-scale instruments it is difficult for both numbers and access to have enough of a sample of elites to draw conclusions from, and in general who we are interested in (the very elite) are lumped together with others that do not quite belong within the category of "elite."[3] Furthermore, elites are difficult to identify and access for social scientists. Yet, luckily there has been an increasing amount of work that gives us the sense of elite policy preferences that we can compare with other work on elite political activity. Combining these two literatures helps us better understand elite attitudes and how such attitudes are enacted.

While Stuart Soroka and Christopher Wlezien have suggested that the preferences of the affluent and others are not that different (2008), there is mounting evidence against such a position (Gilens, 2009, 2012; Page, Bartels, & Seawright, 2013). Looking at data over the last 40 years, scholars have consistently found that, "Relatively affluent Americans tend to be more liberal than others on religious and moral issues, including abortion, gay rights, and prayer in school, but much more conservative than the non-affluent on issues of taxes, economic regulation, and social welfare" (Page et al., 2013, p. 52; see also Page & Hennessy, 2010; for more on overall policy preferences of all Americans, see Page & Jacobs, 2009 and Page & Shapiro, 1992; for more on political responsiveness to such different preferences see Bartels, 2008 and Schlozman, Verba, & Brady, 2012).

Yet "affluent" is a broad category. In the case of Martin Gilens' work, it encapsulates up to the top 20% of Americans. By my definition (see note 1), this does not constitute "elite." I do not mean this as a criticism of the important work by scholars like Gilens and Bartels, I simply mean that it does not accurately fit the categories I am interested in for my own arguments. But recently Page et al. (2013) have fielded a survey/interview study of high net worth Americans; their sample has a median wealth of $7.5 million and an average of $14 million.[4] Their work shows that such elites have different priorities than those of average Americans particularly on economic issues of taxation and redistribution. In short, the trend we see at the beginning among upper-middle class voters — divergent attitudes from the rest — continues as we move up the income distribution.

Although Americans' overwhelming favor the expansion of government support for health care and social security, elites strongly favor shrinking these programs. And where Americans express strong support for policies wherein governments ensure jobs, a minimum wage, a baseline standard of living, and tax credits for middle and working class Americans, elite support for such policies is far more tempered.[5] Importantly, Page et al. find that the richer people get, the more different their views are from everyday Americans; "the top one-tenth of 1 percent of wealth holders (people with $40 million or more in net worth) may tend to hold still more conservative views that are even more distinct from those of the general public." They favor less regulation of (their) economic interests and cutting back support for social programs. This is not surprising. But its documentation is important. Furthermore, there is evidence that such expressed attitudes are actually enacted in voting behavior. In his work with various colleagues, Andrew Gelman (Gelman, Shor, Bafumi, & Park, 2007; Gelman et al., 2008) shows that wealth is associated with voting behavior — the wealthier you are the more likely you are to vote for the Republican party, and the less well-off you are the more likely you are to vote for Democrats. These are robust results, but they are strongly tempered by context — particularly the context of whether or not you live in a rich or a poor state. In poorer states, the rich are much more likely to vote for the Republican party than the poor; in rich states, there is relatively a low correlation with income and vote preference (Gelman et al., 2007). Yet still, the basic finding is important for it shows that elites vote in ways that are consistent with the attitudes, *particularly in relation to economic issues*. Though they tend to diverge on social issues from the rest of the society (being more liberal), when it comes to the voting booth, they more often than not vote with their wallets.

In the following section of the paper, I draw upon Gelman's point about context to draw out some of the differences between the context of elite and average Americans. The reader should be aware, however, that where Gelman uses multilevel models to give a fine-grained account of the varying contexts across states, I write in far broader terms. Drawing upon the recent work of economists, I argue that the material experiences of elites have been considerably different than that of other Americans. This is not so say that "The rich are different than you and I; they have more money." Instead, it is to say that the dynamics of the material worlds that the rich and the rest inhabit are often very different from one another.

The Counter-Cyclical Character of the Elite

Since the publishing of Thomas Piketty and Emmanuel Saez's seminal paper (2003), economists have been using social security, tax return, and other administrative data to uncover the inequality and mobility in America dating back to 1917 (1937 for mobility data). These data give us some of the longest runs we can expect from reliable sources in terms of the relationship between Americans to one another (inequality) and both the intergenerational transfer of wealth and the intragenerational capacity to develop such wealth through wage gains over the life course. The broad story is that inequality declined in the postwar period and then increased in the 1970s. Today, inequality is what it was at the tail end of the gilded age – which is to say that America is a very inequitable nation compared to other industrialized countries and even its recent past. One of the more specific take-aways from the account provided by Piketty and Saez is that the engine of inequality has been the rich rather than the poor or middle classes. We cannot explain a variable by a constant. And while the level of inequality in America has varied considerably over time, the relative position of the poor and middle classes has remained roughly the same since the 1960s. The fate of the rich, however, has waxed and waned. Within economics, this combination of data that address long-run inequality and mobility and a somewhat novel empirical finding (to understand inequality we should study the rich not the poor) has led to an enormous growth of new studies on elites. And as this paper is due for publication, these findings have become the subject of major national debate – with the publication of Thomas Piketty's book, *Capital in the Twenty-First Century* (2014).

While the inequality story is relatively well known, until recently less attention has been paid to mobility. The mobility patterns follow a somewhat similar trajectory to those of inequality – though the story is more complicated. There are numerous reasons for this. First, there is a distinction between intragenerational mobility (of which there has been a considerable amount) and intergenerational mobility (which has been stagnant). Furthermore, a nontrivial amount of the intragenerational mobility story is due to women's entry into the labor market. So, as Kopczuk and his colleagues have shown (2010), mobility among all workers has increased since the 1950s, but if we look at the experience of men, we see that it has declined among this group. As women have made up considerable ground in the labor market, they have driven the overall mobility upward.

How one reads such a finding is largely a product of one's political orientation. That is, some might argue that this is simply an experience of market equilibrium, with men's wages declining as the discriminatory practices of excluding women create wage adjustments. Others, by contrast, might find that the increase in women's position is a product of the decline of real wages for families, whereby women are still discriminated against as they enter labor markets, and families lose both women's labor time in the household and men's wages in the markets. My orientation causes me to tend toward latter explanation, but for my overall argument it does not matter which position you adopt.

As for intergenerational mobility, the findings have been continually reassessed as new data are gathered and made available. While mobility estimates once suggested a high degree of intergeneration movement (Becker & Tomes, 1979, 1986), such estimates have been revised. Today, economists have access to better data – both administrative data and panel studies that eliminate the assumptions of earlier models and follow actual families to explore intergenerational mobility. While about a decade ago work suggested a decline in mobility (Mazumder, 2005) over the last 40 years, a recent major study suggests that Americans born from the 1970s through the 1990s have experienced roughly equivalent mobility (Chetty, Hendren, Kline, Saez, & Turner, 2014). There are reasons to be thankful (and surprised) that as inequality has increased, mobility has remained largely unchanged.[6] However, there are three important caveats. First, the overall levels of mobility in America are among the lowest among industrialized nations. And second, while the increase in inequality has not influenced the rate of mobility, as Chetty et al. note, "because inequality has risen, the consequences of the "birth lottery" – the parents to whom a child is born – are larger today than in the past." And finally, Chetty's results rely upon imputed wages for workers under the age of 30; there are many reasons to believe that such imputations, while expertly done, will prove to be in error.

These general trends suggest that inequality declined in the immediate postwar period and began increasing sometime in the mid-1970s, that inequality and mobility are inversely related (cross-nationally), that in America as inequality increased intergenerational mobility remained stagnant (but intragenerational mobility continued to be stable or increasing, largely driven by the entry of women into labor force). However, missing from our story is breaking down these findings to look more carefully at the position of the elite. That is, while I have described here the trends for the society overall, what about that small sector – say the 1% or 0.1% – that we have seen to be so consequential to the dynamics we're interested in?

Here, again I turn to the work of economist Wojciech Kopczuk, who, along with a series of colleagues, has explored this question extensively. And yet again, the findings are more complex than with our simple equality story (and consequential for our argument). There are two basic findings of interest: one on wealth concentration and the other on wealth mobility. In exploring wealth shares of the top 1%, Kopczuk and Saez find that, "there has been a sharp reduction in wealth concentration over the 20th century: the top 1 percent wealth share was close to 40 percent in the early decades of the century but has fluctuated between 20 and 25 percent over the last three decades. This dramatic decline took place at a very specific time period, from the onset of Great Depression to the end of World War II, and was concentrated in the very top groups within the top percentile, namely groups within the top 0.1 percent" (2004, p. 446). However, unlike Piketty and Saez's finding (2003) that income inequality continued to increase dramatically after the 1980s, largely driven by the income gains of the top 1% and even 0.1%, Kopczuk and Saez find that while wealth concentration increases from the 1970s into the 1980s, this tendency basically ceases in the mid-1990s. They explain this by arguing that the recent growth in income among the elite has been driven by employment and not capital returns. This leads them to suggest that, "the rentier class of the early century is not yet reconstituted" (2004, p. 445; for more on wealth inequality see also Keister, 2000, 2005; Kennickell, 2003; Spilerman, 2000; and Wolff, 1998, 2002).

This finding, no doubt, will come as a surprise to readers (or those who have heard) of Piketty (2014). Indeed, Piketty reports a very similar finding (Figure 6.5, pp. 222), where we see the capital share remaining relatively stagnant from 1995 to 2010 in most rich countries. Piketty's argument, to be clear, is that such capital share will increase under two conditions: as massive income of the elite is converted to capital and as we move to a low-growth regime. While I am highly sympathetic to these arguments, it is important to note that they are highly speculative (anticipating the rest of the 21st century rather than describing the immediate past).

What this suggests is that *at present* the elite are certainly outpacing the rest in terms of wages but not in the rates of wealth acquisition. This might indicate comparatively low savings rates or the lack of time for the increase in income inequality to build the relatively similar disparity in wealth (indeed, it seems that this latter explanation is the strongest and that forthcoming data will suggest a rise in wealth inequality keeping pace with income inequality – though slightly lagged). I will return to this point. But first I wish to highlight another important finding about wealth; it comes from Lena Edlund's work with Kopczuk. Using estate tax return data, Edlund and Kopczuk (2009) look at the share of women among the very wealthy in America (0.01%); they take this as an indicator of dynastic wealth. The logic here is that the more women there are among the elite, the more likely it is that the elite has inherited rather than made their wealth (this is a plausible assumption). They find that share of women within the top 0.01% peaked in the late 1960s – when women made up nearly half of the wealthiest people in America. In recent years, the share has declined to about one-third. The finding suggests that wealth mobility into the elite *declined* through the early 1970s, only to increase in the subsequent period. Elites had less mobility into their group through the early 1970s and more mobility into it more recently.

This brings us to the main point of this paper: the experience of the elite, then, and the rest of America, has been considerably different. I will now turn to this observation in order to highlight how, in important respects, the elite experience and the "mass" experience are different. The implication of this difference is that elites and everyday Americans may understand their own experiences quite well, but elites might overgeneralize from their experience – believe that others live in the same world that they do.

Such availability bias could well produce some of the disparities in political attitudes I outlined in the previous section. I write in speculative terms here, but the following section establishes this point more firmly by drawing upon my own work. Regardless of the strength of that argument, the general point about the counter-cyclical nature of the elite still has important implications for understanding this group.

The basic observation I hope to draw out is that elites in America have had what I call a "counter-cyclical" experience: when most Americans experienced mobility they experienced stagnation; while most Americans have been locked in place, elites have experienced considerable mobility. Although the previous data discussions were somewhat dense, centered around discussions of economic data, here I move to a more speculative narrative so that the implications of this experience can be better understood.

Much of the increase in attention to elites has been driven by political rather than empirical concerns. Piketty and Saez's paper was published five years before the great recession of 2008. But its importance increased after chants of "We. Are. The 99%" echoed through Zuccotti Park and other outposts of the Occupy Wall Street movement. When we talk about the difference between the 1% and the 99%percent, the implicit argument is that the experience of the 1% is quite different than the experience of the 99%. That is, these two groups are not part of a singular entity that has a kind of flow between all its parts like a "market" but instead live in fractured or separate worlds. While this is often our implicit presumption, we are rarely explicit about its consequences.[7]

We might ask ourselves, what is the experience of the world from 1945 until the 1970s for two groups: average Americans and very, very wealthy Americans? From our discussion of the economics literature, we can begin to see the outlines of our story. If you were an average American in the immediate postwar period, you would experience some of the lowest levels of inequality our nation has ever seen. You'd also experience modest mobility – particularly as social programs provided both a safety and access to institutions like education, which aided advancement. In the postwar period, you'd enjoy substantial mobility over your lifetime and be less hindered or advantaged by your parents' wages than your parents were by theirs. Hard fought battles over racial and gender oppression also meant that the relative position of nonwhites and women was beginning to advance. I would argue that we often read our American experience through this moment: one where rights were fought over and won, where opportunity was relatively available, and where inequalities were comparatively low.

But if we were to look within, say, the top 0.01%, we would find something different. Elites experienced less of both kinds of mobility than in previous eras. That is, their wages were comparatively stagnant – to a large degree, this is because of incredibly high marginal tax rates (Piketty & Saez, 2003). But not only were wages stagnant so, too, was membership within the elite – as Edlund and Kopczuk show, dynastic wealth was the most dominant in this moment (more so than any other moment we have data for in the 20th century). This means that movement in (and out of) the elite was comparatively rare.

This is what I mean by the counter-cyclical nature of elites. In the immediate postwar period, the average American lived in a world of comparatively low levels of inequality and modest mobility; the very, very wealthy lived in a world of relative wage stagnation and comparatively low levels of turnover. Overall, the elite lived in the same world, but if we were to look at elites alone (which is to say, elites looking in the mirror or around their neighborhoods), the story is quite different.

But what if this postwar period was exceptional? Perhaps the elite is not counter-cyclical; instead, I have identified a unique period in our social and economic history and generalized too broadly from it. There is something to this claim but overall we still find strong currents to the trend I have suggested. Unfortunately, our data sources are not particularly good for the periods well before the postwar era, but we can look more closely at the period immediately after. And so we might ask: what has happened to the elite and the average American over the last three decades?

The average American has experienced comparative wage stagnation and stagnant mobility. Intragenerational (or life course) mobility has increased, though this is largely an artifact of women's increased labor market participation; women have made real wage gains, but male workers (which is to say, the majority of workers) have tended to be locked in place, even declining slightly.

However, if we were to look in the elite, we would observe something quite different. While the overall wealth concentration of the elite did not return to its prewar levels, along other dimensions the elite experience was very much a return to a previous era. So the likelihood of being in the top 0.01% is not so strongly related to having parents that were within that group as it was in the 1960s. There are more "new rich" today than in the immediate past. And the wage gains that we observe within the top 0.01% are dramatic. Even though some of these gains were eliminated with the great recession of 2008, the recovery has been dramatic in favor of the elite, returning them to their prerecession standing.

Try, for a moment, to put yourself in the position of the American elite. Let's say you're fortunate enough to be in the top 0.01%. If you look at someone slightly beneath you economically, you find that your wages are growing much faster than theirs. That is because wage growth is considerable among the elite, and the growth function is almost exponential. But that also has an important implication. The satisfaction of looking down is only met with the anxiety of looking up. That's because if you look at those above you, you see that those who make more money than you do are outpacing your wage gains at an even greater rate than you are outpacing the person beneath you. In short, for the elite the recent experience is one of more mobility and more wage growth than in the past. And this material experience is bound to a lived one of seeing movement all around you: growing wages, more new members who join your ranks because of wage work not capital rewards, with distances between people growing every day. This is an experience of growth and movement — a vital economy.

But if you're in the middle of the American wage distribution, you don't see this at all. What you see is a relative stagnation, all around. The exception here, of course, is women and nonwhites. But increasingly, the evidence seems to show that even among these groups, the gains have mostly ceased (particularly for Black Americans). And so perhaps the postwar period was not a typical American moment, but in general an exception is in that the majority of Americans enjoyed low levels of inequality and some mobility and unexceptional in that the elite experience and the experience of the average American were markedly different.

My argument here is not contra-Smith or other economic models that economic resources are finite or zero-sum and therefore when one group does well other groups are necessarily constrained (which is to say that there are no rising tides). The data I have presented are too limited to make such a broad claim. But there is an implicit argument here that there is no "economy" in the sense of a unified experience of market conditions. Instead, there are economies within national markets, and those economies may well have radically different characters. This is certainly true across race and gender; in this paper, I am arguing that it is also likely true across class lines. Furthermore, there are other indices than inequality and mobility. We might look, for example, at standard of living, life expectancy, happiness, or any litany of other measures. I have chosen inequality and mobility because they have been shown to be important to society relative to a host of indicators (Jencks, 2002). And monetary units are relatively objective in their measurement, making them ideal for the kinds of analyses we have just undertaken. Furthermore, as I mentioned before, the data drawn upon represent a very small range of time and should our temporal parameters shift, so too would our story. I do not wish to back off my claims, only to acknowledge some of their limitations. But the observation seems important enough that I will build upon them and outline their implications for understanding elites. Here, I move away from elite literatures in political science and economics and focus more concretely on my own work within the sociological tradition.

The Cultural Implications of These Observations for our Understanding of Elites

Americans are comparatively segregated in terms of where we live, not just racially, but also economically. Perhaps, the best look at the global elite today comes from journalist Freeland (2012), whose access to elites provides the reader an acute sense of a world that is often more imagined than observed. Traveling with them from penthouses to boardrooms to the streets of Davos, Switzerland, Freeland combines ethnographic skill with journalistic prose in conveying how it is that elites understand and live in the world. In her work, Freeland argues that the plutocratic elite think of neighborhoods not relative to physical proximity or national bounds; they think of neighborhoods globally in terms of those they feel closest to in spirit rather than geography – in this sense, the Upper East Side may be closer to Tokyo's Ginza district than it is for Spanish Harlem. While elites may be proximally close to nonelites, their tendency to occupy different worlds means that encounters are few and relatively unsustained.

If we are to follow our earlier story, one of the things that we see is a radical change in the social conditions of the elite.[8] One of those aspects is their "opening" – by which I mean that there is more mobility into the group than before. But such an experience has been mirrored by other declines in what we might think of as social closure. An example would be the tremendous opening of a broad range of social institutions in much of the West over the past 40 or so years. We cannot underestimate these radical changes to society – access to opportunities that the majority of the population were once excluded from (women, minorities) is more than just window dressing. This opening has not meant anything close to equality. But its impact on the ways in which people understand their worlds is profound. Institutions like my own elite university have opened up to Black students – going from 0.8% of the student body 40 years ago to about 13% today – and transformations like this have influenced how students at such elite schools understand themselves and the world around them.

We often associate social closure with inequality. In both theoretical and lay conceptualizations, we suggest that inequality emerges because of disparate access. Yet, in the last 40 years inequality has increased dramatically and by almost every measure, access to elite institutions by those formerly excluded has increased.

The reason is simple enough. Elite institutions are those that seem to have most forcefully embraced the language of openness. In the United States, we can point to the Ivy League's tremendous commitment to affirmative action, or if you visit the website of any major corporation, all will have statements of their "diversity initiatives." And when such programs are subject to legal challenge – as affirmative action programs have been in the elite public university system – a powerful *amicus curiae* brief in favor of these policies was written by that most sacred of American institutions: its military.

But as we saw in our discussion of the economics literature at the same time that elites have embraced openness, they have also been the engines of inequality (Piketty & Saez, 2003). And they have been willfully blind to problems of increased inequality (Jencks, 2002), and hostile to programs that might help alleviate it (Page et al., 2013). It has been the growth of wages of those at the top that has resulted in the rise of inequality in most of the Western world (Atkinson & Piketty, 2007, 2010). A general observation, then, is that the democratic embrace among the elite has been accompanied by a similar rise in their fortunes.

There are many explanations to the rise of inequality, from the declines in unionization (Western & Rosenfeld, 2011) to the financialization of the economy (Tomaskovic-Devey & Lin, 2011), to the increased capacity for managers to leapfrog one another (DiPrete, Eirich, & Pittinsky, 2010, but see also Gabaix & Landier, 2009). Underplayed in this literature, and at the core of my interest, are the cultural rhetorics that have facilitated these processes. I seek to establish such rhetoric through an account of my own work as well as show how it is grounded in the elite experience itself. The core of this rhetoric is the idea of the rise of the talented, deserving, meritorious individual. And mobility among the elite supports such a cultural framework.

In my earlier work (Khan, 2011), I argued that the culturally important shift in the elite identity has been from being a "class" to a collection of individuals – the best and the brightest. That is, rather than identifying themselves as a group constituted through institutions and organizations (families, schools, clubs, a shared cultural–historical legacy, etc.), today's elites consider themselves as becoming elites because of their individual talents. What "groups" elites is the fact that they have worked hard and gotten ahead; they are the cream that has risen to the top. In embracing this individual work ethic rather than class narrative, elites think of themselves as meritocrats.

One of the consequences of the collectivist movements of the 1960s has been the triumph of the individual and the death of the collective. Groups gathered together – Blacks, women, gays, and immigrants – to argue that the properties that grouped them and were then used to explain or justify their disadvantage should not matter. It should be human capital that matters; we should all have opportunities based on our capacities, not on characteristics ascribed to us. I developed this argument in the context of an ethnography of St. Paul's School – one of the most elite boarding schools in the nation (and my alma mater).[9]

My interest in my ethnographic work on St. Paul's was to better understand a place that vigorously embraces the importance of being an "open" or representative institution, and yet under such moral commitments to a kind of equality was a tight coupling with a context where inequality is increasing (the cost of access climbed at a rate at least twice that of economic growth).

When talking to students at St. Paul's School I found them forthcoming and almost universally consistent about how they made sense of their success. For example, Stan was from a wealthy but not particularly established family and seemed well liked by other students and faculty. He gave a typical answer when asked how far he had come since he started at St. Paul's. "I worked hard to get here, I learned in class, I worked to make the varsity team. And it was hard. But I earned it. We all earned it. And I feel good when I [...] see how far I've come .... I've come a long way. It wasn't easy .... I mean ... it's still not easy. It might even be harder ... but I did it .... Not everyone does this, gets this far. It takes a lot. I know I'm not done," he added cheerfully, "I've sorta just begun. But now I know that I can do it. I've got what it takes."

Stan's framing of his achievements as the result of hard work – whether conscious or not – works against a common suspicion of entitlement and the nagging feeling that the rich succeed just because of who they are. St. Paul's students seek to replace that frame with one that is based on merit. Stan was not alone in talking about how hard he worked to earn what he has achieved. For example, there is a set of couches on campus that only seniors are allowed to sit on (this is not an official rule but is nonetheless an accepted practice). When the senior class graduated, and the rest of the school remained to take their finals, the juniors began aggressively taking over these couches to mark themselves as the new seniors on campus. I asked them why it was so important for them to immediately occupy this space. A junior, Emily, said, "This is going to sound ridiculous. But life here is tough. And this place, this was a goal for me. I mean, I would walk by every day and see seniors sitting here. And at first I thought, 'I'll never get there .... I don't think I can do it.' But that motivated me. It's not just some 'forbidden fruit' for me. It was a goal. Something I could work toward. I'd see it every day and think to myself, 'I am going to get there .... I can do it.' And guess what? Here I am. I've done it. I honestly don't care about the couch. But this is important for me. It proves that I did it. That all that work got me somewhere. That it was worth it."

Emily deploys the same frame for the couches as Stan did for his personal achievements. Her ascension was a goal that came through work not a deserved acquisition that came from time logged or inheritance. And in achieving their newfound status, Emily and Stan both appeal to their own capacity: Emily finds that she "can do it"; Stan notes that he can achieve tasks he sets himself to in a way that not everyone can.

Such students are not completely naive. They know that not everyone who works hard gets ahead. They see many at their school who suffer this fate. These people are the staff, the men, and women who make the school function day in and day out. Not surprisingly, students spoke fondly of staff members. They are the caretakers and cheerleaders for students while parents are away. Jessica, who praised a cleaning woman in her dormitory for her demeanor, her seemingly limitless memory, and her work ethic, could only come up with "bad luck" as the reason for the cleaner's station in life. Another student explained, "Forty years ago, women weren't allowed into places like this. We've come a long way. Things are different now." Gathering all of the students' interview responses together, we learn that staff are unlucky, have different priorities, or — most commonly — are casualties of an unjust era that we have since overcome. Importantly, students maintain a belief in meritocracy throughout these accounts.

Students also know that being talented and hardworking may not make them the best at everything. In fact, students consistently bring up other students who are better than they are. Students told stories about a violinist on campus who might soon have a premiere at Carnegie Hall, a mathematician who would win one of the greatest prizes in that discipline (the Fields Medal), an artist who would sell paintings for millions, and a squash player who would soon take home gold in the junior Olympics. There is, no doubt, a certain teenage mentality to this — students assume that the school is the whole world. But still, it was not simply that the students thought of themselves as having a sense of potential — that the world was theirs to contribute to; they also recognized that certain people had extraordinary talents, skills that far exceeded their own. At St. Paul's School, the students believed that they were surrounded by such talents; as a result, that which was extraordinary became a part of their ordinary reality. Their school was a collection of some of the hardest working, most talented kids in the world.

Talking to students, I overwhelmingly heard about their hard work, and how much they earned their success. The students similarly expressed a commitment to social justice and a narrative of just how far the world had come. The lessons from their accounts were of past injustices, present opportunities, and the necessity of work, discipline, and talent to make it. The world is a meritocracy. This does not mean that it is equal — some people are better than others, and these talents are important to recognize. The view is that inequalities are increasingly acquired by the action of individuals and decreasingly ascribed by belonging to a class, race, or gender.

My basic finding was that those who have most vigorously adopted the stance of an open meritorious society have been the elite. They look more diverse, including some of those they formerly excluded. And while they certainly know that their individual traits, capacities, skills, talents, and qualities are cultivated, they suggest that this cultivation is done through hard work, and access is granted through capacity rather than birthright.

IMPLICATIONS AND CONCLUSIONS

If I were to talk about elite culture today, then, I would talk about a culture of "individual self-cultivation." And the argument of this paper is that this cultural framework is not simply a delusional presentation of self or a hegemonic attempt to blind the masses but instead it has an experiential basis. Yet, the narrative of openness and talent may help elites explain themselves to themselves, but as we have seen from our discussion of overall patterns of mobility and equality, it obscures the broader American experience. And the result might not be pernicious,[10] but the consequences are important. Society has recessed in the minds of the elite; if anything, it is a producer of social problems. What society did was to create the biases of old institutions based in categorization — racism, sexism, and exclusion. The resulting view is one where society must be as benign as possible, sitting in the background as we play out our lives in a flat world. And the result of such a stance is a new efficiency, the market.

Such a view suggests that social problems are the result of processes whereby we thought in terms of collectivities. With such barriers removed, market equality can take over. We live the results of this triumph today, and I would argue that it has been a world with less equality and mobility for the Average American and a more empowered elite.

Meritocracy is a social arrangement like any other: it is a loose set of rules that can be adapted in order to obscure advantages, all the while justifying them on the basis of shared values. Markets allow elites to limit investments in all by undermining public goods and shared, socialized resource allocations. This allows them to increase their own advantage by deploying their economic spoils in markets; they receive returns to these investments, those without resources to invest are left behind. As Miles Corak (2013b) has shown in his work, those societies with higher returns to education tend to be less mobile. This is an associational finding, but it might be explained by high inequality regimes wherein those with resource surpluses purchase additional education thereby solidifying advantages for their offspring. In suggesting that it is their work and not their wealth, and that it is their talents and not their lineage, elites do three things. First, they draw on the elite experience to generate a cultural architecture. Yet these experiences are relative — it's not that *all* elites have achieved from nothing, only that a few have and most have achieved an enormous amount from the position of already considerable advantage. Second, they have applied a cultural view of *their* world to *the* world. Third, the result is effectively to blame inequality on those whom our democratic promise has failed.

One of the most fascinating things we see if we compare elites from the tail end of the Gilded Age to those of today is that in the Gilded Age, the richer you were, the more likely you were to rely upon capital for your income (Kopczuk, Saez, & Song, 2010; Piketty & Saez, 2003). Gilded Age elites were far more likely to do something like own a factory and therefore they engaged in a fundamentally different enterprise than most Americans (who relied upon employment earnings, not capital ownership). But today what rich people do for their wealth primarily is to earn it through wages. We shouldn't push this argument too far. But psychically — or at least culturally — the experience of thinking that you're rich because you receive a massive paycheck for your work rather than for the fact that you own something means that you're likely to think of yourself as not different from everyone else. You're actually just like them. You get up in the morning, you go to work, and you earn a living. And your paycheck is way bigger because while everyone is doing the same thing (working); you're just more skilled than everyone else.

This helps elites believe something that's not true – that they are the engines of their own achievement and that their individual characteristics explain the outcomes that they're experiencing. One way that elites are like all other people is that they overgeneralize from their own experience. Their wages have grown so there is wage growth. They see more mobility around them so the American Dream is alive and well (provided you're willing to work hard enough). Harvard is terribly diverse so race doesn't matter anymore. Each of these stories helps justify an individualistic approach to the world, identifying collectivist policies like affirmative action or redistribution from one class to another as problematic. And because of their social power, elites have been successful in imposing their particularistic cultural logic much more broadly, arguing that it helps us better understand how markets and states should work.

We can think of elites as manipulative, or we can think of them as being like others: products of their particular locations and likely to overgeneralize from them. Elites are not completely accurate in understanding their own world – they overestimate their own contributions to their position and underestimate their structural advantages. They are not wrong in thinking that there is more mobility and growth today than there was a generation ago; they simply fail to recognize it's only a tiny fraction of Americans for whom that is true. The solutions to such a situation are simple enough to imagine but hardly easy to achieve. Economic conditions might be made consistent rather than the inverse of one another, particularistic experiences could be revealed for what they are, or social isolation might give way to greater social encounters with different worlds. But my conclusion is simple enough: elites and the rest live in different worlds. And there is a deeper meaning to this claim than we often recognize. For the dynamics of their economic experiences might often be inconsistent. And such counter-cyclical experiences may well make the world of difference.

NOTES

1. In this piece I will define "elites" as those with vastly disproportional access to or control over resources (social, cultural, symbolic, economic, or even human capital), where such resources have a transferable value. This definition is

elaborated in a longer review essay I have written on the sociology of elites (Khan, 2012a).

2. A good example of such an approach would be that of Malcolm Gladwell's *Outliers* (2008), which seeks to explain those tails of distributions by looking at their common attributes.

3. For example, if a survey has an upper-bound income category of $200,000, many within this category would be well-off but hardly elite.

4. This study has severe limitations; it is truly more of a pilot, focusing on the city of Chicago. Yet given that its findings are supported by a range of other observations from studies with different populations using different data and methodological instruments, I feel somewhat secure in its findings.

5. For example, take two questions: (1) The government should provide a decent standard of living for the unemployed and (2) The government in Washington ought to see to it that everyone who wants to work can find a job. For the first, 23% of elites favor the statement, whereas 50% of the general public does; for the second, 19% of elites favor the statement whereas 68% of the public does (Page et al., 2013, p. 57).

6. This finding suggests we re-evaluate some of the work that has suggested a "Great Gatsby Curve," a finding where countries with more inequality at one point in time also experience less earnings mobility across the generations (Corak, 2013b). This term was coined by Alan Krueger in a speech, "The Rise and Consequences of Inequality," to the Center for American Progress on January 12, 2012. As Corak notes, Krueger made this speech in his capacity as the Chairman of the Council of Economic Advisors, and Kreuger is hardly alone in his noting this relationship; we can see also Andrews and Leigh (2009), Björklund and Jäntti (2009), Blanden (2013), Corak (2006, 2013a), and Ermisch, Jäntti, Smeeding, and Wilson (2012). Such a curve is not so much a causal story as an associational one: that high inequality and low mobility associated could be explained by a range of phenomena (see Brunori, Ferreira, Peragine, 2013 for a particularly good review of this point). At the time of publication, the literature in this area is far from settled.

7. In the following several paragraphs I have drawn on a previously published essay that I wrote in response to Chrystia Freeland's book, *Plutocrats*. See Freeland (2012) and Khan (2013).

8. In the following paragraphs I draw upon a series of earlier published works, most deeply Khan (2011, 2012b) and Khan and Jerolmack (2013).

9. Founded in 1855, St. Paul's School is one of the top preparatory boarding schools in the country. It has one of the largest endowments of any educational institution in the world (nearly one million dollars per pupil), and in recent years, 30 percent of graduating classes attended an Ivy League University. If one takes a cursory look at the student body of this coed institution, there can be no doubt that the school is a place where privileged youths spend their adolescent years – although a quick glance will also show a fairly diverse student body. I was permitted to conduct my study of St. Paul's School in 2004–2005 academic year, during which I worked as a faculty member and lived at the school (located in Concord, New Hampshire). This position allowed me to observe the school's workings and talk to its faculty, students, staff, and alumni. My project was public knowledge. I was interested in getting a broad sense of the life of the place –

namely how its 500 students, its faculty, and its staff experienced their lives there and were formed (or transformed) by their experiences at the institution.

10. Here I break from earlier work (Khan, 2012), which suggested that such cultural logics were pernicious. A broader reading of the economics literature, as presented in this paper, has led me to this view.

REFERENCES

Andrews, D., & Leigh, A. (2009). More inequality, less social mobility. *Applied Economics Letters, 16*(15), 1489–1492.

Atkinson, A. B., & Piketty, T. (2007). *Top incomes over the 20th century*. Oxford: Oxford University Press.

Atkinson, A. B., & Piketty, T. (2010). *Top incomes in global perspective*. Oxford: Oxford University Press.

Bartels, L. M. (2008). *Unequal democracy: The political economy of the new gilded age*. New York, NY: Russell Sage Foundation and Princeton University Press.

Becker, G. S., & Tomes, N. (1979). An equilibrium theory of the distribution of income and intergenerational mobility. *Journal of Political Economy, 87*, 1153–1189.

Becker, G. S., & Tomes, N. (1986). Human capital and the rise and fall of families. *Journal of Labor Economics, 4*, 1–39.

Björklund, A., & Jäntti, M. (2009). Intergenerational income mobility and the role of family background. In W. Salverda, B. Nolan, & T. M. Smeeding (Eds.), *The Oxford handbook of economic inequality*. Oxford: Oxford University Press.

Blanden, J. (2013). Cross-country rankings in intergenerational mobility: A comparison of approaches from economics and sociology. *Journal of Economic Surveys, 27*(1), 38–73.

Brunori, P., Ferreira, F. H. G., & Peragine, V. (2013). *Inequality of opportunity, income inequality and economic mobility: Some international comparisons*. Policy Research Working Paper No. 6304, The World Bank, Development Research Group.

Chetty, R., Hendren, N., Kline, P., Saez, E., & Turner, N. (2014). *Is the United States still a land of opportunity? Recent trends in intergenerational mobility*. NBER Working Paper No. 19844. Retrieved from http://www.nber.org/papers/w19844

Corak, M. (2006). Do poor children become poor adults? Lessons for public policy from a cross country comparison of generational earnings mobility. In *Research on economic inequality* (Vol. 13, pp. 143–188). Dynamics of Inequality. Amsterdam, The Netherlands: Elsevier Press.

Corak, M. (2013a). Inequality from generation to generation: The United States in comparison. In R. Rycroft (Ed.), *The economics of inequality, poverty, and discrimination in the 21st century*. Westport, CT: Praeger Publishers Inc.

Corak, M. (2013b). Income inequality, equality of opportunity, and intergenerational mobility. *The Journal of Economic Perspectives, 27*(3), 79–102.

DiPrete, T., Eirich, G., & Pittinsky, M. (2010). Compensation benchmarking, leapfrogs, and the surge in executive pay. *American Journal of Sociology, 115*(6), 1671–1712.

Edlund, L., & Kopczuk, W. (2009). Women, wealth, and mobility. 2007. *American Economic Review, 99*(1), 146–178.

Ermisch, J., Jäntti, M., Smeeding, T. M., & Wilson, J. A. (2012). Advantage in comparative perspective. In J. Ermisch, M. Jäntti, & T. M. Smeeding (Eds.), *From parents to children: The intergenerational transmission of advantage*. New York, NY: Russell Sage Foundation.
Frank, T. (2004). *What's the matter with Kansas?* New York, NY: Henry Holt and Co.
Freeland, C. (2012). *Plutocrats: The rise of the new global super-rich and the fall of everyone else*. New York, NY: Doubleday.
Gabaix, X., & Landier, A. (2009). Why has CEO pay increased so much? *The Quarterly Journal of Economics*, *123*(1), 49–100.
Gelman, A., Park, D., Shor, B., Bafumi, J., & Cortina, H. (2008). *Red state, blue state, rich state, poor state: Why Americans vote the way they do*. Princeton, NJ: Princeton University Press.
Gelman, A., Shor, B., Bafumi, J., & Park, D. (2007). Rich state, poor state, red state, blue state: What's the matter with Connecticut? *Quarterly Journal of Political Science*, *2*, 345–367.
Gilens, M. (2009). Preference gaps and inequality in representation. *PS: Political Science & Politics*, *42*(2), 335–341.
Gilens, M. (2012). *Affluence and influence: Economic inequality and political power in America*. Princeton, NJ: Russell Sage Foundation and Princeton University Press.
Gladwell, M. (2008). *Outliers*. New York, NY: Little Brown.
Jencks, C. (2002). Does inequality matter? *Deadalus*, (Winter), 49–65.
Jerolmack, C., & Khan, S. (2014). Talk is cheap ethnography and the attitudinal fallacy. *Sociological Methods and Research*, *43*(2), 178–209.
Keister, L. (2000). *Wealth in America: Trends in wealth inequality*. Cambridge: Cambridge University Press.
Keister, L. (2005). *Getting rich: America's new rich and how they got that way*. Cambridge: Cambridge University Press.
Kennickell, A. B. (2003). A rolling tide: Changes in the distribution of wealth in the U.S., 1989–2001. Board of Governors of the Federal Reserve System, Finance and Economics Discussion Series 2003–24.
Khan, S., & Jerolmack, C. (2013). Saying meritocracy and doing privilege. *The Sociological Quarterly*, *54*, 8–18.
Khan, S. R. (2011). *Privilege: The making of an adolescent elite at St. Paul's school*. Princeton, NJ: Princeton University Press.
Khan, S. R. (2012a). The sociology of elites. *Annual Review of Sociology*, *38*, 361–377.
Khan, S. R. (2012b). Elite identities. *Identities*, 19(4), 477–484.
Khan, S. R. (2013). *Virtual panel on plutocrats with Robert Frank and Shamus Khan*. Public books. Retrieved from http://publicbooks.org/nonfiction/virtual-panel-on-chrystia-freelands-plutocrats
Kopczuk, W., & Saez, E. (2004). Top wealth shares in the United States, 1916–2000: Evidence from estate tax returns. *National Tax Journal*, *57*(2 Part 2), 445–487.
Kopczuk, W., Saez, E., & Song, J. (2010). Earnings inequality and mobility in the United States: Evidence from social security data since 1937. *The Quarterly Journal of Economics*, *125*(1), 91–128.
Lin, K.-H., & Tomaskovic-Devey, D. (2013). Financialization and US income inequality, 1970–2008. *American Journal of Sociology*, *118*, 1284–1329.
Mazumder, B. (2005). Fortunate sons: New estimates of intergenerational mobility in the United States. *Review of Economic Statistics*, *87*(2), 235–255.

Page, B. I., Bartels, L. M., & Seawright, J. (2013). Democracy and the policy preferences of wealthy Americans. *Perspectives on Politics, 11*(1), 51–73.
Page, B. I., & Hennessy, C. L. (2010). What affluent Americans want from politics. Paper Presented at the annual meeting of the American Political Science Association, Washington, DC, September 2–5. WP-11-08, Institute for Policy Research, Northwestern University.
Page, B. I., & Jacobs, L. R. (2009). *Class war? What Americans really think about economic inequality*. Chicago, IL: University of Chicago Press.
Page, B. I., & Shapiro, R. Y. (1992). *The rational public: Fifty years of trends in Americans' policy preferences*. Chicago, IL: University of Chicago Press.
Piketty, T. (2014). In A. Goldhammer (Trans.), *Capital in the twenty-first century*. Cambridge: Harvard University Press.
Piketty, T., & Saez, E. (2003). Income inequality in the United States, 1913–1998. *Quarterly Journal of Economics, 118*, 1–39.
Sartori, G. (1969). Politics, ideology and belief systems. *American Political Science Review, 63*, 398–411.
Schlozman, K. L., Verba, S., & Brady, H. E. (2012). *The unheavenly chorus: Unequal political voice and the broken promise of American democracy*. Princeton, NJ: Princeton University Press.
Soroka, S. N., & Wlezien, C. (2008). On the limits to inequality in representation. *PS: Political Science & Politics, 41*(2), 319–327.
Spilerman, S. (2000). Wealth and stratification processes. *Annual Review of Sociology, 26*, 497–524.
Tomaskovic-Devey, D., & Lin, K.-H. (2011). Economic rents and the financialization of the US economy. *American Sociological Review, 76*, 538–559.
Western, B., & Rosenfeld, J. (2011). Unions, norms, and the rise in American earnings inequality. *American Sociological Review, 76*, 513–537.
Wolff, E. N. (1998). Recent trends in the size distribution of household wealth. *Journal of Economic Perspectives, 12*(3), 131–150.
Wolff, E. N. (2002). *Top heavy: A study of increasing inequality of wealth in America*. New York, NY: New Press.

THE FIELD OF POWER:
THE CHANGING NATURE OF
ELITE NETWORKS

UNDERSTANDING THE CHANGING NATURE OF THE RELATIONSHIP BETWEEN THE STATE AND BUSINESS ELITES

Ali Ergur, Sibel Yamak and Mustafa Özbilgin

ABSTRACT

In this study, we aim to understand how the relationship between state and business elites and underlying power dynamics develop in the face of neoliberalism and globalization in a state-dependent context. For this purpose, we draw on a qualitative research with in-depth interviews with elites from 65 companies which are ranked among the 500 largest Turkish firms by the Istanbul Chamber of Industry. Major contribution of this work is that we illustrate how globalization or internationalization provides a limited tool for business elites to escape the domination of the state in a state-dependent context. The only exceptions to this rule of state domination among business elites are the elites who hold double citizenships and whose initial investment background is in a foreign country. This exceptional group of elites enjoyed higher latitude of action in their interactions with the state. For the rest, state remains as an influential mechanism of coercive power to which elites are subjected.

Last but not least, in spite of the connections between business growth and the state, the business elites are generally distrustful of politics and politicians and this mistrust is manifested in different ways. Overall, we illustrate the significance of the historical context and turning points in accounting for the changing nature of the relationship between elites and the state in Turkey.

Keywords: Globalization; business elites; Turkey; state dependence; business—state relations

INTRODUCTION

The nature of the relationship between business elites and the state seems to have attracted scant attention in the management literature (Yamak, Nielsen, & Escriba-Esteve, 2014). The nature of the relationship would vary across countries and regions. Storey and Lawton (2010) explain that different types of capitalism are rooted in different cultures and states, and this unique combination in turn may influence how business elites perceive the state and interact with it. In this study, we aim to understand the relationship between business elites and the state in the context of globalization in a state-dependent country. For this purpose, we draw on qualitative research, which was conducted among business elites in Turkey. This study aims to provide an answer to the following question: Given the history and nature of the Turkish state and its role as a shaper of the economy, how do the different business elites relate to the state and what is the impact of globalization on this relationship? A major contribution of this work is that we illustrate how globalization or internationalization provides a limited tool for business elites to escape the domination of the state in a state-dependent context. The only exceptions to this rule of state domination among business elites are the business elites who held double citizenships and whose initial investment background was in a foreign country. This exceptional group of elites enjoyed higher latitude of action in their interactions with the state. For the rest, the state remains as an influential mechanism of coercive power to which elites are subjected. Another interesting finding is that Turkish business elites do not form a coherent group and old and new elites' attitudes toward and relationship with the state differ significantly. Last but not least, in spite of the connections between business growth and the state, business elites are generally distrustful of politics and politicians and this mistrust is manifested in different ways.

Overall, we illustrate the significance of the historical context and turning points in accounting for the changing nature of the relationship between elites and the state in Turkey.

CONFIGURATIONS OF RELATIONSHIP BETWEEN THE STATE AND BUSINESSES

In a recent work, political scientists, Coen, Grant, and Wilson (2010) identified four major debates in relation to state−business interaction. While the first debate is concerned with the relative power of the market over governments, the second focuses on the unfair returns that business may receive in politics. The third debate is on understanding the suboptimal public policy outcomes of business−government interaction. Finally, the last debate suggests that the state is the major determinant of markets and businesses. Institutional and historical properties of the context lead to a specific state−business interaction and influence organizational forms, practices, actors, and business systems as a whole (Whitley, 1994). In his typology, Whitley (1994) identifies state-dependent contexts as settings where the impact of the state on business is viewed as dominant. Political and bureaucratic elites allocate resources and coordinate investment policies and activities which render business−state relations essential for access to opportunities and thus for the survival of the businesses. In the context of state domination, the state plays a determinant role in production and reproduction of corporate elites in the country. The fragility of relations with the political and bureaucratic elites, in turn, leads to centralized organizations characterized by strong owner control (Whitley, 1994). Business elites in these contexts, as in the Turkish one for example, are predominantly composed of owners who are able and may be forced to use their personal relations in their interaction with state elites (Buğra, 1994).

Some commentators explain that the increasing pace of globalization may limit state domination in a business system. For example, Camerra-Rowe and Egan (2010) argue that globalization has accelerated the intensity and the variety of flows of goods, services, and capital across different territories, serving to challenge and lessen the regulatory authority of nation states on businesses. Although Vogel (2010) agrees that the regulatory capacities of states are challenged in this process, yet he explains that the extent of state regulations is still expanding in many countries. Given the conflicting views over the impact of globalization on state dominance, it is worth investigating how globalization modifies business elites' attitudes toward and interactions with the state.

Elites are defined as "groups that hold or exercise domination within a society or a particular area of life" (Scott, 2008, p. 32). Scott (2008) also explains that an elite group may also be segregated by lines of ideology, religion, ethnic origin among others, as such unity and social consciousness need to be explored to understand these divisions. In responding to a call for identifying and plotting the relations between different groups of elites (Savage & Williams, 2008; Scott, 2008), in this study we focus on different groups of business elites. Thus, we investigate "people holding positions of dominance in business organizations and who may under certain circumstances have certain additional powers available to them" (Scott, 2008, p. 37). One of the major criticisms of elite theory is that elites are supposed to be "all-powerful" without an effective counteraction to their domination (Scott, 2008). It is thus, worth investigating how business elites' power is contested in the state-dependent context of Turkey. It is known that business elites cleave to the state in late industrializing countries (Bellin, 2000). Turkey's late industrialization and state dependence created a setting where the state dominated business life. Different studies (Buğra, 1994; Greenwood, 2008; Moore, 2004; Öniş & Türem, 2001) mention the co-opting of political authority with a limited number of business elites in similar state-dependent and late industrializing contexts which leads to the formation of an established elite. However, following new opportunities like liberalization (Buğra & Savaşkan, 2010), economic growth (Greenwood, 2008), increasing land and commodity prices (Greenwood, 2008), and changing regulations (Moore, 2004), new groups of elites may emerge, and established elites may lose power. These new developments may alter the composition and relations of business elites. How business elites' power is contested by different actors (like the state or new groups rising from middle class to elite positions) needs further clarification. Therefore, we aim to understand how the relationship between state and business elites and underlying power dynamics develop in the face of neo-liberalism and globalization in a state-dependent context.

TURKISH CONTEXT

State control is a historically entrenched concept in the context of Turkey. Berkes (1978) claims that the concept of state is a reflection as well as an instrument of the cosmic order created by God (*nizâm-âlem*) in early central Asian Turkish states before the adoption of Muslim religion. Since it is created by God it is perfect; it does not need any intervention by humankind. Every artificial extension to it may deteriorate its fundamentals and may mean defying God's will which in turn is considered to be a sin. Therefore, to keep God's order unchanged is a mission semi-divinely attributed to the state which is not only perceived as the organization of public functions but also as a source of sacredness. Thus, the state assumes an eternal life (*devlet-i ebed-müdded*). Hassan (1986, p. 163) pointing to the linguistic roots in the ancient Turkish societies finely demonstrates that traditional law (töre) together with sacredness (kutsallık) and rules (kurallar) is part of an interdependent system of being that assures the collective life. In the Turkish state concept, law-making is directly associated with ban (*yasa, yasağ*), indicating the capacity to rule (Hassan, 2005, p. 71). The Ottoman Empire which was established later in the 13th century inherited the central Asian Turkish state structure. Although it was an Islamic state it kept some basic peculiarities of the early Shaman Turkish political functions. Consequently, the notion of sacredness has also acquired, through centuries, a visibly Islamic connotation.

Saydam (1997, p. 170), in a social psycho-analytical perspective, stresses that a traumatic break point appeared in Turkish society during the passage to Islam, which is, in Freudian terms, a dramatic shift from *mother-orientation to father-orientation*, symbolized in epics of the period, meaning also the establishment of a forbidding father, the omnipotent state. Thus, the place and the role of the state in Ottoman-Turkish lineage imply not only a highly centralized bureaucracy but also a notion of the sacred which is attributed to the state. The concept of "state" in the Turkish context seems to have some *emic* peculiarities, which makes it difficult to analyze using preexisting Western notions, such as feudalism and theocracy (Berkes, 1978). According to Berkes (1978, p. 26), *traditionalism* rather than religiosity preserved the Ottoman system which he describes as an oriental despotism. In the Ottoman state, another factor that assured the consolidation of the system was what Weber (1995, pp. 303–312) defined as *patrimonialism*, which accentuated the concentration of power in the person of the ruler (*padishah*) (Berkes, 1978, p. 29). The Ottoman political order thus offers a good example of the Weberian concept of power concentration. The key political actors do not only comprise the *padishah* himself or the dynastic circle but also a stratum of elites, mostly of bureaucratic origin that hold a privileged role in the redistribution of economic assets. In patrimonial states, then, authors such as Bellin have argued that business elites' financial gains are dependent on "shady relations with state elites" (Bellin, 2000, p. 181).

The Ottoman state became an empire and a well-established dynasty after the conquest of the Constantinople (Istanbul) by Mehmed II the Conqueror in 1453, who also adopted the principle of the juxtaposition of the right to reign and being physically at the ruling position. That means that access to the throne needs to be secured if necessary, by force and once it has been taken over this signifies also having the right to be at the ruling position. This rule existed in Turkish as well as Byzantine state tradition. Thus, the traditionalism, on which the state is built, was once again strengthened during the passage from a nomadic-military political structure to an established super-power (İnalcık, 2009, p. 111).

The accumulated wealth of the Ottoman dynasty was transferable from one monarch to his son as inheritance. The main question then was which one of the existing sons would acquire, if not confiscate the sacred throne (Divitçioğlu, 1981). This is why conflicts were not between social classes and the political power but rather between actors of the state apparatus. Indeed, according to Divitçioğlu (1992, p. 62), the sacredness of the khan (Turkish monarch) is a fragile reverse-image of the regicide practice in favor of the continuity of the state as an independent center of power. As a consequence, though the monarch and the dynasty were represented with sacred signs of reign, in fact, they were only considered as such because they carried the state's sacred eternal power as symbolized in their possession of the throne.

A historical turn was the modernization process in Ottoman Empire, from the 18th century to the early 20th century, when the older rules and system of values were progressively dismantled eventually giving birth to an ethnic-based national-state concept. In the late 18th century, a social transformation had begun not only in economic system but also in the values and the worldview of the society (Ortaylı, 1999). The adoption of French civil law by the Ottoman Empire in the 19th century (La Porta, Lopez-De-Silanes, & Shleifer, 2008) enhanced state tradition based on the centralized distribution of resources (Yamak & Ertuna, 2012). As ideologies and culture deeply influence the choices of legal and political infrastructure (La Porta et al., 2008), the adoption of the civil law tradition was in fact in line with the country's centralized state tradition, compared to the Anglo-American tradition of common law. In fact, the structuring of the social domain has always been organized in terms of the authoritative role and monopolistic place of the state at the expense of the individual actors.

The fundamental problem in the economic history of the Ottoman state was the nonexistence of private property until 1858. Although exceptions existed in private property restrictions (Çiftçi, 2011), the state's servants had the right to obtain rents from soil and accumulate wealth, without possessing a private property claim over the land. They thus lacked the right to inherit the territory. Instead the state retained its central role in the distribution of privileges in the economy (Timur, 1989), which constituted an obstacle for the accumulation of capital that could be reinvested, creating the cycle of growing investment that was essential to the establishment of capitalism in other countries. Given that the concept of sacred state systematically prevented the rise of surplus value that stimulates capital accumulation and thus capitalistic activity, an autonomous lane of capitalist evolution could not survive (Küçükömer, 2001). Those involved in business activities remained highly dependent on the resource distribution of the political power and had limited autonomous power. Although Keyder argued that the economic policies of the state were not absolute and that the farmers could indirectly resist by controlling the production process, and therefore shaping the amount of surplus which was generated (and therefore available for the state elites to expropriate) (Keyder, 1983, pp. 194–195), the system in general, could not be considered, until the mid-20th century, as a system of market exchange. According to Mardin (1990), the Ottoman political system generated a center-periphery disconnectedness, in spite of the centralized character of the state. State servants had power to raise taxes in their localities and built family fortunes but these positions were not inheritable and were only granted by the state which could withdraw them. Whilst the state was highly powerful, powerful state servants in particularly rich regions could also be significant (e.g., as in Ottoman Egypt); it would be a mistake therefore to consider the entire imperial territory as a homogenized social and juridical entity; different forms of power partaking had been developed in different estates, especially around the provincial aristocracy.

The fact that state was still keeping its regulatory force (even in the 19th century during which a modernization process started) resulted in the formation of a second type of relationship between the political power and the gentry, an economic one based on the expansion of capitalist relations besides the traditional political link (Mardin, 1990). Mardin argues that the redistribution of resources in republican Turkey as well as in Ottoman Empire was based on an *unchanging cake* (immobile sum of wealth) except for the protectors, those who controlled the state's economic possibilities and who, then, identified themselves as the state class (Mardin, 2004, pp. 198–199). Thus, the state kept its historically central position in the economy, in spite of the formal differentiation of state, civil society and the economy in the Republican secular era when the focus was on producing a national capitalist state based on Republican principles. The omnipresent legitimacy of the state remained a basic motivation for almost all economic actors.

The Turkish Republic that was founded in 1923 had a very limited industrial capacity at the beginning (for a detailed analysis of economic development and business elites in Turkey please see Yamak, 2006). Concessions which were granted to different countries during the Ottoman period were still in force and they acted as an important factor inhibiting industrialization and protection of the nascent industries (Clark, 1969). In the early 1920s, there were only 130 industrial companies in the country (Saylan, 1974; Yamak, 2006). Following the foundation of the Turkish republic, the state assumed a central role in the process of industrialization. For that purpose, the Law for the Encouragement of Industry was adopted in 1927 (Yamak, 2006). Atatürk, the founder of the Republic and the President at the time, personally encouraged potential local investors (Clark, 1969; Yamak, 2006) and took the initiative to establish İş Bankası (the "Business Bank") (Roos & Roos, 1971). In the mid-1930s, the Soviet model of planned development was adopted and state economic enterprises were established in order to boost industrialization. This period was also characterized by an influx of former state employees into the private sector as founders of businesses (Soral, 1974; Yamak, 2006). The state adopted in the 1950s an import substitution policy to create and preserve local industries (Buğra, 1994). These efforts protected the latter from foreign competition. Through its subsidies, credits, and different types of resource allocation, the state assisted the development of the private sector (Buğra, 1994) which was organized primarily along family business groups (Guillén, 2001). Hence, the state continued to play a major role in the formation of a local business elite. Therefore, in a highly institutional environment where government–business interrelations and the role played by the government in economic life was crucial, business activity was more dependent on the competence in dealing with the bureaucratic ranks in Ankara rather than the uncertainties of demand and supply. Creating a new business or the introduction of a new product was only vaguely related to consumer behavior. They were highly influenced by government decisions and incentives (Buğra, 1994).

A radical policy shift took place in 1980, when Turkey adopted a trade liberalization policy focusing on export promotion (Kazgan, 1994; Yurtoglu, 2000). This was a clear move toward integration with the global markets by privatizing state enterprises, establishing a stock market, abandoning controls over foreign currency and capital mobility (Öniş, 2004). The Association Agreement which was signed in 1963 (but not activated) with the then European Economic Community was revived at the end of the 1980s (Türkmen, 2008). Several factors, such as increases in inward and outward foreign direct investment, advances in the position of Turkey in the global value chains, and improvements in relationships with historically significant links to Central Asian Turkic Republics, contributed to the development of economic activity in Turkey. The policies of liberalization and integration with European Union was supported by the largest businessmen association, TÜSİAD (Association of Turkish Industrialists and Businessmen) which was founded in 1971 in order "to react to the disfunctioning and crisis generating closed economy" (TÜSİAD, 2014) and to represent the established elite. Türkmen (2008, p. 151) perceives support as a "necessity for business circles to avoid the ever-present possibility of arbitrary state intervention, so much a part of Turkish political tradition." This shift in economic policy enabled the access of local firms to international markets (Kazgan, 1994) and the growth of small- and medium-sized companies in Anatolia (Gümüşçü, 2008).

These developments stimulated the creation of new business elites alongside the old ones (Buğra & Savaşkan, 2010; Yamak, Ergur, Ünsal Özbilgin, & Çoker, 2011). MÜSİAD (Association of Independent Industrialists and Businessmen) was founded in 1990 to represent smaller scale industrialists with Islamic values who could not enter TÜSİAD (Gümüşçü, 2008). In the period following liberalization, there were also attempts to incorporate Islamic identity into the liberal economy (Özcan & Turunç, 2011), a process which was eased by the victories of Islamist parties in Turkish General Elections beginning in 2002. As Buğra and Savaşkan argued, the rise of new business elites is a direct consequence of neo-liberal policies adopted by governments since the 1980s, but particularly those of pro-Islamist government in the 2000s. The opening up of the Turkish economy and its tendency for parts of the economy (e.g., textiles and clothing manufacture) to become rapidly being integrated into global markets triggered the astonishing growth of Anatolian middle-scale industrialists in a free-competing national market. This did not mean that the importance of the state had diminished but it had changed form. Instead of intervening directly in the process of shaping capitalist firms and markets, the state in Turkey preferred, since the 1980s, to reinforce the proliferation of businessmen associations which in turn supported the formation of business networks in international activities as well as on a national scale

(Buğra & Savaşkan, 2010). New business people networks such as TUSKON made their appearance during the last decade. The high economic growth rate of Turkey during the second half of 2000 contributed to the integration of different business elite clusters into global markets and into globalization more generally. Yet, the state continues to exert considerable influence in Turkish society and business. The state is socially referred to as "the father state" and its coercive patriarchal power remains inherent in this discourse. In this study, we aim to understand whether these globalization effects have had an impact on the centrality of the state in Turkish economic life, on state notion and the relationship of business elites with the state.

METHODOLOGY

This study investigates the following questions: Given the history and nature of the Turkish state and its role as a shaper of the economy, how do the different business elites relate to the state? What is the impact of the globalization on this relationship? This work is a part of a larger research on Turkish business elites. A comprehensive study headed by Sibel Yamak, Ali Ergur, and Artun Ünsal on Turkish business elites was conducted with the grant provided by the Scientific and Technological Research Council of Turkey between 2009 and 2011. The research investigated elites along different dimensions such as relations with the state and globalization, entrepreneurial attributes, business and society interactions, among others. This paper is based on the part of the data investigating elite, state and globalization relations. Elites from 65 companies among the 500 largest Turkish firms ranked by the Istanbul Chamber of Industry constituted our sample. Stratified random sampling according to the regional breakdown of the 500 largest companies was used to assure the country-wide representativeness of the sample. Our data collection methods comprised interviews, non-participant observation, and documentary searches during this study. We have conducted 65 open-ended interviews with key informants who have such executive roles as CEO, chair, or vice chair of the board. We have defined business elites as "a configuration of capitalists (major shareholders and top executives) and organic intellectuals occupying positions of ultimate authority within leading corporations" (Carroll, 2008, p. 47).

The life stories of the person and the company and the questions related to the relations with the state and globalization constituted the basis of this analysis. Two of the researchers participated in each interview with the exception of two cases where there was only one researcher. Interviews were tape-recorded except in two cases during which detailed notes were taken. Interviews lasted two to three hours. Each researcher has also taken independently observation field notes. An extensive documentary search has been conducted in relation to each interviewee and firm.

RESULTS

Common Traits

Our findings show that a considerable degree of state domination still continues in the Turkish business system. The unpredictable, non-egalitarian, opaque, paternalistic, partisan nature of the business allocations provided by the state seems to have reduced the trust mechanisms between political and economic elites. The discourses of business elites, which are investigated in this study, reveal distrust toward politics and politicians in Turkey. This often led to ambivalent attitudes, urging business elites to assume a distanced approach toward the state, while having to preserve good relationships with it. Almost all of the interviewees showed implicit or explicit signs of fear, in describing their interactions with the state. Even those admiring the government expressed an obedient attitude, akin to a child—adult relationship, like the adoration of a child for his/her father. It is not uncommon in the Turkish language to refer to the state as "the father". Therefore, in the relationship of the businessmen with the state, the use of power appears to be rather asymmetrical. One participant explained the significance of compliance and conflict avoidance for large corporations in Turkey:

> If you are small it's okay, but if you are large firm you should not have conflict with politicians. (Chairperson, 69, male, industrial firm)

Another participant hinted at the fear of deeper involvement with the state and state politics in Turkey. It is also interesting to note that the responsibility of the business is to the state, which presents a contrast to the relationship of responsibility to shareholders and a wider range of stakeholders in advanced economies of Europe. The state is still considered as the source of the moral and material control in commercial activity.

> We aimed not to have any political dimension. While we kept our distance with the state, we never forgot our responsibilities to it. (Chairperson, 61, male, industrial firm)

In spite of the opportunities, the relationship between the business and the state is precarious and tense. The state is feared and revered and the businesses are made to feel that they owe their wealth and longevity to keeping good relations with the state. In general businessmen seem to be reluctant in doing business with the state as the following quote among many similar ones implies:

> Don't take back your own hat, if it falls in government's garden! (Chairperson, 70, male, industrial firm)

Even those who won government bids, often tended not to reveal it. Doing business with government seems often to be equated with favoritism in the discourses of the business people. Doing business with the state is also interpreted as revealing an inferiority, an incapability of being successful in properly competitive markets.

> If you do your work properly (...) you won't need any help. Asking support for the government bids means humiliating yourself. The result these persons will get will be zero. (Chairperson, 63, male, industrial group)

Although the state has considerable power in creating and chastising business elites in Turkey, there is a well-established and dynamic private sector. Indeed we can argue that the business world seems to be relatively autonomous, due to its relatively recent integration with international markets, especially in Middle East, Central Asia, and Africa. However, they are still very sensitive about their relations with the state in relation to their domestic operations. Business elites often argue that politicians rarely listen to their needs and that their expectations are often unfulfilled. The state is often thought to be indifferent to the requests of businesses and business associations. We were repeatedly told that even if the requests are recorded by the state, they are not implemented. A businessman, who once acted also as a minister, told:

> We used to listen to the businessmen's requests like a sheep listening to the flute. (Chairperson, 67, male, industrial group)

Although we have identified a typology to describe different stances toward state, *fear* emerges as a common feeling among our interviewees. Some of them have explicitly criticized the government. However they have also felt the need to balance their claims by conveying positive messages with praising words:

> We love the government, but everything depends on RTE [initials of the Prime Minister]. You need to be a flatterer to get in. (Chairman, 71, male industrial firm)

The significance of the Prime Minister as a figure head has been stated across a number of interviews. One participant's quote pointed to the fact that the political system breeds authoritative power, even though the politicians are elected representatives of the nation:

> All the politicians know us. But I don't know whether Tayyip [first name of the Prime Minister] does. The governments elected by our people are revered by us. (Chairman, 73, male, industrial group)

On the other hand, some of our interviewees avoided openly criticizing government or politicians. They have rather differentiated politics from bureaucracy and have pointed to the latter as a source of the inefficient functioning of the state. They have blamed bureaucrats for being indifferent to the demands of the business world:

> The government enacted a law. However the bureaucracy did not transfer it [about an energy facility] to us. We suffered so much ... (Chairperson, 63, male, industrial group)

Another participant explains that centralization of authority in the government stifles the bureaucratic process. However, as they explain this is not solely due to the demand of the government but the desire of the bureaucrats to defer responsibility:

> The system in Turkey requires having access to the highest decision-maker. You need to go to the minister; you need to tell about your problem. Sometimes you need to go to the Prime Minister; because the decision is made there, you know it. Why? Because the bureaucrat does definitely not want to enter into the responsibility domain; s/he doesn't want; s/he is afraid, s/he doesn't want to take responsibility. This is something which blocks Turkey very much. (CEO, 64, male, industrial group)

Last but not least, some interviewees were so scared that they couldn't voice their expectations of the governments. They didn't even dare to criticize it. These businessmen seem to perceive the state more like a *retaliator* than a regulator and a resource allocator:

> You shouldn't bother first, your associates, second, your employees, third, the state. (Executive director, 50, female, industrial group)

However, forms, doses, and expressions of, and the discursive strategies developed around this fear differ depending on the extent of internationalization and the size of the firm. Only the managers of the foreign-based companies present an apparently independent, if not indifferent attitude. For example, the CEO of a global firm appeared to feel immune to government pressure. This was also observed in the case of the elites, who had started their business abroad and had double citizenship. Their possible mobility granted some kind of security against state retaliation.

> During the crisis, we were negatively affected especially from the state banks. As a response, we started up production units abroad. (Chairperson, 56, male, industrial group)

For the rest, the state induced a considerable level of stress and fear which seemed to increase as the company is more locally oriented. The common experience among elites, except for those with robust international business connections, appears to be fear in our study. This suggests that the state continues to exert disciplinary and coercive force on corporate elites in the country. This presents a contrast to post-industrialized countries of Europe, where states are known to foster positive supportive relationships with corporate elites.

Divergences

Beyond these common traits, we have also identified different groups in which business people's attitudes and perceptions regarding the state differed. There emerge four categories: (1) Sidelined; (2) Critical; (3) Follower; (4) Politically embedded.

Sidelined
Those are the businesspersons whose businesses have been suffering considerable losses because of their poor relationship with the state. The interviewees in this group have reported that they were severely harmed by the actions of the state. They have complained about the fact that the state treated them harshly when they were seeking support. "Uncooperative state" was a commonly reported theme by these sidelined business people. They have been subject to indifference and punishment from the state apparatus, either because of bureaucratic mismanagement or political retaliation, which also suggests an *instrumentalization* of the legal system by the state during the redistribution of the resources.

> When it [business and consequently a businessperson] reaches a certain size, it should be beheaded, and its assets should be recorded as revenue to state treasury. This tradition is deeply penetrated into the Turkish bureaucracy.

One participant viewed the state and bureaucracy as synonymous devices to slow down business activities.

Relationship between the State and Business Elites 121

> Then I realized that the state means bureaucracy, the take-over of the country by the bureaucracy is called state. (Chairperson, 75, male, industrial group)

Another participant viewed the state as a wealth grabbing mechanism:

> Certain laws of the state take over all your wealth. (Chairperson, 61, male, industrial firm)

Business elites feeling threatened by the state appear as another variant of respondent in the "sidelined" category. They seem to feel the state power as the sword of Damocles in their business practices. These businesspersons feared counteractions of and felt threatened by the state. They often narrated an anxious relation with state authorities:

> After that important incident [government's financial operation against a large group] my friends told me not to criticize the government. (Chairperson, 61, male, industrial group)

Another participant expressed his fear which he often experienced in his interactions with the state:

> If you are not on the same side with the state, it can destroy you. (Chairperson, 72, male, industrial firm)

It is interesting to note that the interviewees categorized as "sidelined" are all from old, pro-western, established elite.

Criticals

Our second category, labeled as *criticals*, comprises business elites who are critical of the state as a system. They emphasize the substandard functioning of the state, its involvement in corruption, and its potential costs to the society and business. Some are more critical about the bureaucracy, while others focus on the inefficiencies of the politics.

> In Turkey, collaboration occurred between bad bureaucrats, bad politicians and bad businessmen. (Chairperson, 61, male, industrial group)

Several participants reported incidents for which they were rather critical of the state's role in their business dealings. A *critical* participant reported, for example:

> A bureaucrat told us not to claim this incentive which might be against the interests of a competitor. This competitor who was a relative of the minister, was mostly known for operating unlawfully. Instead he proposed us to have research collaboration with that competitor and apply together for another incentive. (Executive director, 57, female, industrial company)

Some of those who are critical toward the system of allocations try to adopt a nuanced attitude by distinguishing state and government. Those, who have concerns about government policies, often point to the corruption and the incapacity of the staff and ministers surrounding the Prime Minister.

> Things [corruption] done in Turkey during the last ten years would cause the dismissal of a Prime Minister in Europe. (Chairperson, 56, male, industrial company)

These elites come from different backgrounds and ideologies. They seem to be able to critically evaluate the actions and policies of government. The latter's lack of understanding and support constitutes the main argument in this group. They often state that they need a government which backs them up in their international endeavors.

> [A businessperson asked to the Minister of Energy to cite the name of his company while talking with the minister of the hosting country during an official visit, and he expected therefore to have a commercial superiority or privilege among his rivals.]
>
> I told to our minister: "The Minister of Energy is the most powerful man there [an oil-exporting country]. (...) [Sir] 'You [the minister] can have an interview with him, I cannot. It would be enough for us, if you could only pronounce the name of our company once or twice' He [the minister said] said. 'Give it to me as written'. There is no written form for this. This is only a word he could have pronounced during the conversation." (Chairperson, 52, male, industrial group)

Another participant was critical of the cabinet and the general government. The level and focus of criticism varied depending on the nature of the relationship that the business had with the state:

> May be such a Prime Minister is an opportunity for Turkey, but there is not even one correct man in his surroundings. (Chairperson, 63, male, industrial company)

Followers

Our third category comprises the persons who assume a balanced stance to the policies and actions of the government. They may be opposing to government ideologically however, they point both positive and negative aspects. They usually tend to evaluate favorably the actions of the government.

> I evaluate the AKP (Justice and Development Party) as successful in many domains, even if I have hesitations to vote for it. (Executive director, 61, female, industrial and service group)

Some have developed a more favorable view about the state or state actors through sustained interaction with them over the years:

> Politicians have bombed us, especially during the period of this AKP [Adalet ve Kalkınma Partisi – Justice and Development Party: Pro-islamist, purely lberalist rulng party]. (...) The minister of Industry was an industrialist; he was the chair of the Chamber of Commerce of Ankara. I appreciate now what he does actually. (Chairperson, 72, industrial company)

Politically Embedded
The fourth category includes elites who are usually satisfied with their relations with the state. In this category, a multinational's CEO reported that the state regularly consults them and what they propose is usually taken into consideration and implemented. The domination seems to be reversed in the case of multinationals which enjoy privileges from the state. Yet politically embedded local firms are subject to state domination but, at the same time, they receive favors. An example in this category is a locally based company, close to government circle:

> When we talked to our minister of energy, he declared to us that energy prices will be kept as they are. For example, we were estimating big rises in prices of natural gas. Thanks to them, they didn't do that. We are talking about these issues. When they come [to our city] they come [to see us]. (Chairperson, 67, male, industrial company)

In this group, we can distinguish those who explicitly praise government's policies, more precisely the Prime Minister as person. These business elites seem to be highly supportive of government's policies and they almost act as its spokespersons. It is interesting to note that the great majority of these individuals are from the new elite whose companies was either established after the adoption of liberal policies in the 1980s or grew during the same period. Their admiration is more like dedication to the ideas, action, and policies of the government.

> I admire the mastery of our Prime Minister on his own work. (Chairperson, 51, male, industrial group)

They often express their confidence on the future of Turkey in admiration of the state, as if the economic future of the country relies solely on it. This belief underscores the significance of the real and perceived role of the state in controlling economic relations closely in Turkey:

> If ten more years pass like this, I swear we will be ranked among the first great ten countries in the world. I mean it is not necessary to wait for 2023 [targets for the centenary anniversary of the Turkish Republic]. We will get there in a short time. [But]

all that is done [by the government] is under-esteemed. (Chairperson, 53, male, industrial group)

There are striking differences between the first and last categories. The first category is totally composed of old elites whose companies were established and ranked among the largest ones since before the liberalization in 1980. In contrast, the last category is mainly composed of owners of newly established companies. The relative inexperience of newcomers with the state apparatus is also observed in their discourses since they focus solely on government. We can even observe another divide between the followers and politically embedded: while the former display more international experience the latter seems to be more focused on Turkish market.

In sum, our results demonstrate four unique patterns of relationship between business elites and the Turkish state. These major themes combine positions toward the state and perceptions regarding the ways of doing business in Turkey from which strategies of survival and coexistence with the political power are derived. Thus, four kinds of interactions and positions, with their internal variations indicate different orientations of the business elites toward state domination on national market. Although we classify four unique themes, there are cross-overs among these themes and the relationships do change over time. Therefore, we present ideal types, based on evidence-based generalization of observed patterns in our data. The state functions as controlling actor through direct allocation of resources or indirect facilitation of the access to the latter. Consequently, business elites continuously create ways of coping with the changing face of the political power, sometimes too much fluctuating. They display therefore various feelings and attitudes regarding the negotiation with the politics and politicians: Fear, gratitude, mistrust, distinction, articulation, and obedience.

DISCUSSION

Although most of our interviewees presented themselves as globally integrated economic actors, they usually did not deny the importance of maintaining good relationships with the world of domestic politics. Business elites displayed a state of mind with an underlying fear toward the state as the main bureaucratic corpus and political power in Turkey. They believe that the state can enrich a company but also destroy it completely. Recent cases of credit allocations, company sales, and shares in privatizations to businessmen who are willing to support the government provide examples of an enriching state. On the other hand, tax penalties, increased supervisions are frequently used as tools of government intervention to companies which do not act according to the directions and expectations of political authority. Therefore, fear emerges as historically rooted guideline for businesspersons for two reasons: (1) The commonly shared and legitimized idea of coercive and intervening state; (2) possible penalties that the state can create against those who do not obey its mostly hidden, unwritten rules.

As it has been discussed in the literature review, the notion of sacred state has very deep roots in the Turkish state tradition and its social perceptions. Although important changes occurred in Turkey's political and cultural climate from the 1980s onwards, our study reveals that some fundamental notions such as the sacred nature of the state and its imposing status persist in the eyes of businesspersons. Therefore, a coercive state which is a central resource allocator still preserves a legitimate position. Furthermore, the state, with its bureaucratic apparatus and political relations coalescing or conflicting according to the characteristics of the context, still holds the latent capacity of sanctioning its subordinates, through the political use of the legal system. The business world, on the other hand, seems to reproduce such an image of omnipotent state, because it is both a historical construct and fact. However, increasing integration of some Turkish companies with the international/global markets seems to provide their owners with a relative freedom. Globalization acts as a way to resist to or avoid state's coercive power.

In fact, when business elites were asked whether it is imperative to establish relationships with the politics and politicians for doing business in Turkey, they often answered negatively. The frequently repeated reason for such a response was often related to the presence of their company in the international arena. Indeed, a great majority affirmed that since they have expanded their business activities and networks with different actors in the global market, they do not need to manage business within national territories. Consequently the question of scale, the size of the company is often considered as a matter of pride: Those with sufficiently developed international links and respectful foreign partners consider themselves relatively immune to the limitations of national scale. In their mind, doing business at national level is implicitly associated with an obligation to keep organic relations with the State apparatus and its actors. Economic elites having already surpassed this national scale with their business capacity firmly underlined that they never do business with the State, not only as a result of a question of size but also that of principle. Both working with the State and having economic relationships with the politicians are perceived as inefficient and revealing a lack of dignity. It also implies a lack of know-how in doing business at international scale. Indeed this "know-how" (frequently pronounced in English) emphasized by our interviewees seems to have a double meaning. First this implies a technical capability and experience. Second, it also appears as a criterion of distinction among economic elite. In other words, integration with the global market is not only a matter of material capacity. It also delineates an ideologically loaded sign of moral (non-material) superiority. Thus, cultural and symbolic capitals play a major part in the development of a world-scale business perspective and a certain ethical framework in the eyes of business elites.

Our comparison of old and new elite in terms of relations with the state reveals interesting insights. As the established, old elites become more internationalized and thus relatively autonomous, they are targeted by the political power. The newly emerging business elites need much more political support for doing business; first, to benefit from the pushing effect of the dominant political current and second to compensate for their lack of technical ability to conduct internationally connected business, even though the latter is not expressed openly.

Business elites always added that doing business under the tutelage of a ruling political party can help to a company to grow rapidly. Nevertheless, it can also trigger a process of rapid decline, given the possibility of dramatic changes in the political climate. They often illustrated such politically driven attitudes with examples from the near past, while emphasizing the importance of knowing to conduct business out of the range of current politics, as the golden principle of endurance.

Although the rise of a discourse about the eventual disappearance of the state in economics seems to be dominant, our study diagnosed a continuity of the state's role in the redistribution of allocations even in the face of increasing internationalization. Nevertheless, this may appear as a direct and material support, but often it is a much more invisible, indirect, and symbolic tutelage. The more the volume of capital increases and the company has access to the global market, the more its relationship with the political actors becomes abstract, or more latent. The overwhelming majority of the interviewees affirm that they never do business with the state, as a principle, but, a series of discursive clues, archival and iconographic materials showed that, even when they operate on a global scale, their dependence on the political apparatus and state actors in Turkey continues and government bids and privatizations are still lucrative sources of revenue.

We see a kind of gradual transformation of the direct and material relationship in resource allocation between the state and businesses in Turkey toward a latent and symbolic one. The main implication of the change in the nature of the relationships is that latent and symbolic relationships are harder to reveal than relations based on allocation of material resources.

The findings delineate the fact that state–business relationship is a very delicate one in state dependent late industrializing countries like, for example, the ones in Middle East. The companies are usually subject to state intervention which may not always be in line with the requirements of democracy and property rights. The state dependence in late industrializing countries is an enduring characteristic. The power of business elites is a restricted one first, when there is a powerful state and second, when there are fault lines (in terms of ideology, belief, cultural, and economic capitals, etc.) among the elites. The power of the business elites is contested by different sub groups and the state. This contestation of the power does not necessarily lead to a better balance between society and business nor between state and business. In a state-dependent context such a contestation brings about better protected state elites. As an over-view evaluation of our data, we can stress that the relationships between business elites and the State in Turkey are still astonishingly asymmetrical, a kind of parent–child organic and hierarchic link. A total independence from the State, its allocations, and political power can only be possible under conditions of global competition and mobility. Immunity against oppressions from the national political apparatus can only be realized, as a few examples are signaling, if the capital structure is economically powerful and physically distanced enough from it.

ACKNOWLEDGMENT

The authors are grateful for the support provided by the Galatasaray University Research Fund.

REFERENCES

Bellin, E. (2000). Contingent democrats: Industrialists, labor and democratization in late developing countries. *World Politics, 52*, 175–205.

Berkes, N. (1978). *Türkiye'de çağdaşlaşma*. [The development of secularism in Turkey.] Istanbul: Doğu-Batı.

Buğra, A. (1994). *State and business in modern Turkey: A comparative study.* Albany: SUNY Press.
Buğra, A., & Savaşkan, O. (2010). Yerel-sanayi ve bugünün Türkiye'sinde iş dünyası. [Local industry and the business world in today's Turkey.] *Toplum ve Bilim, 110,* 92–109.
Camerra-Rowe, P., & Egan, M. (2010). International regulators and network governance. In D. Coen, W. Grant, & W. Graham (Eds.), *The Oxford handbook of business and government* (pp. 404–421). Oxford: Oxford University Press.
Carroll, W. K. (2008). The corporate elite and the transformation of finance capital: A view from Canada. In M. Savage & K. Williams (Eds.), *Remembering elites* (pp. 44–63). London: Blackwell.
Çiftçi, M. (2011). Osmanlı imparatorluğu döneminde özel mülkiyet ve yapısal özellikleri. [Private property in period of Ottoman Empire and its structural characteristics.] *Turkish Studies, 6,* 623–644.
Clark, E. C. (1969). *The emergence of textile manufacturing entrepreneurs in Turkey 1804–1968.* Unpublished doctoral dissertation, Princeton University, Princeton, NJ.
Coen, D., Grant, W., & Wilson, G. (2010). Political science: Perspectives on business and government. In D. Coen, W. Grant, & W. Graham (Eds.), *The Oxford handbook of business and government: Perspectives on business and government* (pp. 9–34). Oxford: Oxford University Press.
Divitçioğlu, S. (1981). *Asya üretim tarzı ve Osmanlı Toplumu.* [The Asiatic type of production and the Ottoman society.] Kirklareli: Sermet.
Divitçioğlu, S. (1992). *Nasıl bir tarih? (Kök Türkler, Karahanlılar).* [What kind of history? Kök Turks, Karahanids.] Istanbul: Bağlam.
Greenwood, S. (2008). Bad for business?: Entrepreneurs and democracy in the Arab world. *Comparative Political Studies, 41,* 837–860.
Guillén, M. F. (2001). *The limits of convergence: Globalization and organizational change in Argentina, South Korea, and Spain.* Princeton, NJ: Princeton University Press.
Gümüşçü, S. (2008). *Economic liberalization, devout bourgeoisie, and change in political Islam: Comparing Turkey and Egypt.* EUI Working Papers: RSCAS 2008/19 Florence, European University Institute.
Hassan, Ü. (1986). *Eski Türk toplumu üzerine incelemeler.* [Studies on the ancient Turkish society.] Ankara: Verso.
Hassan, Ü. (2005). *Osmanlı, örgüt-inanç-davranış'tan hukuk-ideoloji'ye.* [The Ottoman, from organization-believing-behavior to law-ideology.] Istanbul: İletişim.
İnalcık, H. (2009). *Devlet-i 'Aliyye, Osmanlı İmparatorluğu üzerine araştırmalar – I.* [The great state, researches on the Ottoman Empire – I.] Istanbul: İş Bankası.
Kazgan, G. (1994). *Yeni ekonomik düzende Türkiye'nin yeri.* [The position of Turkey in the new economic order.] Istanbul: Altın Kitaplar Yayınevi.
Keyder, Ç. (1983). *Toplumsal tarih çalışmaları.* [Studies in social history.] Ankara: Dost.
Küçükömer, İ. (2001). *Düzenin yabancılaşması, Batılılaşma.* [The alienation of the order, Westernization.] Istanbul: Bağlam.
La Porta, R., Lopez-De-Silanes, F., & Shleifer, A. (2008). The economic consequences of legal origin. *Journal of Economic Literature, 46*(2), 285–332.
Mardin, Ş. (1990). *Türkiye'de toplum ve siyaset.* [Society and politics in Turkey.] Istanbul: İletişim.
Mardin, Ş. (2004). *Türk modernleşmesi.* [Turkish modernization.] Istanbul: İletişim.
Moore, P. (2004). *Doing business in the Middle East: Politics and economic crisis in Jordan and Kuwait.* New York, NY: Cambridge University Press.
Öniş, Z. (2004). Turgut Özal and his economic legacy: Turkish Neo-liberalism in critical perspective. *Middle Eastern Studies, 40*(4), 113–134.

Önis, Z., & Türem, U. (2001). Business, globalization and democracy: A comparative analysis of Turkish business associations. *Turkish Studies*, 2(2), 94−120.
Ortaylı, İ. (1999). *İmparatorluğun en uzun yüzyılı*. [The longest century of the Empire.] Istanbul: İletişim.
Özcan, G. B., & Turunç, H. (2011). Economic liberalization and class dynamics in Turkey: New business groups and Islamic mobilization. *Insight Turkey*, 13(3), 63−86.
Roos, N. P., & Roos, L. L. (1971). Managers of modernization: Organizations and elites in Turkey (1950−1969). Cambridge, MA: Harvard University Press.
Savage, M., & Williams, K. (2008). Elites: Remembered in capitalism and forgotten by social sciences. In M. Savage & K. Williams (Eds.), *Remembering elites* (pp. 1−24). London: Blackwell.
Saydam, M. B. (1997). *Deli Dumrul'un bilinci*. [Deli Dumrul's consciousness.] Istanbul: Metis.
Saylan, G. (1974). *Türkiye'de kapitalizm, bürokrasi ve siyasal ideoloji*. [Capitalism, bureaucracy and political ideology in Turkey.] Ankara: TODAIE.
Scott, J. (2008). Taking stock of elites: Recognizing historical changes. In M. Savage & K. Williams (Eds.), *Remembering elites* (pp. 27−43). London: Blackwell.
Soral, E. (1974). *Özel kesimde Türk müteşebbisleri*. [Turkish entrepreneurs in private sector.] Ankara: AITIA.
Storey, J., & Lawton, T. (2010). The global dynamics of business-state relations. In D. Coen, W. Grant, & W. Graham (Eds.), *The Oxford handbook of business and government* (pp. 89−120). Oxford: Oxford University Press.
Timur, T. (1989). *Osmanlı çalışmaları*. [Ottoman studies.] Ankara: Verso.
Türkmen, F. (2008). The European Union and the democratization in Turkey: The role of the elites. *Human Rights Quarterly*, 30, 146−163.
TÜSİAD. (2014). Retrieved from. http://www.tusiad.org.tr/tusiad/. Accessed on January 10, 2014.
Vogel, D. (2010). Civil regulation and corporate capitalism. In D. Coen, W. Grant, & W. Graham (Eds.), *The Oxford handbook of business and government* (pp. 472−494). Oxford: Oxford University Press.
Weber, M. (1995). *Économie et société/1, Les catégories de la sociologie*. Paris: Plon.
Whitley, R. (1994). Dominant forms of economic organization in market economies. *Organisation Studies*, 15, 153−182.
Yamak, S. (2006). Changing institutional environment and business elites in Turkey. *Society and Business Review*, 1, 206−219.
Yamak, S., Ergur, A., Ünsal, A., Özbilgin, M., & Çoker, E. Ü. (2011). New Turkish business elites: Resources, networks, boundaries, and mobility. In A. Kakabadse & N. Kakabadse (Eds.), *Global elites: The opaque nature of transnational policy determination* (pp.130−156). Basingstoke, UK: Palgrave.
Yamak, S., & Ertuna, B. (2012). Corporate governance and initial public offerings in Turkey. In A. Zattoni & W. Judge (Eds.), *Corporate governance and initial public offerings* (pp. 470−498). Cambridge: Cambridge University Press.
Yamak, S., Nielsen, S., & Escriba-Esteve, A. (2014). The role of external environment in upper echelons theory: A review of existing literature and future research directions. *Group and Organization Management*, 39(1), 69−109.
Yurtoglu, B. B. (2000). Ownership, control and performance of Turkish listed firms. *Empirica*, 27, 193−222.

IMPACTS OF GLOBALIZATION PROCESSES ON THE SWISS NATIONAL BUSINESS ELITE COMMUNITY: A DIACHRONIC ANALYSIS OF SWISS LARGE CORPORATIONS (1980–2010)

Eric Davoine, Stéphanie Ginalski, André Mach and Claudio Ravasi

ABSTRACT

This paper investigates the impacts of globalization processes on the Swiss business elite community during the 1980–2010 period. Switzerland has been characterized in the 20th century by its extraordinary stability and by the strong cohesion of its elite community. To study recent changes, we focus on Switzerland's 110 largest firms' by adopting a diachronic perspective based on three elite cohorts (1980, 2000, and 2010). An analysis of interlocking directorates allows us to describe the decline of the Swiss corporate network. The second analysis focuses on top managers' profiles in terms of education, nationality as well as participation in national community networks that used to reinforce the cultural cohesion of the Swiss elite community, especially the militia army. Our results highlight a slow but profound transformation of top management profiles, characterized by a decline of traditional national elements of legitimacy and the emergence of new "global" elements. The diachronic and combined analysis brings into light the strong cultural changes experienced by the national business elite community.

Keywords: Switzerland; corporate network; business elite; globalization; transnational community

INTRODUCTION

In empirical cross-national research, national business elite have traditionally been defined as a group of managers exercising dominant positions at the top of the largest companies of a country (Bauer & Bertin-Mourot, 1999; Hartmann, 2007; Maclean, Harvey, & Chia, 2010). In Europe, comparative research on elite has long been dominated by studies about "national career models" and national forms of assets or capital hold by top managers, which are mostly related to the educational systems or to other institutionalized processes that select and develop so-called high potentials (Bauer & Bertin-Mourot, 1996; Evans, Lank, & Farquhar, 1989). In recent years, however, these approaches have been increasingly challenged by the "globalization" of the business environment and by the growing international circulation of top managers (Ruigrok & Greve, 2008; Staples, 2007). In Europe, traditional modes of recruitment and the selection of top managers, which were deeply embedded in national career models, have undergone significant changes in the context of the increasing internationalization of companies and markets. The national business elite of smaller countries like Switzerland seem to have been impacted more by these changes than the elite of bigger European countries (Davoine & Ravasi, 2013). The purpose of our contribution is therefore to focus on the Swiss business elite with a diachronic approach and, by crossing different sources of data, to gain a better understanding of how globalization processes impact the national business elite. We understand globalization by following the definition of Djelic and Quack (2003, p. 305); we understand it not only as the increasing internationalization of economic exchanges or the increasing interconnectedness of national economies, but also, first and foremost, as a set of processes transforming the institutional rules of the economic game – both structural and normative/cognitive – in national business systems as well as elaborating new rules and new institutional frames.

Most studies focusing on the career profiles of national elites have tried to identify national specific mechanisms or national specific assets, which facilitate the access to top management positions. Some authors and studies (e.g., Maclean et al., 2010; Mayrhofer et al., 2004) use the concepts of capital of Bourdieu (1986) to analyze career assets and resources that are necessary for the ascension of a small minority of corporate agents to power positions. Besides economic capital, which still legitimates the authority and the power positions of shareholder family members, Bourdieu differentiates between social capital and cultural capital. Social capital involves relationships of mutual recognition and acquaintance, while cultural capital represents durable social predispositions of the agents and appears in an institutionalized form with academic titles and degrees. Symbolic capital is related to the forms of capital that are recognized within a specific field or a social space as legitimate. In many European countries, institutions of secondary or higher education provide managers with institutionalized cultural and symbolic capital. For example, this is the case of public schools in the United Kingdom; universities delivering doctorates in Germany; and *Grandes Ecoles* in France (Bauer & Bertin-Mourot, 1996). These institutions are also social spaces in which crucial social capital can be acquired for the access to a power position. This is particularly true for British public schools and French *Grandes Ecoles* and is probably less important for German universities. Other elements of career paths, outside of the education system, might bring important resources, in terms of social and symbolic capital. For example, this is the case of the belonging to the *Grands Corps de l'Etat*, like the *Inspection des Finances* for the French civil servants who want to become future top managers; in a similar way, a knighthood or a peerage could facilitate or accompany the access to dominant management positions in the United Kingdom (Maclean et al., 2010, p. 342). Another element can be the social and symbolic capital acquired within a company career path, as it was detected and recognized by corporate processes of talent management. Globalization processes have brought a certain trend of standardization against the national specificities of the educational path of elites (Godelier, 2005). Fioole, van Driel, and van Baalen (2008) observed that, at the end of the 20th century, the educational backgrounds of German and Dutch managers tended to converge.

They noticed, for example, an increase in university degrees in economic sciences and MBAs at the expense of national law degrees. To understand the changes implied by globalization, in terms of the rules of the game in accessing the business elite, it is important to change the perspective from a national social space to a transnational social space. This refers to an arena of social interaction in which the main modes of connection between agents and groups cross national boundaries (Morgan, 2001, p. 115). New rules and new institutional frames are emerging in these transnational spaces, in which symbolic capital valued in national fields can be depreciated. New international sources of legitimacy (i.e., cosmopolitan careers and/or MBAs from prestigious − often US − universities) begin to compete with the state and national vision of excellence that had long prevailed in the national social spaces.

Within these transnational social spaces, transnational communities are emerging as well. Network analysis specialists showed that the interrelationships between boards have increasingly internationalized over the past 20 years (Carroll, 2010; Heemskerk, 2013; Kentor & Jang, 2004). Forms of cooperation between firms in the same country would thus be weakened in favor of transnational networks. The hypothesis of the emergence of a transnational network and a transnational capitalist class during the last two decades of the 20th century sparks an important debate that puts scholars against each other. Examples of this are the discussion with Kentor and Jang (2004, 2006) on the one side and Carroll and Fennema (2002, 2004, 2006) on the other side. Kentor and Jang have highlighted the increasingly stronger interlocking among the boards of directors of the 500 largest firms on the planet during the last two decades of the 20th century. According to these authors, national networks of companies have become progressively less important and in favor of growing transnationalization in a global corporate network. However, their results are criticized by Carroll and Fennema (2006), who posit that this transnational network remains moderate and thus unlikely to undermine interlocking national networks. This is as well a critical view of Hartmann (2009), who believes that interlocking directorates are superficial, functional links that do not replace longer learning and socialization processes in companies or institutions of the national education system.

Morgan (2001), Djelic and Quack (2010), and Harvey and Maclean (2010) propose to study the impact of globalization processes on "transnational communities," rather than on transnational networks. A community is defined as a set of individuals with shared values, assumptions, and beliefs, as well as common interests (Harvey & Maclean, 2010, p. 107).

Morgan (2001, pp. 120–121) explains that transnational communities may emerge in the transnational spaces of global firms through, for example, the interactions between agents from the headquarters and agents from the subsidiaries. "Ideological" transnational communities also emerge through the practices of business education, management consultancies, and other global professional service firms. Djelic and Quack (2010, p. 384) emphasized the importance of a common culture in transnational communities, expressed by "common meanings," "references," and "identity markers." Harvey and Maclean (2010) show that in spite of increasing transnational activities and a growing presence of non-nationals in the boards of directors in French and British companies, business elites of both countries continue to be forged primarily within the context of the national elite communities. This might be different for smaller countries, where globalization processes may induce stronger cultural changes within the business elite community.

The Swiss case is therefore particularly interesting to reflect on these dynamics. This country was characterized by its extraordinary stability in most of the 20th century. While it was spared by the two world wars, Switzerland experienced great continuity, in terms of its economic and political institutions, which have little equivalence in Europe. This relative strong political and economic stability was associated with stable mechanisms in the selection and development of Swiss economic elites. Historically, large Swiss corporations were characterized by a high level of interrelations among their boards of directors, particularly between large banks and industrial firms (see Nollert, 1998; Rusterholz, 1985; Schnyder, Lüpold, Mach, & David, 2005; Schreiner, 1984). The strong density of these interlocking directorates has revealed the high degree of cohesion among the members of the Swiss business elite.

Cohesion and stability of the elite community have been also promoted by the militia principle that traditionally concerns both the military sphere and the political sphere (Bühlmann, David, & Mach, 2012). The militia army constitutes one of Switzerland's specificities, with the obligation of male Swiss citizens to enroll in military service, starting from the age of 18 – with basic training for four months and subsequently three weeks of yearly training until the age of 42–52. The militia army has a profound integrating effect on interpersonal relationships of Swiss citizens, who come from different regions and different social groups, and this effect carries over later in the citizens' work lives (Erten, Strunk, Gonzalez, & Hilb, 2004, pp. 120–121). This effect is especially true for the Swiss business elite. Various studies have revealed that more than half of the top executives in

Swiss firms also held the rank of officer in the army, which is the case in the higher echelons of civil service and in the political world (Jann, 2003, pp. 139−140). This predominance of officers among Swiss elites underlines the role of the army as a major institution; the army delivers legitimate authority, promotes meeting and networking opportunities, and reinforces the cultural cohesion of the Swiss power elite. Having the army as a central institution for selecting and developing managerial elites is not "neutral"; it brought a stronger identification to the Swiss business community with national territory; a stronger solidarity with national interests; and a stronger relationship with the local (male) citizens involved in military activities, which means that it also created bridges and common ground with many politicians and civil servants.

Considering the strong cohesion of the Swiss corporate network and, from a cultural point of view, of the business elite community at the beginning of the 1980s, globalization should have been a major threat. Therefore, we aim to shed light on how different processes associated with globalization have challenged and changed key elements of the elite community between 1980 and 2010. First, studies show a strong decline of the corporate network between 1980 and 2000 (Schnyder et al., 2005) and connects this decline with profound transformations of the business environment. However, interlocking directorates only indicates the existence of functional interactions among board members that can be too superficial to describe the cultural changes of the community linked with transnationalization processes. We, therefore, confront the evolution of the Swiss corporate network with the evolution of top managers' profiles in order to identify how different processes at different levels impact the recruitment of top managers, as well as what the changes of the profiles reveal about the changes of the Swiss business elite community. Secondly, the period covered by our contribution is spread over 30 years (1980−2010), a period marked by important shifts in the economic organization of Switzerland (David, Lüpold, Mach, & Schnyder, 2014). To illustrate these changes, cohorts of managers of the 110 largest Swiss companies were compared between three different dates (1980, 2000, and 2010) with a combination of two approaches: corporate network analysis and individual profile analysis. The first section focuses on the decline of the corporate network, observed between 1980 and 2010. In the next sections, we consider three changes related to the top managers' characteristics in the same period − the growing number of foreigners, the educational backgrounds, and the decline of their engagement in military careers − as well as in other local political and social activities.

Our samples

Our research relies on an important database of Swiss elites,[1] including members of the boards of directors and chief executive officers (CEOs) from Switzerland's 110 largest firms in 1980, 2000, and 2010. For each of these years, these corporations represent the most important firms in the industrial, banking, insurance, and service sectors. They were selected on the basis of their turnover, stock market capitalization, and number of employees. More precisely, our sample consists of 107 firms and 891 people in 1980; 109 firms and 853 people in 2000; and 109 firms and 884 people in 2010. Network analysis included these broad samples for each year in order to show the evolution of interlocking directorates among Swiss largest firms.

The network analysis was then supplemented with an analysis of the profiles of selected top managers (i.e., board of directors' chairs and CEOs). The chairs of the board of directors and the CEOs represent indeed the most influential people, with regard to the strategic and operational management of the companies. By law, in Switzerland, the most important board of a company is the board of directors, which is responsible for both the strategic and executive management of a company. However, the board of directors generally delegates daily executive tasks to an executive committee managed by a CEO. Since there has been no legal obligation for a strict separation of tasks between the strategic management and the executive operations, the board of directors' structure and role, as well as those of the executive committee, can vary considerably from one company to another. Members of the board of directors are also often involved in executive tasks by assuming the role of an executive director. With an average of two persons per firm for each year, this second sample is composed of approximately 600 top managers. The sample contents include the following: in 1980, 189 individuals holding 208 executive positions; in 2000, 184 individuals holding 199 executive positions; and in 2010, 200 individuals holding 207 executive positions. For the profile analysis, we have collected basic biographical data (e.g., age, nationality, education) and career-related information (career path within the firm, number of executive positions held in other firms). This second sample is practically and exclusively composed of men because only four women are presented in the three benchmark years that we took into account (one in 1980 and three in 2010).

THE DISINTEGRATION OF THE SWISS CORPORATE NETWORK

Historically, large Swiss corporations were characterized by a strong level of interrelations between their boards of directors, particularly between large banks and industrial firms (see Nollert, 1998; Rusterholz, 1985; Schnyder et al., 2005; Schreiner, 1984). For a long time, the strong density of these interlocking directorates has revealed the high degree of cohesion within the Swiss business elite community. Former publications based on the evolution of interlocking directorates in Switzerland between 1980 and 2000 have shown an important disintegration of interfirm ties, and more generally, a decline of the corporate network (David et al., 2014; Schnyder et al., 2005). The graphical representations (Figs. A1–A3, in appendix) of the network, composed of all firms that share at least two common directors (2-Slices), clearly illustrate this disintegration of the interfirm ties. Fig. A3 shows that the disintegration went further in the last decade. Two basic indicators (de Nooy, Mrvar, & Batagelj, 2005) clearly express this evolution (Table 1), namely the *average degree* (indicating the average number of ties per firm in the network) and the network *density* (which measures the number of links in the network as a proportion of the maximum possible number of links). Meanwhile, in 1980, a firm was linked on average to more than eight firms due to shared directors; this number decreased to about two ties in 2010. Furthermore, the network density, which was about 8% in 1980, has considerably decreased in 30 years, reaching only 2% in 2010.

Two phenomena directly linked to globalization and the growing financialization of the economy seem to be at the origin of this decline (David et al., 2014; Schnyder et al., 2005). On the one hand, there was a transformation of banking activities, which has led to the disengagement of bankers from the boards of directors in other firms. On the other hand, companies that reoriented their strategies toward shareholder value

Table 1. The Swiss Corporate Network: Density and Degree.

	1980 (N = 107)	2000 (N = 109)	2010 (N = 109)
Average degree	8.6	4.2	2.3
Density	8.1%	3.9%	2.2%

Note: Calculation on 1-mode network (firms).

promoted the adoption of new governance practices that were implemented in the Anglo-Saxon model. This has led to the erosion of ties between corporations, making the presence on several boards particularly difficult.

These correlated phenomena began in the mid-1990s, signaling a clear departure from the past, which had been characterized by the central position occupied by banks within the network (see Fig. A1). The disengagement of banks in the corporate network can be explained by the increasing importance of financial markets, new financial market profit opportunities, and the increasing competition between banks and financial service companies at an international level. The strategy adopted by Switzerland's main banks was therefore meant to reinforce investment banking activities, while reducing traditional credit activities; to extend banking activities into the insurance business; and to expand internationally. Swiss banks have increasingly oriented their activities toward stock exchange markets (initial public offerings, mergers and acquisitions, investment trusts) and wealth management, which offered higher rates of return. As a consequence of this transformation, Swiss banks increasingly behaved as traders and market operators, rather than traditional credit companies. For these banks, granting credit was not as attractive as before, especially since stock exchange activities were generating growing revenues (Baumann & Rutsch, 2008; Mazbouri, Guex, & Lopez, 2012).

These strategic transformations caused banks to decrease their presence on the boards of directors in industrial companies. As Swiss banks were increasingly operating as investment banks, they tried to preserve their credibility within the investment banking sector. In this sector, the presence of close and privileged ties with industrial companies generally undermines this credibility. Moreover, the bankers' representation on the boards of directors in industrial firms was perceived as a conflict of interest. In addition, the development of financial markets provided banks with a source of income, which was much more profitable than those offered by credit activities. As a result, banks allocated credit to companies in a more restrictive and selective manner. Traditionally, the presence of bankers on the boards of directors in industrial companies allowed financial establishments to gain a privileged position; this allowed the financial establishments to monitor their investments and make sure that credits were managed appropriately (Rusterholz, 1985). The granting of credit was considered to be an activity based on a long-term relationship of trust between banks and companies. Sharing the members of board of directors contributed to the preservation of this relationship. At the opposite end of the spectrum, the activities of investment banks, based on isolated transactions, did not require stable and long-term relationships between banks and customers.

The corporate network decline is also explained by the strong decrease in the ties among industrial companies. This evolution was due to a major transformation in Swiss corporate governance regulations, which have developed a stronger orientation toward shareholder value; this was because of the increasing pressure from international financial markets and international institutional investors, starting from the second half of the 1980s. This pressure brought two major changes. On the one hand, it led to a reduction in the size of the boards of directors (smaller boards were considered to be more efficient), and on the other hand, it created higher professional performance standards and expectations for board members, making the holding of several board seats more difficult. From the mid-1990s, a reduction in the size of the boards of directors of Switzerland's largest 110 companies has been observed (David et al., 2014).

The decline of the Swiss corporate network was also correlated with a major change in the recruitment of board members. In examination of the evolution in top management profiles between 1980 and 2010, the increasing number of foreigners in the board of directors of Swiss companies is impressive; the increasing number represents a major change regarding the tradition of the Swiss business elite community. During the 20th century, Swiss economic elites relied on protective mechanisms to safeguard against the outside world, especially foreigners. Switzerland has even been called the "fortress of the Alps" by some representatives of the financial community (Monks & Minow, 1995, p. 320). Among these safeguarding tools, in particular, the *Vinkulierung* instrument allowed boards of directors to prevent foreign investors from taking control of Swiss companies. This legal practice consisted of binding registered shares and limiting their transferability, thus excluding unwanted buyers, including foreigners (see Kaufmann & Kunz, 2001; Kläy, 1997). This process was especially relied upon after World War II and continued until the 1991 reform in the corporate legislation; this, among other changes, precluded the exclusion of shareholders based solely on the investor's nationality (Schnyder, 2007). Moreover, until recently, another clause required the majority of members on a board of directors to be of Swiss nationality, and this clause was finally repealed during a partial revision of the country's corporate legislation.

In our 2010 sample, approximately one-third of the members in the boards of directors were foreigners (300 out of 884 records). In our 2000 sample, the percentage of foreign board members was approximately 20% (180 foreigners out of 853 records). We do not have systematic information concerning the nationality of all members of the boards of directors in 1980, but according to the data that we have, there were only 4% of foreigners at that time. This growing internationalization reveals deep changes within the recruitment process of members of boards of directors from large Swiss companies. On the one hand, this strong presence of foreigners might be viewed as the consequence of a stronger transnationalization of the Swiss corporate network. Because of the lack of systematic data within our sample, regarding the presence of individuals on the boards of directors of non-Swiss companies, we cannot document further the emergence of a transnational network of interrelations. Regardless, we can refer to studies by Kentor and Jang (2004, 2006), which underlined a strong presence of Swiss companies in transnational corporate networks. According to these authors, the Swiss-Swedish company ABB would have been, in 1998, the most central company of a globalized corporate network (Kentor & Jang, 2004, p. 366). On the other hand, the new foreign members were less integrated in the Swiss networks of boards of directors, and therefore contributed (statistically) to the decline of the Swiss corporate network. In 2010, only three of them held at least two seats on boards of directors, while, among Swiss nationals, more than 50 were in at least two boards.

This growing proportion of foreigners in the Swiss business elite represents a challenge for the cultural cohesion of the national business elite community. Therefore, in the next section, we focus on different dimensions of the evolution of top management profiles by using collected data on the top management (chairs and CEOs) of the largest Swiss companies.

EVOLUTION OF TOP MANAGERS' PROFILES

After analyzing the evolution of the network of interconnections between boards of directors in the last three decades, we now look more closely at the major social agents of the Swiss business elite community. The second part of our analysis is therefore based on the comparison of profiles (in terms of nationality, educational background, military, and civil and political engagements) of three samples of top managers (i.e., board of directors' chairmen and CEOs) from Switzerland's 110 largest companies in 1980, 2000, and 2010. The evolution of key elements in the profiles of top management might reflect important evolutions in the elements that legitimatize the authority of the Swiss business elite, as well as reflect changes in the values and cognitive frames that were traditionally shared by the national elite community.

We proceed in three steps for our three samples by analyzing: (1) the presence of foreign managers; (2) the changes in the educational background; (3) the implication of top managers in national social networks, especially in political and military networks, two traditional elements of the Swiss business elite community.

GROWING PRESENCE OF FOREIGN TOP MANAGERS

In 1980, the proportion of foreigners among the top managers in Switzerland's 110 largest companies was less than 4%, and this percentage reached 24% in 2000. This proportion continued to grow during the first years of the 21st century: in 2010, one top manager out of three was not a Swiss national (see Table 2). The significantly lower rate seen in 1980 can be explained by the persistence of the protectionist mechanisms for most of the century, which is mentioned above ("*Vinkulierung*" and the limitation of the number of foreigners on boards of directors).

In 2000, German nationals represented the main foreign nationality (11 top managers, 5.8% of the sample), followed by French nationals (6 top managers, 3.2%) and Austrians (3.2%). Ten years later, we notice an increase in top managers coming from Germany (28 top managers, 14% of the sample) and the stability of French nationals (7 top managers, 3.5%); on the other hand, we observe a greater presence of top managers coming from the United States (8 top managers, 4%) and the United Kingdom (5 top managers, 2.5%). Thus, an increase in top managers coming from Anglo-Saxon countries has been observed during the past decade.

Table 2. Foreigners among the Top Managers.

	1980 ($N=189$)	2000 ($N=184$)	2010 ($N=200$)
Board of directors' chairs	3.4%	16.2%	30.5%
Chief executive officers	4.3%	29.7%	39.1%
Total	3.7%	23.9%	35.5%

Note: A person holding a position as board of director's chair and CEO at the same time is included in both categories.

As can be observed in Table 2, in 2000, internationalization concerns mainly the executive positions (CEOs), and the chair of boards of directors tends to be more frequently occupied by Swiss nationals. In 2007, the repeal of the clause that limited the number of foreigners serving on boards of directors allowed for more freedom in the recruitment of members to serve on the boards of directors. In 2010, the proportion of foreigners reached 30% among the chairs of board of directors and 40% among the CEOs.

Other studies with various samples have shown that managerial elites have experienced a substantial internationalization. Dyllick and Torgler (2007, p. 78) wrote that the level of foreigners among top managers in Switzerland's 500 largest firms was at 28% in 2004. For Davoine (2005, p. 95), half of all executive committee members on Swiss firms listed on the Swiss stock exchange index SMI in 2005 were foreigners. Based on a large sample including managers in an executive role, Ruigrok and Greve (2008, pp. 65–66) noticed that 49% of all managers in Switzerland were foreigners, compared to 34% in the Netherlands, 20% in the United Kingdom, 17% in Sweden, 13% in Finland, 7% in Norway, and 1% in Denmark. Therefore, the degree of internationalization in Switzerland can be assumed to be particularly high, and Ruigrok and Greve (2008, p. 67) conclude that "Swiss firms appear to be at the forefront of the development of an international market for executive labor."

In order to understand how foreign top managers have been appointed to the top positions of large Swiss companies, we conducted a more qualitative and detailed analysis of our database for 2000 (David, Davoine, Ginalski, & Mach, 2012) and 2010 samples (Ravasi, 2013). We could identify four categories of career logics among foreign top managers of the Swiss business elite. The first category identified is that of *founders/owners*: this category could already explain the presence of some foreign managers in the 1980 sample. In the 2000 sample, they were the most represented group of foreign managers (about 30%), but this proportion declined sharply in 2010 (about 15%). Enterprises created by foreign top managers in our sample in 2010 generally belong to sectors that are considered as traditional for the Swiss economy, such as banking and finance, watch manufacturing, or pharmaceutical − for example, the French president of Actelion group Jean-Paul Clozel or the American naturalized Swiss Nicolas Hayek, president of Swatch. The second category of foreign top manager career path identified was that of *mountain climbers within Swiss multinational companies*. This type of career path, in which top managers integrated the company very early and climbed one by one all the corporate levels, is typical of certain Swiss multinationals, such as the Austrian Peter Brabeck-Letmathe (president) and the Belgian Paul Bulcke (CEO) of Nestlé in 2010. This category was also already present in 1980 (15%) and accounted for 10% of the sample in 2000. Its proportion has increased slightly over the last decade and in 2010 they represented almost 17% of the sample. The third category is that of *Mergers & Acquisitions' mountain climbers*: top managers who come from companies that have merged with or been acquired by a Swiss company. This category was not represented in the 1980 sample, represented about 20% in the sample of foreign top managers in 2000, and declined sharply in 2010 (5% of the sample). An example of this category was the German citizen Carsten Schloter (CEO of Swisscom in 2010) who was on the management board of the German firm Debitel when it was acquired by Swisscom and then became CEO after a brief career path within Swisscom. The last category identified is that of *externally recruited international managers*. Like the previous category, it could be identified for the first time in our 2000 sample and represented approximately 20% of the sample. During the decade 2000−2010, the proportion of this category increased significantly and in 2010, it corresponded to almost 50% of the 71 foreign top managers of the 2010 sample. We counted in this category foreign top managers who had no ties with the company they managed, either with regard to the property (through family ties with the founder or through a merger/acquisition) or professional career experience within the firm that they managed.

Observing the career path profiles allowed us to link the growing presence of foreign top managers to the transnationalization of the Swiss business environment. In 2010, Switzerland was indeed a major host country for foreign direct investments (UNCTAD, 2011), and larger Swiss cities were the site of several headquarters and subsidiaries for numerous multinational, international, and financial organizations (Naville, Walti, & Tischhauser, 2007; Steiner & Wanner, 2011), which facilitate social interactions between agents as well as the development of a local "transnational executive labor market." Though many Swiss multinational companies have a traditionally high transnationalization index, which seems to be a recurrent phenomenon for multinational companies coming from smaller countries with smaller internal markets (Katzenstein, 2003; Morgan, 2011, p. 420), the recent liberalization of the Swiss business environment has certainly facilitated foreign direct investments and attracted entrepreneurs from foreign countries who decided to found their company in Switzerland. More liberal rules have also led to an increased activity of mergers and acquisitions with the resulting transfer of top managers from foreign companies to Swiss firms. The increased transnationalization experienced by large Swiss multinational corporations has also facilitated the arrival of top managers that had career paths, depending less on national institutional mechanisms than on multinational corporate talent management programs (Al Ariss, Cascio, & Paauwe, 2014; Mayrhofer et al., 2004).

CHANGES IN EDUCATIONAL BACKGROUND

Education is the second criterion used to analyze the internationalization of Swiss business elites. On one hand, we studied the education level achieved, and on the other hand, the different fields of study chosen. Regarding the first criterion (Table 3), top managers of large Swiss companies generally have a high level of education: 69% had a university degree in 1980, and 79% in 2000 and 2010. And 40% of them attended a postgraduate program (doctorate, masters, or business school executive education program) in 1980, 47% in 2000, and 50% in 2010. The proportion of executives who undertook an apprenticeship, negligible at the beginning, decreased somewhat during the observation period. We generally noticed an increase in education levels between 1980 and 2000, and the percentages remained similar in the 2010 sample.

The most remarkable change during the period under scrutiny concerns the fields of study (Table 4). Among the three dominant academic areas (technical sciences, law, and economics/management), a decline is noticed in the 2000 sample in the percentage of law graduates, who were predominant in the 1980 sample. We also observe in the 2000 sample an increase of degrees obtained in management or economics. The percentage of graduates

Table 3. Educational Level of the Top Managers.

	1980 ($N=189$)	2000 ($N=184$)	2010 ($N=200$)
Apprenticeship	11.6%	7.1%	6.0%
University degree	68.8%	78.8%	78.5%
Other higher education (professional schools)	5.8%	9.2%	7.5%
Postgraduate degree	40.2%	46.7%	49.5%
Unknown	18.5%	4.9%	5.0%

Note: The different categories are not exclusive so the sum of percentages in each column may exceed 100%.

Table 4. University Degree Achieved by Top Managers, by Field of Study.

	1980 (N = 130)	2000 (N = 145)	2010 (N = 157)
Engineering/Technical sciences	30.8%	32.4%	29.9%
Law	33.8%	22.8%	16.7%
Economics	18.5%	24.8%	48.1%
Other	1.8%	2.8%	10.2%
Unknown	16.9%	17.2%	1.3%

Note: The different categories are not exclusive so the sum of percentages in each column may exceed 100%.

Table 5. Postgraduate Degree Achieved by Top Managers, by Field of Study.

	1980 (N = 76)	2000 (N = 86)	2010 (N = 99)
Engineering/Technical sciences	15.1%	15.1%	11.1%
Law	52.0%	26.7%	17.2%
Economics	26.0%	55.8%	71.7%
Other	2.7%	5.6%	5.0%
Unknown	6.8%	3.5%	1.0%

Note: The different categories are not exclusive so the sum of percentages in each column may exceed 100%.

in technical and natural sciences, mainly from the Swiss Federal Institutes of Technology (EPFZ in Zurich and EPFL in Lausanne), remained stable from the 1980 sample to the 2000 sample. The most important change occurred between 2000 and 2010 samples, with a clear decline of top managers with law degrees, a slight decrease in technical and natural sciences, and a significant increase of managers with degrees in economics or management. Thus, in 2010, almost half of the top managers having achieved an academic degree had graduated in economics or management.

Regardless, the most striking changes appear at the postgraduate level (master and PhD) (Table 5). Between 1980 and 2010, a clear decline was observed in law studies (from 52% in 1980 to 17% in 2010), and at the same time, a very strong increase in economics and management degrees was noted (from 26% in 1980 to 72% in 2010). Meanwhile, the proportion of postgraduate degrees achieved in technical sciences remained rather stable and was less important compared to the two other fields of study (15% or less).

Thus, the main change concerning postgraduate education lies in the important rise of economics and management in the education background of the Swiss business elite. This evolution is mainly due to the high number of managers having attended an MBA or another similar executive management education program: out of 71 top managers in 2010 with a postgraduate degree in economics or business administration, 59 of them attended an MBA or similar program (33 in 2000 and 11 in 1980). Several authors that studied the education backgrounds of top managers have emphasized the increasing importance of undergraduate and postgraduate education in the fields of economics, management, or finance – in particular, MBAs or similar executive programs from Anglo-Saxon business schools (Barrial, 2006; David, Ginalski, Rebmann, & Schnyder, 2009; Davoine, 2005; Dyllick & Torgler, 2007; Widmer, 2012). This evolution can be explained by the increasing importance of stock exchange markets and the growing influence of international investors: that is, of the approach of shareholder value to business strategy. In this sense, an education background in economics, particularly in business administration, can be interpreted as a sign of expertise or as an element of legitimate authority linked to the growing importance of financial markets. Other recent studies (e.g., on German and Dutch managers) have shown that top managers are increasingly trained as financial experts rather than as jurists or engineers. This trend is clearly correlated with the reorientation of companies' strategies toward shareholder value (Fioole et al., 2008; Höpner, 2004). Brezis (2010) radically stated that a consequence of globalization has been the standardization of the elite's education following the internationalization of universities, the development of transnational knowledge, and the growing importance of finance and economic issues in the management of companies.

Parallel to the increase of the number of degrees in economics and management, the decline of Law degrees is interesting because law education is traditionally more nationally bounded than management education, which is often considered an internationally recognized element of legitimate authority, especially in the case of business school courses like MBAs (Bühlmann, David, & Mach, 2013). Most of the institutions delivering postgraduate degrees in the 2010 sample were business schools in the United States like Harvard Business School or in European countries like IMD or INSEAD, which are European business schools with programs, organization, and faculty profiles following the US model. Considering the changes in the educational background, from law to management, new global or cosmopolitan elements of legitimate authority slowly replaced the more national bounded one. Following Vaara and Faÿ (2012, p. 1028) and using Bourdieu's terminology (Bourdieu, 2000), education — management and MBA education in particular — plays a central role in the (re)production of "nomos" (i.e., the principle of vision and division of a social order) and "doxa" (i.e., a set of fundamental beliefs that does not even need to be asserted in the form of an explicit, self-conscious dogma). The growing importance of "Anglo-Saxon" business school education among national elites can also be seen as a vector of diffusion for Anglo-Saxon or global management concepts and ideologies, values, and cognitive frames that impact directly corporate strategies and facilitate indirectly the transformation of the business environment (Godelier, 2005; Morgan, 2001).

DECLINE OF INVOLVEMENT IN TRADITIONAL NATIONAL COMMUNITY NETWORKS

Useem (1980, p. 58) has underlined that among American economic elites, "business, associational, educational, and kinship networks comprise mutually reinforcing strands of cohesion." A traditional feature of the cohesion of the Swiss business elite community was its strong involvement in other social activities. Following the militia principle, Swiss top managers showed a strong involvement in the army and in political mandates at federal (national) and cantonal (regional) levels.

As an illustration, 15% of the managers of the 1980 sample had a political mandate, and 57% were involved in a parallel military officer career. De Weck (1983), former CEO of UBS and member of several boards of directors during the 1980s, described his military career experience in the general staff of the Swiss army as excellent managerial training: "*For my generation, the general staff of the Swiss army really provided our 'management' training.*" Even if we can consider that a parallel military career is helpful to develop general management skills, studies show that it is first and foremost useful to develop relationships and social capital (Jann, 2003). In the past, various sociological factors, such as bonds of friendship or proximity developed during academic studies or military service, have played an important role in the cooptation of boards of directors (see discussion in Mizruchi, 1996). A similar militia spirit, and a similar development of social networks, could be observed in the political field, with a strong involvement of Swiss top managers in political responsibilities.

Military careers and political mandates reinforced the ties within the business elite community as well as the ties between military, economic, and political elites.

The Swiss national elite had been traditionally characterized by a strong cohesion (David et al., 2014), certainly a stronger cohesion than that of the US "power elite" described by Wright Mills (1956) because of a lower heterogeneity and stronger solidarity mechanisms among the different elite spheres. First, the deep roots of the militia principle in Swiss society, especially in the political and military spheres, promoted weak political professionalization, a low number of directorships in the hands of single individuals, and more generally, an incomplete differentiation of elites into different spheres. Second, Katzenstein (2003) showed that national elites of small European countries, including Switzerland, have learned to "stick together" at a national level to face an international environment on which they depend. This sense of vulnerability has promoted various modes of collaboration between political and economic elites, especially in the form of neo-corporatist cooperation instances. Strong cohesion within the employers has so long relied on various forms of collaboration, such as the many interconnections between corporate boards and highly representative employers' organizations (David et al., 2009; Widmer, 2012). De Weck (1983) described clearly the "club mentality" that influenced the Swiss business elite until the 1980s and helped maintain the network of interrelations: *"There is in human nature a tendency towards clubs and this tendency is maybe more marked in Switzerland than anywhere else. (...) And we also have clubs of boards of directors. (...) In several places within the German-speaking part of Switzerland, the mentality of the population is still marked by corporatism; a history of many centuries steeped in the* Zünfte *(corporations) can still be felt."* Despite early internationalization of the Swiss economy, the control mechanisms of firms and their leaders have thus remained embedded in the national framework.

From 1980 to 2010, through an analysis of the military ranks obtained by top managers in Switzerland's large companies (Table 6), we clearly observe the decline of the military experience in top managers' profiles. When compared to the 1970s or 1980s, the importance of this kind of experience has decreased even if it remained significant among Swiss managers in 2010. If we consider the whole sample of company managers, we notice that more than half of the managerial elite held an officer's rank in 1980 while the same indicator fell to one quarter in 2010. However, this decline must be put into perspective. If we only take Swiss nationals into consideration, we merely notice a slight erosion: the percentage of Swiss

Table 6. Officers among Top Managers.

	1980 (N = 189)	2000 (N = 184)	2010 (N = 200)
Lower ranking officers (lieutenant and 1st lieutenant)	11.1%	8.2%	8.0%
Specialist officers	0.5%	4.3%	1.5%
Captains	18.0%	4.3%	7.0%
Higher ranking officers (major, lieutenant-colonel and colonel)	23.8%	22.8%	10.0%
General officers (brigadier, major general, lieutenant general)	1.1%	1.1%	0.0%
Total	54.5%	40.8%	26.5%
Total among Swiss top managers only	56.6%	53.6%	43.4%

managers holding an officer's rank in the Swiss army falls from 57% to 43%. It still represents a high proportion, even if in 2010 officers' ranks were lower than in 1980, thereby illustrating the fact that parallel careers in both the army and in the business world are less common. The end of the Cold War and the recurrent criticism toward the Swiss army contributed to the constant decline noticed during the 1990s. The skills acquired during military service are progressively less valued within the corporate world, also because of the greater prevalence of women in middle management. Furthermore, the absences caused by annual training periods bring a growing criticism from the corporate world (Jann, 2003).

Another distinctive feature of Switzerland was the strong involvement of corporate managers in politics, which is linked to the size of the country, to its political system of direct democracy, and to the militia principle (Bergmann, 1994). Traditionally, a position of Member of Parliament was considered a side activity to a professional career, at least until the 1990s, a period marked by some Parliamentary reforms and by the increase of the remuneration of Members of Parliament, which led to a certain professionalization of the Federal Parliament (for more details, Pilotti, Mach, & Mazzoleni, 2010). Consequently, more than 15% of the managers within the 1980 sample concurrently held a political mandate (mainly at the cantonal and federal level) before or after being appointed to a top executive position at one of Switzerland's largest 110 companies. Afterward we noticed a significant decrease in political mandates: the proportion reached only 3% in 2010 (5% for managers of Swiss origin). This collapse can only be partially linked to the stronger presence of foreign managers. The evolution is the result of Parliament reforms on the one hand and of a certain managerial professionalization on the other hand. This makes more difficult – and less legitimate – to concurrently hold positions in both politics and the business world. When broadening the sample to include all members of boards of directors, we noticed that in 1980, 91 directors (10%) out of the 891 held a mandate in the federal Parliament. In 2010, they were only 28 out of 884.

This withdrawal of business elites was also observed in the decrease of the involvement of managers in other community activities. This evolution was confirmed within our sample by data concerning Rotary Club memberships during the last 30 years. With more than 200 local clubs, the Swiss Rotary Club has more than 12,000 members (approximately 6,000 in 1980) and is characterized by a strongly decentralized structure and deep regional ties. It brings together people who occupy higher echelons within various professional fields. While 36% of managers were members of the Rotary Club in 1980, the percentage fell to only 23% in 2000 and 17% in 2010. It should be recognized that membership within the Rotary Club is, in fact, a contestable criterion because it is not a "real" Swiss institution, because its success (and its less elitist recruitment methods) can make it less attractive to managers, and also because competition with other similar associations (the Lion's Club, for example) would necessitate a deeper analysis and more thorough statistics, including membership within other associations. Nevertheless, the decreasing involvement of top managers in the Rotary Club can be taken as an additional sign of the lower importance given to local involvement in other social activities, as well as a sign of changing value orientations in the Swiss business elite community.

To conclude, we observe a clear decline in our 2010 sample of the involvement in other traditional social activities, especially activities and responsibilities in the military and political fields, which were characteristic of the Swiss business elite before the 1980s. Regular social interactions in boards of directors, employers' associations, philanthropic societies, clubs, or, in the case of Switzerland, parallel military careers reinforced the political and social cohesion of Swiss elites. On one hand, the decline of involvement observed across our three samples is partly due to the increasing number of foreign top managers who have been socialized outside from the Swiss business system and who therefore do not share the same representations and values of military prestige or of political involvement in a system of direct democracy. On the other hand, the transformations or the globalization of the business environment have changed the rules of the game for the access to top management positions in large Swiss companies. During our research, we interviewed an anonymous 58-year-old Swiss CEO with a parallel military career, who declared, "*Another point is that the internationalization of the Swiss economy has made the national network less important as it used to be, less important than international networks. And this means that a national network institution like the army has become less important. An international MBA is the ideal advantage to know new people from other countries, whom you can use if you need contacts in their countries*" (quoted in Schmalz, 2012, p. 141). This last quote clearly illustrates the rationale of the decline. Today, an MBA education, as an asset and as a socialization process, has become more important to get access to and to legitimate a position in the Swiss business elite. Traditional national institutions, which were, like the army, a source of (national) social capital, legitimate authority, shared values, cognitive frames, and identity within the national elite community have been challenged and weakened by the new constraints and demands of today's more "globalized" environment.

CONCLUSIONS

We have investigated the impact of globalization on the top managers in Switzerland's 110 largest firms by adopting a diachronic perspective based on three elite cohorts (1980, 2000, and 2010). In order to unravel the changes undergone by the Swiss business elite community, we have carried out two types of analyses which have rarely been combined in the academic literature. First, we illustrated the decline of the national business elite community with the perspective of the corporate network, identifying different elements and processes of the environment, which could explain the sharp decline of the Swiss national corporate network in a period of three decades. Second, focusing on top manager samples in 1980, 2000, and 2010, we analyzed the evolution of top managers' profiles in terms of nationality and education and observed the decline of involvement in other associative, military, and political networks, all important elements for the cohesion of the community. This double approach allowed us to reveal correlated phenomena, as well as interplays between changes occurring in the national environment parallel to changes occurring in the development, selection, and socialization of the main agents of the Swiss business elite community.

Our diachronic analysis illustrates various interrelated structural changes that we can link to the globalization and the financialization processes of the Swiss national economy. First, on a macro-level, related to these processes, major changes have occurred in the formal institutions regulating Swiss corporate governance, relations between banks and companies, and relations between corporate boards. These changes explain to a great extent the disintegration of the Swiss corporate network. The openness to foreign direct investments and to foreign board members relates to the increase of foreign managers appointed to boards and top management positions. An important proportion of new foreign members of the Swiss business elite came to Switzerland as investors, founders, or high potential managers selected in the headquarters or in the subsidiaries of Swiss or foreign multinational companies. This new afflux of foreigners (a third of our 2010 sample) reflects as well the growing importance of companies with multinational activity in our sample of the 110 largest Swiss companies. Multinational companies often use their own corporate processes of talent management to detect, to select, and to develop their future top managers. These corporate processes come in confrontation with the traditional Swiss processes of selection and development of the national business elite, which were embedded in the national institutions and rooted in the values and the cognitive frames of the national Swiss elite community. On a micro-level, the decrease in the traditional key elements of symbolic, social, or cultural capital (military careers, law degrees, political responsibilities) in the top managers' profiles of our samples certainly reflects that these elements became less important in 2010 to legitimate managerial authority and to give access to elite positions. The emergence of new recurrent elements like MBAs or business school education in the individual profiles – of the Swiss as well as of the foreign top managers – clearly shows that new "global" or "cosmopolitan" elements of symbolic capital have gained weight to gain access to or to legitimate a position in the highly transnational social space of the Swiss business elite.

The weakening of the national network of interrelations and the growing appointment of foreigners as members of boards of directors and as executive managers can be interpreted in two ways. On the one hand, they can be seen as consequences of drastic changes occurring in the governance model that led to a more international openness and a more systematic use of international financial markets and managerial labor (Ruigrok & Greve, 2008). Recent empirical studies have shown that the appointment of international managers is not automatically seen as a positive signal by financial markets (Schmid & Dauth, 2014). On the other hand, and we would like to insist on that dimension, these phenomena can also be viewed in a more constructivist perspective, so we can argue that the recruitment of international managers (whose legitimacy, networks, identities, values, and cognitive frames are different from those of the traditional Swiss managerial elite) also influences governance models, strategies, and forms of cooperation between economic actors. We consider also that the transnationalization of members of boards of directors and executive managers in Switzerland helped reinforce the general process of transnationalization of capital and the transformations of corporate governance practices. The growing presence of foreigners and of local managers with standardized business school education helped the diffusion of new cognitive and normative frameworks (Morgan, 2001) and weakened national specificities in the elite community culture. As an example for this process, a large number of Swiss top managers belonging to the new business elites worked at McKinsey, the consulting firm that has contributed directly and indirectly to the promotion of the notion of shareholder value in Switzerland (Mach, David, & Bühlmann, 2011, pp. 94−95).

Another element that we could not show with our data is the growing transnational openness of the Swiss corporate network, with new links from Swiss boards to foreign company boards. The social space of a transnationalized community could certainly find a fertile ground in a country where there is a strong geographical proximity between the headquarters of Swiss multinational companies and banks, many European headquarters of US multinationals, consulting and auditing companies, as well as international organizations and regulatory bodies (like the World Trade Organization or the International Labor Organization in Geneva or the Committee on banking supervision in Basel). The geographical proximity can facilitate social interactions between the members of the Swiss business elite and other agents, as well as the development of new, transnational networks that our data does not take into account. The traditional Swiss elite club mentality could find new venues for social encounters within transnational clubs, such as the International Chamber of Commerce, the Bilderberg Group, the World Economic Forum, or the European Round Table of Industrialists (Nollert, 2005). Nestlé, one of the largest multinational companies in the country, has been strongly involved in these kinds of transnational clubs since the 1980s. For example, Helmut Maucher, CEO and chairman of the board of directors of Nestlé, gave up his management position at the main Swiss employers' association in 1996 to become president of the European Round Table of Industrialists. The following year, he was appointed president of the International Chamber of Commerce. The World Economic Forum in Davos is a good example of a transnational club where many members of the Swiss business elite play a major role. Our contribution should therefore support on the one hand a similar view as that of Carroll and Fennema (2006, pp. 608–609): a transnational business community is emerging, but the process is complex, tentative, and embedded in national specificities and path dependencies. It is also building upon established "domestic" networks rather than displacing them.

On the other hand, transnationalization processes can have negative consequences for the cultural cohesion in the elite community. They could create potential conflict between (the local and the "global") subgroups of the elite, or bring simply a "denationalization" of the community (see discussion in Djelic & Quack, 2010, p. 390). In our samples, some Swiss top managers have solved this potential conflict and combined both kinds of assets or socialization elements (e.g., MBA and Swiss military career), a phenomenon observed in other European countries like France or Germany (Hartmann, 2007, p. 212), where some top managers transform accumulated local symbolic capital into global symbolic capital by gaining an MBA after a first traditional local socialization process. But looking at the new generation of top managers in the Swiss 2010 sample, there are only rare cases of managers who cumulate company and military careers, international assets, and local political responsibilities. In comparison with other European countries, the Swiss specificity is that the army seems to be the national traditional institution, which played a major role in the development of human, cultural, and social capital of the Swiss business elite. In other European countries, the prestige of national institutions that traditionally played a major role in the elite selection and development (e.g., public schools in the United Kingdom, German universities, and French *Grandes Ecoles*) was less challenged in the last decades than the one of the army. The prestige of the army, associated with masculine values, as well as with nationalist values that are not always compatible with transnational communities, has decreased in most European countries, probably since the end of the Cold War period (Jann, 2003), and many European countries, for example Germany and France, abandoned the conscription principle in the 1990s, which definitely made the opportunity of following a military officer career less attractive compared to a civilian career. Even in Switzerland, where a popular vote or referendum in September 2013 demonstrated that a militia will not be abandoned in the near future, the institution has lost some of its prestige in the last decades, and parallel military careers definitely seem to be less adapted to contemporary companies' human resource management principles and policies. The clear but surprisingly slow decline of military socialization within the Swiss business elite will therefore probably carry on. This trend will likely make the Swiss business elite community increasingly at risk of being disconnected from the rest of the Swiss population, a risk that had been mitigated through regular interactions (at least with the male part of the population) during the military service periods.

NOTE

1. This paper was prepared as part of a larger research project on Swiss elites in the 20th century, financed by the Swiss National Science Foundation (grant no. 100012-113550/1). The database for this research project includes more than 14,000 people having a management function in the political, economic or administrative sectors in Switzerland at different key dates in the 20th century. For more details: http://www.unil.ch/iepi/page54315.html

ACKNOWLEDGMENTS

We would like to thank Thomas David, University of Lausanne, for his collaboration on the first version of this paper, presented at the 2012 EGOS Conference in Helsinki, as well as the Swiss National Science Foundation for its financial support.

REFERENCES

Al Ariss, A., Cascio, W. F., & Paauwe, J. (2014). Talent management: Current theories and future research directions. *Journal of World Business*, *49*(2), 173–179.

Barrial, F. (2006). *Evolution du profil sociologique de l'élite managériale suisse entre 1980 et 2000*. Master's thesis, University of Lausanne, Switzerland.

Bauer, M., & Bertin-Mourot, B. (1996). *Vers un modèle européen de dirigeant?* Paris: CNRS-Boyden.

Bauer, M., & Bertin-Mourot, B. (1999). National models for making and legitimating elites. A comparative analysis of the 200 top executives in France, Germany and Great-Britain. *European Societies*, *1*(1), 9–31.

Baumann, C., & Rutsch, W. E. (2008). *Swiss banking — Wie weiter? Aufstieg und Wandel der Schweizer Finanzbranche*. Zürich: NZZ Verlag.

Bergmann, A. (1994). *The Swiss way of management*. Paris: Eska.

Bourdieu, P. (1986). The forms of capital. In J. G. Richardson (Ed.), *Handbook of theory and research for the sociology of education* (pp. 241–258). New York, NY: Greenwood Press.

Bourdieu, P. (2000). *Pascalian meditations*. In R. Nice (Trans.). Stanford, CA: Stanford University Press.

Brezis, E. S. (2010). *Globalization and the emergence of a transnational oligarchy.* UNU-WIDER Working Paper No. 2010/05.

Bühlmann, F., David, T., & Mach, A. (2012). Political and economic elites in Switzerland: Personal interchange, interactional relations and structural homology. *European Societies, 14*(5), 727–754.

Bühlmann, F., David, T., & Mach, A. (2013). Cosmopolitan capital and the internationalization of the field of business elites: Evidence from the Swiss case. *Cultural Sociology, 7*(2), 211–229.

Carroll, W. (2010). *The making of a transnational capitalist class: Corporate power in the 21st century.* London: Zed Books.

Carroll, W., & Fennema, M. (2002). Is there a transnational business community? *International Sociology, 17*(3), 393–419.

Carroll, W., & Fennema, M. (2004). Problems in the study of the transnational business community: A reply to Kentor and Jang. *International Sociology, 19*(3), 369–378.

Carroll, W., & Fennema, M. (2006). Asking the right questions: A final word on the transnational business community. *International Sociology, 21*(4), 607–610.

David, T., Davoine, E., Ginalski, S., & Mach, A. (2012). Elites nationales ou globalisées? Les dirigeants des grandes entreprises suisses entre standardisation et spécificités helvétiques (1980–2000). *Swiss Journal of Sociology, 38*(1), 57–76.

David, T., Ginalski, S., Rebmann, F., & Schnyder, G. (2009). The Swiss business elite between 1980–2000: Declining cohesion, changing educational profile and growing internationalization. In C. Boyer & F. Sattler (Eds.), *European economic elites. Between a new spirit of capitalism and the erosion of state socialism* (pp. 197–220). Berlin: Duncker & Humblot.

David, T., Lüpold, M., Mach, A., & Schnyder, G. (2014 forthcoming). *De la «Forteresse des Alpes» à la valeur actionnariale: histoire de la gouvernance d'entreprise suisse au 20e siècle.* Zurich: Seismo.

Davoine, E. (2005). Formation et parcours professionnel des dirigeants d'entreprise en Suisse. *Revue économique et sociale, 3,* 89–99.

Davoine, E., & Ravasi, C. (2013). The relative stability of national career patterns in European top management careers in the age of globalization: A comparative study in France/Germany/Great Britain and Switzerland. *European Management Journal, 31*(2), 152–163.

de Nooy, W., Mrvar, A., & Batagelj, V. (2005). *Exploratory social network analysis with Pajek.* New York, NY: Cambridge University Press.

De Weck, P. (1983). *Un banquier suisse parle, Entretiens avec François Gross.* Fribourg: Editions M. Michel.

Djelic, M.-L., & Quack, S. (2003). *Globalization and institutions. Redefining the rules of the economic game.* Cheltenham: Edward Elgar Publishing.

Djelic, M.-L., & Quack, S. (2010). Transnational communities and their impact on the governance of business and economic activity. In M.-L. Djelic & S. Quack (Eds.), *Transnational communities: Shaping global economic governance* (pp. 377–413). Cambridge: Cambridge University Press.

Dyllick, T., & Torgler, D. (2007). Bildungshintergrund von Führungskräften und Plazierungsstärke von Universitäten in der Schweiz. *Die Unternehmung, 1*(61), 71–96.

Erten, Ch., Strunk, G., Gonzalez, J.-C., & Hilb, M. (2004). Austria and Switzerland. Small countries with large differences. In C. Brewster, W. Mayrhofer, & M. Morley (Eds.), *European human resource management – Evidence of convergence?* (pp. 95–122). Oxford: Elsevier.

Evans, P., Lank, E., & Farquhar, A. (1989). Managing human resources in the international firm: Lessons from practice. In P. Evans, Y. Doz, & A. Laurent (Eds.), *Human resource management in international firms*. London: Macmillan.

Fioole, W., van Driel, H., & van Baalen, P. J. (2008). Europeanisation and Americanisation? Converging backgrounds of German and Dutch top managers, 1990–2005. In H. G. Schröter (Ed.), *The European enterprise. Historical investigation into a future species* (pp. 155–167). Berlin: Springer.

Godelier, E. (2005). Les élites managériales entre logiques nationales endogènes et globalisation exogène. *Entreprise et histoire, 41*, 6–14.

Hartmann, M. (2007). *Eliten und Macht in Europa. Ein internationaler Vergleich.* New York, NY: Campus Verlag.

Hartmann, M. (2009). Die transnationale Klasse – Mythos oder Realität? *Soziale Welt, 60*(3), 285–303.

Harvey, C., & Maclean, M. (2010). Transnational boards and governance regimes in Britain and France. In M.-L. Djelic & S. Quack (Eds.), *Transnational communities: Shaping global economic governance* (pp. 107–129). Cambridge: Cambridge University Press.

Heemskerk, E. (2013). The rise of the European corporate elite: Evidence from the network of interlocking directorates in 2005 and 2010. *Economy and Society, 42*(1), 74–101.

Höpner, M. (2004). Was bewegt die Führungskräfte? Von der Agency-Theorie zur Soziologie des Managements. *Soziale Welt, 55*(3), 263–282.

Jann, B. (2003). Old-boy network. Militärdienst und ziviler Berufserfolg in der Schweiz. *Zeitschrift für Soziologie, 32*(2), 139–155.

Katzenstein, P. (2003). Small states and small states revisited. *New Political Economy, 8*(1), 9–30.

Kaufmann, H., & Kunz, B. (2001). *Vinkulierung von Schweizer Aktien. Teil 1.* Zurich: Bank Julius Bär.

Kentor, J., & Jang, Y. S. (2004). Yes, there is a (growing) transnational business community: A study of global interlocking directorates 1983–98. *International Sociology, 19*(3), 355–368.

Kentor, J., & Jang, Y. S. (2006). Different questions, different answers: A rejoinder to Carroll and Fennema. *International Sociology, 21*(4), 602–606.

Kläy, H. (1997). *Die Vinkulierung. Theorie und Praxis im neuen Aktienrecht.* Frankfurt: Helbing & Lichtenhahn.

Mach, A., David, T., & Bühlmann, F. (2011). La fragilité des liens nationaux. La reconfiguration de l'élite du pouvoir en Suisse, 1980–2010. *Actes de la Recherche en Sciences Sociales, 190*, 78–107.

Maclean, M., Harvey, C., & Chia, R. (2010). Dominant corporate agents and the power elite in France and Britain. *Organization Studies, 31*(3), 327–348.

Mayrhofer, W., Iellatchitch, A., Meyer, M., Steyrer, J., Schiffinger, M., & Strunk, G. (2004). Going beyond the individual. Some potential contributions from a career field and habitus perspective for global career research and practice. *Journal of Management Development, 23*(9), 870–884.

Mazbouri, M., Guex, S., & Lopez, R. (2012). Finanzplatz Schweiz. In P. Halbeisen, M. Müller, & B. Veyrassat (Eds.), *Wirtschaftsgeschichte der Schweiz des 20. Jahrhunderts* (pp. 467–518). Basel: Schwabe.

Mizruchi, M. (1996). What do interlocks do? An analysis, critique, and assessment of research on interlocking directorates. *Annual Review of Sociology, 22*, 271–298.

Monks, R., & Minow, N. (1995). *Corporate governance*. Cambridge: Cambridge University Press.
Morgan, G. (2001). Transnational communities and business systems. *Global Networks, 1*, 113−130.
Morgan, G. (2011). Reflections on the macropolitics of micropolitics. In Ch. Dörrenbacher & M. Geppert (Eds.), *Politics and power in the multinational corporation* (pp. 415−436). Cambridge: Cambridge University Press.
Naville, M., Walti, A., & Tischhauser, P. (2007). *Multinational companies on the move: How Switzerland will win the battle!* Zurich: Swiss-American Chamber of Commerce and The Boston Consulting Group.
Nollert, M. (1998). Interlocking directorates in Switzerland. A network analysis. *Schweizerische Zeitschrift für Soziologie, 24*(1), 31−58.
Nollert, M. (2005). Transnational corporate ties: A synopsis of theories and empirical findings. *Journal of World-Systems Research, 11*(2), 289−314.
Pilotti, A., Mach, A., & Mazzoleni, O. (2010). Les parlementaires suisses entre démocratisation et professionnalisation, 1910−2000. *Revue suisse de science politique, 16*(2), 211−245.
Ravasi, C. (2013). Les top managers internationaux des grandes entreprises suisses: profils et parcours de carrière. *Revue Economique et Sociale, 71*(4), 107−119.
Ruigrok, W., & Greve, P. (2008). The rise of an international market for executive labour. In L. Oxelheim & C. Wihlborg (Eds.), *Markets and compensation for executives in Europe* (Vol. 24, pp. 53−78). International Business & Management. Bingley, UK: Emerald Group Publishing Limited.
Rusterholz, P. (1985). The banks in the centre: Integration in decentralized Switzerland. In F. Stokman, R. Ziegler, & J. Scott (Eds.), *Networks of corporate power* (pp. 131−147). Cambridge: Polity Press.
Schmalz, A. (2012). *Impact d'une carrière militaire à la carrière civile. Etude sur le rôle de la carrière militaire dans la carrière civile des élites et des dirigeants économiques suisses à travers les 30 dernières années*. Master's thesis, University of Lausanne, Switzerland.
Schmid, S., & Dauth, T. (2014). Does internationalization make a difference? Stock market reaction to announcements of international top executive appointments. *Journal of World Business, 49*(1), 63−77.
Schnyder, G. (2007). *Corporate governance reform in Switzerland: Law, politics and the social organization of business, 1965−2005*. Doctoral dissertation, University of Lausanne, Switzerland.
Schnyder, G., Lüpold, M., Mach, A., & David, T. (2005). *The rise and decline of the Swiss Company network during the 20th century* (Travaux de Sciences Politique, Université de Lausanne No. 22).
Schreiner, J.-P. (1984). Le capital financier et le réseau des liaisons personnelles entre les principales sociétés en Suisse. *Revue d'économie industrielle, 29*(1), 78−95.
Staples, C. L. (2007). Board globalisation in the world's largest TNCs 1993−2005. *Corporate Governance: An International Review, 15*(2), 311−321.
Steiner, I., & Wanner, P. (2011). Dimensions démographiques des flux migratoires récents en direction de la Suisse. *La Vie économique: Revue de politique économique, 12*, 8−11.
UNCTAD. (2011). Investment country profiles: Switzerland (United Nations Conference on Trade and Development Report).
Useem, M. (1980). Corporations and the corporate elite. *Annual Review of Sociology, 6*, 41−77.

Vaara, E., & Faÿ, E. (2012). Reproduction and change on the global scale: A Bourdieusian perspective on management education. *Journal of Management Studies*, *49*(6), 1023–1051.

Widmer, F. (2012). La coordination patronale face à la financiarisation. *Les nouvelles règles du jeu dans l'industrie suisse des machines*. Zurich: Seismo.

Wright Mills, C. (1956). *The power elite*. New York, NY: Oxford University Press.

Globalization Impacts on the Swiss National Business Elite Community 161

APPENDIX

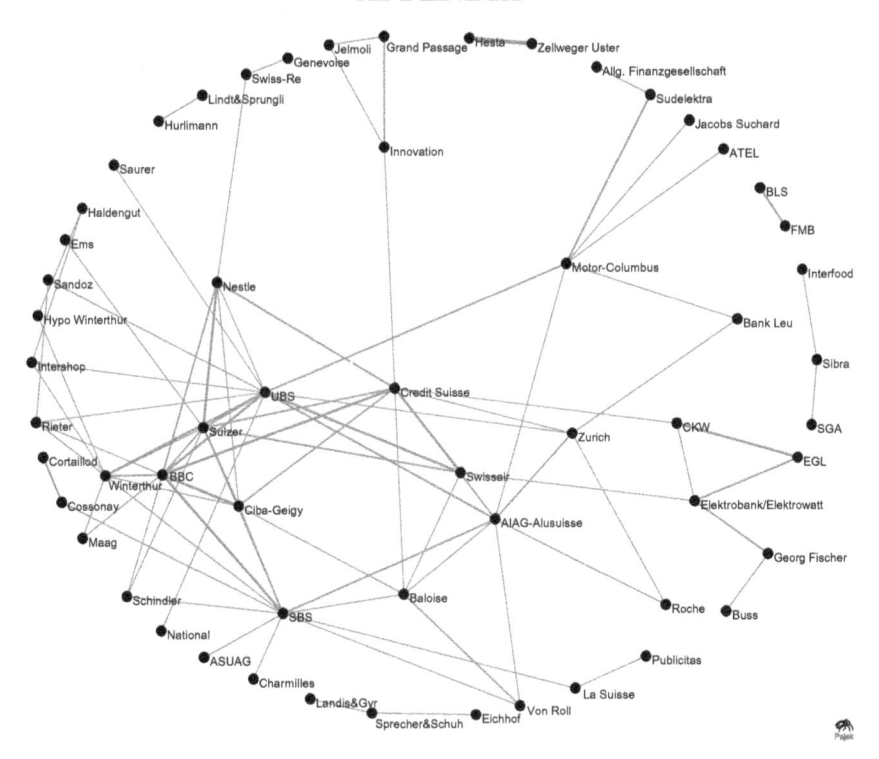

Fig. A1. 2-Slices in the Swiss Corporate Network, 1980.

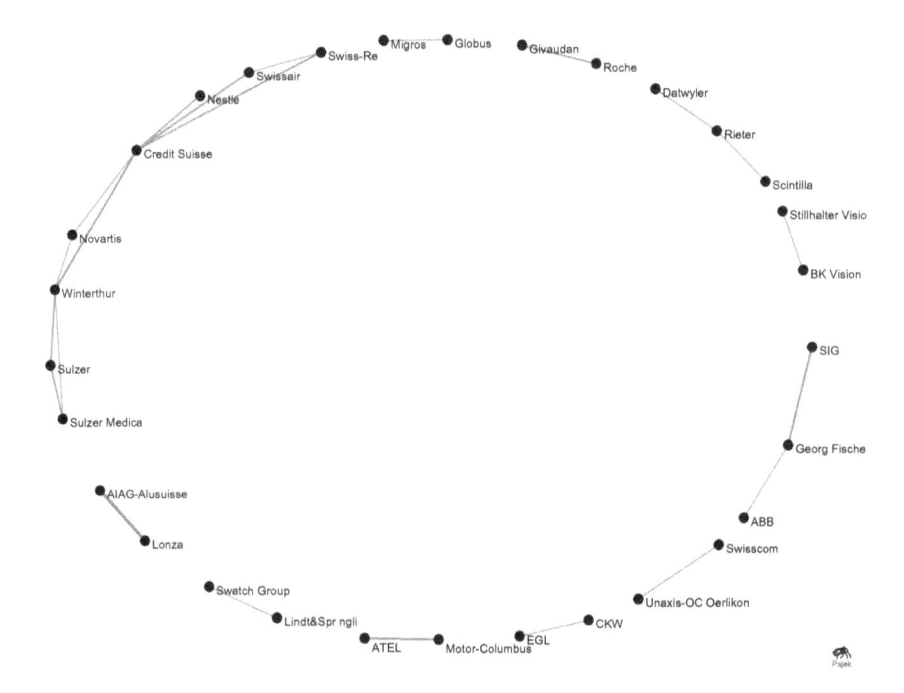

Fig. A2. 2-Slices in the Swiss Corporate Network, 2000.

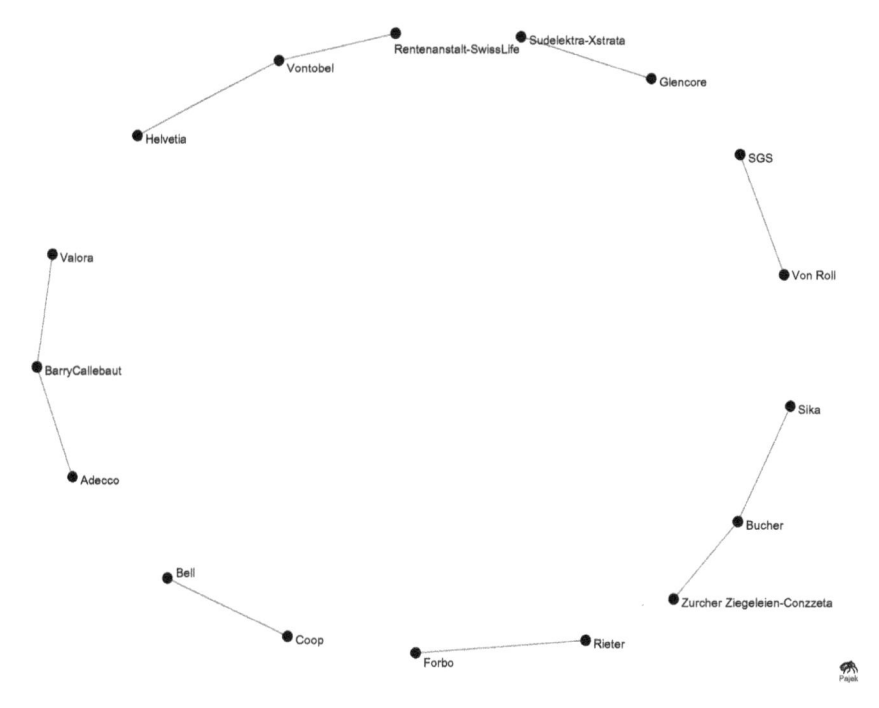

Globalization Impacts on the Swiss National Business Elite Community 163

Fig. A3. 2-Slices in the Swiss Corporate Network, 2010.

THE EURO ZONE CORPORATE ELITE AT THE CLIFF EDGE (2005−2008): A NEW APPROACH OF TRANSNATIONAL INTERLOCKING

Antoine Vion, François-Xavier Dudouet and Eric Grémont

ABSTRACT

The paper examines the degree of interlocking directorships across the major Eurozone economies. It uses the major stock market indices in France, Germany, Italy, the Netherlands, and Belgium to identify the top of the corporate elite in each country. For the period of 2005−2008, it studies transnational links between European companies. The paper draws attention to a number of features of these interlocks. Firstly transnational interlocks remain relatively low but secondly they do vary considerably. An important issue here is the degree of bilateral integration which is occurring between some countries within the Eurozone, for example France and Belgium, and the degree to which other countries, most notably, Italy are increasingly disconnected, whilst the two most powerful economies, France and Germany, are very weakly connected. This variability reflects a series of structural divides between big business in the Eurozone that makes it difficult for this corporate elites to be cohesive at the European level.

Keywords: Interlocking directorates; Eurozone; stock market indices; integration

INTRODUCTION

The financial crisis revealed how fragile the Economic and Monetary Union could be and how overriding national reactions could remain. In the Eurozone, as soon as the crisis of 2007−2008, bank defaults were treated on a national basis, except where there was clear evidence that the institutions were jointly owned such as Dexia (Franco-Belgian financial group) and Fortis (a Benelux firm). As state defaults became possible (Greece, Portugal, Ireland), financial solidarity amongst the Eurozone states as a whole was controversial and difficult to achieve. Only when it became clear that such defaults would impact throughout the Eurozone and threaten the Euro itself, did some form of cooperation emerge that stabilized the situation. These Eurozone difficulties have mainly been discussed in terms of financial shock impacts on sovereign spreads (Mody & Sandri, 2011; Reinhart & Rogoff, 2011) and what they reveal about failures in coordinating different policies within the EU and the Eurozone (Dinan, 2011; Donnelly, 2014). However, they also reveal in stark form the lack of an organized European business elite capable of influencing the formulation and implementation of common strategies towards the first step of the crisis. In this sense, the dominance of national reactions and negotiations amongst national actors could be said to reflect the absence or the fragmentation of a transnational Eurozone business community, contrary to the expectations of some authors that over the period of the last 50 years, such an elite community had been emerging. In this paper, we examine this integration from the perspective of interlocking directorships where individuals are affiliated to companies located in two or more EU countries.

This approach is one of four main perspectives which have been developed to assess these processes of transnational integration. First, a classical strategic perspective has focused on the transnational rescaling of corporate structures through mergers, joint-ventures (Meynaud & Sidjanski, 1967) or the internationalization of corporate governance bodies (Lee & Park, 2006; Maclean & Harvey 2010). This first perspective assumes that transnational integration is encompassed in a firm's strategies as its business moves from operating predominantly within its home base to becoming more internationalized though concentrated in specific regional locations such as the EU (Rugman, 2004, 2012) A second perspective has consisted in looking for the advent of a transnational capitalist class (TCC) through the internationalization and globalization of firms which dominate over states by virtue of their command of massive financial resources. States become dependent on these resources and become suppliants to the firms and their leaders. Such a class is supposed to be emancipated from States (Cox, 1987; Robinson & Harris, 2000; van der Pijl, 1998) and consists of top managers in the largest global firms. However, the internationalization of capital is not a sufficient basis to identify a transnational capitalist class which acts as a class for itself separate from any embedded national or regional interests. These elites may interact on a global scale, for example at Davos etc. but do they really act in concert (Therborn, 2000)? If we except Leslie Sklair's approach, which emphasizes the role of global consumerism as a driving ideology behind such a social process (Sklair, 2001), few studies manage to provide evidence of the development of such a class for itself.

A third approach, based on Mills' theory on elite (Mills, 1999 [1956]), has gradually emerged which focuses on identifying the formation of a transnational business community by considering the degree of cohesion that corporate leaders around the world could achieve. Carroll and Fennema (2002), for example, contested the empirical evidence of the TCC and proposed to test the transnational cohesion of the corporate elite through the well-tried methodology of interlocking directorate studies (Mizruchi, 1996; Scott, 1997; Useem, 1984). Though they did not pretend to reduce transnational business community to inter-corporate relations, they underlined that the network formed by them has structural properties that overstep each particular link: "By mapping the international network of corporate interlocks we investigate whether or not these interlocks connect the world's largest firms in one connected component or whether the network falls apart in separate national components" (Carroll & Fennema, 2002, p. 397). This approach has been tested at the European scale (Dudouet, Grémont, & Vion, 2012; Guieu & Meschi, 2008; Heemskerk, 2011; Nollert, 2005), and this is the one we follow in this paper.

As underlined by a new wave of new institutionalist perspectives (Fligstein, 2008; Morgan, 2001; Radaelli & O'Connor, 2009), Europeanization processes have created a range of institutions (political, bureaucratic, legal, and regulatory) which may support social integration among managers in Europe, even when they remain anchored to their national origins. As far as interlocking directorate studies are worth be expanded, an important methological challenge addressed by new institutionalist approaches is to avoid the decoupling of the transnational and national levels. Too often, methodologies developed in national contexts have simply been rescaled on a transnational level, in order to prioritize the relevant levels of integration. As Morgan (2001) argued, the issue is not to prioritize one over the other, insofar as "it is possible to retain a view of business as being deeply socially embedded in national institutional contexts, while recognizing that it has necessarily begun to create forms of transnational social space" (Morgan, 2001, p. 127). Djelic and Quack (2010) also underlined quite well that business communities could be embedded in national and transnational spaces simultaneously and non-exclusively, so that elite circles could cross through a multiple membership phenomenon. As scholars in international sociology suggested (Devin, 1995; Dezalay & Madsen, 2009), this calls for a relational analysis of the different spaces of power.

In this paper, we will thus try to renew transnational interlocking directorate studies by paying attention both to the national embeddedness of corporate networks and how these are evolving and changing and to how transnational links connect together different national arenas. This reveals that within the transnational framework of the EU, bilateral corporate linkages across countries are highly differentiated. There has not fully been the creation of an integrated EU corporate elite but what has emerged consists of specific pockets of interconnectedness.

The approach here is predominantly structural. Directors and top managers of the largest firms tend to form a business elite, also named corporate elite (Scott, 1997; Mizruchi, 2013). One of the main advances of interlocking directorate studies is to measure its cohesion from the density of the network they form on the basis of directors' multiple affiliations (Mizruchi, 1996; Scott, 1997). A corporate elite is said to be national or domestic when top managers belong to firms anchored in a same country of origin.[1] It is considered as transnational when the latter belong to firms which are embedded in different business milieus. Our purpose is to measure both these milieus relationally.

RENEWING TRANSNATIONAL INTERLOCKING DIRECTORATE STUDIES

If we except the pioneering study edited by Meindert Fennema in 1982, transnational interlocking studies mainly emerged in the early 2000s (Carroll & Carson, 2003; Carroll & Fennema, 2002; Kentor & Jang, 2004), when the debate about the existence of a transnational capitalist class was reformulated (Robinson & Harris, 2000; Sklair, 2001). This allows us to draw some temporary conclusions on what has been done, but also to spot recurring difficulties and propose new perspectives.

Transnational Interlocks and National Anchorage

The main purpose of these early studies was to question the emergence of a transnational business community from the measurement of interlocks by comparing national and transnational links throughout time. Carroll and Fennema (2002) witnessed a light increase in transnational interlocks between 1976 and 1996, which was mainly due to increasing cross-border links in the European context. They also proved that these links were more connective in 1996 than in 1976. But they contradicted John Scott's expectations (1997), as they found no decline in domestic links compared to transnational ones between 1976 and 1996. As was the case in 1976, the 1996 global network was primarily built around a North Atlantic core network, with a key role played by European firms, between which 2/3 of transnational links were concentrated. Their conclusion was that one could talk about the emergence of a transnational business community, but they did not assume that such a class would be a substitute for national business worlds – as Robinson and Harris (2000) and Sklair (2001) had suggested earlier.

At a different level, Carroll and Carson (2003) have explored what they called the global corporate elite. They combined an interlocking directorate study with the study of policy groups,[2] and stressed the political cohesion of these managers and their influence on States and education policies. Their study brought out a core structured by North-American and European elites and a periphery constituted by the rest of the world. This led them to question the existence and the power of an Atlantic ruling class. Carroll (2010), from measuring interlocks between the 500 biggest companies ranked by Fortune between 1996 and 2006, showed a relative increase in transnational interlocks and claimed the persistence of the Atlantic ruling class. Burris and Staples (2012), with a similar corpus for 1998 and 2006, provide similar observations. But, focusing on density rather than on the total amount of raw links, they claim this global corporate elite has increased more at a transatlantic level than within Europe.

Existing literature on transnational interlocks has generally been built on a global sample of firms, for example from the *Fortune 500*. Comparing national and transnational interlocking from such a global sample, however, tends to distort the picture of interlocks inside national contexts because so many firms in that national context are missing from the global sample. Thus comparing degrees of interlocks at the national and the transnational level from within such a sample is misleading. For instance, it makes a difference to consider the top of the Belgian business community formed by the twenty firms listed in the BEL 20 index or to retain only three Belgian firms because they are the ones listed in Fortune Global 500. Following the first method, one tries to identify what the top of the Belgian business community could be and then how this elite is connected to other countries through interlocking directorates; following the second approach it is impossible to draw any conclusions about the degree of national/transnational interlocks from just three firms. Instead the focus is on a few countries which have giant firms, such as the United States, a process which potentially over-emphasizes transnational interlocks. Burris and Staples (2012) are right to underline that the increase of transnational interlocks in such studies (and the perceived relative decline in the significance of national interlocks) may result because of the selective nature of the global sample. The proportion of transnational links tends to increase when the number of countries taken into account is higher and the number of firms in each of them lower.

However, such data is difficult to interpret because of its limited nature (Table 1). When they claim that transnational interlocks represent 30% of the whole set of links, they neither mean that all firms maintain one third of their corporate links to foreign companies nor that every domestic business community is open at a level of a third. The fact that transnational links fluctuate between 13.7% and 30.9% does not tell us much about the places and the forms of transnational integration. These averages conceal national specificities and the particularities of what is occurring. For example, there may be firms from one country with huge transnational interlocks and firms from another with no transnational link. Is this significant? How do we understand these differences? Global samples lead to very different samplings of data at the level of national sets making comparisons about

Table 1. Percentage of Transnational Links in Main Former Studies.

Studies	Years	# Firms	National	Trans.	Global	Transnational/ Global
Fennema (1982)	1970	176	303	101	404	25.0%
	1976	176	318	152	470	32.3%
Carroll and Fennema (2002)	1976	176	284	84	368	22.8%
	1996	176	267	88	355	24.8%
Kentor and Jang (2004)	1983	500	755	120	875	13.7%
	1998	500	916	181	1097	16.5%
Carroll (2010)	1996	500	1285[a]	319[a]	1604	19.9%
	2006	500	750[a]	336[a]	1086	30.9%
Burris and Staples (2012)	1998	500	916	181	1097	16.50%
	2006	498	761	307	1068	28.70%

[a]We recalculated this from percentages and global numbers (Carroll, 2010).
National: Links between firms from the same country only.
Transnational: Links between firms from different countries only.
Global: Global set of links, be they national or transnational.

the degree of transnational integration between different countries very difficult. This has led authors to find ad hoc ways of correcting the problems. Fennema (1982), for example, had to correct his initial sampling because of the overrepresentation of US firms (92 over 150). So did Carroll and Carson (2003) to obtain sufficient number of firms from emerging countries. Even when rescaling the sample on a European basis (Guieu & Meschi, 2008; Heemskerk, 2011; Nollert, 2005), problems are of the same kind. Eelke Heemskerk's study on the 300 firms which compose the Eurostoxx 300 had to face the problem of the heterogeneity of national communities retrieved from this set of firms (from 4 for Austria, Denmark, and Portugal to 78 for the United Kingdom). Such a heterogeneity makes comparative network studies problematic using a global sample of the largest companies in the world (Table 1).

A fundamental methodological issue is therefore to determine the minimal number of firms which are required to make sense of a domestic business milieu and to link this to the issue of transnational integration. Furthermore ideally this study needs to be longitudinal, to see trends in levels of integration and how easily these trends can be shaped by a few individuals leaving the network (Dudouet et al., 2012).

In this paper, we will define transnational interlocks by adapting Mark Mizruchi's initial definition (1996): a transnational interlocking directorate occurs when a person affiliated with one organization anchored in one country sits on the board of directors of another organization anchored in another country. Rather than attempt this task at a global level, we will focus on the Eurozone, addressing the question presented at the start of the paper; what evidence is there of the emergence of a Eurozone corporate elite, that is strong, stable, and significant cross-national interlocks amongst the largest Eurozone companies, and how if at all does this relate to changes in national corporate elites and their degree of integration and cohesion?

We have defined national corporate sets firstly in terms of large firms anchored in particular countries. Using the term "large firms," we more precisely mean that a corporate elite sets up in firms which are present in national stock market indices. Financial institutions develop such indices as ways to package ready-made products for investors who want to ensure that their returns match those of the market. Directors appreciate to have their company listed in indices, as this guarantees liquidity for their shares and shareholder wealth maximization as well as notoriety. Every national stock exchange develops multiple indices for all sorts of financial products, but each marketplace establishes a flagship index which concentrates both the highest volume of exchange and the highest social prestige. The number of quoted companies included in this index varies across the main European markets in part depending on the total number of companies listed on the exchange. Thus the London Stock Exchange which is the largest market has the FTSE100 as its main index. In Belgium by contrast, a much smaller stock exchange, the index is the BEL20. As stated, size of capitalization is the main criteria for membership of the index though there are some variations in this. Nevertheless, by taking as our sample of companies in each country those companies that appear in the main Stock Exchange index we are confident that we are examining the heart of the national corporate elite.[3] Stock exchange indices are a very useful gateway to the social structure of national core business circles. Because being present in a commonly used index is so advantageous to public companies, all the leading organizations pay the highest attention to their strategy of affiliation of entering and staying in an important index (Rao, Davis, & Ward, 2000). Belonging to such an index means being part of the business elite that counts in terms of revenue, economic power, media, and political influence.

The way the composition of indices is decided upon is everything but transparent. Whilst exchanges which encourage significant foreign listings such as London and New York set criteria for entry into an index strictly from the point of view of market capitalization at a particular point in the year, many Eurozone exchanges operate other criteria alongside market capitalization. Broadly however, indices suit the purpose of this research as they are relatively stable over time, and are generally recognized as being composed of the largest and most important firms on a particular country.

From this point of view, our purpose is to examine how integrated the Eurozone corporate elites was prior and at the first steps of the financial crisis. Following previous studies (Dudouet et al., 2012), we will argue that a Eurozone corporate elite exists, but it does not dominate over national contexts, which remain the main space of socialization into business milieus. Secondly, we will show again that this European corporate elite can only be assessed from the national business communities that underpin it. People who act at a transnational level always come from a national milieu: there is no elite in weightlessness conditions. Thirdly, we will show that the transnational integration within the Eurozone is not homogeneous (equal for all firms and indices) and that there are different patterns of transnational bilateral integration.

We will compare the degree, cohesion, and stability of linkages which directors in these firms have through directorships in other firms, both within the same index and within the indices of other EU countries (Dudouet et al., 2012). This perspective allows us to study interlocks at several levels simultaneously, national, international, and bilateral. In this way, we can analyze and compare the strength of these different levels of integration over time.

METHODOLOGY

Levels of Transnational Integration

Building an analytical framework of transnational interlocking means taking into account different levels of relations: Board interlocks within each national community, transnational links between firms anchored in various national communities, transnational interlocking within the whole zone considered (here the Eurozone), and transnational interlocking within bilateral relations between national communities. These different levels are analyzed relationally. In order to appraise how integrated business communities are into transnational spaces, bilateral dimensions should also be taken into account. We thus suggest to assess integration by distinguishing between national anchorage (i), internationalization (ii), transnational openness (iii), and transnational bilateral integration (iv).

(i) *National anchorage*
How far are firms which are affiliated to the same index connected to each other? Do they form a dense or loose network? Cohesion can be measured by the density of the network, which corresponds to the sum of the ties observed divided by the number of possible ties (Scott, 1992).

(ii) *Internationalization of national communities*
By internationalization of a corporate elite, we mean the sum of transnational links which go out from an index to another related to the sum of links counted within this index. This allows us to assess the degree of internationalization from the perspective of the national corporate elite.

(iii) *Transnational openness of national communities*
Comparing levels of internationalization, however, does not allow us to judge the openness of a community in terms of transnational connections. For example, most of the transnational links may be held by just a few firms. In order to assess openness, we will measure the percentage of the firms stated in the index which have at least one transnational link.

(iv) *Transnational bilateral integration*
By bilateral integration, we mean the degree of interpenetration of two national business milieu in terms of board interlocks. This follows a continuum that goes from no relation at all to a complete fusion or absorption. This is measured by the sum of links existing between two indices divided by the sum of links existing within each index. This brings out a score for each index toward each others. If scores between two indices are comparable, bilateral integration will be symmetric, if they are not, integration will be qualified as asymmetric. As absolute equivalence of scores is unlikely, we will simplify the reading of the results by distinguishing between six types of scores (see Table 2): 0%, minor to 10%, 10–19%, 20–49%, 50–99%, 100% and plus. If index A and index B both maintain under 10% of bilateral relations, very weak symmetric integration will be brought out. If bilateral relations correspond to less than 10% for index A and 20–49% for index B, one will talk of a very weak asymmetric integration from A to B and of a medium asymmetric integration from B to A. If a stock exchange

Table 2. Patterns of Transnational Bilateral Integration.

			Index B			
		0%	<10%	10–19%	20–49%	50–99%	≥100%
Index A	0%		Very weak symmetric integration	Very weak asymmetric integration	Very weak asymmetric integration	Very weak asymmetric integration	Absorption of B by A
	<10%	Weak asymmetric integration	Weak symmetric integration	Weak asymmetric integration	Weak asymmetric integration	Absorption of B by A
	10–19%	Medium asymmetric integration	Medium asymmetric integration	Medium symmetric integration	Medium asymmetric integration	Absorption of B by A
	20–49%	Strong asymmetric integration	Strong asymmetric integration	Strong asymmetric integration	Strong symmetric integration	Absorption of B by A
	50–99%	Absorption of A by B	Absorption of A by B	Absorption of A by B	Absorption of A by B	Merging
	≥100%					

index shows bilateral integration score over 100% under non reciprocal conditions, one can talk of a process of absorption. If both the indices reach 100%, one can talk of a process of fusion.

Data

Our data is based on the set of companies, which is composed of five stock exchange indices of the Eurozone from December 31, 2005 to December 31, 2008 (see Table 3). These five indices are the AEX 25 (the Netherlands), the BEL 20 (Belgium), the CAC 40 (France), the DAX 30 (Germany), and the MIB 40 (Italy). All of them belong to the Eurozone and are among the founders of the EC. Therefore if there is to be evidence of the emergence of a European corporate elite (as measured by interlocking directorates), we should see some signs in this sample.

195 companies have been analyzed after we took into account merging initiatives (which were particularly numerous in the Italian banking sector in 2007), change of name, usual entrance, and exit activity within these indices. Indices are composed of a finite number of firms : a maximum of 25 for the AEX, 20 for the BEL, 40 for the CAC and the MIB, 30 for the DAX. Yet, in our sample, indices are not absolutely complete: stock exchange authorities may not have filled in all slots of an index at a given date, or we may have had to arbitrate. Indeed, in order to prevent redundancy, we have been compelled to select an index of reference for companies which are registered in two or more indices. To this end, we have used the dominant nationality of the management. We also subtracted a given company – ArcelorMittal – because of the quasi-impossibility to affiliate it.[4]

Table 3. Sample.

	December 31, 2005	December 31, 2006	December 31, 2007	December 31, 2008
#Individuals	1975	1986	1984	2011
#Firms	148	148	144	148
AEX 25	22	23	20	22
BEL 20	18	18	18	19
CAC 40	38	37	37	37
DAX 30	30	30	30	30
MIB 40	40	40	39	40

The managers we retained are all members of the Board, including Censors, Representatives of employees and States, and observers, but not honorary Chairmen and Secretaries. We added some Executive Managers who are not members of the Board of Directors or Supervisory Board such as members of Boards of Management, Chief Executive Officers (CEO), and Deputy CEOs. Annual reports and corporate press releases were used to collect manually all the data.

RESULTS

Global Structure of the Eurozone's Business Community

A very high majority of firms (between 92% and 93%) are connected to each other in a same network during the four-year period (Table 4). So a Eurozone corporate elite exists but at this step we know very little about its structure. Tables 5 and 6 present a more detailed view of the types of links and their longitudinal evolution.

These results show that transnational links represent about a fifth of valued links and a quarter of binary ones; the majority of interlocks are with other firms in the same index. However, the European corporate elite is still significantly divided into national communities.

This is confirmed by scores of density calculated on the basis of both the whole sample and indices (Fig. 1). Density is very often used to

Table 4. Main Properties of the Network.

	2005	2006	2007	2008
Firms	148	148	144	148
Links	1244	1080	1030	1014
Diameter	7	9	9	7
Firms in the main component	137	137	133	136
Firms in secondary components[a]	4	2	2	2
Isolates	7	9	9	10

[a]For 2005 there are two secondary components.
Diameter is the shortest path (number of firms) between the two most distant firms.
Main component is the network grouping the most numerous firms.
Secondary components are firms connected to each others without connections with the main component.
Isolates are firms without any connections.

Table 5. Evolution of the Links (Binary).

	2005	2006	2007	2008	2005–2008
Total links	1244	1080	1030	1014	−18%
Inside index links	936	788	780	760	−19%
Transnational links	308	292	250	254	−18%
% Transnational links	25%	27%	24%	25%	0%

Table 6. Evolution of the Links (Valued).

	2005	2006	2007	2008	2005–2008
Total links	1616	1376	1288	1246	−23%
Inside index links	1274	1062	1020	962	−24%
Transnational links	342	314	268	284	−17%
% of transnational links	21%	23%	21%	23%	2%

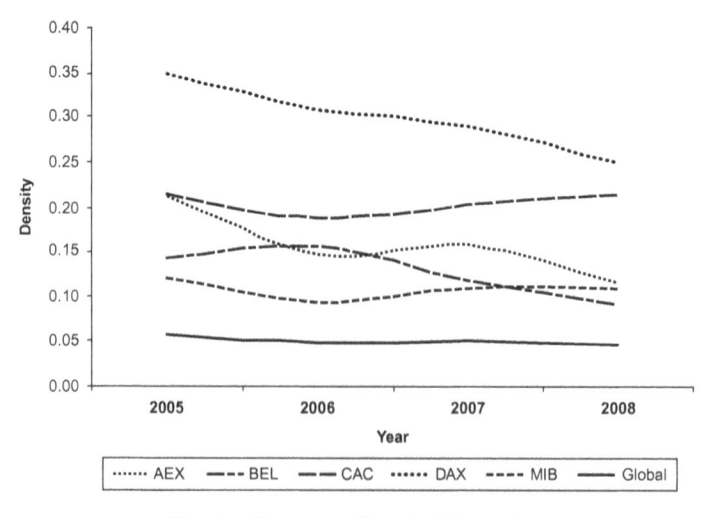

Fig. 1. Eurozone Density Networks.

assess the cohesion of a business milieu.[5] Overall density is rather weak (between 0.05 and 0.06). Even though we take into account the size of the whole network, which is substantially higher than a given domestic network, overall density is systematically inferior to intra-index density scores. The DAX has a very high score, and even if it decreases over the period studied, it remains much higher than those of other indices. This reveals that the German business community is still very cohesive and interlinked compared to other European business communities. The CAC is rather stable with a score of 0.21 at the early and late stages of the period. It is less cohesive than the DAX but represents a relatively strong set of links. The three other indices have comparable scores at the end of the period, but with very different processes of change to reach the same point. The density of the AEX has been reduced dramatically (0.21−0.12) between 2005 and 2008; the BEL has also reduced in density (0.14−0.09), while the MIB is rather stable, though at a relatively low level.

These results show that we do not have homogenous business milieus in the Eurozone, but various social structures, of capitalism with different levels of cohesiveness.

Internationalization of Business Communities

Table 7 presents the percentage of transnational links compared with the total of domestic links. The BEL shows a level of transnational links, which is equivalent and even higher than domestic links, with a record high of 145% in 2008. Transnational links in other indices are less than 100% and often less than 50% if we except the AEX for 2007 and 2008. The Dutch index is the only one where the proportion of transnational links continuously increases (32−62%). The CAC, conversely, shows a decrease (35−28%), while the DAX and the MIB have lower and more stable scores of cohesiveness.

The different degrees of internationalization reveal the continued heterogeneity of the European corporate elite. The Dutch and the Belgian contexts have become more internationalized whilst the French has become less so, whilst Germany and Italy have remained roughly the same over this period.

Table 7. Percentage of Transnational Links (Valued) Compared to Domestic Ones.

	2005	2006	2007	2008
AEX	32%	43%	50%	62%
BEL	102%	90%	116%	145%
CAC	35%	36%	29%	28%
DAX	20%	19%	15%	20%
MIB	15%	18%	15%	14%

Transnational Openness

For each index, Table 8 indicates the proportion of firms which maintain at least one transnational link. In general, the proportion of the firms holding transnational links tends to decrease, except in the case of the AEX, where it increases and the CAC where it remains stable. Drawing comparisons of openness from each index leads us to underline the limits of averages. The average for the whole sample in terms of what percentage of firms have transnational links is about 60%. However there are huge differences. The MIB varies from 38% to 28% whilst on the CAC the variation over time is minimal going from 82% to 81% over the period, with a minimum of 78% in 2006.

The strong openness of the DAX and the BEL tends to decrease slightly, whilst that of the AEX increases. The stability of the very strong openness of the CAC contrasts with the situation of the MIB which gradually becomes more closed over the period.

Bilateral Integration

The heterogeneity of corporate elite in the Eurozone does not mean that there is no process of integration but it appears that this is primarily through the development of bilateral relations. Table 9–12 give percentages of transnational links over domestic ones toward a single index over the four years of the study. The tables should be read from rows to the column. For example, in 2005, AEX (from the row) has transnational links with BEL (on column) counting for 7% of AEX domestic links. In the same time BEL (from the row) has transnational links to the AEX equaling 17% of BEL domestic links. Following our methodology these percentages show the degree of bilateral integration of each index toward all the others. We signal in bold the highest score of bilateral integration for each index.

Table 8. Percentage of Firms with Transnational Links.

	2005	2006	2007	2008
AEX	50%	48%	60%	68%
BEL	67%	72%	67%	63%
CAC	82%	78%	81%	81%
DAX	73%	73%	67%	63%
MIB	38%	33%	33%	28%

Table 9. 2005 Score of Bilateral Integration.

	AEX	BEL	CAC	DAX	MIB
AEX		7%	**15%**	7%	3%
BEL	17%		**69%**	15%	2%
CAC	5%	9%		**14%**	7%
DAX	2%	2%	**12%**		4%
MIB	1%	0%	**8%**	5%	

Table 10. 2006 Score of Bilateral Integration.

	AEX	BEL	CAC	DAX	MIB
AEX		10%	**19%**	8%	6%
BEL	16%		**59%**	12%	3%
CAC	5%	11%		**13%**	6%
DAX	2%	2%	**11%**		4%
MIB	2%	1%	**9%**	6%	

Table 11. 2007 Score of Bilateral Integration.

	AEX	BEL	CAC	DAX	MIB
AEX		14%	**23%**	10%	3%
BEL	23%		**77%**	11%	5%
CAC	5%	**10%**		8%	6%
DAX	2%	1%	**8%**		4%
MIB	1%	1%	**8%**	5%	

Table 12. 2008 Score of Bilateral Integration.

	AEX	BEL	CAC	DAX	MIB
AEX		17%	**22%**	20%	3%
BEL	24%		**102%**	19%	0%
CAC	4%	**12%**		6%	5%
DAX	4%	3%	**8%**		4%
MIB	1%	0%	**8%**	5%	

Once again, bilateral integration scores show strong heterogeneity: they go from 0% (BEL-MIB and MIB-BEL in 2008) to 102% (BEL-CAC in 2008). However, scores are generally less than 25%. All indices have their highest score of bilateral integration with the CAC though there is large

Table 13. Trends of Bilateral Integration.

	Weakening	Stability	Reinforcement
Symmetric	BEL-MIB MIB-BEL CAC-DAX DAX-CAC	AEX-MIB CAC-MIB DAX-MIB MIB-AEX MIB-CAC MIB-DAX	
Asymmetric		CAC-AEX DAX-AEX DAX-BEL	AEX-BEL AEX-CAC AEX-DAX BEL-AEX BEL-CAC BEL-DAX CAC-BEL

variation. From 2005 to 2008 the most remarkable results are the progressive absorption of the BEL by the CAC and the weakening bilateral integration between the CAC and the DAX. Table 13 summarizes the different scores in trends from 2005 to 2008.

Overall, bilateral relations remain at similar levels throughout the four years. Only the BEL-MIB on one hand, and the CAC-DAX on the other hand, reduce significantly in the period. The indices which how most evidence of increased integration with one other index are the AEX and the BEL, in relation to their interlocks with the CAC and the DAX. Table 13 shows that European integration is a very dynamic and differentiated process. The weakening of the CAC-DAX relations (the two leading indices of the Eurozone), the absorption of the BEL by the CAC, as well as the relative isolation of the MIB, are essential dimensions of the structuration of the Eurozone corporate elite.

DISCUSSION

This study aimed to embrace the complexity of the transnational integration of blue chips' managers in the Eurozone, by relating the three dimensions of national, bilateral, and multilateral integration during four consecutive years. Managing this kind of longitudinal studies helps understand how different national business circles are evolving in terms of integration nationally and in the Eurozone.

Firstly, our methodology seems helpful to assess the corporate elite's integration from the perspective of the most central institutions they are embedded in, namely national stock exchange indices. On one hand, it is a way to avoid top-down explanations. Top-down theoretical frameworks of European business structures tend to prioritize the level of multilateral integration over others. Fligstein (2008) nuances this dominant perspective by taking into account bilateral integration through joint-ventures. However, European data on joint-ventures are very partial. Moreover, by the fact they limit bilateral integration to the strict perimeter of firms' structures, they do not tell us much about the social integration of top managers at the inter-firm level. Finally, even though Fligstein turns to a more sociological discourse to argue that "the patterns of shared culture and interaction that have occurred across European borders have exactly followed social class lines" (Fligstein, 2008, p. 137), he does not provide better evidence than a few Eurobarometer results. What our comparison shows is that such a persistence of national cohesion tends not to decline at the same degree or at the same pace across the countries studied. The Eurozone between 2005 and 2008 appears as a weakly socially integrated zone, based on a mish-mash of transnational links.

Secondly, taking bilateral integration into account, together with the transnational openness of indices, provides many counterintuitive results. The first one is the relatively low degree of Franco-German integration. The decrease that occurred in 2007–2008 is totally decoupled from the intensification of intergovernmental cooperation in the same period (Vion, 2012). As noted before, minor shifts in Franco-German transnational relations have had major effects on the structure of their links (Dudouet et al., 2012). Our study shows that the Franco-German axis is much more a political construction than a process driven by business life. This makes institutional explanations of transnational integration (Risse-Kappen, 1995) fall short, except if intense intergovernmental cooperation is conceived as a game of rival associates. The second counterintuitive result is that national differences, regarding the internationalization of national business communities, are much higher than expected. Belgium and the Netherlands are increasingly internationalizing. This may indicate an absorption of the periphery by the center (here the powerful indices DAX and CAC). In the Belgian case, the achievement of what we call absorption into the CAC is unexpected and has to be confirmed by data for the more recent period. Moreover it is interesting that in the context of the French speaking/Walloon speaking political, economic, and social fissure within Belgium it is the very old business association between the

Belgian Walloon businessman Albert Frère and the French bank Paribas (BNP-Paribas since 2000) that is probably the best example of socio-economic integration between Walloon and French capitalisms (Dudouet & Grémont, 2010). The connection of Frère's companies (GBL and CNP) with the CAC firms explain almost half of the BEL-CAC links in 2008. Another good example of Belgian internationalization is provided by a firm like Solvay, which was connected in 2008 to 6 firms from the CAC (AXA, Société Générale, Alstom, Carrefour, Saint-Gobain, Vivendi), 3 firms from the BEL (Umicore, Fortis, Agfa), 3 firms from the DAX (K + S, Munich Re, RWE), and 2 from the AEX (Philips, Akzo Nobel). Solvay took over the French Rhodia in 2011 and was listed in the CAC 40 in 2012.

Thirdly, regarding bilateral processes, our results show that there is no convergence between the internationalization and the transnational openness of national communities. Our examination of transnational openness indicates big variations between countries. On one side, the Belgian case is quite different from the Dutch one, because its increasing internationalization is managed in a context of decreasing transnational openness. The internationalization of the BEL increased between 2005 and 2008, while the number of firms which managed transnational links regularly decreased. This indicates a decoupling process within Belgian business communities, with an internationalized side of the BEL and another more isolated one, even though both sides are still connected, but in a less tight way. From this perspective of openness, the CAC and the DAX show very contrasting patterns. The French index is very stable as a strongly open community. Conversely, German openness appeared to have fallen into some kind of withdrawal from 2005 to 2008. This is all the more interesting in that the symmetric integration between these two communities has weakened. German firms have turned from their Western partners. Admittedly, this picture might be modified if the database included the ATX (Austrian index). Similarly, a wider empirical project including the SMI (Switzerland), the FTSE100 (United Kingdom), and the Ibex 35 (Spain) would help further clarify these processes. But manual collection is a demanding task.

Fourthly, these results may help to explain how the corporate elite responded to bank problems at the early stages of the financial crisis. Similar to states, corporations had huge difficulties in converging on transnational organizational solutions to bank defaults. Except for the Franco-Belgian case, all the measures were national in the early stages. In the case of Dexia's default, Belgian and French elites tried to save the bank before managing its splitting. In the case of Fortis, the Dutch managed the repatriation of the bank's insurance branch. But BNP-Paribas took the control of the company's remaining bank activities with the help of the Belgian government – the latter consequently became the largest shareholder of BNP-Paribas. By doing so, BNP-Paribas became the main financial institution in Belgium. This translated existing links into financial ones and led to the absorption of Belgian capitalism by the French one. In other cases, transnational relations were unilaterally dismantled, without any efforts at negotiation. The alliance between CommerzBank (Germany) and Generali (Italy) was curtly broken by a German decision to merge Dresdner Bank with CommerzBank, and to turn Allianz into the main shareholder of the new group. So, except for Dexia and Fortis, bank defaults were dealt with on a national basis and not on a transnational one. Of course, later, the solutions provided by the ECB as the sovereign debt crisis developed in the Eurozone could be defined as transnational ones, but the decision to merge or liquidate a bank was always taken at the national level. Finally, our results show that the structural basis for the formation of a corporate elite in the Eurozone has not been achieved given the evidence from the interlocking directorships. Even though the national anchorage of business elites has declined, transnational linkages have not grown much and thus the capacity for acting cohesively at moments of crisis does not exist.

NOTES

1. For us, someone like Lindsay Owen-Jones, a British citizen who was Chairman and CEO of L'Oréal from 1986 to 2006, belongs to the French corporate elite.
2. The policy groups retained were the International Chamber of Commerce, the Trilateral Commission, Bilderberg Conference, World Business Council for Substainable Development and World Economic Forum.
3. It is not uncommon for very large firms to have multiple listings and to be quoted on a number of stock exchanges in order to access foreign capital etc. but the depth and liquidity of trading is usually highest in one of those – generally the historic home base of the company.
4. ArcelorMittal is a company ruled by the Luxemburger law, quoted in Amsterdam, Brussels, Luxembourg, Madrid, New York, and Paris while most of the shares is hold by the Indian Citizen Lakshmi Mittal and his family, who is also Chairman and Chief Executive Officer of the company. ArcelorMittal was present on the AEX and CAC 40 in 2007 and 2008. Somehow, Arcelor Mittal can be considered as fully a transnational firm.

5. Of course, it is always risky to compare scores of density when networks do not have the same size (Scott, 1992), but we consider that, except for the Eurozone network, ours have close enough sizes to allow comparisons. Moreover, let us stress that in our corpus, density scores are not correlated to the size of the networks: the DAX and the CAC with 30 and 37 firms systematically bring out higher scores than the AEX and the BEL do (respectively less than 25 and 20 firms).

REFERENCES

Burris, V., & Staples, C. L. (2012). In search of a transnational capitalist class: Alternative methods for comparing director interlocks within and between nations and regions. *International Journal of Comparative Sociology*, *53*(4), 323−342.

Carroll, W. (2010). *The making of a transnational capitalist class. Corporate power in the 21st century*. London: Zed Books.

Carroll, W., & Carson, C. (2003). The network of global corporations and elite policy groups: A structure for transnational capitalist class formation. *Global Networks*, *3*(1), 29−57.

Carroll, W., & Fennema, M. (2002). Is there a transnational business community? *International Sociology*, *17*, 393−419.

Carroll, W. K., & Sapinski, J. P. (2010). The global corporate elite and the transnational policy-planning network, 1996−2006 a structural analysis. *International Sociology*, *25*(4), 501−538.

Cox, R. (1987). *Production, power and world order*. New York, NY: Columbia University.

Devin, G. (1995). Norbert Elias et l'analyse des relations internationales. *Revue française de science politique*, *45*(2), 305−327.

Dezalay, Y., & Madsen, M. R. (2009). Espaces de pouvoirs nationaux, espaces de pouvoirs internationaux. In A. Cohen, B. Lacroix, & P. Riutort (Eds.), *Nouveau manuel de science politique*. Paris: La Découverte.

Dinan, D. (2011). Governance and institutions: Implementing the Lisbon treaty in the shadow of the Euro crisis. *Journal of Common Market Studies*, *49*, 103−121.

Djelic, M.-L., & Quack, S. (2010). *Transnational communities: Shaping global economic governance*. Cambridge: Cambridge University Press.

Donnelly, S. (2014). Power politics and the undersupply of financial stability in Europe. *Review of International Political Economy*, *21*(4), 980−1005.

Dudouet, F.-X., & Grémont, E. (2010). Les grands patrons en France. Du capitalisme d'Etat à la fianciarisation, Lignes de repères.

Dudouet, F.-X., Grémont, E., & Vion, A. (2012). Transnational business networks in the Eurozone. A focus on four stock exchange indices. In G. Murray & J. Scott (Eds.), *Financial elites and transnational business: Who rules the world?* Cheltenham: Edward Elgar.

Fennema, M. (1982). *International networks of banks and industry*. The Hague: Martinus Nijhoff Publishers.

Fligstein, N. (2008). *Euroclash. The EU, European identity and the future of Europe*. Oxford: Oxford University Press.

Guieu, G., & Meschi, P.-X. (2008). Conseils d'administration et réseaux d'administrateurs en Europe. *Revue française de gestion*, *185*, 21−45.

Heemskerk, E. (2011). The social field of the European corporate elite: A network analysis of interlocking directorates among Europe's largest corporate boards. *Global Networks*, *11*(4), 1−21.

Kentor, J., & Jang, Y. S. (2004). Yes, there is a (growing) transnational business community. In: *International Sociology*, *19*, 355−368.

Lee, H., & Park, J. (2006). Top team diversity, internationalization and the mediating effect of international alliances. *British Journal of Management*, *17*(3), 195–213.

Maclean, M., & Harvey, C. (2010). Transnational boards and governance regimes. A Franco-British comparison. In M.-L. Djelic & S. Quack (Eds.), *Transnational communities: Shaping global economic governance* (pp. 107−127). Cambridge: Cambridge University Press.

Meynaud, J., & Sidjanski, D. (1967). *L'Europe des Affaires*. Paris: Payot.

Mills, C. W. (1999). *The power elite* (New ed.). Oxford: Oxford University Press.

Mizruchi, M. S. (1996). What do interlocks do? An analysis, critique, and assessment of research on interlocking directorates. *Annual Review of Sociology*, *22*, 271−298.

Mizruchi, M. S. (2013). *The fracturing of the American corporate elite*. Cambridge, MA: Harvard University Press.

Mody, A., & Sandri, D. (2011). *The Eurozone crisis: How banks and sovereigns came to be joined at the hip*. IMF Working Paper n°269.

Morgan, G. (2001). Transnational communities and business systems. *Global Networks*, *1*(2), 113−130.

Nollert, M. (2005). Transnational corporate ties: A synopsis of theories and empirical findings. *Journal of World-systems Research*, *11*(2), 289−314.

Radaelli, C., & O'Connor, J. (2009). How bureaucratic elites imagine Europe: Towards convergence of governance beliefs. *Journal of European Public Policy*, *16*(7), 971−989.

Rao, H., Davis, G., & Ward, A. (2000). Embeddedness, social identity and mobility: Why firms leave the NASDAQ and join the New York stock exchange. *Administrative Science Quarterly*, *45*(2), 268−292.

Reinhart, C. M., & Rogoff, K. S. (2011). From financial crash to debt crisis. *American Economic Review*, *101*(5), 1676−1706.

Risse-Kappen, T. (Ed.). (1995). *Bringing transnational relations back in. Non-state actors, domestic structures and international institutions*. Cambridge: Cambridge University Press.

Robinson, W. I., & Harris, J. (2000). Towards a global ruling class? Globalization and the transnational capitalist class. *Science & Society*, *64*, 11−54.

Rugman, A. M. (2012). *The end of globalization* (2nd ed.). New York, NY: Random House.

Scott, J. (1992). *Social network analysis*. London: Sage.

Scott, J. (1997). *Corporate business and capitalist classes*. Oxford: Oxford University Press.

Sklair, L. (2001). *The transnational capitalist class*. Oxford: Blackwell.

Therborn, G. (2000). Globalizations dimensions, historical waves, regional effects, normative governance. *International Sociology*, *15*(2), 151−179.

Useem, M. (1984). *The inner circle*. New York, NY: Oxford University Press.

van der Pijl, K. (1998). *Transnational political economy and international relations*. New York, NY: Routledge.

Vion, A. (2012). Franco-German friendship: A sequential analysis. Paper presented at the international conference Friendship in IR: Conceptions and Practices, Harvard University, February.

BUSINESS ELITES AND THE FIELD OF POWER IN FRANCE

Mairi Maclean, Charles Harvey and Gerhard Kling

ABSTRACT

Bourdieu's construct of the field of power has received relatively little attention despite its novelty and theoretical potential. This paper explores the meaning and implications of the construct, and integrates it into a wider conception of the formation and functioning of elites at the highest level in society. Drawing on an extensive dataset profiling the careers of members of the French business elite, it compares and contrasts those who enter the field of power with those who fail to qualify for membership, exploring why some succeed as hyper-agents while others do not. The alliance of social origin and educational attainment, class and meritocracy, emerges as particularly compelling. The field of power is shown to be relatively variegated and fluid, connecting agents from different life worlds. Methodologically, this paper connects biographical data of top French directors with the field of power in France in a novel way, while presenting an operationalization of Bourdieu's concept of the field of power as applied to the French elite.

Keywords: Bourdieu; elite careers; field of power; French business elites; hyper-agency; power

INTRODUCTION

This paper considers the nature and practice of elite formation among top French directors. Elite formation as an object of study cannot be separated from the study of power, hence the primary focus of this paper is on French business leaders and the pathways taken by the most powerful amongst them into what Bourdieu (1993, 1996) terms the 'field of power' (FoP hereafter). We define this as the integrative social domain that transcends individual fields and organizations, which functions as a metafield of contestation and struggles for dominant agents – individuals who hold a controlling position within an organizational field – from different professional backgrounds (Maclean, Harvey, & Kling, 2014). Wacquant (1993, p. 21) describes the FoP as a 'configuration of power relations within which the dominants ... of a society are arrayed and pitted against one another'. The study of power is fundamental to the social sciences and to organization studies in particular (Clegg, 1989a; Clegg, Courpasson, & Philips, 2006; Courpasson, 2000; Courpasson & Golsorkhi, 2009; Reed, 2012; Zald & Lounsbury, 2010). Access to power (or lack of it) sets limits to organizational strategy as well as to individual career paths, while the outcome of power struggles at the societal level helps to determine government policies, resource flows and the trajectories of social movements (Fligstein, 1997). This paper contributes to research on this important topic.

Mills' (1956) seminal study of the power elite was centred on the United States, and other eminent scholars have followed in his footsteps in examining the American super elite (e.g. Davis, 2009; Domhoff, 2006, 2009; Lindsay, 2008; Mills, 1956; Useem, 1979; Useem & Karabel, 1986). The identification of board interlocks regularly assumes centre stage (Brass, Galaskiewicz, Greve, & Tsai, 2004; Burris, 2005; Burt, 1980; Davis & Greve, 1997; Mizruchi, 1996; Mizruchi & Stearns, 1988; Palmer, 1983; Palmer, Friedland, & Singh, 1986). Interlocking directorships, however, as Zald and Lounsbury (2010, p. 967) point out, represent only one aspect of the study of the elite occupants of 'institutional and societal command posts'. This paper is intended as a response to the call for more research on hyper-agency and on the nature and functioning of the FoP (Schervish, 2003). The empirical domain is contemporary France, but our conceptualization of the FoP has, we believe, wider implications. We focus on the social origins, careers and networking strategies of the French business elite, those serving as a full member of the board or executive board of at least one of France's top 100 largest companies, differentiating between those whose careers are made within the corporate world and the minority of hyper-agents who assume a more pivotal role in wider society.

Careers are the products of both institutional structures and individual agency (Inkson, 2007). They illuminate the 'structuring social context' (Goffman, 1963, p. 18) where societal history meets individual life stories, combining micro and macro perspectives and casting light on linkages with wider society (Iellatchitch, Mayrhofer, & Meyer, 2003). Human activity is recursive and self-reproducing, resulting in the relative imperviousness of social structures to social change; yet to be an agent is also to have the capacity for action, 'to "make a difference" to a pre-existing state of affairs or course of events' (Giddens, 1984, p. 14). We identify 386 of the 1,160 individuals studied, near exactly a third, as hyper-agents: that is to say that they emerge as multi-positional actors within the FoP who regularly make common cause with others in issue-based coalitions formed to secure favourable legislative and resourcing decisions or to conceive alternative possibilities in the struggles of the moment (Bourdieu, 1996; Emirbayer & Mische, 1998). We deem them 'multi-positional' because the most powerful amongst them populate boardrooms drawn from different life worlds, including public bodies, business associations, top cultural and sports organizations and charities. Hyper-agency is linked to the dynamics of power, since agents occupying 'strategic command posts' (Mills, 1956, p. 4) in society tend to act in such a way as to further their personal and organizational interests and in this way to legitimate desired outcomes (Brown, 1994, 1998; Clegg et al., 2006; Fligstein, 1997; Schervish, 2003; Suchman, 1995; Zald & Lounsbury, 2010).

THE CONCEPT OF POWER

'Power', according to Giddens (1981, pp. 28−29), 'is an integral element of all social life ... All social interaction involves the use of power, as a necessary implication of the logical connection between human action and *transformative capacity*'. It is a *relational* concept (Clegg et al., 2006; Foucault, 1980). As such it is central to the study of power and politics in organizations and to contemporary organizational theory (Clegg, 1989a, 1989b; Courpasson, 2000; Courpasson & Golsorkhi, 2009; Hardy & Clegg, 1996; Hickson, Hinings, Lee, Schneck, & Pennings, 1971; Hindess, 1982; Pfeffer, 1992). Weber (1978) in particular recognized that through the process of rationalization bound up with organization, individuals risked becoming trapped in an 'iron cage' of bureaucracy, restricting their power and room to manoeuvre (Courpasson & Clegg, 2006).

Building on Weber's insights, Dahl (1961), who investigated community politics in New Haven, argued that democratic decisions were ultimately the outcome of contestation among a plurality of elites. Bachrach and Baratz (1962), however, asserted that the study of power should include examination of a second, concealed 'face' of power, embracing non-decision making and institutional bias (Haugaard, 2002). Lukes (1974/2005) stated that power had to be thought about more widely still, as three-dimensional, to include control over the political agenda, being at its most efficacious when least apprehensible. In this, his views resonate with those of Foucault (1980), who demonstrates that power works most effectively when it is least visible, being exercised through social micro-practices rather than through the deliberate intentions of autonomous agents (Lukes, 1974/2005; Oakes, Townley, & Cooper, 1998).

Concerned with the practices and mechanisms of domination which abound in human living, Foucault confirms that there is no escape from power, which is ubiquitous, decentred and polymorphous. In *Discipline and Punish* (1979), he explores its disguise through seemingly neutral institutions whose control mechanisms are internalized by the individuals they seek to dominate, inducing conformity to social norms. Bourdieu (1991, p. 167) likewise conceives of power as perpetuated by institutions whose 'structured and structuring' symbolic systems bring 'their own distinctive power to bear on the relations of power which underlie them ... contributing, in Weber's terms, to the "domestication of the dominated"'.

For many scholars, including Bourdieu, Foucault and Clegg, the relational embeddedness of power implies that it is mistaken to think in terms of cause and effect. For Clegg (1989b, p. 99), power is at once a 'property of relations' and a '"capacity" premised on resource control'. Elsewhere, we have defined power as 'command over resources' (Maclean, Harvey, & Press, 2006). In the present paper, we broaden this definition to include as a vital resource the capacity of elite occupants of command posts to bring together diverse groups of high-status social actors to make common cause within the FoP. Clegg et al. (2006, pp. 31–32), in their excellent study of power in organizations, accord particular focus to what is implied by the terms 'power to' and 'power over'. Quack (2013, pp. 661–662) defines these as 'expertise as a practical capacity' and 'expertise as an instrument of domination,' respectively. What we are essentially dealing with here, however, is arguably 'power with', which concerns the power to mobilize in that it encompasses 'the transformative potential of collective action' (Quack, 2013, p. 661), which in turn feeds into 'power to'. Lindsay (2008, p. 62) describes this as a form of 'convening power', stating that the power to convene is the significant 'structural advantage' elite actors can exploit. Leading elites use this form of convening power to help them define reality, employing their social skills strategically to fashion and ultimately determine institutional arrangements (Fligstein, 1997). However, it is important to note as a caveat that they need to keep this particular type of power active, safeguarding their legitimate right to convene power by retaining place as an active agent within the FoP (Courpasson & Golsorkhi, 2009).

This relational, dynamic aspect of power is therefore fundamental to success in the FoP, as members of the business elite assemble various resources and channels to exert influence on their way into the FoP. The world Bourdieu (1986) depicts, however, is material as well as relational. In addition to this dynamic aspect of power, power also derives from material wealth and position, as elite agents draw on their different capitals (economic, cultural, social and symbolic) to enhance their positioning in the social structure (Anheier, Gerhards, & Romo, 1995).

THE FoP

Bourdieu's work has attracted much interest from organizational theorists (e.g. Anheier et al., 1995; Emirbayer & Johnson, 2008; Harvey, Maclean, Gordon, & Shaw, 2011; Kerr & Robinson, 2012; Mutch, 2003; Oakes et al., 1998). Yet his concept of the FoP remains under explored relative to his more popularized concepts of field, capital and habitus, in spite of its theoretical and empirical potential (Bourdieu, 1996). In Fig. 1, we introduce our conceptualization of the FoP which, as part of our original contribution, seeks to explicate and develop the ideas and terminology first put forward by Bourdieu (1993, 1996, 2011). This depicts society as divided vertically into fields, each defined by the legitimate activities conducted within a particular social space delineated by prevailing rules of competition, practices and actor dispositions. As individual agents undergo career progression, they may gradually ascend the hierarchy within their chosen field, eventually, should they continue to progress, penetrating the *field elite*. This conceptualization of the FoP is intended to be more generic than the French context alone, with wider implications, being designed to explicate and operationalize elite formation in the West more generally.

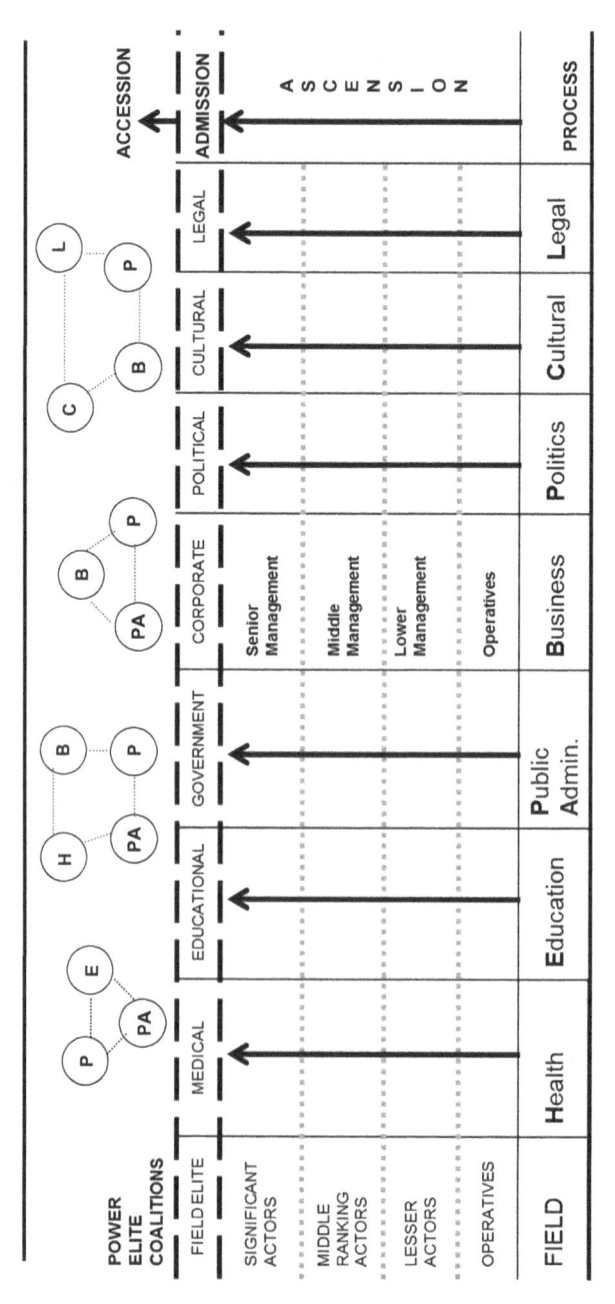

Fig. 1. Elite Actors in the Field of Power.

In Fig. 1, we show various pathways to the top which might be followed within individual fields, including those of health, education, public administration, politics, the cultural and legal fields, as well as the organizational field. In the French context, Bourdieu's writing on the FoP refers specifically to the business elite closely intersected with those who serve the State. In this regard, our empirical study, as a comprehensive survey of all directors of the top 100 companies, classified by type, covers only one facet of the FoP, albeit a very important one, focusing namely on entrance achieved through membership of the business elite (including those who began their careers in public administration and professions and then moved into the business arena). In the interests of clarity, it is worth pointing out that our study does not cover those who made their way into the FoP exclusively through the administrative pathway (which is not uncommon in France), nor those who might have made it exclusively through a professional pathway or from other fields.

The concept of the *power elite*, informed by the seminal studies of Mills (1956) and Useem (1984), refers to a network of dominant agents operating collectively within the FoP above individual field level and within the topmost strata transcending distinctive organizational fields. This depiction of the power elite in Fig. 1 as horizontal, boundary spanning, effectively sitting above and buttressed by individual field elites, shifts the emphasis away from the 'vertical differentiation of perceived power' (Hickson et al., 1971, p. 217) to the inter-organizational; the social space where different types of dominant agent engage as equals with their peers from different life worlds to form *power elite coalitions* in pursuit of specific economic, social and political objectives. These coalitions, as Fig. 1 implies, are not 'hard-wired', but, as the dotted lines suggest, may form and disband in response to pressing issues of the day. Elevation or *ascension* to the level of field elite represents a *sine qua non* for the potential entry of an agent into the FoP, boardrooms in particular representing the ultimate loci of power in organizational settings (Pettigrew & McNulty, 1998). *Accession* to the FoP, however, is an arduous process which cannot be taken for granted; membership of what Mills (1956, p. 281) dubs the 'fraternity of the successful' depending crucially on subsequent engagement with other dominant agents within broader societal networks (Maclean, Harvey, & Chia, 2010).

The careers of elite actors in the FoP regularly transcend organizational boundaries (Ancona & Caldwell, 1992; Geletkanycz & Hambrick, 1997; O'Mahony & Bechky, 2006), connecting contests within the organization with broader power struggles in society-at-large. To transcend their particular organizational field, dominant agents must achieve voice beyond the confines of their respective organization and field. Individual organizational fields may be viewed as sites of contestation, playgrounds or battlefields, where agents or institutions are defined as dominant or subordinate according to their positioning within the field (Bourdieu & Wacquant, 1992; Iellatchitch et al., 2003; Rosenbaum, 1984). The FoP, conversely, functions as a 'macro-level arena of struggle' (Swartz, 2008, p. 50), affording access to substantial volumes of capital (economic, social and symbolic in particular) to the most dominant agents (Anheier et al., 1995; Harvey & Maclean, 2008). It both sets elite agents from different fields (such as health, public administration, politics, intelligentsia, art and culture, law or the media) against one another; while at the same time providing the necessary structural conditions for them to collaborate through forming time-limited, issue-based coalitions of interests (O'Mahony & Bechky, 2008). Players cannot rely on their various capitals alone, nor solely on the hand that they have been dealt in life; playing the game skilfully being instrumental to eventual success (Fligstein, 1997).

Through alliances and networks forged within the FoP, elite agents seek to influence societal decision-making processes, resource flows, opinion formation and wider logics of action by strengthening commitment to particular projects or objectives. They 'make accounts', as Giddens (1984, p. 29) puts it, becoming the purveyors of legitimizing narratives or scripts designed to inform collective systems of meaning in order to effect or impede institutional change (Creed, Scully, & Austin, 2002; Lindsay, 2008; Lounsbury & Glynn, 2001; Mills, 1940; Scott, 2001; Scott & Lyman, 1968; Vaara, 2002). Fligstein (1997) explains how they exploit their social skills in order to direct authority and frame action. It is crucial, however, that their actions are legitimized by wider public perceptions of their civic-mindedness and disinterestedness (Bourdieu, 1996, p. 389; Harvey et al., 2011), since, as Fligstein (1997, p. 400) argues, 'If others think that one wants something and that it is narrowly for selfish purposes, then they are unlikely to try to negotiate'. Through playing the game with skill, elite agents are able to influence their own positioning within the '"supra-individual" structuration of social institutions' (Giddens, 1984, p. xxv). In asserting their 'right' to discourse in a Foucauldian sense (Bourdieu, 1987; Domhoff, 2009; White, 1979), the most powerful amongst them 'struggle to impose their particular capital … as the most legitimate for dominating an entire social order' (Swartz, 2008, p. 50), eventually forcing action through legislative or quasi-legislative means. In this way, through hyper-agency, they seek to counter such countervailing power and resistance to their agendas as might arise in order to pursue their interests, personal and organizational.

METHODOLOGY

Our methodology is prosopographical. We gathered data on the social origins, education, careers, networks, affiliations, distinctions and interests of the executive and non-executive directors of the top 100 companies in France (with the exception of employee representatives who lack power for the reason that, while they are entitled to attend board meetings, they are not permitted to speak and therefore effectively have no voice) in post for part or all of the period 1998–2004, since 'sampling large firms best represents the population to which the sociology of the corporate elite is most applicable' (Davis, Yoo, & Baker, 2003, p. 314). Composition of the top 100 French companies was determined by size by computing an equally weighted composite measure based on total capital employed, turnover, profit-before-tax and employment (Grant, 1997); market capitalization having been rejected as a selection criterion because of its susceptibility to short-term fluctuations.

To profile individual members of the elite, data were gathered from five main sources: company annual reports and accounts; *Le Guide des Etats Majors des grandes enterprises* for 1999 to 2004; *Who's Who in France* for 2004 and its online version, which furnished on data social origins, education, careers, interests, honours and distinctions; extensive web searches, including standard business sources for director information such as company websites, *Business Week*, Forbes and the *Financial Times*, newspaper and periodical articles sourced using the Highbeam research service. The project database was built through the addition of data on a case-by-case basis using multiple tables in an integrated relational structure. We ran consistency routines for data recorded in the database and then populated fields in the project spreadsheet. Finally, two of the authors coded the spreadsheet separately, debating and reconciling problematic cases as these arose, including any partly subjective judgements such as parental social class, to ensure reliability.

Individual cases are defined uniquely using their last name and forenames. Titles, gender, age and nationality were recorded, and the year he or she first joined the main board of a top 100 French company. With regard to social class, a four-way classification was adopted: upper class, upper-middle class, lower-middle class, and lower class (Halsey, 1995). Classification was undertaken mainly on the basis of parental occupation, supplemented by information on place of upbringing and family circumstances. Upper class was reserved for those with parents holding high office or having large fortunes. Upper-middle class was reserved for top professionals such as lawyers, medical doctors, graduate engineers, senior state officials, and business men and women in senior but not the very highest positions. Lower-middle class was applied to those from white-collar occupations such as school teachers, sales people, lesser officials and technicians; while lower class was reserved for parental occupations such as worker (*ouvrier*), van driver and miner.

Place of birth was coded as falling into one of eight regions on the French mainland, with additional categories for those born in a French colony or in another country. Educational data were coded by attendance or not at an elite school and by attendance or not at one or more elite higher education institution. Many individuals attended more than one secondary school, with substantial numbers being educated locally before entering an elite institution to prepare for the examinations (in *classes préparatoires*) for entry into elite higher education institutions. Top academic qualifications by grade and subject type are recorded for each individual, in addition to professional qualifications. Declared or revealed involvement in sport and culture was recorded in each case; though under-recording is likely, given that not all individuals report their personal pursuits and pastimes.

Data on state honours were collected for the *Légion d'Honneur* (LdH) and the *Ordre National du Mérite* (ONM), each of which has the same ranking system. Membership of a *grand corps* is a signifier of membership of the French civic elite at the very highest level (Bourdieu, 1996). Known data were gathered for the Conseil d'Etat, Corps des Mines, Cour des Comptes, Inspection des Finances and the Corps des Ponts et Chaussées, the most prestigious of these within business being arguably the Corps des Mines and the Inspection des Finances.

Individuals are classified according to their career type: those who spend most or almost all their careers in the private sector; those whose careers commenced within government departments (public administration) before entering business and finally those who began their career in a profession (academia, law, medicine, etc.) before entering the corporate sector. They are also classified according to the type of activity that served as a foundation for their subsequent advancement. The number of top 100 company main board memberships and non-top 100 main board memberships held by an individual on both 1st January 1998 and 1st January 2004 are recorded, but subsidiary board memberships are disregarded on the basis that we are here concerned with discrete and separate organizations. Non-top 100 French companies are included if recognized as large companies by inclusion in *Le Guide des Etats Majors*. Non-French companies are also recorded, but only those that might be classified as large companies.

Given our interest in the FoP, the specific nature of the power base, the primary organizational field in which each director is embedded is recorded. Power bases include academia, banking and finance, the corporate sector excluding banks and finance houses, family trusts as the vehicles used by owner families to maintain control, the law, and the State. Likewise, the type and extent of engagement in external networks is noted, including involvement in charities, public bodies, business organizations, higher education, sports and culture. To gauge an individual's activities in the FoP, network size is captured by recording both the total number of corporate and extra corporate board memberships.

EMPIRICAL ANALYSIS

Characteristics of the French Corporate Elite

The French business class is often depicted as a relatively small, close-knit world (cf. Davis et al., 2003), surrounded by a relatively impermeable social boundary, and typified by high-density 'strong' or 'closure ties' which foster local cohesion and at times also promote concerted action by elites (Bauer with Bertin-Mourot, 1987; Bauer & Bertin-Mourot, 1997; Burt, Hogarth, & Michaud, 2000; Comet & Finez, 2010; Hartmann, 2000, 2007; Kadushin, 1995; Maclean, 2002; Maclean, Harvey, & Press, 2007; Oh, Chung, & Labianca, 2004; Suleiman, 1978). This 'social closure' (Ramirez, 2001) is in contrast to the weaker ties of lower-density networks identified by Granovetter (1973), more typical of the United States or the United Kingdom (Maclean et al., 2006). This is a corporate world closely allied to a supportive State apparatus, which facilitates connections through the *grands corps*, such as the Inspection des Finances, the Corps des Mines or the Cour des Comptes, the pinnacle of France's civil service elite, as well as through key organs of government, especially the Treasury, or ministerial Cabinets. As many as 27% of top French directors included in our sample moved from the public to the private sector, that is they began their career working for the State. The *grands corps* fosters an *esprit de caste*, likened to forms of extended family or freemasonry (Barsoux & Lawrence, 1990). Suleiman (1978, p. 197) describes the *grands corps* as 'placement bureaux', commenting that no one ever entered the Inspection des Finances to inspect finance or the Corps des Mines to fashion a career in mining. As Bourdieu observes, the *grands corps* consecrate social identities that are both in competition and complementary, such that, despite the rivalry between individual *corps*, all *corpsards* are 'united by a genuine organic solidarity' (1996, p. 142).

Yet, while many members of the French business elite have at times identified more readily than in other countries with the State agenda, it would be mistaken to think of the corporate elite as monolithic and homogenous. A more accurate representation is that the elite has a number of defining characteristics, but at the same time is relatively diverse in several crucial aspects. The upper echelon of the French business system, like many others, is largely a male preserve (96% in 1998), is mainly composed of people born and bred in the country (88% in 1998), is drawn predominantly from people from upper and upper-middle class backgrounds (62% in 1998), and is highly educated (96% to first degree level, 71% to master's degree level and 10% holding a doctorate in 1998) in elite institutions (75% in 1998). This picture has changed relatively little over recent decades (Comet & Finez, 2010). However, alongside these similarities there are also interesting differences. Members of the elite may be educated and work in Paris, but they are drawn there from all parts of France. Moreover, as French business has internationalized, significant minorities are gradually but increasingly being appointed to French boards from Belgium, Germany, Italy, Switzerland, Spain, the United Kingdom and the United States (Davoine & Ravasi, 2013; Harvey & Maclean, 2010; Wagner, 2011). Likewise, while science, engineering and mathematics (36% in 1998) and law, business, economics and management (53% in 1998) are the two main higher education platforms for business elite careers, there is considerable subject variation within those broad categories.

We suggest that as for many national business systems, there has in the French case been a tendency to simplify and over generalize with respect to matters relating to elite selection, reproduction, networking and the exercise of power (Barsoux & Lawrence, 1990). In what follows we suggest that the business elite is slightly more differentiated and pluralist than has been portrayed, highlighting in particular the different pathways to power taken by those who come to exercise power at the very highest level in society.

Entering the FoP

We identify members of the business elite operating within the FoP in France as those satisfying a minimum of two of four criteria: (i) appointment as a *top tier executive* (y_1), the CEO or Executive Chairman of a top

100 company, including those styled Président Directeur-Général (PDG) and Président du Directoire; (ii) a *corporate networker* (y_2), defined as holding at least two board memberships of top 100 French companies or one top 100 company and at least two other directorships of medium to large-sized companies; (iii) an *extra corporate networker* (y_3), signified by membership of two or more national or international non-business boards or equivalent high office outside business; (iv) an *entrepreneur* (y_4), with significant ownership rights. In effect, application of the four differentiating criteria divides the French business elite into two categories, those who become power brokers at the wider societal level within the FoP (386 individuals) and those whose careers remain confined in large measure to the corporate world (774 individuals).

This method of determining which members of the business elite are operating within the FoP acknowledges that those occupying high office in the business sphere have different power bases (including academia, banking, finance, business, a family trust, the law or the State) and recognizes that individuals who can meet more than one criterion are those most likely to function effectively at the societal level. The four individual pathways (y_1, y_2, y_3, y_4) were identified as embracing the most vital aspects of power, in that through their positions of top tier director, corporate networker, extra corporate networker and entrepreneur, they enjoy both managerial control (CEO) and ownership (y_1 and y_4), while reflecting other aspects of power which connect them with other life worlds, emphasizing the importance of networks, and suggestive of the notion of 'power with' and the power to convene (y_2 and y_3) (Fligstein, 1997; Lindsay, 2008; Quack, 2013).

In Table 1 we display our findings on the pathways taken by individuals acceding to the FoP in France. Part A of the table relates to entry qualifications, the four individual pathways to power that individuals might follow. It can be seen that of the 1,160 individuals profiled, just 17% of the elite qualified as *top tier executives* of a top 100 French company (pathway y_1). However, the individuals pursuing this pathway almost certainly (with 91% probability) entered the FoP. The second pathway (y_2), *corporate networker*, characterized by multiple directorships of top 100 and other large companies, were more numerous (32% of the elite), 84% of whom made it into the FoP. An even larger number (48% of the elite) qualified as an *extra corporate networker* (y_3), but only 68% of them entered the FoP. The fewest number (4.5% of the elite) qualified by having significant *ownership* (y_4) rights in large companies, of whom 90% entered the FoP.

In Part B of the table, the frequencies are exhibited in rank order for each of the nine discrete pathway combinations followed by the 386

Table 1. Entry of Corporate Agents into the Field of Power in France.

A: Entry qualifications (observations = 1,160)

Pathway	Code	No. Qualifying	% Qualifying	No. within FoP	% Qualifying within FoP
Top tier executive	y_1	198	17.1	180	90.9
Corporate networker	y_2	366	31.6	309	84.4
Extra corporate networker	y_3	555	47.8	379	68.3
Ownership	y_4	52	4.5	47	90.4

B: Entrants into the Field of Power (386 of 1,160)

Type of Actor in FoP	Pathway Combination	No. of Entrants into FoP	% of Entrants into FoP
Corporate and extra corporate networker	$y_2 + y_3$	182	47.2
Top tier corporate and extra corporate networker	$y_1 + y_2 + y_3$	94	24.4
Top tier extra corporate networker	$y_1 + y_3$	58	15.0
Top tier owner corporate and extra corporate networker	$y_1 + y_2 + y_3 + y_4$	15	3.9
Owner corporate and extra corporate networker	$y_2 + y_3 + y_4$	12	3.1
Owner extra corporate networker	$y_3 + y_4$	12	3.1
Top tier owner extra corporate networker	$y_1 + y_3 + y_4$	6	1.6
Top tier corporate networker	$y_1 + y_2$	5	1.3
Top tier owner corporate networker	$y_1 + y_2 + y_4$	1	0.3
Top tier owner	$y_1 + y_4$	1	0.3

individuals entering the FoP. This specifies more clearly the composition of the elite within the French business elite, identifying by type the hyper-agents who represent the business community within the FoP in France. Our empirical findings have shown that the predominant type (47%), while not the most powerful, concerns senior executives below the rank of CEO in large companies who have extensive networks within the corporate and other life worlds (Maclean et al., 2010, pp. 334–335). The most powerful agents, in the main, are the top tier executives and owner-executives who combine three or four pathways in acceding to the FoP (Maclean et al., 2010, pp. 336–337). The most numerous (24%) are the *top tier corporate and extra corporate networkers* who lead (CEO, Executive Chairman or Chairman and CEO) large companies and who sit on the boards of other large companies and national or international organizations outside the corporate sector. These individuals are rivalled only by the 15 (4%) *top tier owner corporate and extra corporate networkers* who bestride the FoP in France. Other pathway combinations reveal interesting variations on the theme. A large minority of top tier executives, for instance, are not corporate networkers, preferring instead to channel their energies within their own companies and build networks within the field as *top tier extra corporate networkers* (15%). A further six business owners, as *top tier owner extra corporate networkers* (1.6%) likewise steer clear of corporate networking while building extensive extra corporate networks as engaged actors operating within the FoP.

Education, Social Origins and the FoP

The French business elite has at times been perceived as united by a shared education, being educated on the same benches of the same elite schools (Barsoux & Lawrence, 1990; Eymeri, 2001). Table 2 confirms that graduation from an elite higher education institution is the norm for those who progress to the top in French business. The degree of concentration in attendances even within the set of elite *grandes écoles* and universities is noteworthy, with 52% of all attendances being at just one of ten institutions. It is common to progress from one elite higher education institution to another, and for scientists, engineers and mathematicians to progress to study economics, business, management or social sciences at postgraduate level. Those wishing to work for the State for some time and having sufficiently high grades might gain admission to the elite national college of public administration, the Ecole Nationale d'Administration (ENA). Others might work in business for a few years and then apply to a prestigious business school at home or abroad such as Harvard. Increasingly, in a change from previous decades, more are studying at business schools which were not initially considered as leading to top tier positions, such as ESSEC Business School, established in 1907, or HEC Paris, founded in 1881 by the Paris Chamber of Commerce and Industry. The curricula these schools offer reflect the diverse knowledge needed to lead and manage successfully in global enterprises, including the study of international political economy and cross-cultural management, alongside more traditional business school subjects. The emphasis on integrated learning, engagement with practice and practitioners, problem solving and decision making increasingly has been picked up from leading US schools by elite institutions in

Table 2. Higher Education and the French Business Elite.[a]

Institution Name	Institution Type	Year Founded	No. of Attendances	% of All Attendances
École Polytechnique	Engineering, Sciences and Mathematics	1794	222	11.8
Institut d'Études Politiques de Paris (IEP) (Sciences Po)	Social Sciences	1872	174	9.3
École National d'Administration (ENA)	Public Administration	1945	144	7.7
HEC Paris	Business and Management	1881	96	5.1
Université Paris 1 – Panthéon Sorbonne	Law, Humanities and Social Sciences	1252	93	4.9
École des Mines de Paris (ENSMP)	Engineering, Sciences, Economics and Management	1783	73	3.9
Université Paris 2 – Panthéon-Assas	Law, Management, Social and Information Sciences	1252	64	3.4
Harvard Business School	Business and Management	1908	39	2.1
ESSEC Business School	Business and Management	1907	38	2.0
École Centrale Paris	Engineering, Science and Technology	1829	35	1.9

Source: French business elites database. This contains data on the 1,160 directors (executives and non-executives) of the Top 100 companies in France in 1998.

[a]Data are available for 1,064 individuals with a combined attendance of 1,880, and a mean attendance rate of 1.77 attendances per head. The top 10 institutions account for 52.1% of all attendances.

France, including institutions with a primarily technological identity, such as the Ecole des Mines de Paris, which now offers an Executive MBA (2014).

Having an elite education of one type or another is virtually a necessary condition of reaching the pinnacle of French business, but it is by no means sufficient. Even though the numbers attending elite institutions are relatively small when set against the total number of university and college graduates, there is nevertheless still a surfeit of individuals with the most prized qualifications from the supposedly best places. Outstanding academic performance at an elite institution of higher education, we reason, is not what differentiates between members of the corporate field elite who enter the FoP and those who do not. The 'X-factor', we propose, stems from the compelling combination of *coming from the right place* (social origin) and *personal accomplishment* (merit). Following Bourdieu (1986, 1996), we hypothesize that being born into an upper or upper-middle class family imparts the dispositions, distinctions, cultural and social capital necessary to take full advantage of opportunities that arise as careers unfold. In particular, active networking and social capital accumulation within and without corporate organizations is facilitated by the social polish, ease of manner and expectation of inclusion that stems from being born into the habitus of existing power brokers (Le Wita, 1994). Those from a well-to-do background, we suggest, come better equipped to recognize and realize opportunities than equally talented colleagues from less privileged backgrounds (Dezalay, 1995; Hartmann, 2000; Maclean, Harvey, & Chia, 2012).

Evidence in support of our hypothesis is presented in Table 3. This suggests that social class is strongly implicated in helping to determine those

Table 3. Social Class and the Field of Power in France.

	\multicolumn{4}{c}{Social Class}			
	1	2	3	4	Total
Panel A: column percentage					
Not in FoP	105	267	298	46	716
	(48.4)	(57.8)	(86.1)	(80.7)	(66.2)
In FoP	112	195	48	11	366
	(51.6)	(42.2)	(13.9)	(19.3)	(33.8)
Total	217	462	346	57	1,082
	(100)	(100)	(100)	(100)	
Panel B: row percentage					
Not in FoP	105	267	298	46	716
	(14.7)	(37.3)	(41.6)	(6.4)	(100)
In FoP	112	195	48	11	366
	(30.6)	(53.3)	(13.1)	(3.0)	(100)
Total	217	462	346	57	1,082
	(20.1)	(42.7)	(32.0)	(5.3)	(100)
Chi-square test					
Statistic	112.09				
p-value	0.000				

Source: French business elites database. This contains data on the 1,160 directors (executives and non-executives) of the Top 100 Companies in France in 1998. Of these we know the social class of 1,082 individuals.

who enter the FoP, as confirmed by the Chi-square test statistic. The overall probability of an agent's entering the FoP is 33.8% (see Panel A). However, those originating from classes one and two exhibit a much higher probability of entry, 51.6% and 42.2%, respectively. Her~e, an agent in class one, the upper class, is 3.72 times more likely to enter the FoP compared to an individual in the third social class (i.e. 51.6% divided by 13.9%). In stark contrast, agents from the third and fourth social class have only a slim chance of entering the FoP. Panel B considers row percentages, displaying the distribution of social class both inside and outside the FoP. From this, we observe that 83.9% of members of the FoP belong to social classes one or two. Viewed in this light, the relationship between high social status and ultimate accession to the FoP emerges as especially close.

Networks and the Functioning of the FoP

In Table 4 we present the results of our analysis by director type and corporate connectivity of the main board directors of France's top 100 companies

Table 4. Corporate Connectors in France ($n = 1,160$).

Director Type	Single Board	Connecting 2–4 Boards[a]	Connecting 5 Boards[a]	Total
Executive networker				
Number	0	344	77	421
Row %	0.0	81.7	18.3	
Dedicated executive				
Number	433	0	0	433
Row %	100.0	0.0	0.0	
Non-executive networker				
Number	0	81	27	108
Row %	0.0	75.0	25.0	
State representative				
Number	36	28	1	65
Row %	55.4	43.1	1.5	
Dedicated non-executive				
Number	133	0	0	133
Row %	100.0	0.0	0.0	
All directors				
Number	602	453	105	1,160
Row %	51.9	39.1	9.1	

Source: French business elites database. This contains data on the 1,160 directors (executives and non-executives) of the Top 100 Companies in France in 1998.
[a]Includes both top 100 and non-top 100 (medium or large) French and Non-French companies.

in 1998. This is revealing in two main aspects. First, it demonstrates that the members of the business elite play different roles within the national business system. As many as 854 of the 1,160 member of the elite are corporate executives, divided almost equally between those who serve a single company and those who connect the company they serve as an executive with others. These corporate connectors add value to firms within their corporate network through knowledge exchange, calibration against norms, developing consensus and the initiation of collaboration or joint action in relation to common threats or opportunities (Bühlmann, Thomas, & Mach, 2012; Geletkanycz & Hambrick, 1997). The remaining three types of director within the business elite constitute small but substantial minorities. One group is made up of non-executives who serve a single company. Some of these are former executives who remain on the board after retirement; others are specialists who bring expertise from different walks of life; and others are shareholder representatives, quite often senior members of family-owned firms. A second group comprises senior public servants who represent the interests of government on the boards of firms in which the State has retained a significant shareholding. These people are the 'eyes and ears' of officialdom, directly connecting the State with the business sector. The third group is composed of non-executives who serve more than one company. Typically these are individuals who prolong their careers following retirement from executive responsibility and who are prized as advisors, communicators and influencers, often within the political realm.

The second main point emerging from Table 4 is that the degree of connectivity varies considerably between members of the business elite. A majority of State representatives sits on just a single board, although a sizeable minority have more extensive networks, connecting between two and four boards. Just one of them is in the super corporate connector class of five or more boards. This class is made up of just over 9% of the business elite drawn mainly from the ranks of executive and non-executive networker directors. Of the 105 super corporate connectors identified, almost three-quarters of these are executive networkers, the ultra-powerful individuals who dominate the French corporate system and who qualify as hyper-agents, typically the chief executives of the largest companies who are invited to join the boards of other pillars of the French business establishment (Comet & Finez, 2010; Denord, Lagneau-Ymonet, & Thine, 2011; Dudouet & Joly, 2010; François, 2010).

Further insights concerning the connectivity of the French business elite emerge from the analysis presented in Table 5. In this, the French business elite is divided into six categories by primary current association: French corporate board (77.4%), international (non-French) corporate board (9.9%), banking and finance (5.2%), law and other professions (0.7%), politics and public administration (5.6%) and academia (1.2%). Table 5 makes clear the interpenetration between State and business elites, confirming that a high proportion of those whose power base is now within the business sector was once employed by the State. However, the extent to which

Table 5. Connectivity by Non-Executive Appointments of the French Business Elite[a] ($n = 1,160$).

Appointment by Organization Type	Power Base[a]					
	CB ($n=898$)	ICB ($n=115$)	B&F ($n=60$)	L&P ($n=8$)	STATE ($n=65$)	ACAD ($n=14$)
Top 100 companies						
Number[b]	98	10	21	0	18	3
% in class	10.9	8.7	35.0	0.0	27.7	21.4
Non-top 100 companies						
Number[b]	305	107	60	3	17	1
% in class	34.0	93.0	100.0	37.5	26.2	7.1
Charity						
Number[c]	64	35	10	1	5	2
% in class	7.1	30.4	16.7	12.5	7.7	14.3
Public body						
Number[c]	204	61	40	6	65	11
% in class	22.7	53.0	66.7	75.0	100.0	78.6
Business associations						
Number[c]	253	77	48	5	19	6
% in class	28.2	67.0	80.0	62.5	29.2	42.9
Education						
Number[c]	96	44	19	2	24	11
% in class	10.7	38.3	31.7	25.0	36.9	78.6
Culture/sport						
Number[c]	64	35	10	1	5	2
% in class	7.1	30.4	16.7	12.5	7.7	14.3

Source: French business elites database. This contains data on the 1,160 directors (executives and non-executives) of the Top 100 Companies in France in 1998.
[a]Power base is defined by current primary association. CB = French corporate board; ICB = international (non-French) corporate board; B&F = investment bank or the investment banking arm of a large bank; L&P = law or other profession; STATE = politics or public administration; ACAD = academic world.
[b]Total number of appointments held.
[c]Number of individuals holding such an appointment.

French companies have welcomed foreign nationals on to their boards as they have extended their international reach is less well known (Davoine & Ravasi, 2013; Wagner, 2011). Likewise, growth at home and abroad, often through mergers and acquisitions, has required the close support of the investment banks, leading to their partners and senior employees being appointed to numerous corporate boards. The appointment to boards of a small number of individuals from the law, academia (scientists and economists) and other professions is interesting, reflecting an appreciation of the specialist talents of top people within those fields.

It can be observed that individuals with different power bases (to wit academia, banking, finance, business, a family trust, the law or the State) bring with them their own network of connections from within and outside the corporate world, broadening the potential sphere of access and influence available to Top 100 companies. At any one time, a director will likely have a portfolio of appointments to boards, advisory groups, government commissions, representative bodies and the like. The value of such connectors lies in knowing from the inside what is going on in high places, and how to access influencers and decision makers (O'Mahony & Bechky, 2006, 2008). Charities, public bodies, business associations, educational institutions, sporting clubs and cultural organizations are all places where participation in governance makes for connection within the FoP. The mingling of elites in diverse settings helps to attune minds and form a consensus as a basis for action by power elite coalitions, as depicted in Fig. 1. Table 5 confirms just how well connected are those with a power base in international business and banking and finance (Kadushin, 1995; Kerr & Robinson, 2012), demonstrating further the reach of the business elite into the public sphere and its connectivity in the governance of business associations. The connectivity of the business elite with higher education, most often with schools attended, serves to reinforce the hegemony and ideological unity imparted by the most highly prized French educational establishments (Comet & Finez, 2010; Dudouet & Joly, 2010; Eymeri, 2001).

DISCUSSION AND CONCLUSION

The study of elites is arguably downplayed in the social sciences literature, especially relative to its critical importance to the workings of society and to 'world-making' by elite agents (Bourdieu, 1987; Clegg et al., 2006;

Maclean, Harvey, Gordon, & Shaw, 2012; Savage & Williams, 2008). Given that the cogency of organizational research lies first and foremost in its data (Courpasson, Arellano-Gault, Brown, & Lounsbury, 2008, p. 1387), a quintessential aspect of a reinvigorated examination of power and elites is the need to 'obtain the evidence ... and to think of each [social] phenomenon as paradoxical or counter-intuitive' (Courpasson & Golsorkhi, 2009, p. 62). This we have endeavoured to do.

There is arguably a common perception that the French corporate elite is relatively undifferentiated, comprising a self-reproducing oligarchy who act and think alike (Barsoux & Lawrence, 1990; Bauer with Bertin-Mourot, 1987, 1997; Eymeri, 2001; Milesi, 1990; Suleiman, 1978). This is arguably how the French corporate elite has traditionally appeared to the outside world (Burt et al., 2000; Kadushin, 1995). Our study demonstrates that, despite forming a relatively small world, 'particularly closed in on itself', the French corporate elite is in fact slightly more nuanced and differentiated than it is at times assumed to be (Comet & Finez, 2010, pp. 9–10; Davis et al., 2003; Useem & Karabel, 1986). Although our empirical study ended just before the onset of the financial crisis in 2007, nevertheless we can speculate that one effect of the crisis on the corporate elite may be to spur it to become more differentiated, in particular to admit more international directors into its fold (Wagner, 2011). In the continuing grip of a global crisis (at the time of writing, France is not yet out of recession), it makes sense for the boards of top French companies to spread their risks and capture a broader perspective by becoming more internationalized (Davoine & Ravasi, 2013; Harvey & Maclean, 2010). Of the 1,160 dominant corporate agents profiled, 386, approximately one third, were found to have acceded to the FoP as 'dominant dominants'. We find this group of hyper-agents to be differentiated by power − in terms of whether they accede to the FoP or not; whether they achieve top tier or next-best positions; and whether they extend their reach into different life worlds or remain confined to the business sphere. They are also differentiated by actor type and career trajectory. In other words, a reasonably large and diverse cast of actors is found to represent business within the FoP in France.

Three interesting observations emerging from this study require emphasis and point to the necessity for further research. The first is that the four pathways to power identified are interlinked, illustrative in part of the 'contemporary fluidity of elites' highlighted by Zald and Lounsbury (2010, p. 971). This might be a reflection of structural changes in the French economy, given the increasing proportion of financial and professional services amongst the largest French companies (Ramirez, 2010). Our inclination, however, is to interpret this as suggesting that the FoP requires diversity, albeit perhaps a rather limited form of diversity within the parameters of 'very strong social endogamy' (Denord et al., 2011, p. 37), and that there may in fact be different ways of linking the French business system with the body politic. The implication is that the FoP is more of a 'mixed bag' than it may initially appear. There are other dominant agents in the system with interesting and varied roles to play in society. This corresponds with the need for dominant agents to 'convene power' by forming provisional issue-based coalitions of interests in the FoP with players from different backgrounds and power bases, in the manner of 'power with' outlined above (Lindsay, 2008; O'Mahony & Bechky, 2008; Quack, 2013). Viewed on this light, contemporary coalitions of interests are not fixed or 'hard-wired' but rather emerge in response to issues which arise, despite residual loyalties based on shared schools and *grands corps*. Hence we might see them as more flexible than might at first appear, more akin to 'wi-fi', as depicted in Fig. 1, being able to reconfigure, reform and regroup as the need arises in pursuit of diverse personal, political and organizational interests and agendas on a case-by-case basis (Clegg et al., 2006; Zald & Lounsbury, 2010). This depiction of the FoP, we acknowledge, goes beyond our empirical findings, being informed by our interpretation of our data. To this end, while the organizational field has attracted some interest from scholars in terms of its capacity to lead to the FoP (Denord et al., 2011; Maclean et al., 2014), there is a need for future research to be conducted into elites recruited in particular from other sub-fields, who pursue alternative pathways to the top, and who serve as members of these coalitions of power, including those identified in Fig. 1.

Our second observation concerns causality regarding who does and who does not succeed in penetrating the FoP in France. A basic requirement clearly is the need to be well schooled in the French system, and Table 2 reveals some positive relations in this regard. When a high-status background is lacking, an elite educational grounding is all the more precious to the individual concerned (Reay, Crozier, & Clayton, 2009). Nevertheless, attendance at a *grande école* does not emerge as the ultimate discriminator it is often assumed to be, for the simple reason that many people attend *grandes écoles*. What matters more, we suggest, is the alliance of social origin and educational attainment, the union of class and meritocracy. Transparently, corporate agents from less well-to-do backgrounds must run harder and faster to acquire the dispositions, skills and know-how to ascend the corporate ladder and break out to accede to the FoP, as Table 3 confirms (Maclean, Harvey, & Chia, 2012). In a meritocracy, the game may be open to all comers, theoretically at least. However, how games are constructed in the first place forms an important part of the equation (Fligstein, 1997), and the game is stacked in the favour of the sons and daughters of the rich and powerful (Dezalay, 1995; Hartmann, 2000).

Our final observation relates to the importance of corporate and extra corporate networking to the composition and functioning of the FoP. Corporate agents acceding to the FoP, the majority serving executives, exhibit considerable diversity of type and connectivity. They are confirmed as multi-positional agents, whose reach extends into different life worlds by dint of their external ties (Geletkanycz & Hambrick, 1997; O'Mahony & Bechky, 2006), enabling them more readily to form the issue-based coalitions and pressure groups that have the capacity to frame action, direct agendas, shape public opinion, influence resource flows, and even, on occasion, to (re)set the rules of the game at the societal level (Fligstein, 1997; Lindsay, 2008). Corporate and extra-corporate networking activities are complementary, and those who accumulate the highest levels of social and symbolic capital within this milieu invariably wield the most power and influence. In this regard, we propose that the most successful agents in building and exploiting networks, insinuating themselves in positions of power and influence, are those emerging from the upper and upper-middle classes. Once established as hyper-agents within the FoP, they are able more readily to prolong their careers, picking up significant appointments on a serial basis. The implication is that incumbents are not easily ousted from the system, the FoP exhibiting a considerable degree of 'stickiness' in this regard.

This paper contributes to the relatively sparse literature on business elites entering and operating within the FoP, generally and specifically. We concentrate in this regard on the organizational field, that is to say on accession to the FoP achieved through membership of the business elite, rather than via other possible routes highlighted in Fig. 1, such as the legal or medical field. We break new ground theoretically through our conceptualization of the FoP which articulates and develops the concept and terminology first propounded by Bourdieu (1993, 1996, 2011), exploring the meaning and implications of the construct, and integrating it into a wider conception of the formation and functioning of elites at the highest level in society more generally. Methodologically, we connect biographical data of top French directors with the FoP in France in a novel way. Using a detailed dataset, our study takes a closer look at the composition of the FoP in France, comparing and contrasting those who enter the FoP with those who fail to qualify for membership. In this way, our analysis connects micro and macro levels of analysis, linking the careers of individual agents with the bigger picture of the functioning of elite groups within society (Iellatchitch et al., 2003). In focusing on the business sphere, as opposed to other potential pathways to the FoP featured in Fig. 1, it is understandable that the group under study might ostensibly exhibit social closure (Eymeri, 2001; Ramirez, 2001). However, we found in the course of this study that the French corporate elite is actually slightly more nuanced and differentiated than traditional perceptions might imply, suggestive of the multidimensional nature of power in the French corporate world. We suggest that this is a trajectory which is likely to continue, given the financial crisis, as the net of expertise is by necessity cast more widely to meet global challenges in the future.

Given the close relationship between high social status and the probability of entering the FoP, as highlighted in Table 3, we further suggest that organization theorists should look afresh at issues of social class. The language of class has been quietened in recent decades, overridden by notions of a 'classless', individualized society and a seemingly ever-enlarging middle class; and by the politics of identity, gender and ethnicity which have arguably taken centre stage (Bennett et al., 2009; Pakulski & Waters, 1996; Scott, 2002). As a result, the broader ramifications of inequality viewed as hierarchy have tended to be overlooked (Bottero, 2004). Class processes, however, increasingly operate through 'individualized distinction' (Savage, 2000, p. 102). Widening inequalities, exacerbated by the current crisis (Godechot, 2011), throw down the gauntlet to society to produce and nurture a more inclusive leadership; in this sense too, elites are 'on trial'. It therefore seems to us that the continuing effects of class differentiation on processes of hierarchy merit re-examination (Bottero, 2004; Maclean et al., 2014; Reay et al., 2009).

ACKNOWLEDGEMENTS

The authors would like to thank the convenors and participants of the sub-theme on 'Elites and the Design of Institutions, Industries and Organizations' at the 28th European Group for Organizational Studies (EGOS) colloquium held in Helsinki in July 2012 for their perceptive and helpful comments. We wish to thank Sigrid Quack in particular for her insightful comments which further strengthened this paper.

REFERENCES

Ancona, D. G., & Caldwell, D. F. (1992). Bridging the boundary: External activity and performance in organizational teams. *Administrative Science Quarterly, 37*, 634–665.
Anheier, H. K., Gerhards, J., & Romo, F. P. (1995). Forms of capital and social structure in cultural fields: Examining Bourdieu's topography. *American Journal of Sociology, 100*(4), 859–903.
Bachrach, P., & Baratz, M. S. (1962). Two faces of power. *American Political Science Review, 56*(4), 947–952.
Barsoux, J.-L., & Lawrence, P. (1990). *Management in France*. London: Cassell.
Bauer, M. with Bertin-Mourot, B. (1987). *Les 200: Comment devient-on un grand patron?* Paris: Seuil.
Bauer, M., & Bertin-Mourot, B. (1997). *Radiographie des grands patrons français: Les conditions d'accès au pouvoir*. Paris: L'Harmattan.
Bennett, T., Savage, M., Silva, E., Warde, A., Gayo-Cil, M., & Wright, D. (2009). *Culture, class, distinction*. London: Routledge.
Bottero, W. (2004). Class identities and the identity of class. *Sociology, 38*(5), 985–1003.
Bourdieu, P. (1986). *Distinction: A social critique of the judgement of taste*. London: Routledge.
Bourdieu, P. (1987). *Choses dites*. Paris: Minuit.
Bourdieu, P. (1991). *Language and symbolic power*. In G. Raymond & M. Adamson (Trans.). Cambridge: Polity.
Bourdieu, P. (1993). *The field of cultural production*. In R. Johnson (Trans.). Cambridge: Polity.
Bourdieu, P. (1996). *The state nobility: Elite schools in the field of power*. In L. C. Clough (Trans.). Cambridge: Polity.
Bourdieu, P. (2011). Champ du pouvoir et division du travail de domination. *Actes de la Recherche en sciences sociales, 190*, 126–193.
Bourdieu, P., & Wacquant, L. J. D. (1992). *An invitation to reflexive sociology*. Chicago, IL: University of Chicago Press.
Brass, D. J., Galaskiewicz, J., Greve, H. R., & Tsai, W. (2004). Taking stock of networks and organizations: A multilevel perspective. *Academy of Management Journal, 47*(6), 795–817.
Brown, A. D. (1994). Politics, symbolic action and myth making in pursuit of legitimacy. *Organization Studies, 15*(6), 861–878.
Brown, A. D. (1998). Narrative, politics and legitimacy in an IT implementation. *Journal of Management Studies, 35*(1), 35–58.
Bühlmann, F., Thomas, D., & Mach, A. (2012). The Swiss business elite (1980–2000): How the changing composition of the elite explains the decline of the Swiss company network. *Economy and Society, 41*(2), 199–226.
Burris, V. (2005). Interlocking directorates and political cohesion among corporate elites. *American Journal of Sociology, 111*(1), 249–283.
Burt, R. S. (1980). Cooptive corporate actor networks: A reconsideration of interlocking directorates involving American manufacturing. *Administrative Science Quarterly, 25*, 557–582.
Burt, R. S., Hogarth, R. M., & Michaud, C. (2000). The social capital of French and American managers. *Organization Science, 11*(2), 123–147.

Clegg, S. R. (1989a). *Frameworks of power*. London: Sage.
Clegg, S. R. (1989b). Radical revisions: Power, discipline and organizations. *Organization Studies*, *10*(1), 97–115.
Clegg, S. R., Courpasson, D., & Philips, N. (2006). *Power and organizations*. London: Sage.
Comet, C., & Finez, J. (2010). Le coeur de l'élite patronale: Reproduction sociale et réseaux de gouvernance. *Sociologies Pratiques*, *21*, 49–66.
Courpasson, D. (2000). Managerial strategies of domination: Power in soft bureaucracies. *Organization Studies*, *21*(1), 141–161.
Courpasson, D., Arellano-Gault, D., Brown, A., & Lounsbury, M. (2008). Organization studies on the look-out? Being read, being listened to. *Organization Studies*, *29*(11), 1383–1390.
Courpasson, D., & Clegg, S. R. (2006). Dissolving the iron cages? Tocqueville, Michels, bureaucracy and the perpetuation of elite power. *Organization*, *13*(3), 319–343.
Courpasson, D., & Golsorkhi, D. (2009). Les productivités du pouvoir. *Revue française de gestion*, *193*, 61–71.
Creed, W. E. D., Scully, M. A., & Austin, J. R. (2002). Clothes make the person? The tailoring of legitimating accounts and the social construction of identity. *Organization Science*, *13*(5), 475–496.
Dahl, R. (1961). *Who governs? Democracy and power in an American city*. New Haven, CT: Yale University Press.
Davis, G. F. (2009). *Managed by the markets: How finance re-shaped America*. Oxford: Oxford University Press.
Davis, G. F., & Greve, H. R. (1997). Corporate elite networks and governance changes in the 1980s. *American Journal of Sociology*, *103*(1), 1–37.
Davis, G. F., Yoo, M., & Baker, W. E. (2003). The small world of the American corporate elite, 1982–2001. *Strategic Organization*, *1*(3), 301–326.
Davoine, E., & Ravasi, C. (2013). The relative stability of national career patterns in European top management in the age of globalisation: A comparative study in France/Germany/Great Britain and Switzerland. *European Management Journal*, *31*(2), 152–163.
Denord, F., Lagneau-Ymonet, P., & Thine, S. (2011). Le champ du pouvoir en France. *Actes de la Recherche en sciences sociales*, *190*, 24–57.
Dezalay, Y. (1995). 'Turf battles' or 'class struggles': The internationalization of the market for expertise in the 'professional society'. *Accounting, Organizations and Society*, *20*(5), 331–344.
Domhoff, G. W. (2006). *Who rules America? Power, politics and social change* (5th ed.). New York, NY: McGraw-Hill.
Domhoff, G. W. (2009). The power elite and their challengers: The role of nonprofits in American social conflict. *American Behavioral Scientist*, *52*(7), 955–973.
Dudouet, F.-X., & Joly, H. (2010). Les dirigeants français du CAC 40: Entre élitisme scolaire et passage par l'Etat. *Sociologies Pratiques*, *21*, 35–46.
Ecole des Mines de Paris. (2014). *Théorie et pratique*. Retrieved from http://www.mines-paristech.fr/. Accessed on January 25.
Emirbayer, M., & Johnson, V. (2008). Bourdieu and organizational analysis. *Theory and Society*, *37*, 1–44.
Emirbayer, M., & Mische, A. (1998). What is agency? *American Journal of Sociology*, *103*(4), 962–1023.

Eymeri, J.-M. (2001). *La fabrique des énarques*. Paris: Economica.
Fligstein, N. (1997). Social skill and institutional theory. *American Behavioral Scientist*, *40*(4), 397–405.
Foucault, M. (1979). *Discipline and punish: The birth of the prison*. In A. M. Sheridan (Trans.). Harmondsworth: Penguin.
Foucault, M. (1980). *Power/knowledge: Selected interviews and other writings 1972–1977*. Harlow: Longman/Harvester Press.
François, P. (2010). Les guépards du capitalisme français? Structure de l'élite patronale et modes d'accès aux positions dominantes. Paper presented at 'Les élites économiques en France et en Europe', DRM-IRISSO, Université de Paris Dauphine, November.
Geletkanycz, M. A., & Hambrick, D. C. (1997). The external ties of top executives: Implications for strategic choice and performance. *Administrative Science Quarterly*, *42*(4), 654–681.
Giddens, A. (1981). *A contemporary critique of historical materialism*. London: Macmillan.
Giddens, A. (1984). *The constitution of society: Outline of the theory of structuration*. Cambridge: Polity.
Godechot, O. (2011). *Finance and the rise of inequalities in France*. Working Paper 13. Paris School of Economics.
Goffman, E. (1963). *Behaviour in public places*. New York, NY: Free Press.
Granovetter, M. S. (1973). The strength of weak ties. *American Journal of Sociology*, *78*, 1360–1380.
Grant, R. R. (1997). Measuring corporate power: Assessing the options. *Journal of Economic Issues*, *31*(2), 453–460.
Halsey, A. H. (1995). *Change in British society* (4th ed.). Oxford: Oxford University Press.
Hardy, C., & Clegg, S. R. (1996). Some dare call it power. In S. R. Clegg & C. Hardy (Eds.), *Handbook of organization studies* (pp. 622–641). London: Sage.
Hartmann, M. (2000). Class-specific habitus and the social reproduction of the business elite in Germany and France. *The Sociological Review*, *42*(2), 241–261.
Hartmann, M. (2007). *Eliten und Macht in Europa*. Frankfurt: Campus.
Harvey, C., & Maclean, M. (2008). Capital theory and the dynamics of elite business networks in Britain and France. *The Sociological Review*, *56*(s.1), 105–120.
Harvey, C., & Maclean, M. (2010). Transnational boards and governance regimes in Britain and France. In M.-L. Djelic & S. Quack (Eds.), *Transnational communities: Shaping global economic governance* (pp. 107–129). Cambridge: Cambridge University Press.
Harvey, C., Maclean, M., Gordon, J., & Shaw, E. (2011). Andrew Carnegie and the foundations of contemporary entrepreneurial philanthropy. *Business History*, *53*(3), 424–448.
Haugaard, M. (2002). *Power: A reader*. Manchester: Manchester University Press.
Hickson, D. J., Hinings, C. R., Lee, C. A., Schneck, R. E., & Pennings, J. M. (1971). A strategic contingencies' theory of intraorganizational power. *Administrative Science Quarterly*, *16*(2), 216–229.
Hindess, B. (1982). Power, interests and the outcomes of struggles. *Sociology*, *16*(4), 498–511.
Iellatchitch, A., Mayrhofer, W., & Meyer, M. (2003). Career fields: A small step towards a grand career theory? *International Journal of Human Resource Management*, *14*(5), 728–750.
Inkson, K. (2007). *Understanding careers: The metaphors of working lives*. London: Sage.
Kadushin, C. (1995). Friendship among the French financial elite. *American Sociological Review*, *60*, 202–221.

Kerr, R., & Robinson, S. (2012). From symbolic violence to economic violence: The globalizing of the Scottish banking elite. *Organization Studies, 33*(2), 247−266.
Le Wita, B. (1994). *French bourgeois culture.* Cambridge: CUP.
Lindsay, D. M. (2008). Evangelicals in the power elite: Elite cohesion advancing a movement. *American Sociological Review, 73,* 60−82.
Lounsbury, M., & Glynn, M. A. (2001). Cultural entrepreneurship: Stories, legitimacy, and the acquisition of resources. *Strategic Management Journal, 22*(6−7), 545−564.
Lukes, S. (1974/2005). *Power: A radical view* (2nd ed.). London: Palgrave Macmillan.
Maclean, M. (2002). *Economic management and French business from de Gaulle to Chirac.* Basingstoke: Palgrave Macmillan.
Maclean, M., Harvey, C., & Chia, R. (2010). Dominant corporate agents and the power elite in France and Britain. *Organization Studies, 31*(3), 327−348.
Maclean, M., Harvey, C., & Chia, R. (2012). Reflexive practice and the making of elite business careers. *Management Learning, 43*(4), 385−404.
Maclean, M., Harvey, C., Gordon, J., & Shaw, E. (2012). World-making and major philanthropy. In CGAP (Ed.), *Philanthropy and a better society?* (pp. 2−3). London: Alliance Publishing Trust.
Maclean, M., Harvey, C., & Kling, G. (2014). Pathways to power: Class, hyper-agency and the French corporate elite. *Organization Studies, 35*(6), 825−855.
Maclean, M., Harvey, C., & Press, J. (2006). *Business elites and corporate governance in France and the UK.* Basingstoke: Palgrave Macmillan.
Maclean, M., Harvey, C., & Press, J. (2007). Managerialism and the postwar evolution of the French national business system. *Business History, 49*(4), 531−551.
Milesi, G. (1990). *Les nouvelles deux cents familles.* Paris: Belfond.
Mills, C. W. (1940). Situated actions and vocabularies of motive. *American Sociological Review, 5,* 904−913.
Mills, C. W. (1956). *The power elite.* Oxford: Oxford University Press.
Mizruchi, M. S. (1996). What do interlocks do? An analysis, critique, and assessment of research on interlocking directorates. *Annual Review of Sociology, 22,* 271−298.
Mizruchi, M. S., & Stearns, L. B. (1988). A longitudinal study of the formation of interlocking directorates. *Administrative Science Quarterly, 33,* 194−210.
Mutch, A. (2003). Communities of practice and habitus: A critique. *Organization Studies, 24*(3), 383−401.
Oakes, L. S., Townley, B., & Cooper, D. J. (1998). Business planning as pedagogy: Language and control in a changing institutional field. *Administrative Science Quarterly, 43,* 257−292.
Oh, H., Chung, M.-H., & Labianca, G. (2004). Group social capital and group effectiveness: The role of informal socializing ties. *Academy of Management Journal, 47*(6), 860−875.
O'Mahony, S., & Bechky, B. A. (2006). Stretchwork: Managing the career progression paradox in external labor markets. *Academy of Management Journal, 49,* 918−941.
O'Mahony, S., & Bechky, B. A. (2008). Boundary organizations: Enabling collaboration among unexpected allies. *Administrative Science Quarterly, 53,* 422−459.
Pakulski, J., & Waters, M. (1996). *The death of class.* London: Sage.
Palmer, D. (1983). Broken ties: Interlocking directorates and inter-corporate coordination. *Administrative Science Quarterly, 28,* 40−55.

Palmer, D., Friedland, R., & Singh, J. V. (1986). The ties that bind: Organizational and class bases of stability in a corporate interlock network. *American Sociological Review*, *51*, 781−796.

Pettigrew, A., & McNulty, T. (1998). Sources and uses of power in the boardroom. *European Journal of Work and Organizational Psychology*, *7*(2), 197−214.

Pfeffer, J. (1992). *Managing with power: Politics and influence in organizations*. Boston, MA: Harvard Business School Press.

Quack, S. (2013). Regime complexity and expertise in transnational governance: Strategizing in the face of regulatory uncertainty. *Oñata Socio-Legal Series*, *3*(4), 647−678.

Ramirez, C. (2001). Understanding social closure in its cultural context: Accounting practitioners in France (1920−1939). *Accounting, Organizations and Society*, *26*(4−5), 391−418.

Ramirez, C. (2010). Promoting transnational professionalism: Forays of the 'Big Four' accounting community into France. In M.-L. Djelic & S. Quack (Eds.), *Transnational communities: Shaping global economic governance* (pp. 174−196). Cambridge: Cambridge University Press.

Reay, D., Crozier, G., & Clayton, J. (2009). 'Strangers in paradise'? Working-class students in elite universities. *Sociology*, *43*(6), 1103−1121.

Reed, M. I. (2012). Masters of the universe: Power and elites in organization studies. *Organization Studies*, *33*(2), 203−221.

Rosenbaum, J. E. (1984). *Career mobility in a corporate hierarchy*. London: Academic Press.

Savage, M. (2000). *Class analysis and social transformation*. Oxford: OUP.

Savage, M., & Williams, K. (2008). Elites: Remembered in capitalism and forgotten by social sciences. *The Sociological Review*, *56*(s.1), 1−24.

Schervish, P. G. (2003). *Hyperagency and high tech donors*. Boston, MA: Social Welfare Research Institute.

Scott, J. (2001). *Power*. Cambridge: Polity.

Scott, J. (2002). Social class and stratification in late modernity. *Acta Sociologa*, *45*(1), 23−35.

Scott, M. B., & Lyman, S. M. (1968). Accounts. *American Sociological Review*, *33*, 46−62.

Suchman, M. C. (1995). Managing legitimacy: Strategic and institutional approaches. *Academy of Management Review*, *20*, 571−610.

Suleiman, E. (1978). *Elites in French society: The politics of survival*. Princeton, NJ: Princeton University Press.

Swartz, D. L. (2008). Bringing Bourdieu's master concepts into organizational analysis. *Theory and Society*, *37*, 45−52.

Useem, M. (1979). The social organization of the American business elite and participation of corporate directors in the governance of American institutions. *American Sociological Review*, *44*(4), 553−572.

Useem, M. (1984). *The inner circle: Large corporations and the rise of business political activity in the US and UK*. Oxford: Oxford University Press.

Useem, M., & Karabel, J. (1986). Pathways to top corporate management. *American Sociological Review*, *51*(2), 184−200.

Vaara, E. (2002). On the discursive construction of success/failure in narratives of post-merger integration. *Organization Studies*, *23*(2), 211−248.

Wacquant, L. J. D. (1993). From ruling class to field of power: An interview with Pierre Bourdieu on *La noblesse d'état*. *Theory, Culture and Society*, *10*, 19−44.

Wagner, A.-C. (2011). Les classes dominantes à l'épreuve de la mondialisation. *Actes de la Recherche en sciences sociales*, *190*, 4–9.
Weber, M. (1978). *Economy and society: An outline of interpretive sociology*. Berkeley, CA: University of California Press.
White, H. (1979). Michel Foucault. In J. Sturrock (Ed.), *Structuralism and since: From Lévi Strauss to Derrida* (pp. 81–115). Oxford: Oxford University Press.
Zald, M. N., & Lounsbury, M. (2010). The wizards of Oz: Towards an institutional approach to elites, expertise and command posts. *Organization Studies*, *31*(7), 963–996.

ELITES AND THE PROBLEM OF LEGITIMACY

ns as moral actors or the development of a "business creed." American
THE DEMOCRATIC DILEMMA: ALIGNING FIELDS OF ELITE INFLUENCE AND POLITICAL EQUALITY

Elisabeth Clemens

ABSTRACT

Regardless of whether "elite" is defined with respect to social status, economic wealth, or professional accomplishment, these sources of advantage are blunted by democratic political commitments to equality. This durable dilemma has shaped the institutional development of the American polity and the economy, as those with extra-political advantages have sought new forms of political influence, at times subverting rules or advancing cultural projects that elaborate an image of corporations as moral actors or the development of a "business creed." American elites have also worked at the margins of the formally democratic policy to construct fields of public action that are accepted as public, legitimate, and admirable, but not strictly democratic. Corporate philanthropy has been central to these efforts. Organizations like the Community Chest can be understood as practical responses to the constraints of ideological commitments to political egalitarianism. This line of response to

Elites on Trial
Research in the Sociology of Organizations, Volume 43, 223−241
Copyright © 2015 by Emerald Group Publishing Limited
All rights of reproduction in any form reserved
ISSN: 0733-558X/doi:10.1108/S0733-558X20150000043020

the democratic dilemma is "constructive" in the nonnormative sense that it produces new fields of social action and reconfigures institutional arrangements. By linking economic position to civic influence, organizations of this type translate economic power into elevated influence over public affairs through the constitution and stabilization of partially hybridized forms or fields.

Keywords: Elites; democracy; field alignment; corporate philanthropy; Community Chest

In a democratic age, elites face a deeply structured dilemma. Regardless of whether "elite" is defined with respect to aristocratic descent, social status, economic wealth, or even educational and professional accomplishment, each of these sources of advantage is blunted by democratic political commitments to equality. So long as the scope of the democratic polity is more expansive than that of elite membership, these obstacles to the exercise of social privilege exist whether political standing is restricted to white, property-owning men or is extended more broadly. This mismatch between unequal social or economic resources and formal commitments to equality of political standing constitutes a persistent democratic dilemma.[1]

This durable dilemma has shaped the institutional development of both the American polity and the economy. Setting aside those who make no political effort in support of their privilege, citizens possessing advantages of standing or wealth have responded in diverse ways. Some deploy whatever opportunity for leverage is afforded within the rules of the institutions: making contributions at the top end of an allowable range, making use of interpersonal networks,[2] publicizing one's political preferences through a free press in the hope (or, indeed, the expectation) that others will shift their preferences accordingly out of either admiration or dependence. An alternative possibility of this general type involves subverting the rules by channeling illicit funds to candidates or making payments to legislators through corrupt lobbyists. Each of these alternatives may be accompanied by efforts to work within the framework of rules to change the rules of political participation and influence, by pushing for changes in the regulation of lobbying, the conduct of elections, or the status of money as speech. All of these options are central to debates within political science.

The tensions between democratic equality and economic privilege may also provoke adaptive responses. Within business history and economic sociology broadly construed, this durable tension between political democracy and market capitalism has been understood as a catalyst for cultural or ideological projects. In their classic postwar study, *The American Business Creed* (1956), Francis X. Sutton and his coauthors grasped this possibility in terms of an analysis of ideology understood as a selective portrayal of reality that engages both understanding and emotion. Working within the broadly social psychological functionalism of the time, they argued that businessmen elaborated an understanding of the American economy that helped to relieve the strains generated by the contrast of political commitments to individual liberty and the exercise of economic power. In this analysis, one of the important features of any ideology is its selective representation of the world and, above all, its selective silences. The "business creed" portrays business enterprises as if they were all relatively small firms in a competitive market and omits mention of the role of power in economic relationships, whether between employers and employees, producers and consumers, or senior and junior executives.

A variation on this primarily cultural response to the democratic dilemma centers on reconstructing the image of the firm as profoundly *moral* rather than simply small and competitive. Whereas the U.S. Supreme Court smuggled in the concept of corporate personhood in a late nineteenth-century opinion, generations of industrialists, financiers, and consultants took this charge quite seriously. In the spirit of Roland Marchand's felicitous phrase (1998), they sought to create "the corporate soul" through expressions of high-minded intentions, acts of corporate generosity, and the constitution of "familial" or "team" relationships between employers and employees (Jacoby, 1997). As I have argued elsewhere (Clemens, 2009), these efforts represented a repair of the analogy drawn by the concept of "corporate personhood" in liberal political theory. In the texts that are foundational to that tradition, the moral sensibility of natural persons is required to limit the potential rapaciousness of individual appetites and the pursuit of self-interest. Adam Smith, after all, built his theory not only on the invisible hand of *The Wealth of Nations* but also on the "omnipotent observer" of *The Theory of Moral Sentiments*. Following this response to the democratic dilemma, the advantages of economic wealth and power would be tempered by the acknowledged morality and public interest of business leaders.

The coauthors of *The American Business Creed* (1956, p. 23) captured this sensibility in a quotation taken from *USA, The Permanent Revolution* (Davenport, 1951), a volume published by the editors of *Fortune* magazine: "There are times, as I sit behind a desk piled high with the day's unread correspondence, when I stare darkly out of the window." Walter H. Wheeler, Jr., President of Pitney Bowes, Inc., of Stamford, Connecticut, was speaking on the *Social Responsibility of Business*: "Trying to see me are three conscientious executives, who would like to remind me, if they dared, that we're in business to make a profit and that I must spend *some* time on the problem of sales, manufacturing, and development. There is a Community Chest meeting in five minutes, and a directors' meeting tomorrow morning, neither of which I am prepared for ... It seems to me that none of us can look forward with hope over the years unless all of us can find solutions to problems bigger than our immediate material progress." By the postwar era, this executive's lament reflected the dual identity of corporations as loci for profit-making and platforms for civic responses to "problems bigger than our immediate material progress." The salience of these mixed motives was sustained by distinctive types of organizations established at the intersections of politics with other domains of social life: the economy, community relations, social standing. Thus the erosion of constraints on the conversion of economic wealth into political influence was accomplished through a particular sort of institution-building project. Organizational innovation must be added to strategic action and cultural adaptation as an important line of response to the democratic dilemma of elites.

While socially responsible executives served to exemplify a particular moral orientation in the argument of *The American Business Creed*, Walter H. Wheeler, Jr. associated this responsible civic engagement with a specific organizational vehicle: the Community Chest. A closer examination of these federated fund-drives and their colocation in economic and civic fields illuminates the capacity of organizational innovation to sustain effective – if often partial and less than permanent – responses to the democratic dilemma of elites. At the margins of the formally democratic organized polity, elites have worked to construct fields of public action that are accepted as public, legitimate, and admirable, but not strictly democratic. In these fields, "leading citizens" are constituted through non-electoral means, through deployments of eloquence, charisma, celebrity, heroism, altruism, longevity, social standing, and wealth. Each of these aspects of social distinction, although admirable in its own right, rests on principles that are at odds with strict interpretations of the equality of democratic citizens. Eloquence and charisma may slip into demagoguery, altruism and wealth into the creation of forms of dependency that undercut the democratic dignity of those who receive while elevating those who give.

The organization of power and leadership in these public but not formally political fields has the potential to undercut the authority of democratic representation as well as commitments to equality by facilitating the translation of advantage in one domain into unearned advantage in another. As Verba and Orren (1985, pp. 7–8, quoted in Bartels, 2008, p. 24) insightfully explain: "The aim of egalitarianism is not the elimination of all differences, which would be impossible, nor even the elimination of differences within any one of these spheres, which might also be impossible unless the state continually intervened. Rather, the goal is to keep the spheres autonomous and their boundaries intact. Success in one sphere should not be convertible into success in another sphere. Political power, which is the most dangerous social good because it is the easiest to convert, must be constrained against transmutation into economic power, and vice versa."

Organizations like the Community Chest, therefore, can be understood as practical responses to the constraints of ideological commitments to political egalitarianism. Rather than directly subverting democratic rules or developing cultural adaptations that elide the tension, this line of response to the democratic dilemma is "constructive" in the nonnormative sense that it produces new fields of social action and reconfigures institutional arrangements. By linking economic position to civic influence – if not necessarily all the way to electoral or legislative power – organizations of this type facilitate the "transmutation" of economic power into elevated influence over public affairs. In this way, the economically powerful are transformed into "leading citizens" (Clemens, 2010a) despite the formally democratic architecture of elections and representation.

In organizational terms, this third type of response – unlike the deployment of resources within existing institutions or ideological projects of moral self-fashioning – involves the constitution and stabilization of partially hybridized forms or fields. Here, the "partial" constitutes the theoretical puzzle. Precisely because work on institutional logics has tended to emphasize the internal coherence and constraining consistency of a particular model of relationships,[3] the question of relationships across logics (or domains structured by different logics) is a core puzzle of institutional and organizational theory. In response, scholarship has focused on the role of gate-keepers or brokers in transporting elements across organizational boundaries as well as on the role of hybrids in articulating relationships across domains with conflicting commitments (Murray, 2010). An analytic vocabulary of terms such as "liminality" and "trading zones" has developed to describe zones of action at the margins or peripheries of fields structured by a dominant logic. But the democratic dilemma requires these puzzles to be moved to center field: how is the articulation of logics-in-conflict stabilized and even institutionalized? How has democratic capitalism developed to sustain the interconnections of fields structured around economic inequality and those premised on formal political equality?

Because we lack strong theories of the conditions of possibility of durable hybridized fields, I turn to slightly extended but decidedly stylized cases to develop a provisional theoretical argument. The argument builds on Verba and Orren's analysis of the incompatibility between economic inequality and political egalitarianism, between competitive capitalism and democracy as models of social organization. Absent a demonstrated incompatibility between images of organization, the concept of hybridity lacks significant theoretical interest. The mutual repulsion of incompatible social logics, however, can be relaxed through multiple mechanisms. Two have already been sketched: the selective attention of the *ideological* analysis offered by Sutton et al. in *The American Business Creed* and the *identity-based* approach of public relations practitioners, their clients, and historians (Jacoby, 1997; Marchand, 1998). The third approach, central to the account here, is more essentially organizational in that it turns on the capacity to reorient and reconfigure these relational geometries such that the contradiction is muted if not entirely resolved.

In the historical sketch that follows, three mechanisms of institutional change recur. First, the alignment of partially hybridized fields involves the linking of networks of influence in one domain to projects understood to address a distinct set of social concerns or values. In this specific case, the organization of municipally centered business networks allowed the extension of business influence over organized charity and social service. Second, the identities of the organizations involved were reshaped to reflect this linkage; businessmen expressed civic commitments while social service organizations adopted a new vocabulary of efficiency. Both these processes crosscut well-established distinctions between the principles organizing diverse activities and appropriate to different kinds of actors. Firms, particularly when they were owned by stockholders, were responsible for making profits rather than doing good. Languages of sentiment, altruism, and religiosity had long been central to the field of charity and social provision. Consequently, the linkage of these two fields through new organizational forms generated a concomitant set of tensions and inconsistencies that were, at least to an extent, realigned and contained by new institutional rules. In time, however, these settlements and configurations of fields were undermined by further developments in their component parts. As the American corporate elite fractured in the postwar decades (Mizruchi, 2013), so too did the capacity of these partial hybridizations to sustain the conversion of business leader into leading citizen. So as economic inequality escalated in the last decades of the twentieth century, business and financial elites were once again faced with crafting new organizational vehicles to convert wealth into political influence.

CONSTRUCTING A CIVIC WORLD FOR AMERICAN BUSINESS

Ironically, the path toward institutionalizing the civic role of American business began with an effort to consolidate the ties among businessmen, often in opposition to other political forces. Although this characterization is unquestionably oversimplified, the early nineteenth century economic world can be described as one of relatively small firms oriented toward one another in relations of small scale collaboration and intense competition. While individual businessmen – then more likely to describe themselves as merchants, traders, or manufacturers if not by the name of a specific craft – were often leading citizens in their roles in local government, religious life, and benevolent activities, business *qua* business was relatively unorganized as an element of the civic society. In particular places, however, a move toward the greater coordination of business efforts and their alignment with projects of civic improvement was already evident. In New England, a new form of jointly business and civic endeavor was exemplified by the formation of the "Boston Associates" which joined the wealth derived from the merchant trade of that city into a sustained investment in the development of the textile industry inland from the city's great harbor. The regular returns on that investment sustained family fortunes begun in the risky world of overseas training through generations in which sea captains were replaced by industrialists and then ministers, lawyers, and scholars. The establishment, in 1818, of the closely linked Massachusetts Hospital Life Insurance Company provided a vehicle through which benevolent trusts and associations could also participate in the relatively predictable revenue stream generated by this jointly industrial and investment project (Dalzell, 1987, p. 135). Beyond the close circle of the Boston Associates, other influential citizens advanced the use of private corporations – linked to projects of education, charity, road-building, and bridge-construction – to promote both public goods and their private benefit (Neem, 2008).

Although the leading residents of Boston were unmatched in the scale and effectiveness of their early co-construction of economic and civic influence, they were not alone in exploring the possibilities of this type of hybrid field. Charleston, for example, was the site of multiple charitable organizations sustained by its wealthier citizens in the hope of overcoming deep divisions of race and class. In that city, "the connection of poor relief to the parish government established a link between civic and religious duty never formed in Virginia or North Carolina, where the courts, remote and inchoate institutions, haphazardly distributed almost from the general tax fund to the most desperate" (Bellows, 1993, p. 4; see also Lockely, 2007, p. 50). These linkages of economic advantage, civic position, and religious obligation were understood to forestall a more dangerous interpenetration of fields in which civic "rights" would extend to the workings of the market. This concern was evident in Boston where those "most engaged in charity [were] those who most feared creating an extensive dependence of the poor on the rich. ... They were haunted by the possibility that growing numbers of the poor had learned to thrive on alms and live without labor" (Pease & Pease, 1985, p. 150). These civic institutions linked economic and civic positions among the advantaged in order to police the separation of civic standing and economic aid among the poor. And, as these early elites were displaced from positions of political power in the early nineteenth century cities (Bridges, 1982; Heale, 1976), new strategies were deployed to gain civic or political leverage from charitable or social organizations.

The entwined processes of business development and civic mobilization were not restricted to the most-advantaged and established cities of the eastern seaboard, although comparable projects required the passage of time necessary for settlement and the founding of firms. As these processes took hold across the Appalachians by mid-century, the pattern so prominent in Boston was echoed, perhaps faintly and always with variations, in booming towns that became the nation's new cities. As migrants flowed down the Ohio River into territory newly wrested from Native Americans for agrarian settlement, cities-in-the-making were marked by a layering of new economic and civic organizations that created an extra-electoral capacity to advance public projects and meet public crises (Hall, 1982, pp. 151–77; Haydu, 2008, pp. 41–60). As American industry and finance grew in scale and burgeoning wealth, new infrastructures of sociability linked nascent elites into self-consciously distinctive status groups (Almond, 1998 [1938]; Roy, 1997). These new formations enhanced the capacity for collective – or at least loosely coordinated – action and trust among economic elites but simultaneously aggravated the democratic dilemma that confronted the newly privileged.

Responses to the situation varied. Some of the very wealthy retreated into a trans-Atlantic aristocratic fantasy. The two men whose wealth was unmatched by the late nineteenth century — Andrew Carnegie and John D. Rockefeller — pioneered a new model of philanthropy and foundation-based public works that would have a major influence on American civic life and public policy debates for decades to come (Zunz, 2012). But below these highest peaks of wealth, a broad tier of the economically powerful faced practical challenges of leveraging economic advantage in political settings often controlled by party organizations and political circles rather than by networks of important businessmen and leading citizens.

Among the most significant practical responses to this aspect of the democratic dilemma was the invention of a new hybrid form that linked wealth and social status to social service within many American cities. Building on the establishment of Charity Organization Societies in the late nineteenth century (themselves the projects of reform-minded rationalizers), local elites and businessmen contributed to the private voluntary funding of services to those in need in their communities, following the pattern familiar from the time of the Boston Associates forward.[4] Business organizations, exemplified by the new Chambers of Commerce appearing in cities across the country, stepped in to vet the multiplying requests for donations that were directed at many of their members. Delegating authority to investigate the worthiness of various organized causes to a committee on charities, the Chambers of Commerce developed a role as the legitimating authority for a field of private, civic organizations. This capacity of the leaders of one field to accredit organizations in another field represented a first important step toward hybridization.

This business accreditation of charitable organizations was soon followed by an additional rationalizing move: the creation of annual federated fund drives. Business leaders brokered an arrangement whereby charitable organizations that were recognized as being central to the concerns of the community as a whole — as opposed to sectarian or specialized — were required to abjure independent fund drives in return for a negotiated share of the proceeds from an annual federated fund-raising campaign. This guarantee came with additional requirements for financial standardization and auditing of charities (Cutlip, 1965, p. 143) by the Community Chest (and, by extension, to the businessmen sitting on the Charities Endorsement committees of their local Chamber of Commerce). Through such organized, rationalized systems of community-wide fund-raising, private businessmen constructed a position of influence over a wide range of private charitable organizations, many of which might have earlier been dependent on a handful of major donors or the support of a particular constituency of social reformers (Barman, 2006, pp. 19–25). This financial centralization reinforced the linking of fields through the effective authority of business organizations to accredit charitable institutions. It also sought to lodge "ownership" of a major piece of the problem of social provision for the poor securely within a field open to the influence of organized business while limiting the extent to which this problem would be addressed by party organizations and electoral processes – forms of organization in which the economically advantaged were positioned as large (and potentially larger) taxpayers rather than in positions of control.

The role of peak business organizations in brokering relations between fields also allowed for those who controlled the Chambers of Commerce to impose or strengthen status orders among industrialists, financiers, on down to small business owners (Clemens, 2010a). Occupational expertise in assessing the finances of going concerns was turned to the task of creating schedules of expected donations from firms throughout a community (Todd, 1932). Personal networks – sometimes of friendship, sometimes of the patron-client variety – were activated during fund-raising campaigns. The largest potential contributors carefully monitored what had been given by other men of wealth, wanting to ensure that their own large contribution did not become an excuse for others to shirk their civic responsibilities. Chain stores recognized the strength of this mode of community membership, recommending that their local franchises set aside funds to participate actively in such federated drives to forestall growing political pressure for anti-chain store regulation (Russell, Lyons, & Flickinger, 1931, p. 32). Overall, the introduction of the Community Chest or federated campaign model tended to increase the number of contributors, incorporating a broader swathe of residents into the donative networks that ran through the nexus of the business community and the field of voluntary social provision.[5] The vision of community-centered voluntary fund-raising was not limited to annual drives, but took a more durable form in the Community Trusts which were another innovation of the time. In both, business and financial leaders occupied central nodes in the network of community self-provisioning through charitable fund-raising.[6]

These developments did not go unnoticed and a backlash developed, fueled by charges that these arrangements offended both democratic and voluntary principles. The centralization of control by economic elites, some contended, represented a form of "plutocracy." The intensification of social pressure linked to federated fund-raising threatened to transform voluntary gifts into a form of privately managed "taxation without representation" (Lee, 1928). This was particularly salient for industrial workers who were increasingly solicited for contributions to community funds that would support privately managed systems of social support insulated from the pressure that could be brought to bear through open elections.

These arrangements were simultaneously challenged on a second front as shareholders objected to managerial decisions to divert funds that might have been invested or redistributed as profits to stock owners. Even without this line of objection, it was not clear how to handle business charitable contributions within the tax law. In practice, many firms treated such contributions as regular business expenses linked to the cultivation of "good will" for the firm, an accounting that also helped to forestall shareholder objections that such community contributions were illegitimate deviations from managers' obligation to maximize value for the company's owners. But these objections, whether on principles of democratic governance or shareholder value, only highlighted the accomplishment of this newly constructed hybridized field. By linking central business organizations to the financing of community social services through federated fund-raising, economic elites had established the organizational machinery for supplying a limited level of social support without setting in train political dynamics that would generate demand for increases in tax revenues. The result, at least from the perspective of many leading businessmen, admirably combined civic values with appropriate thrift in public spending.

ALIGNING THE TAX CODE WITH THE COMMUNITY CHEST

Although the invention and diffusion of the Community Chest model had provided a powerful bridge between economic advantage and civic influence, this partial linkage of fields was vulnerable to disputes regarding the legitimacy of a central resource: the business contribution. As economic enterprises increasingly took the form of publicly owned corporations, rather than personal or family firms, top management lost the discretion to treat company resources as a means to express their own commitments to community.

Prior to the onset of the Great Depression, some efforts had been made to unravel this apparent contradiction. As early as 1917, a handful of states adopted legislation allowing business charitable contributions on the part of corporations that held charters from that state (Guthrie, 2010, p. 184). During the same moment of response to wartime mobilization, Congress approved charitable deductions from the federal income tax for individuals (Zunz, 2012, p. 88) while some state legislatures made special provisions for chartered banks and public utilities to contribute to the war fund drives. Suggestions were floated to allow the incorporation of a new kind of benevolent organization that would pool contributions for social benefit. But, in large part, this tangle at the intersection of business, charity, and taxation had not been resolved when the onset of depression radically shifted the premises of the discussion. After the tremendous – and all too obviously inadequate – effort to contain the consequences of mass unemployment and drought by relying on a combination of private donations and social service agencies, public programs expanded into the fields of social service where the efforts of Community Chests had once established a bulwark against further increase in services funded by public spending.

Although privately funded charity would continue to be an important source of support for "unemployables," business leaders found their responsibility for maintaining a level – however basic – of support for the workers of their community who had been forcefully preempted by new government programs (Clemens, 2010b). This loss of responsibility, however, freed businessmen to think more expansively about the possible uses of corporate philanthropy now that their contributions would no longer be tied so closely to community needs (Himmelstein, 1996, p. 148).[7] But this would require resolving the legal uncertainties surrounding the principle of business charitable contributions.

One important element of this tangle was relaxed by the Wealth Act of 1935. Introduced to Congress as an administration bill, the one amendment to the final version established the now-familiar 5 percent deduction for business charitable contributions. But legitimation in the eyes of the Internal Revenue Service was not sufficient. Corporations held charters by virtue of state law and it was not until 1953 when the State Supreme Court of New Jersey definitively allowed corporate contributions to charitable enterprises that were not in some way related to business activities. Turning down a shareholder challenge to a donation to Princeton University, the court declared that "There is now widespread belief throughout the nation that free and vigorous nongovernmental institutions of learning are vital to our democracy and the system of free enterprise and that withdrawal of corporate authority to make such contributions within reasonable limits would seriously threaten their continuance" (Muirhead, 1999, p. 20).

With this move, the claim for the moral personhood of the corporation was matched by judicial license for corporations to make donations that were no longer constrained by a strictly profit-oriented sense of what would benefit business. The law could now accommodate the understanding of firms as moral actors, directed by executives committed to some vision of the public good or civic community that could be enacted through contributions. Firms, Emily Barman has argued, extend "their own models of philanthropy to their workplace campaigns. Different models of philanthropy possess differing degrees of elective affinity with different conceptions of community" (2006, p. 12). With respect to charitable contributions, the civic influence of corporations was no longer constrained by distributional obligations to shareholders.

A further organizational development helped to secure these new possibilities as a durable feature of organized systems of voluntary or nonprofit social provision. Prior to the Second World War, only four company foundations had been established. But during the 1950s alone, 160 companies established new foundations which then helped to anchor the philanthropic ecologies of communities across the nation (Muirhead, 1999, p. 34). But if the foundation stabilized flows of funds, other developments undercut the closely connected circuits of coordination that had characterized the earlier Community Chest-Chamber of Commerce configuration. Shortly after the *Smith* decision of 1953, General Electric inaugurated the first employee matching-gift program which transferred control over the direction of a fraction of corporate contributions out of the executive suites (Muirhead, 1999, p. 25).

This contestation of executive control over corporate philanthropy had a political edge. During the Second World War, President Roosevelt had insisted the representatives of organized labor be included in the community councils that oversaw federated fund drives and the distribution of their receipts to local community services as well as to the war effort. After the end of the conflict, and the president's death, business leaders reacted against this forced collaboration with labor. In the course of expelling labor representatives from such deliberations, some corporate leaders also parted way with the broader community elites that had long been central to the organization of community fund-raising (Fones-Wolf, 1994) and opted instead to run "United Fund" campaigns within the workplace. An embrace of urban heterogeneity also threatened the centralized community fund-raising model that had been critical to linking business and civic leaders; members of ethnic communities or activist movements demanded that their causes be represented in the list of beneficiaries of the drives, leading to an expanding practice of donor-choice systems within federated drives (Barman, 2006).

The picture at the national level resembled the heightened contestation of the linking of business power to philanthropic influence within communities. This expansive phase of corporate philanthropy, perhaps inevitably, triggered a political backlash as critics charged that the tax code effectively constituted an overly large and subsidized sphere of business influence over public affairs. During the 1960s, Congressional hearings and revisions to the tax code threatened the arrangements that had developed during the postwar era. This threat, in turn, provoked a defense by philanthropists and nonprofit organizations who combined not simply to protect the situation as it existed but to bolster the concept of a distinct, identifiable nonprofit sector that could be linked to claims for a distinctive role in providing public goods (Barman, 2013, pp. 112−115). In some cities, the strained alliance of business and civic leadership was further challenged by urban riots and demands for corporate transparency in the distribution of their tax-subsidized contributions.

As if the film was playing in reverse, this political backlash against the linking of business influence to civic endeavors was joined by renewed pressure on this hybrid arrangement from markets. From the 1970s onwards, the ability of business leaders to enact broad visions of philanthropy was under renewed attack by shareholders and the threat of mergers and acquisitions as well as by new forms of policing by advocacy organizations concerned over the allegedly liberal tilt of corporate giving (Himmelstein, 1996, pp. 150−56). By the 1990s, "Forced to explain why businesses should give away money while laying off workers, contributions managers at hundreds of companies have come up with an approach that ties corporate contributions directly to strategy. In those and other companies, contributions departments and other and business units are using 'strategic philanthropy'" (Muirhead, 1999, p. 41). In an interesting reversion to the 1920s, corporate philanthropy was once more becoming aligned to cultivating "good will" for specific firms rather than as a means to participate in the collective but private governance of municipal affairs.

TOWARD A THEORY OF HYBRIDIZED FIELDS

Among the classics of business history one can find powerful accounts of how business leaders have managed the tensions between corporate power and democratic norms. In *The American Business Creed*, Francis X. Sutton and his coauthors delineated a distinctive ideological formation which operated through selective silences, notably when the power was involved, whether of firms over customers, of employers over employees, or senior executives over their juniors. A related line of work traces the construction of the corporation as a moral actor or, in Roland Marchand's fine phrase, "creating a corporate soul" (1998). As I have argued here, these ideological and cultural projects were augmented and sustained by a history of institutional development which steadily relaxed the contradictions between democratic citizenship and organized civic benevolence. If the damage to the democratic dignity of individual citizens had produced predictable waves of backlash against business control over community fund-raising, that could be remedied – or at least moderated – by removing those with the greatest political voice from the categories that were vulnerable from such civic diminution.

Ironically, the very success of the New Deal social insurance programs did just this, precisely because of the exclusions along lines of gender and race (specifically domestic and agricultural workers) that have been documented by scholars and deplored by advocates of a more complete realization of civil rights. Whereas encompassing fund-raising campaigns predictably produced arguments in favor of programs supported by public taxation, the introduction of a corporate charitable deduction secured a new and substantial source of funding. Adding further irony, the increasingly progressive character of individual and estate taxation that produced "the Great Compression" of the 1950s and 1960s (Goldin & Margo, 1992) also intensified the incentives for the wealthy to dispose of their funds in a tax-privileged manner. Thus with respect to both the receipt and the funding of benevolence, the great progressive reforms of these decades also disarmed the feedback mechanisms that limited the role of organized benevolence and through it the exercise of political influence by business leaders, the wealthy, and other elites.

At a more analytic level, this history makes an important point about the possibilities of converting economic power into political influence. To the extent that the economy and the polity are organized along different principles – and, surely, the combination of capitalism and democratic egalitarianism constitutes just one such pairing – the conversion of one source of advantage into another will not necessarily be easy or straightforward. In this particular case, networks had to be forged, identities reimagined, and laws changed in order to stabilize the hybridized arrangement that was so effective at equating business leaders and leading citizens for much of the twentieth century. But this stabilization never overcame the underlying differences between the fields of activity that were linked by organizations such as the Community Chests and War Funds. Politics shifted, undermining the capacity of such centralized efforts to be taken as representative of some unified "community." Slowing growth and new fashions in business management steadily constrained the capacity of corporate leaders to promote a broader civic business while juggling the needs of making a profit for the firm.

Thus, at century's end, economic elites again face the democratic dilemma in terms made starker by the growing concern for inequalities of income, wealth, and influence. The felt need for new methods of conversion of wealth into political erupted in business commentary in 2013−2014. Billionaires decried the apparent outbreak of class warfare; one venture capitalist even asserted that the wealthy should be given more votes than others. In response to a growing political debate over inequality − exemplified by the Occupy movement and the furor over Mitt Romney's comments about "the 47 percent" who are "dependent upon government" and "pay no income tax" − there has also been a reenergized pattern of experimentation with new vehicles and networks of elite political influence[8] in parallel with celebrations of "philanthrocapitalism" (Bishop & Green, 2008) and "social entrepreneurship" as extra-political means of addressing the ills of the nation and the world. This cacophony of celebratory and critical debate over new varieties of "public-private partnerships" signals the felt absence of a reliable means for converting one source of power into another, the insufficiency of hybrid arrangements linking the economic and the civic in polities that remain formally and ideologically democratic.

NOTES

1. Larry Bartels begins his recent *Unequal Democracy* (2008) by quoting the first line of Robert Dahl's classic *Who Governs?* (1961): "In a political system where nearly every adult may vote but where knowledge, wealth, social position, access to officials, and other resources are unequally distributed, who actually governs?" (2008, p. 1).
2. This claim is foundational to the influential work of Mills (1956) and Domhoff (1967).
3. But see Crawford and Ostrom (1995) on the importance of "may" statements within institutional grammars.
4. This linkage of the corporate model of organization to charitable causes had appeared in the eighteenth century in England. As Linda Colley describes Britain's

first hospital for foundlings, organized by Thomas Coram: "the charity was run in their commercial image. As a voluntary corporate body with its own directors and legal identity, it was modeled on London's joint-stock-companies, the first time an organization of this kind had been extended to the work of philanthropy. The hospital's avowed aim was mercantilist as well as humanitarian; to rescue young lives that would otherwise be wasted and render them useful to the state" (1992, p. 59). Playing out in a democratic rather than mercantilist context, American economic elites faced a similar challenge of harnessing economic advantage to public projects.

5. "Community Chest Corollaries," *The Survey* (June 15, 1925), p. 344; Homer W. Borst, "Community Chests and Relief: A Reply," *The Survey* (October 15, 1930), p. 74.

6. This configuration of power was noted by contemporary observers. As Philip Klein, Director of Research at the New York School of Social Work, wrote to Julius Rosenwald, a noted philanthropist, opponent of endowments in perpetuity, and president of Sears, Roebuck: "the so-called Community Trusts, which beginning with the Cleveland Foundation, organized by the farsightedness of Judge Goff and his dread of the 'dead hand,' have spread over the country until there are scores of them now in existence. These Trusts seem to me to substitute for the well intentioned and sincerely motivated 'dead hand' one that is not technically dead but whose motives are far from those of devoted donors. Funds are being accumulated under the control of financial institutions with only a perfunctory provision for informed and interested guidance by those most intensely interested and informed on the social work problems of the day." P. K. to J. R., May 17, 1929, Box III, Folder 6, Julius Rosenwald Papers, University of Chicago Special Collections. See also Kelso (1932).

7. Tightly linked networks of corporate donors and social services continued to characterize a number of the national's major metropolitan areas including, perhaps most famously, Minneapolis-St. Paul (Galaskiewicz, 1985).

8. See, for example, "Big-Money Donors Demand Larger Say in Party Strategy," *New York Times* (March 2, 2014), p. 1.

REFERENCES

Almond, G. A. (1998 [1938]). *Plutocracy and politics in New York city*. Boulder, CO: Westview Press.

Barman, E. (2006). *Contesting communities: The transformation of workplace charity*. Stanford, CA: Stanford University Press.

Barman, E. (2013). Classificatory struggles in the nonprofit sector: The formation of the national taxonomy of exempt entities, 1969–1987. *Social Science History, 37*(1), 103–141.

Bartels, L. M. (2008). *Unequal democracy: The political economy of the new gilded age*. Princeton, NJ: Princeton University Press.

Bellows, B. L. (1993). *Benevolence among slaveholders: Assisting the poor in Charleston, 1670–1860*. London: Louisiana State University Press.

Bishop, M., & Green, M. (2008). *Philanthrocapitalism: How giving can save the world*. New York, NY: Bloomsbury Press.

Bridges, A. B. (1982). Another look at plutocracy and politics in antebellum New York city. *Political Science Quarterly*, *97*(1), 57–71.

Clemens, E. S. (2009). The problem of the corporation: Liberalism and the large organization. In P. Adler (Ed.), *Handbook of organizational studies and classical social theory*. Oxford: Oxford University Press.

Clemens, E. S. (2010a). From city club to nation state: Business networks in American political development. *Theory and Society*, *39*, 377–396.

Clemens, E. S. (2010b). In the shadow of the new deal: Reconfiguring the roles of government and charity, 1928–1940. In E. Clemens & D. Guthrie (Eds.), 2010 *Politics and partnerships: Voluntary associations in America's political past and present*. Chicago, IL: University of Chicago Press.

Colley, L. (1992). *Britons: Forging the nation, 1707–1837*. New Haven, CT: Yale University Press.

Crawford, S. E. S., & Ostrom, E. (1995). A grammar of institutions. *American Political Science Review*, *89*(3), 582–600.

Cutlip, S. M. (1965). *Fund raising in the United States: Its role in America's philanthropy*. New Brunswick, NJ: Rutgers University Press.

Dahl, R. A. (1961). *Who governs? Democracy and power in an American city*. New Haven, CT: Yale University Press.

Dalzell, R. F., Jr. (1987). *Enterprising elite: The Boston associates and the world they made*. Cambridge, MA: Harvard University Press.

Davenport, R. W. (1951). *U.S.A. The permanent revolution*. New York, NY: Prentice-Hall.

Domhoff, G. W. (1967). *Who rules America?* Englewood Cliffs, NJ: Prentice-Hall.

Fones-Wolf, E. A. (1994). *Selling free enterprise: The business assault on labor and liberalism, 1945–60*. Chicago, IL: University of Illinois Press.

Galaskiewicz, J. (1985). *Social organization of an urban grants economy: A study of business philanthropy and nonprofit organizations*. Orlando, FL: Academic Press.

Goldin, C., & Margo, R. (1992). The great compression: The wage structure in the United States at mid-century. *Quarterly Journal of Economics*, *107*(1), 1–34.

Guthrie, D. (2010). Corporate philanthropy in the United States: What causes do corporations back? In E. S. Clemens & D. Guthrie (Eds.), *Politics and partnerships: Voluntary associations in America's political past and present*. Chicago, IL: University of Chicago Press.

Hall, P. D. (1982). *The organization of American culture, 1700–1900: Private institutions, elites, and the origins of American nationality*. New York, NY: New York University Press.

Haydu, J. (2008). *Citizen employers: Business communities and labor in Cincinnati and San Francisco, 1870–1916*. Ithaca, NY: ILR press.

Heale, M. J. (1976). From city fathers to social critics: Humanitarianism and government in New York, 1790–1860. *Journal of American History*, *63*(1), 21–41.

Himmelstein, J. L. (1996). Corporate philanthropy and business power. In D. F. Burlingame & D. R. Young (Eds.), *Corporate philanthropy at the crossroads*. Indianapolis, IN: Indiana University Press.

Jacoby, S. M. (1997). *Modern manors: Welfare capitalism since the new deal*. Princeton, NJ: Princeton University Press.

Kelso, R. W. (1932). Banker control of community chests. *The Survey* (May 1), *68*(3), 117–119.
Lee, J. (1928). The chest and social work. *The Survey*, *59*(12), 749–750.
Lockley, T. J. (2007). *Welfare and charity in the Antebellum South*. Gainesville, FL: University Press of Florida.
Marchand, R. (1998). *Creating the corporate soul: The rise of public relations and corporate imagery in American big business*. Berkeley, CA: University of California Press.
Mills, C. W. (1956). *The power elite*. New York, NY: Oxford University Press.
Mizruchi, M. S. (2013). *The fracturing of the American corporate elite*. Cambridge, MA: Harvard University Press.
Muirhead, S. A. (1999). *Corporate contributions: The view from 50 years*. New York, NY: The Conference Board.
Murray, F. (2010). The oncomouse that roared: Hybrid exchange strategies as a source of productive tension at the boundary of overlapping institutions. *American Journal of Sociology*, *116*(2), 341–388.
Neem, J. (2008). *Creating a nation of jointers: Democracy and civil society in early national Massachusetts*. Cambridge, MA: Harvard University Press.
Pease, W. H., & Pease, J. H. (1985). *The web of progress: Private values and public styles in Boston and Charleston, 1828–1843*. New York, NY: Oxford University Press.
Roy, W. (1997). *Socializing capital: The rise of the large industrial corporation in America*. Princeton, NJ: Princeton University Press.
Russell, F. A., Lyons, R. W., & Flickinger, S. M. (1931). The social and economic aspects of chain stores. *The American Economic Review*, *21*(1), 27–36.
Sutton, F. X., Harris, S. E., Kaysen, C., & Tobin, J. (1956). *The American business creed*. Cambridge, MA: Harvard University Press.
Todd, A. J. (1932). Some sociological principles underlying the community chest movement. *Social Forces*, *10*(4), 476–484.
Verba, S., & Orren, G. (1985). *Equality in America: The view from the top*. Cambridge, MA: Harvard University Press.
Zunz, O. (2012). *Philanthropy in America: A history*. Princeton, NJ: Princeton University Press.

LEGITIMATION STRATEGIES OF CORPORATE ELITES IN THE FIELD OF LABOR REGULATION: CHANGING RESPONSES TO GLOBAL FRAMEWORK AGREEMENTS

Markus Helfen, Elke Schüßler and Sebastian Botzem

ABSTRACT

Corporate elites are increasingly held responsible for issues of sustainability including working conditions and workers' rights in global production networks. We still know relatively little about how they respond to concrete stakeholder initiatives aiming to restrict corporate voluntarism through transnational regulation. In this paper we report comparative findings on corporate legitimation strategies in response to requests by labor representatives to sign Global Framework Agreements (GFAs). These agreements are intended to hold multinational corporations (MNCs) accountable for the implementation of core labor standards across their supply chains. We propose to broaden management-focused analyses of corporate legitimation strategies by applying a field-oriented perspective that considers the embeddedness of management in a broader web of strategic activity and variable opportunity structures. Our findings suggest that legitimation strategies are developed dynamically along with the rules, positions, and understandings developing around specific regulatory issues in sequences of interactions between elites and challenging groups.

Keywords: Legitimation; sustainability; Global Framework Agreements; transnational regulation

INTRODUCTION

As indicated by the proliferation of terms such as perception and impression management, public affairs management, or corporate social responsibility, legitimizing corporate activities vis-à-vis external expectations has become an important management activity that goes beyond traditional public relations (e.g., Kostova & Zaheer, 1999; Strike, Gao, & Bansal, 2006). Multinational corporations (MNCs) in particular are increasingly scrutinized by civil society groups and nongovernmental organizations (NGOs) criticizing the violation of labor rights or environmental standards. Given that activities of MNCs extend across national jurisdictions, corporate elites are confronted by multiple efforts to regulate their behavior on a transnational level (Waddock, 2008). And yet, in the absence of a state-like authority, corporations are also called upon to participate in creating, shaping, and enforcing emerging environmental and social regulations (Scherer & Palazzo, 2011).

On the one hand, corporate elites try to exploit the existence of multiple regulatory initiatives by avoiding any binding regulation or shifting toward a forum in which rules are set that are in line with their interests (Quack, 2013). On the other hand, corporate elites cannot take their influence within organizational domains or on regulatory policies for granted because different actors, among them even small NGOs and social movements, can raise challenges that make transnational fields contested and fluid (Djelic & Quack, 2008; Djelic & Sahlin-Andersson, 2006). Scherer, Palazzo, and Seidl (2013) have recently argued that in complex global environments corporations use three different, and at times contradictory, legitimation strategies: adaptation, manipulation, and moral reasoning. In so doing, they seek to account for heterogeneity and dynamism in stakeholder expectations, appeasing or co-opting challengers while preserving as much autonomy as possible. While Scherer et al. (2013) discuss how organizations intend to cope with the paradoxical tensions posed by such an approach, they do not study the dynamic interplay and resultant shift in the corporate elites' legitimation strategies over time within a specific field of regulation.

In this paper, we examine how corporate elites dynamically adjust their legitimation strategies in response to legitimacy threats in the field of transnational labor regulation emerging around Global Framework Agreements (GFAs). GFAs are company-based agreements codifying MNCs' commitment to comply with core labor standards defined by the International Labor Organization (ILO) across their supply chains. They are negotiated and signed by Global Union Federations (GUFs) and top management representatives. As such, they can be regarded as a joint attempt of MNCs and civil society actors — specifically trade unions and their global federations — to regulate labor relations transnationally and to monitor compliance. Similar to other attempts of regulating transnational sustainability issues (Palazzo & Scherer, 2006), the actual impact of such negotiated agreements for workers at the bottom of the pyramid is still unclear. However, the range of elite reactions to GFAs indicates that such agreements have the potential to effectively challenge corporate elites' positions in the field of labor regulation. GFAs thus provide a rich empirical setting in which to analyze *how legitimation strategies of corporate elites evolve through the interaction with challenging actors in contested transnational regulatory fields.*

In only two cases of our sample of 12 MNCs engaging in GFA negotiations corporate elites changed their legitimation strategy and shifted from initial resistance toward engagement in moral reasoning with corporate challengers. In the other cases, MNCs only marginally changed their legitimation strategies from resistance toward selective adaptation of GFAs or manipulation of the agreements in order to avoid an actual change in behavior. The extent of change and type of legitimation strategy adopted depended on the enactment of opportunity structures provided by transnational institutional heterogeneity, established patterns of national labor relations, and specific actor constellations. Thus, our study suggests that legitimation strategies need to be understood as developing out of a process of contestation embedded in and impacting on the rules, positions, and understandings around a substantive domain of regulation.

THEORETICAL FRAMEWORK

Corporate Elites in Transnational Regulatory Fields

Transnational regulatory arrangements have emerged in different contexts, ranging from the realm of professional services (e.g., Suddaby, Cooper, & Greenwood, 2007) and financial markets (e.g., Mayntz, 2012) to that of various social and environmental standards (e.g., Overdevest, 2010). They tend to be driven predominantly by private actors such as corporations and NGOs (e.g., Bartley, 2005) but are also impacted by public actors, that is, governments and international organizations (e.g., Schüßler, Rüling, & Wittneben, 2014). In any case, transnational regulation always involves negotiations and struggles among a diverse set of actors with conflicting interests, thereby leading to reconfigurations of rule-setting authority between public and private actors (Botzem & Hofmann, 2010). Central questions in researching transnational regulation thus revolve around who is able to claim and provide legitimacy for rule-setting and monitoring, as well as how other actors in the field respond to these activities (Dezalay & Garth, 2010; Quack, 2010; Zürn, 2004).

Although we know less about the power resources of corporate elites on a transnational level, we know from national contexts that corporate leaders commonly have command over financial and often social capital that allows them to influence important policy decisions (Mills, 2000/1956; Useem, 1984). As recent evidence shows, transnational elites are firmly embedded in national arenas (Carroll, 2009). Such power is often considered structural, based on connections to elite networks and public agencies (e.g., Barley, 2007, 2010; Davis, 1991; Davis & Greve, 1997; Davis & Mizruchi, 1999; Mizruchi, 2004; Pfeffer & Salancik, 2003). Equally, institutions like corporate law, property rights, professions, or social customs (DiMaggio & Powell, 1991; Hensmans, 2003; Lawrence, 2008) are important elements of national elites' power resources. At the transnational level, elite studies using structural network analyses have identified similar groups and overlaps, mainly between European and North American corporations given shared activities on transnational boards (Carroll & Sapinski, 2010). While these studies shed some light on the potential of corporate elites to influence transnational regulatory processes, they largely neglect contestation dynamics in which management practices are being challenged by outside actors.

A field-level approach is useful to capture these dynamics because it recognizes the fluidity of elites in today's globalized, postindustrial society in which legitimate influence is the outcome of specific interaction patterns in complex webs of relationships (Bernstein, 2011; Harvey & Maclean, 2010; Malets & Quack, 2013; Quack, 2013). Regulatory fields typically form around a contested issue and evolve as actors struggle over the rules, positions, and understandings dominating the field (Hoffman, 1999; Levy, 2008; Rao et al., 2000). Business actors participate in these fields in various guises, so we define corporate elites broadly as going beyond the directors of the world's largest 500 corporations who sit on at least two G500 directorates (cf. Carroll, 2009) to also include the supportive stratum of managers occupying positions below the peak level (cf. Kerr & Robinson, 2012), as well as a host of professional business consultants, policy advisors, and representatives from business associations involved in shaping emerging regulations (Zald & Lounsbury, 2010).

Corporate elites are regularly drawn into contest over the rules, positions, and understandings around specific regulatory issues by challengers in the form of advocacy coalitions and social movements (e.g., Lounsbury, Ventresca, & Hirsch, 2003; McAdam & Scott, 2005). Such "strategic action fields" are characterized by dynamism and change, because actors "make moves and other actors have to interpret them, consider their options, and act. Actors who are both more and less powerful are constantly making adjustments to the conditions in the field given their position and the actions of others" (Fligstein & McAdam, 2011, p. 5). Yet, despite this dynamic conception of strategic agency, actors' positions are still often considered as relatively static, with challengers thought to populate niches in the field that ordinarily wield little influence. Both corporate elites and challenging groups, however, need to socially construct and fight for their positions in a regulatory arena through the use and dynamic adjustment of legitimation strategies (Dezalay & Garth, 2010, p. 117).

Toward a Field-Oriented Analysis of Legitimation Strategies

Legitimacy can be understood as a "generalized perception or assumption that the actions of an entity are desirable, proper, or appropriate within some socially constructed system of norms, values, beliefs, and definitions" (Suchman, 1995, p. 574). As such, legitimacy is important for all organizations, because it allows them to acquire material and human resources necessary to survive (Aldrich & Fiol, 1994), grow (Khaire, 2010), and change (Suddaby & Greenwood, 2005). Much of the research on organizational legitimation strategies has focused on the discursive, rhetorical efforts of organizations to rationalize, normalize, or theorize their actions vis-à-vis opponents and the wider public. Corporations, for instance, use legitimation strategies to gain acceptance for organizational changes such as restructuring and downsizing (e.g., Erkama & Vaara, 2010; Vaara, Tienari, & Laurila, 2006). However, legitimacy not only depends on managing public perception, it also rests on the underlying socially constructed system of norms and formal regulations against which such perceptions of legitimacy are defined and challenged. Legitimacy is thus closely tied to the hegemony of those who shape rule systems and demand rule following (Ashforth & Gibbs, 1990; Pfeffer & Salancik, 2003).

The groundwork for research on corporate legitimation strategies has been laid by Oliver (1991), who outlines five possible strategic responses to external expectation: acquiescence, compromise, avoidance, defiance, and manipulation. Building on this concept, efforts to gain, maintain, or repair legitimacy are often broadly classified as either strategic, that is, oriented toward the manipulation of symbols and meaning structures, or institutional, oriented toward adapting to external expectations (Suchman, 1995). In transnational fields, however, there is no unequivocal, stable set of cultural or normative expectations that can serve as a reference point for established legitimation strategies. Instead, organizations — and MNCs and their corporate elites in particular — seek to justify their practices and procedures through processes of moral reasoning with diverse stakeholders (Palazzo & Scherer, 2006; Suchman, 1995). Unlike manipulation tactics that are oriented toward imposing ones' view over others, Scherer et al. (2013) consider moral reasoning as an open-ended discursive process that involves learning and adaptation by incumbents and challengers alike. However, moral reasoning is often employed alongside adaptation and manipulation strategies, and the resulting patterns of legitimation strategies lack empirical elaboration to date.

Moral reasoning and emerging regulations also provide challengers with new options by which to question the corporate elites' legitimacy. For instance, sports manufacturers like Puma or Adidas have adapted to the new behavioral standard established by competitor Nike in increasing supply chain transparency (Frenkel & Scott, 2002), at the same time engaging in a stakeholder dialogue and trying to manipulate public perception with regard to environmental issues (Scherer et al., 2013). In one of the few existing studies examining sequences of interactions between corporations and challenging groups, Bartley (2003, 2007) finds that corporate responses to labor rights campaigns changed from the symbolic adoption of Codes of Conduct to the establishment of independent monitoring bodies in order to defend corporate legitimacy in the face of ongoing stakeholder pressure. Thus, transnational regulatory fields are like other fields a space of possibilities (cf. Bourdieu, 1985, p. 737) for both corporate elites and challenging actors in which opportunity structures are created and enacted dynamically in specific actor constellations and with regard to specific regulatory issues.

EMPIRICAL STUDY: REGULATING LABOR RELATIONS THROUGH GLOBAL FRAMEWORK AGREEMENTS

Research Setting

We draw on empirical data from a large, multi-country study of the emerging field of regulating transnational labor relations through GFAs (Arruda, Fichter, Helfen, & Sydow, 2012; Fichter & Helfen, 2011; Fichter, Helfen, & Schiederig, 2013; Fichter, Helfen, & Sydow, 2011; Fichter, Sayim, & Agtas, 2013; Fichter & Stevis, 2013; Fichter, Stevis, & Helfen, 2012; Fichter, Sydow, et al., 2012; Gartenberg & Bandekar, 2011; Helfen & Fichter, 2013; Helfen, Fichter, & Sydow, 2012; Helfen & Sydow, 2013).[1] The starting point of this research is that GFAs are signed between GUFs and MNCs to implement core ILO labor standards[2] across MNCs' global operations, often including suppliers and joint ventures in the production network (Fichter et al., 2011). GFAs represent a form of regulation situated between voluntary standards (like corporate Codes of Conduct) and international law. They are distinct from accreditation and certification schemes in that they are based on institutionalized mechanisms of labor representation and interest aggregation (Hammer, 2005; Kocher, 2008; Mund & Priegnitz, 2007). For GUFs, GFAs provide an opportunity to influence global labor standards by bilateral, direct dealings with MNCs, as opposed to attempts to influence standards indirectly via the ILO whose conventions are directed at nation states and do not have MNCs as immediate addressees. GFAs thus promise a considerable, strategically important benefit for GUFs to contribute to the extension of industrial human rights, for example, the right to form independent unions or the right to bargain collectively throughout MNCs' global operations. Additionally, GUFs see GFAs as an opportunity for securing their own recognition as a legitimate negotiation partner, since GFAs are, in many cases, the first instances in which MNC accept these union bodies as negotiating on behalf of employees (Fichter, Helfen, et al., 2013).

The transnational business community, represented through bodies like the International Organization of Employers (IOE) or the European Roundtable of Industrialists (ERI), tends to disregard GFAs as an appropriate instrument through which to regulate labor relations. According to our interviews with representatives from these bodies, there is no consensus on supporting GFAs ideationally or actively. If individual MNCs sign a GFA, the issue is tolerated by way of taking a skeptical, but neutral stance. The vast majority of the approximately 80,000 MNCs (UNCTAD) have still not signed a GFA and thus, by and large, follow a strategy of voluntarism. MNCs for their part typically either do not perceive deficits in labor relations as an urgent issue, are entirely satisfied with a unilateral (CSR) approach, or are not convinced that GFAs bring a reliable solution for labor problems. Most MNCs follow a strategy of voluntary self-regulation in the form of Codes of Conduct, encompassing but not focusing on labor-related matters (Bartley, 2005). The corporate elite is in a favorable position in cross-border economic exchanges because social movement pressure by unions is weak, many governments do not enforce workers' rights, and the transnational regulatory body (i.e., the ILO) lacks sanction-based enforcement mechanisms.

Nevertheless, a combination of reputation concerns due to high visibility in consumer markets, CSR policies, the tradition of cooperative labor relations at headquarters, and union pressure can increase the willingness of individual MNCs to sign a GFA (e.g., Helfen & Fichter, 2013; Helfen et al., 2012). The large majority of the 118 GFAs signed from the mid-1990s up until the end of 2013 have been negotiated with MNCs from continental Western Europe (21 Germany, 17 Scandinavia, 13 France, 12 Southern Europe, 9 Benelux), although the last five years have seen a slow increase in the number of agreements with MNCs whose headquarters are located in other parts of the world such as the United States, South Africa, Brazil, Japan, Canada, Indonesia, Australia, and New Zealand (see Table 1).

GFAs are company-specific, but are rooted in a wider transnational regulatory field in which nationally embedded and globally operating actor groups and networks struggle for influence on the employment policies and practices of MNCs. This "GFA arena" (Helfen & Fichter, 2013, p. 556) is similar to other transnational regulatory fields in its multiple layers of regulation (Djelic & Quack, 2003, 2010; Djelic & Sahlin-Andersson, 2006; Morgan & Kristensen, 2006): policy processes related to ILO standards, the presence of regional and national industrial relations institutions and

Table 1. Global Framework Agreements, December 2013 (Own Compilation According to GUFs' Webpages).

Global Union Federations (GUFs)[a]	Sectors	Total No. of GFAs[b]	No. of GFAs with Non-European MNCs
IndustriAll[c]	Car manufacturing, energy, chemical industry, machine tool and metal engineering, apparel and textiles	43	5
UNI global union	Telecommunication, retailing, commerce, property and facility services, temporary work agencies, printing and media, finance	50[d]	16[d]
BWI	Construction and building, building materials, woodworking	17	–
IUF	Hotels and catering, food and beverages	8	3
Total		**118**	**24**

[a]The Public Service International has also been involved in negotiating GFAs, but always as a cosignatory to IndustriAll.
[b]As counted in terms of signing MNCs.
[c]Containing all GFAs originally signed by IMF, ICEM, and ITGWLF.
[d]The total number of agreements within the domain of UNI is difficult to assess. UNI self-declares to have signed its 50th agreement in 2013. Due to various reasons, however, the actual number of GFAs is very likely to be lower. For example, many of the non-European agreements have only a restricted geographical scope; mergers, acquisitions, and liquidations have reduced the agreements still effective; some agreements lack in substantive jurisdiction.

legacies, and realities of company-level formal and informal regulations. In addition, the arena is marked by capital-labor antinomy (Fichter, Stevis, et al., 2012; Helfen & Fichter, 2013). On the labor side, works councils (European, world) are involved along with national affiliates and the GUFs. On the management side, involvement is usually from HR department heads, industrial relations experts, top management, and business associations on different levels.

Combined, the multilateral and multilevel nature of the GFA arena implies complex and heterogeneous actor constellations comprising (organized) labor and management actors at the transnational level (single MNCs and GUFs), national/sectoral level (national/sector unions and employer associations), MNC headquarter level in the home country, and at the level of local subsidiaries/suppliers in host countries. As a research setting, GFAs thus allow us to observe how corporate legitimation strategies are used and change in line with emerging regulations in a complex, multilayered opportunity structures.

Data Collection and Analysis

For this paper, we take a bird's eye perspective on 28 case studies on GFAs conducted by an international research team in different GUF domains and in four different countries (Brazil, India, the United States, Turkey) (e.g., Fichter & Helfen, 2011; Fichter et al., 2011). We reinterpret and summarize this case study material through the lens of legitimation strategies of corporate elites faced with a moral reasoning challenge. We focus in depth on 12 case studies from manufacturing industries for greater comparability.

The original data collection effort between 2008 and 2011 included primary data (interviews with both parties of the agreements at the HQ level as well as with selected subsidiaries) and a host of secondary data (agreements themselves, interviews with third parties like employer associations and NGOs, companies' CSR and sustainability reports, and other documents containing general information about the cases). For the interview data, the aim was to have at least one interview per actor group and country for MNCs in the domains of four GUFs (now three due to the merger of ICEM, IMF, and the ITGWLF to IndustriAll (2012)).

Within this overall approach, the research team conducted 146 semi-structured interviews with representatives of management and labor at the headquarter level and at corporate production sites in India, the United States, Brazil, and Turkey (See Table 2). Taken together, this data material allows us to capture varying perspectives, divergent assessments, and common evaluations among the most relevant actors, above all, MNCs and GUFs across the transnational regulatory field in focus.

Out of all 28 MNCs, 22 already had a signed GFA before the field phase, 1 signed the GFA after the end of 2011, and 5 have not signed a GFA to date. The 12 cases we focus on in this paper are all in the domain of IndustriAll and BWI, actually have a GFA, and are empirically captured by at least one pair of interviews with management and labor representatives involved in the GFA process.

Remaining gaps in the data collection process were filled either through secondary material or the growing literature on GFAs (e.g., Davies, Williams, & Hammer, 2011; Dehnen, 2013; Egels-Zandén, 2009; Hammer, 2005; Niforou, 2011; Williams, Davies, & Chinguno, 2013; for an extensive overview see Papadakis, 2011). For the secondary material, we draw on a text analysis of 73 GFAs (as of 2009). This analysis includes the 12 cases that examine core features of the formal agreements, such as parties'

Table 2. Interview Material.

GUF	Total Sample	Subsample	IndustriAll	BWI
No. of MNCs	28	12	7	5
Management headquarter	28	18	11	7
Unions headquarter	50	19	10	9
Management local	23	18	16	5
Unions local	45	22	17	5
Sum	**146**	**80**	**54**	**26**

goals, the relationship between the parties, substantive content, scope, conflict resolution mechanisms, termination rules, and signatories. In addition, the research team examined numerous sources such as policy statements of GUFs and employer associations, internet pages, and press releases.

In order to identify typical trajectories — historically rooted pathways resulting from repeated interactions (Malets & Quack, 2013) — of how corporate elites respond to the moral reasoning challenge posed by GFAs, we draw on thick case descriptions and coding efforts developed in different stages of the original research process (see above) to derive an overall synthesizing picture for the subsample. We trace MNCs' trajectories from the initial proposal by the unions to sign a GFA, through to the preliminary management reaction, ensuing respective union responses and finally the subsequent managerial reaction. We have hereby applied the three types of corporate legitimation strategies distinguished by Scherer et al. (2013): moral reasoning, manipulation, and adaptation. In presenting our results we abstract from details of single cases to provide an overview of managerial approaches to GFAs.

FINDINGS

Starting Conditions

Although there are a few exceptions, the typical GFA negotiation process unfolds as follows (see also Helfen & Sydow, 2013): (1) the GUFs (more often than not supported and even led by national unions and works councils at the MNC headquarters) try to enter into negotiations with MNC management by applying various soft (and, rarely, strong) pressure tactics;

(2) management initially responds by declining the request on several grounds, but gives in and starts official negotiations if (3) the union side continues pushing for an agreement; (4) during negotiations management either continues to react with resilience through manipulation tactics or opens up a moral reasoning process depending on unions' bargaining position and concessions as well as on the management approach to labor relations. (5) Finally, an agreement is reached which then opens up the space for further (re-)negotiations and debates as the implementation of the agreement is tested, evaluated, and monitored. From there on, a new iteration — somewhat equivalent to the first phase — starts on a very different ground.

In all of our 12 cases, initiating GFA negotiations has been particularly difficult and demanding, since management and labor actors begin with very different perceptions about the need for global labor standards in the first place (Fichter et al., 2011). On the union side, a consent formation process is already required in that the GUFs convince their affiliates of the adequacy of a company-based policy process for dealing with violations of core ILO labor standards (see also Croucher & Cotton, 2009; Hammer, 2005; Papadakis, 2011). On the level of individual MNCs, management reacted with tactics of defiance such as criticizing GFAs as a tool or claiming voluntary CSR initiatives to be sufficient in all but one of our cases. A change in managerial reluctance typically occurred only after several rounds of reiteration between the parties, somewhere between 6 months and three years.

Typical Trajectories of Legitimation Strategies

We can identify essentially three different trajectories of legitimation strategies across our sample of 12 MNCs: (1) a trajectory of responsibility-taking, in which MNCs adopt active measures to implement core labor standards across their supply chains (e.g., ChemCorp, documented in Fichter et al., 2011; Helfen & Sydow, 2013); (2) a trajectory of responsibility delegating and shifting, in which MNCs selectively respond to stakeholder demands (e.g., MetalCorp, documented in Fichter et al., 2011; Helfen & Fichter, 2013; Helfen & Sydow, 2013); and (3) a trajectory of responsibility avoiding, in which there is a hollow agreement (Helfen & Sydow, 2013) followed by almost no active implementation activities (e.g., ResourceCorp, documented in Fichter et al., 2011; Helfen & Sydow, 2013).

Table 3. Classification of Cases and Outcomes.

Avoiding responsibility	ResourceCorp, BWI, France
	RubberCorp, IndustriAll, Germany
	BuildCorp, BWI, Germany
	MaterialCorp, IndustriAll, Germany
Delegating and shifting responsibility	ConCorp, BWI, Scandinavia
	WireCorp, IndustriAll, Germany
	FurnCorp, BWI, Germany
	CarCorp, IndustriAll, Germany
	MetalCorp, IndustriAll, Germany
	PapCorp, IndustriAll, Scandinavia
Taking responsibility	ChemCorp, IndustriAll, France
	PenCorp, BWI, Germany

These trajectories did not evolve in a linear way, but were carried forward by different situational opportunity structures and legitimation strategies on various levels. Table 3 places each of our cases within one of these three trajectories.

Delegating and Shifting Responsibility
The most common trajectory is the middle one in Fig. 1, leading from initial management defiance toward engagement in moral reasoning with labor stakeholders, converting to selective adaptation of stakeholder demands and resulting finally in the delegation and shifting of responsibility where possible (six MNCs). Here, the GFAs tend to outline specific implementation policies and escalation procedures, but exemplary good practices and initiatives in some areas are accompanied by passivity and neglect in others. For example, formalized mechanisms of monitoring and conflict resolution set up by MNCs might not be extended to all facilities. Swedish-based *PapCorp* is an exemplar of this phenomenon: the agreement's implementation is outstanding in one of its North American divisions, where an exceptional multiplant collective agreement with the United Steelworkers has been signed, but implementation is weak in other business divisions and countries. For instance, in Colombia there appears to be a problem with PapCorp shifting responsibility for the agreement's implementation to the management team of a joint venture:

> We have some problems sometimes, but we can't say that PapCorp is the primary trouble maker, because PapCorp is involved in joint ventures in different parts of the world, especially in Latin America, in a country like Colombia. And sometimes we get rumours, more or less, that maybe this joint venture company is not following (…). They don't accept the establishing of trade unions. But we have no proof, and we can't

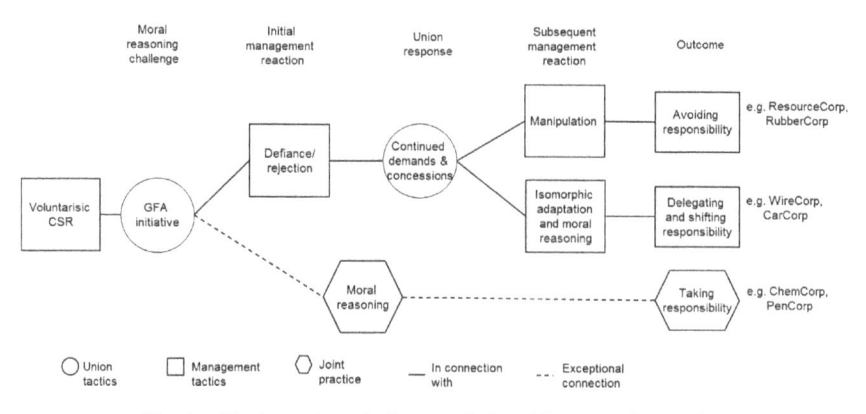

Fig. 1. Trajectories of Changes in Legitimation Strategies.

find people who want to come forward and say: "I lost my job because I tried to organize a new trade union." (PapCorp, union at headquarter)

As mentioned, good policies may also be thwarted by MNC passivity, as exemplified by German-based *WireCorp*. *WireCorp* is a relatively small MNC, but has a high number of global locations. As such, the European works council (EWC) with support from the union operating at *WireCorp's* headquarter has been labor's leading agreement negotiator "in the spirit of constructive and cooperative conflict management" (WireCorp GFA). However, management has called the agreement a "joint declaration" and has insisted on its legally nonbinding character:

> That is a declaration, but not an agreement, and it has been coordinated consensually with the EWC, but not negotiated. (WireCorp, headquarter management)

The works council responded to this approach with a concessionary bargaining style triggering some objections from the union at *WireCorp's* headquarter location:

> At WireCorp, we have a weak works council. And we have many non-unionized sites or sites with weak unions. Against this background one sometimes asks: "Is it worth putting all that effort and energy into negotiating a GFA?" (WireCorp, union at headquarter)

Nevertheless, the same union representative admits that complaint handling produces at least some results:

> (...) for example, we had reports from unions trying to organize at two locations in Romania. The unions tried to get in, but were blocked by local management. We put

this issue on the table in the EWC meetings with central management. And finally, the local unions were able to organize these plants. (WireCorp, union at headquarter)

In fact, many German and Scandinavian MNEs follow this trajectory. In these countries, labor representation at the headquarters is strongly institutionalized and labor relations tend to be cooperative as state regulation is supportive of union rights strengthening the overall bargaining power of labor actors. Even if management initially tries to defy the GFA for the reasons mentioned above, unions continue to exert pressure until, eventually, corporate elites engage in moral reasoning to accommodate and pacify external demands interactively.

Avoiding Responsibility

The second most common trajectory is one that leads from defiance toward the use of manipulation strategies, resulting ultimately in avoidance of responsibility (four MNEs). Essentially, management in these cases strategically drafts a GFA with the aim of avoiding open opposition, but uses various manipulation tactics to avoid an actual change in behavior. For example, we find cases in which management successfully restricted the scope of the agreements by declaring direct control of operations as a necessary precondition, directly excluding joint ventures, majority and minority investments, and subcontractors. In such cases, the GFA is not typically integrated in an MNC's sourcing policy and no responsibility is taken for (deviant) partners in business relationships (e.g., *ResourceCorp*, *BuildCorp*). Furthermore, management often manipulated the scope of an agreement by defining local customs and regulations as a restricting condition. This approach is well illustrated in the case of *ResourceCorp* (cf. Helfen & Sydow, 2013):

It is not our responsibility to operate our sub-contractors. We are not to interfere with the business management of our sub-contractors or either it won't be sub-contracting but ResourceCorp. (ResourceCorp, headquarter management 1)

In other cases, the procedure of complaint handling is underspecified, ad hoc, and informal. This shifts the burden of proof of violations to the unions and opens up leeway for postponing the resolution of problems that emerge. Where neither a formal procedure nor clear-cut organizational accountability for the GFA is defined, the agreement cannot be put into practice locally without difficulty.

Strategic manipulation by corporate elites provides the basis for a weak agreement that delegates responsibility. One path in this direction may be a headquarter-level social partnership in which labor representatives are co-opted as comanagers and the management effectively only negotiates with these representatives (e.g., worker representatives on the supervisory board or works councils) thereby excluding labor actors like GUFs' local affiliates, which might be more sensitive to local problems (e.g., *BuildCorp*). Another manipulation tactic is a paternalistic strategy typical for family-owned firms that claim responsibility for their own actions and neutralize critique by emphasizing how needs are taken care of by a traditional distribution of rights and responsibilities (e.g., *ResourceCorp*, *RubberCorp*). In such cases, the management approach to independent labor representation is characterized by adversarialism, even if mechanisms of labor voice are strongly institutionalized at the headquarters' location as in countries such as Germany or France. Manipulation tactics such as deploying disunity among labor actors or inadequately informing, communicating, and educating subsidiary managers on the contents of the GFA allow corporate elites to maintain internal processes in their extant form in this trajectory. Management signals compliance through the guise of a formal GFA, but shields core activities from external evaluation. By not refusing the GFA, corporate elites establish themselves symbolically as the legitimate actor to influence, control, or monitor the regulation of corporate activities, but effectively circumvent the moral reasoning challenge.

Taking Responsibility
A much more unusual trajectory is that of direct engagement in a moral reasoning process when faced with a demand for a GFA, resulting in a strong agreement and actual behavior change. A good illustration for a trajectory marked by high cooperation in legitimation strategies is that of French *ChemCorp* in the domain of IndustriAll. Here, the initiative to sign a GFA is actually a joint activity by management and unions, because management seeks to increase its responsibility with regard to CSR issues (Fichter et al., 2011). In this case, we can say that management has long engaged in moral reasoning with employee representatives and has developed a highly collaborative labor relations culture at the headquarters including unions. Also, the German *PenCorp* in the domain of the BWI is a good example of a responsibility-taking trajectory. In contrast to *ChemCorp*, *PenCorp* is a committed family-owned company that takes responsibility for its global production as the following quote illustrates:

> There are many firms having a voluntary Code of Conduct, but usually without any external control. For me, the tendency is clear that external ratification and control is the future. And CSR must not be allowed to be a mere "strategy," for PR or marketing.

> We need to face the issue head on. From the start, CSR must be top-down in the sense that the CEO, the company's leadership takes the issue to heart, otherwise it simply does not work. (PenCorp, headquarter management)

In both cases management has positively and constructively reacted to a union initiative for a GFA. In the case of *PenCorp*, well-organized labor representatives reviewed production sites across the world and reported that some sites in Brazil and Asia have very high social standards. Upon this report, the suggestion to improve the situation for all production sites based on the ILO-standards was immediately welcomed by management.

Opportunity Structures for Different Trajectories

These trajectories are influenced by the ways in which contesting actors enacted their institutional environments, relationships, or symbolic resources in the political struggle. Most GFAs to date are European, so the institutionally embedded tradition of employee participation and representation at the country of the headquarter location is an important factor for getting MNCs to the negotiation table. Specifically, continental European MNEs like Scandinavian, German, or French MNCs have been more likely to negotiate GFAs than Anglo-Saxon or Southern European MNCs so far, not to mention MNCs from the Americas or Asia. At the same time, there are important differences between the strategies of GFA-signing MNCs from the same country, so this institutional background does not automatically precondition a certain kind of trajectory. Rather, the way labor actors use their institutionally granted power resources in specific interactions at the MNC headquarters can effect change in legitimation strategies.

Forming and upholding unity among the various labor actors seeking involvement in the GFA process both on the national and transnational level was important for limiting the scope for manipulation by corporate elites. Again, this condition is not static, but develops in the context of specific interactions and actor constellations.

Within the interaction process, unions typically had to accept the dominant influence of MNC headquarter management. They did so through discursive position-taking exemplified by consciously excluding controversial substantive issues like global differentials in wages and material working conditions, even though these were important for explaining unions' motivations to have a GFA in the first place. Similarly, the issue of how to finance implementation was also taken out of negotiations. Such contested issues would have fuelled the fears of their management counterparts about the potential risks of GFAs as a new regulatory instrument. In turn, concessions from the union side made it easier for corporate elites to change their initial resistance, but also opened many doors for opportunistic behavior, most importantly by manipulating agreements' jurisdictions and decoupling the stated intentions from actual behavior.

The final test of the credibility of corporate elites occurs when violations of the agreement are brought to headquarter-level review meetings for discussion. Our evidence indicates that headquarter unions already leading the labor camp at the GFA negotiation stage are also capable of taking up controversial issues and bringing them to the table for effective resolution of later-stage violations, although a more longitudinal perspective is necessary to differentiate structural from situational factors in this observation.

DISCUSSION AND CONCLUSIONS

We have set out to examine changes in the legitimation strategies corporate elites use in response to challenges from societal actors in the field of transnational labor regulation. An analysis of different trajectories of legitimation allows us to elaborate on the combination of strategies and their variability over time. We hereby go beyond existing approaches that study how organizations, and in particular the management of large corporations, deal with conflicting institutional demands (e.g., Greenwood, Raynard, Kodeih, Micelotta, & Lounsbury, 2011; Pache & Santos, 2010). More concretely, we compare how different MNCs respond to one moral reasoning challenge – here, the request to sign a GFA and implement ILO core labor standards across global operations – and the resulting interactions. We have identified three "typical" trajectories of changes in legitimation strategies carried forward by the enactment of relational and institutional opportunity structures in sequences of interactions between elites and challenging groups.

Applying the conceptual framework of corporate legitimation strategies developed by Scherer et al. (2013) we suggest several refinements. First, we observe that in the case of GFAs the initial choice and change of legitimation strategies depends less on the calculated cost of required organizational change or the heterogeneity of demands exhibited by different actors operating within divergent institutional environments, and more on the extent to which challenger groups – trade unions, their confederative bodies, advocacy and charity NGOs, local governments, national policy agencies, and international organizations – are able to collaboratively hold corporate elites accountable across institutional distances (Kostova, 1999). The lack of transnational union collaboration, for instance, was a clear prerequisite for corporate voluntarism or manipulation in countries with weak industrial relations institutions. Generally, the slowly growing, but still very limited spread of GFAs as a regulatory instrument can be attributed to a lack of resources, unclear communication channels, and political or ideological disagreements among the various actors from the labor side, which make such a transnational union collaboration difficult to form in the first place (for a general treatment, see Anner, 2009). On a global level, GUFs are relatively small organizations compared to MNCs. On a national level, the influence of labor actors at MNC headquarters varies strongly between countries, sectors, and even individual companies. Such variations provide the background against which interactions between corporate elites and challenging actors unfold – and influence the extent to which the GFA process is open to corporate maneuvering.

Given this situation, the few cases where GFAs led to a profound strategy change from voluntarism to responsibility-taking can be attributed less to the powerful, united counter-force exhibited by trade unions, and more to a preexisting receptivity of corporate elites to collaborate with unions on issues such as good labor practices. The much more common scenario, however, is that corporate elites de facto avoid engaging in a moral reasoning process by symbolically adopting a GFA that is weak and unspecific so that ultimately they are not held accountable for poor labor standards. Thus, second, we conclude that the propensity for the efficacy of a moral reasoning strategy regarding sustainability issues may be overestimated by Scherer and colleagues (Palazzo & Scherer, 2006; Scherer et al., 2013). By being able to shape the "material" content of regulations (i.e., in our case GFAs) in the process of bargaining with labor representatives, corporate elites can combine a discursive, moral reasoning process with a selective adaptation toward norms emerging collectively within a certain sector. Legitimacy remains important even in cases when management applies manipulation tactics such as restricting the scope of the agreement or leaving implementation measures unspecified and avoiding moral reasoning altogether. Which strategy is chosen depends strongly on the history of labor relations in particular MNCs embedded in particular sectors and countries.

Third, the existence of heterogeneous demands for sustainability highlighted by Scherer et al. (2013) not only constitutes a challenge to, but also a resource for corporate elites. The existence of alternative regulatory instruments such as voluntary Codes of Conduct, for instance, allow many MNCs to avoid engaging in a GFA process altogether. Thus, the more regulatory arenas are opened up and regime complexity increases (Quack, 2013), the more corporate elites can play different initiatives and stakeholder groups against each other so as to defend their legitimacy by symbolically adapting to some demands, while declaring that others are unjustified. Such strategies are particularly relevant in legally ambiguous regulatory fields around the "fictitious commodities" of land, labor, and money (Polanyi, 1944) where implementation into national politics is typically weak or heterogeneous and interactions among elites and challenger groups form in multiple arenas and around multiple regulatory issues (e.g., Keohane & Victor, 2011).

GFAs' effectiveness depends heavily on enforcement, which in turn is influenced by the endurance of countervailing social groups on both national and transnational levels. In our study, the variability of corporate legitimation strategies points to a forceful legacy of national arenas and issue fields in which "old" legitimation strategies such as manipulation and decoupling are still effective — unless challenger groups find opportunities to mobilize a collective stakeholder effort on the transnational level that actually puts elites "on trial."

Given that such transnational coordination among challenger groups is required to create mutually reinforcing pressure on corporate elites from "above" and "below" (Keck & Sikkink, 1998), further research is needed to analyze conflicts in anti-corporate mobilization (cf. Kraemer, Whiteman, & Banerjee, 2013). Further research and models on legitimation strategies should also take different levels of analysis more decidedly into account. In particular, the sectoral level on which norms and practices converge cross-nationally seems to be highly relevant as a unit of analysis. While we expect that legitimation strategies dynamically change through interaction with challenger groups also in other transnational regulatory fields such as the global trade regime forming around the WTO, the trajectories may be different depending on the strength of enforcement mechanisms behind regulations, the legal ambiguity of regulations or regime complexity, and the patterns of coordination and collaboration among challenging groups nationally and transnationally.

Scherer et al. (2013) raise the question of how long manipulation strategies are sustainable. In our case, ongoing stakeholder pressure may well cause another shift in the legitimation strategy of corporate elites that are currently on a "weak" trajectory sustained through manipulation.

Finally, it must be recognized that corporate elites are willing to risk being perceived as illegitimate and, in some instances, use non-legitimate, nonlegal instruments and other instruments of force and domination.

NOTES

1. This work was supported by the Hans-Böckler-Foundation [grant number S-2008-141-2]. Additional support and technical assistance was provided by the Friedrich Ebert Foundation [no grant number].
2. The core labor standards refer to the prohibition of child labor (ILO co. 138 and 182) and forced labor (ILO co. 29 and 105), to nondiscrimination and equal pay (ILO co. 100 and 111), and to freedom of association and collective bargaining (ILO co. 87 and 98).

ACKNOWLEDGEMENTS

We thank the editors and especially Sigrid Quack for invaluable comments regarding the development of this paper. We are also grateful for all the vivid debates with the members of the multinational GFA research team.

REFERENCES

Aldrich, H. E., & Fiol, C. M. (1994). Fools rush in? The institutional context of industry creation. *Academy of Management Review, 19*(4), 645–670.
Anner, M. (2009). Two logics of labor organizing in the global apparel industry. *International Studies Quarterly, 53*, 545–570.
Arruda, L., Fichter, M., Helfen, M., & Sydow, J. (2012). *International framework agreements — A powerful tool for ensuring core labor standards in a globalized world? Insights from Brazil*. Berlin: Friedrich-Ebert-Foundation.
Ashforth, B. E., & Gibbs, B. W. (1990). The double-edge of organizational legitimation. *Organization Science, 1*(2), 177–194.
Barley, S. R. (2007). Corporations, democracy, and the public good. *Journal of Management Inquiry, 16*, 201–215.
Barley, S. R. (2010). Building an institutional field to corral a government: A case to set an agenda for organization studies. *Organization Studies, 31*, 777–805.
Bartley, T. (2003). Certifying forests and factories: States, social movements, and the rise of private regulation in the apparel and forest products fields. *Politics & Society, 31*(3), 433–464.

Bartley, T. (2005). Corporate accountability and the privatization of labor standards: Struggles over codes of conduct in the apparel industry. *Research in Political Sociology*, *14*, 211–244.

Bartley, T. (2007). Institutional emergence in an era of globalization: The rise of transnational private regulation of labor and environmental conditions. *American Journal of Sociology*, *113*(2), 297–351.

Bernstein, S. (2011). Legitimacy in intergovernmental and non-state global governance. *Review of International Political Economy*, *18*(1), 17–51.

Botzem, S., & Hofmann, J. (2010). Transnational governance spirals: The transformation of rule-making authority in internet regulation and corporate financial reporting. *Critical Policy Studies*, *4*(1), 18–37.

Bourdieu, P. (1985). The social space and the genesis of groups. *Theory and Society*, *14*, 723–744.

Carroll, W. K. (2009). Transnationalists and national networkers in the global corporate elite. *Global Networks*, *9*(3), 289–314.

Carroll, W. K., & Sapinski, J. P. (2010). The global corporate elite and the transnational policy-planning network, 1996–2006: A structural analysis. *International Sociology*, *25*(4), 501–538.

Croucher, R., & Cotton, E. (2009). *Global unions, global business: Global Union federations and international business*. London: Middlesex University Press.

Davies, S., Hammer, N., Williams, G., Raman, R., Ruppert, C. S., & Volynets, L. (2011). Labour standards and capacity in global subcontracting chains: Evidence from a construction MNE. *Industrial Relations*, *42*, 124–138.

Davies, S., Williams, G., & Hammer, N. (2011). Organizing networks and alliances: International unionism between the local and the global. In K. Papadakis (Ed.), Shaping global industrial relations. *The impact of international framework agreements* (pp. 201–219). London: Palgrave.

Davis, G. F. (1991). Agents without principles? The spread of the poison pill through the intercorporate network. *Administrative Science Quarterly*, *36*(4), 583–613.

Davis, G. F., & Greve, H. R. (1997). Corporate elite networks and governance changes in the 1980s. *American Journal of Sociology*, *103*(1), 1–37.

Davis, G. F., & Mizruchi, M. S. (1999). The money center cannot hold: Commercial banks in the US system of corporate governance. *Administrative Science Quarterly*, *44*(2), 215–239.

Dehnen, V. (2013). Transnational alliances for negotiating international framework agreements: Power relations and bargaining processes between global union federations and European works councils. *British Journal of Industrial Relations*, *51*(3), 577–600.

Dezalay, Y., & Garth, B. (2010). Marketing and selling transnational 'judges' and global 'experts': Building the credibility of (quasi)judicial regulation. *Socio-Economic Review*, *8*(1), 113–130.

DiMaggio, P., & Powell, W. W. (1991). Introduction. In W. W. Powell & P. DiMaggio (Eds.), *The new institutionalism in organizational analysis* (pp. 1–38). Chicago, IL: The University of Chicago Press.

Djelic, M.-L., & Quack, S. (Eds.). (2003). *Globalization and institutions. Redefining the rules of the economic game*. Cheltenham: Edward Elgar.

Djelic, M.-L., & Quack, S. (2008). Institutions and transnationalization. In R. Greenwood, C. Oliver, R. Suddaby, & K. Sahlin-Andersson (Eds.), *Sage handbook of organizational institutionalism* (pp. 299–323). London: Sage.

Djelic, M.-L. & Quack, S. (Eds.). (2010). *Transnational communities: Shaping global economic governance*. Cambridge: Cambridge University Press.

Djelic, M.-L. & Sahlin-Andersson, K. (Eds.). (2006). *Transnational governance: Institutional dynamics of regulation*. Cambridge: Cambridge University Press.

Egels-Zandén, N. (2009). TNC motives for signing international framework agreements: A continuous bargaining model of stakeholder pressure. *Journal of Business Ethics, 84*, 529–547.

Erkama, N., & Vaara, E. (2010). Struggles over legitimacy in global organizational restructuring: A rhetorical perspective on legitimation strategies and dynamics in a shutdown case. *Organization Studies, 31*(7), 813–839.

Fichter, M., & Helfen, M. (2011). Going local with global policies: Implementing international framework agreements in Brazil and the United States. In K. Papadakis (Ed.), *Shaping global industrial relations. The impact of international framework agreements* (pp. 85–115). London: Palgrave.

Fichter, M., Helfen, M., & Schiederig, K. (2013). Transnational solidarity around global production networks? Reflections on the strategy of international framework agreements. In P. Fairbrother, M.-A. Hennebert, & C. Levesque (Eds.), *Transnational trade unionism: Building union power* (pp. 203–222). New York, NY: Routledge.

Fichter, M., Helfen, M., & Sydow, J. (2011). Employment relations in global production networks – Initiating transfer of practices via union involvement. *Human Relations, 64*(4), 599–624.

Fichter, M., Sayim, K. Z., & Agtas, Ö. B. (2013). *Organization and regulation of employment relations in transnational production and supply networks. Ensuring core labor standards through international framework agreements?* Ankara: Friedrich-Ebert-Foundation. Retrieved from http://www.fes-tuerkei.org/media/pdf/Partnerpublikationen/layouts%20web%20english.pdf

Fichter, M., & Stevis, D. (2013). *Global framework agreements in a union-hostile environment: The case of the USA*. Berlin: Friedrich-Ebert-Stiftung. Retrieved from http://library.fes.de/pdf-files/id/10377.pdf

Fichter, M., Stevis, D., & Helfen, M. (2012). Bargaining for corporate responsibility: The global and the local of framework agreements in the USA. *Business and Politics, 14*(3), 1–31. doi:10.1515/bap-2012-0017

Fichter, M., Sydow, J., Helfen, M., Arruda, L., Agtas, Ö. B., Gartenberg, I., ... Stevis, D. (2012). *Globalising labour relations. On track with framework agreements?* Berlin: Friedrich-Ebert-Foundation. Retrieved from http://library.fes.de/pdf-files/iez/09422-20121129.pdf

Fligstein, N., & McAdam, D. (2011). Toward a general theory of strategic action fields. *Sociological Theory, 29*(1), 1–26.

Frenkel, S. J., & Scott, D. (2002). Compliance, collaboration, and codes of labor practice: The adidas connection. *California Management Review, 45*(1), 29–49.

Gartenberg, I., & Bandekar, S. (2011). Challenges to ensuring core labour standards in transnational corporations: The case of India. *The Indian Journal of Labour Economics, 54*(2), 269–283.

Greenwood, R., Raynard, M., Kodeih, F., Micelotta, E. R., & Lounsbury, M. (2011). Institutional complexity and organizational responses. *The Academy of Management Annals, 5*(1), 317–371.

Hammer, N. (2005). International framework agreements: Global industrial relations between rights and bargaining. *Transfer, 11*, 511–530.

Harvey, C., & Maclean, M. (2010). Transnational boards and governance regimes: A Franco-British comparison. In M.-L. Djelic & S. Quack (Eds.), *Transnational communities. Shaping global economic governance* (pp. 107–129). Cambridge: Cambridge University Press.

Helfen, M., & Fichter, M. (2013). Building transnational union networks across global production networks: Conceptualising a new arena of labour–management relations. *British Journal of Industrial Relations, 51*(3), 553–576.

Helfen, M., Fichter, M., & Sydow, J. (2012). Anfänge einer Institutionalisierung grenzüberschreitender Arbeitsbeziehungen? Zur Paradoxie der Internationalen Rahmenabkommen im globalen Dienstleistungssektor. *Industrielle Beziehungen, 19*(3), 290–313.

Helfen, M., & Sydow, J. (2013). Negotiating as institutional work: The case of labour standards and international framework agreements. *Organization Studies, 34*(8), 1073–1098.

Hensmans, M. (2003). Social movement organizations: A metaphor for strategic actors in institutional fields. *Organization Studies, 24*(3), 355–381.

Hoffman, A. (1999). Institutional evolution and change: Environmentalism and the U.S. chemical industry. *Academy of Management Journal, 42*(4), 351–371.

Keck, M., & Sikkink, K. (1998). *Activists beyond borders: Advocacy networks in international politics*. Ithaca, NY: Cornell University Press.

Keohane, R. O., & Victor, D. G. (2011). The regime complex for climate change. *Perspectives on Politics, 9*(1), 7–23.

Kerr, R., & Robinson, S. (2012). From symbolic violence to economic violence: The globalizing of the Scottish banking elite. *Organization Studies, 33*(2), 247–266.

Khaire, M. (2010). Young and no money? Never mind: The material impact of social resources on new venture growth. *Organization Science, 21*(1), 168–185.

Kocher, E. (2008). Codes of conduct and framework agreements on social minimum standards – Private regulation? In O. Dilling, M. Herberg, & G. Winter (Eds.), *Responsible business: Self-governance and law in transnational economic transaction* (pp. 67–86). Portland, OR: Hart.

Kostova, T. (1999). Transnational transfer of strategic organizational practices: A contextual perspective. *Academy of Management Review, 24*(2), 308–324.

Kostova, T., & Zaheer, S. (1999). Organizational legitimacy under conditions of complexity: The case of the multinational enterprise. *Academy of Management Review, 24*(1), 64–81.

Kraemer, R., Whiteman, G., & Banerjee, B. (2013). Conflict and astroturfing in Niyamgiri: The importance of national advocacy networks in anti-corporate social movements. *Organization Studies, 34*(5–6), 823–852.

Lawrence, T. B. (2008). Power, institutions and organizations. In R. Greenwood, C. Oliver, R. Suddaby, & K. Sahlin (Eds.), *The Sage handbook of organizational institutionalism* (pp. 170–197). London: Sage.

Levy, D. L. (2008). Political contestation in global production networks. *Academy of Management Review, 33*, 943–963.

Lounsbury, M., Ventresca, M., & Hirsch, P. M. (2003). Social movements, field frames and industry emergence: A cultural–political perspective on US recycling. *Socio-Economic Review, 1*(1), 71–104.

Malets, O., & Quack, S. (2013). Projecting the local into the global: Trajectories of participation in transnational standard-setting. In G. Drori, M. Höllerer, & P. Walgenbach (Eds.), *Global themes and local variations in organization and management. Perspectives on glocalization* (pp. 325–338). London: Routledge.

Mayntz, R. (2012). Institutional change in the regulation of financial markets: Questions and answers. In *Crisis and control. Institutional change in financial market regulation* (pp. 7–27). Frankfurt am Main: Campus.

McAdam, D., & Scott, R. W. (2005). Organizations and movements. In G. F. Davis, D. McAdam, R. Scott, & M. N. Zald (Eds.), *Social movements and organization theory* (pp. 4–40). New York, NY: Cambridge University Press.

Mills, C. W. (2000/1956). *The power elite*. New York, NY: Oxford University Press.

Mizruchi, M. S. (2004). Berle and Means revisited: The governance and power of large U.S. corporations. *Theory and Society, 33*, 579–617.

Morgan, G., & Kristensen, P. H. (2006). The contested space of multinationals: Varieties of institutionalism, varieties of capitalism. *Human Relations, 59*, 1467–1490.

Mund, H., & Priegnitz, K. (2007). Soft law – Second best solution or a privatisation of social rights? Some pointers for a future discussion. *Transfer, 13*, 671–677.

Niforou, C. (2011). International framework agreements and industrial relations governance: Global rhetoric versus local realities. *British Journal of Industrial Relations, 50*, 352–373.

Oliver, C. (1991). Strategic responses to institutional processes. *Academy of Management Review, 16*, 145–179.

Overdevest, C. (2010). Comparing forest certification schemes: The case of ratcheting standards in the forest sector. *Socio-Economic Review, 8*(1), 47–76.

Pache, A. C., & Santos, F. (2010). When worlds collide: The internal dynamics of organizational responses to conflicting institutional demands. Academy of Management Review, 35(3), 455–476.

Palazzo, G., & Scherer, A. G. (2006). Corporate legitimacy as deliberation: A communicative framework. *Journal of Business Ethics, 66*(1), 71–88.

Papadakis, K. (Ed.). (2011). *Shaping global industrial relations. The impact of international framework agreements*. London: Palgrave.

Pfeffer, J., & Salancik, G. R. (2003). *The external control of organizations: A resource dependence perspective*. Stanford: Stanford University Press.

Polanyi, K. (1944). *The great transformation: The political and economic origins of our time*. Boston, MA: Beacon Press.

Quack, S. (2010). Law, expertise and legitimacy in transnational economic governance: An introduction. *Socio-Economic Review, 8*, 3–16.

Quack, S. (2013). Regime complexity and expertise in transnational governance: Strategizing in the face of regulatory uncertainty. *Oñati Socio-Legal Series, 3*(4), 647–678.

Rao, H., Morrill, C., & Zald, M. N. (2000). Power plays: How social movements and collective action create new organizational forms. *Research in Organizational Behavior, 22*, 237–281.

Scherer, A. G., & Palazzo, G. (2011). The new political role of business in a globalized world: A review of a new perspective on CSR and its implications for the firm, governance, and democracy. *Journal of Management Studies, 48*(4), 899–931.

Scherer, A. G., Palazzo, G., & Seidl, D. (2013). Managing legitimacy in complex and heterogeneous environments: Sustainable development in a globalized world. *Journal of Management Studies, 50*(2), 259–284.

Schüßler, E., Rüling, C., & Wittneben, B. (2014). On melting summits: The limitations of field-configuring events as catalysts of change in transnational climate policy. *Academy of Management Journal, 57*, 140–171.

Strike, V. M., Gao, J., & Bansal, P. (2006). Being good while being bad: Social responsibility and the international diversification of US firms. *Journal of International Business Studies, 37*(6), 850–862.
Suchman, M. S. (1995). Managing legitimacy: Strategic and institutional approaches. *Academy of Management Review, 30*, 571–610.
Suddaby, R., Cooper, D. J., & Greenwood, R. (2007). Transnational regulation of professional services: Governance dynamics of field level organizational change. *Accounting, Organizations and Society, 32*(4), 333–362.
Suddaby, R., & Greenwood, R. (2005). Rhetorical strategies of legitimacy. *Administrative Science Quarterly, 50*, 35–67.
Useem, M. (1984). *The inner circle: Large corporations and the rise of business political activity in the US and UK*. Oxford: Oxford University Press.
Vaara, E., Tienari, J., & Laurila, J. (2006). Pulp and paper fiction: On the discursive legitimation of global industrial restructuring. *Organization Studies, 27*, 789–810.
Waddock, S. (2008). Building a new institutional infrastructure for corporate responsibility. *Academy of Management Perspectives, 22*, 87–108.
Williams, G., Davies, S., & Chinguno, C. (2013). Subcontracting and labour standards: Reassessing the potential of international framework agreements. *British Journal of Industrial Relations*. doi:10.1111/bjir.12011
Zald, M. N., & Lounsbury, M. (2010). The wizards of Oz: Towards an institutional approach to elites, expertise and command posts. *Organization Studies, 31*, 963–996.
Zürn, M. (2004). Global governance and legitimacy problems. *Government and Opposition, 39*(2), 260–287.

ELITE DISCOURSE AND INSTITUTIONAL INNOVATION: MAKING THE HYBRID HAPPEN IN ENGLISH PUBLIC SERVICES

Mike Reed and Mike Wallace

ABSTRACT

This paper focuses on the strategic role of elites in managing institutional and organizational change within English public services, framed by the wider ideological and political context of neo-liberalism and its pervasive impact on the social and economic order over recent decades. It also highlights the unintended consequences of this elite-driven programme of institutional reform as realized in the emergence of hybridized regimes of 'polyarchic governance' and the innovative discursive and organizational technologies on which they depend. Within the latter, 'leaderism' is identified as a hegemonic 'discursive imaginary' that has the potential to connect selected marketization and market control elements of new public management (NPM), network governance, and visionary and shared leadership practices that 'make the hybrid happen' in public services reform.

Keywords: Elites; polyarchy; leaderism; public services

INTRODUCTION

Our purpose in this paper is to examine the strategic role of elites in managing institutional and organizational change within English public services, framed by the wider ideological and political context of neo-liberalism and its pervasive impact on the social and economic order over recent decades (Gamble, 2009; Harvey, 2005, 2011; Mirowski, 2013; Peck, 2010). Economic strategies in many western countries have long reflected Keynesian principles: frequent government intervention in private sector operation, and extensive public sector spending to maintain the workforce and consumer base on which future prosperity depends. Recent decades have witnessed a radical reorientation guided by variants of a neo-liberal ideology, aiming to restrict the state to a minimum and to maximize the scope of individual freedom. A mix of free and regulated market principles drives the associated neo-liberal political economy, which is thus subject to less direct government intervention.

Elites constitute ruling minorities 'in positions to make decisions having major consequences' (Mills, 1956, p. 1). Those within and around such governments have been prompted by the economic ideological shift to extricate welfare systems from longstanding central and local government-dominated 'club regulation' in favour of 'market regulation'. The consequent institutional transformation of the social and economic system has far-reaching implications for changing inter-organizational and intra-organizational control regimes (Moran, 2007; Richards & Smith, 2004). We illustrate the problematic nature of innovations generating such institutional transformation by examining the contribution of elite agency and discourse to shaping the innovation process and outcomes, referring to English public services. National circumstances have created particularly favourable conditions for different political parties forming successive central governments to put neo-liberal ideas into public service practice. It thus offers an instructive 'extreme case': illustrating how a neo-liberal ideology can be enacted where contextual factors allow a central government unusually extensive room for unilateral manoeuvre.

An unintended consequence of this ideologically and culturally driven endeavour by ruling elites, as powerful contributors to national policy decisions (Reed, 2012a; Scott, 2008), has been the progressive hybridization of organizational forms and service management practices within English public services. Hybridization implies a shifting balance between the longstanding hierarchical operation typical of bureaucratic organizations and the emergence of horizontal relationships amongst different organizations within networks. It flows from the determined attempt to 'open up' these services to market competition and to minimize direct state involvement in planning and operating them.

As part of that effort, government elites have promoted service management practices to enact neo-liberalism in public services reflecting their associated operational ideology of 'managerialism', with its core assumption that 'business knows best'. Jamieson (1996, p. 35) caricatures how the argument runs for education:

> ... part of the problem of poor school performance is poor management. Good quality management ... is largely to be found in private business. This is because only business organizations are both complex and have the discipline of the market place which forces them to be efficient.

Private sector management practices thus offer a dual blueprint: initially, for implementing change to improve the efficiency of public services, as inspired by neo-liberalism; subsequently, for the ongoing operation of more efficient, marketized public services and further evolutionary institutional innovation. We argue that a hegemonic elite discourse of 'leaderism' has emerged out of the initial managerialist discourse of 'management' (in England and elsewhere) over the last two decades. Leaderism provides a new 'discursive imaginary' (Fairclough, 2010) connecting selected marketization and market control elements of new public management (NPM), network governance, and visionary and shared leadership practices that 'make the hybrid happen' (O'Reilly & Reed, 2010, 2011). The new discourse focuses on 'winning hearts and minds' by nurturing collective allegiance to an inspiring vision for radical improvement and motivating synergistic efforts to achieve it. Leaderism has provided the ideological legitimation and cultural representation of the institutional innovation process and consequent organizational hybridization, with the potential radically to reconfigure public service provision.

Alongside forms of 'hard' regulative power, backed by the potential to apply legal sanctions or to withhold resources, elites located in centres of political, administrative and professional authority have mobilized 'soft' cultural forms that work by attraction: 'soft power – getting others to want the outcomes that you want – co-opts people rather than coerces them' (Nye, 2004, p. 5). Co-optation refers to a pre-emptive 'process of absorbing new elements into the leadership or policy-determining structure of an organization as a means of averting threats to its stability or existence' (Selznick, 1966, p. 259). Leaderism is operationalized through leadership development interventions. They embody a form of soft power: getting public service organization managers to want the outcomes that government elites want. The goal is to co-opt managers through their acculturation as leaders, equipped to spearhead local service marketization, and further institutional innovation that is intrinsic to marketized service operation.

In combination, these forms of power have crystallized around a progressively distanced market regulation strategy. State disengagement from direct involvement in public service governance structures and service delivery is coupled with a proliferation of 'remote control' mechanisms, many operated by agencies appointed (and monitored) by government. Most notable are accountability regimes for market regulation that variably link specified service standards, priority targets, surveillance and sanctions. They are designed to pre-empt or quash practices that the elites deem unacceptable. The extent of elite operational disengagement has generated new 'creative space' for institutional fields, within the boundaries imposed by remote control, where new organizational service provision mechanisms and control regimes have emerged. They are increasingly taking on hybrid logics and forms, creating 'polyarchic governance regimes' (Clegg, Courpasson, & Phillips, 2006; Courpasson & Clegg, 2012) that combine selected elements of oligarchic elite power with pluralistic stakeholder engagement.

Our analysis of the way elites manage contemporary public service change is developed in the remaining sections. First, we outline the theoretical framework for grasping the dynamics of elite power and control, and their role in shaping the complex interplay between discursive and institutional innovation. The expression of these elite dynamics in our English case was historically situated and ideologically contextualized. Growing commitment to a neo-liberal ideology amongst ruling political, administrative and professional elites from the 1980s generated a transformed policy environment. Within it, the dominant policy narrative became the marketization of public services. It was supported by accompanying facilitatory governance regimes, and the mechanisms for holding the ensuing diversity of providers to account for the efficiency and effectiveness of their services. Second, we offer a brief overview of the form that discursive and institutional innovation has taken in English public services over the last three decades, highlighting the contribution that leaderism has made to it. Third, we consider how 'managed market' reforms have opened-up delimited 'creative space' for entrepreneurial activity amongst elite groups located at different system levels, and operating within the increasingly fragmented power relations framing contemporary public service operation. We highlight how leaderism emerged out of already well-entrenched managerialism in the mid-1990s, as a 'lubricative imaginary'. It became operationalized through centralized development initiatives designed to get the senior staff in public service organizations to want what government elites wanted: to make their marketization reforms work. Here we refer to our recent study (Wallace, O'Reilly, Morris, & Deem, 2011) of such interventions in school education, healthcare and higher education during the period when leaderism became established from the late 1990s. Finally, we consider the wider theoretical and substantive implications of our study for understanding the strategic institution-building role of elites.

THEORIZING ELITES

The dynamics of elite power and control involve shaping emergent institutional logics and organizational forms in complex domains, not least public services. Analysing these dynamics demands a theoretical framework integrating a focus on hierarchical power structures and a complementary engagement with horizontal network relationships (Reed, 2012a, 2012b; Savage & Williams, 2008; Zald & Lounsbury, 2010). Elites possess significant social power, expressed when they act to influence others, but also embodied in their potential to act (Scott, 2008). They are based at different levels, from the centre to the periphery of a social system. Scott (2001, p. 25) distinguishes between 'strategic', 'intermediate' and 'local' elite groupings. The workings of elite power are intrinsically dynamic. Elites and their supporting associates engage with each other across these levels and interact with non-elites in maintaining the status quo and promoting institutional change.

The first focus, on *hierarchical* power structures or 'structures of dominancy' (Weber, 1978), entails tracing the intricate ways in which elites are embedded within institutionalized, so widely taken-for-granted, relations of superordination and subordination. These power relations establish the location of strategic level elites at the apex of hierarchical bureaucratic structures and their *authority* to affect those lower down. Collectively such elites possess 'corporate agency', the political powers and capacities to change structures and cultures (Archer, 2003). But analytical attention to hierarchically stratified domination structures, and the concentrated elite positional power and authority that flows from them, must be complemented by a second focus. The *horizontal* networks through which strategic level elite domination is mediated by more structurally dispersed, intermediate and local level elite groups and their supporting associates also bear consideration. Power to mediate (Brunetto, 2001; Ferlie, Fitzgerald, Wood, & Hawkins, 2005) entails deploying agency to endorse, faithfully implement, adapt, work around, subvert, avoid or openly challenge practices that such groups are being mandated or invited to adopt (Spours, Coffield, & Gregson, 2007; Wallace, 1998). Elites operating within networks possess various forms of *expertise* necessary to translate strategic policy directives and initiatives adaptively into operational programmes and practices that 'work on the ground' (Clarke, Newman, Smith, Vidler, & Westmarland, 2007; Newman, 2001, 2005; Zald & Lounsbury, 2010).

It is out of the complex interplay between centrally located elite authority and expertise, and more dispersed forms of elite expert power, that hybrid governance regimes and organizational forms emerge. Organizational hybridity is an unintended consequence of strategic-level authoritative and expert elite-driven innovation designed to change the nature of institutions and practices within them. But such innovation has the effect of altering the system-wide balance between hierarchical and horizontal power relationships framing the practice of elites and non-elites within and between intermediate and local levels, and their strategic-level linkage. The governance regimes and organizational forms that ensue reflect the new hierarchical–horizontal balance of power.

In respect of public services, system-wide authority legitimating elite dominancy rests with politicians at the strategic level (in central government), and to a lesser extent at the intermediate level (in local government). Contingently, they may act in concert as corporate agents, or engage in internal or cross-level struggles. They are also ultimately dependent on the support of expert senior administrators and policy advisers at the strategic level, and on the expertise of elites at the apex of intermediate-level agencies and local-level service organizations. Expert assistance is essential to carry forward the implementation of politically driven change, whether centrally initiated neo-liberal reforms encouraging institutional innovation or locally initiated, ongoing improvement efforts. The configuration of organizations involved embodies to, a significant degree, hierarchical power structures that delimit the new scope for institutional innovation afforded by the extension of horizontal power relationships within (and just maybe beyond) these limits. Thus increased hybridity generates the latent capacity to generate new institutional logics and practices differing radically from their predecessors (Clegg et al., 2006; Crouch, 2005). 'The new' will inevitably embody residual material, social and cultural elements of 'the old'. But the new will necessarily entail forms and practices that extensively reconfigure the service provided, how it is to be funded and evaluated, and why it now has to be organized in this way rather than that of the past.

Hybridization, therefore, entails a recombination of different and often contradictory structural and cultural elements, with potential to generate qualitatively new and 'emergent' forms. It encapsulates the capacity for institutional innovation by creating new mechanisms which generate a much wider range of design options and developmental possibilities. As Selznick (1966) recognized long ago, bureaucratic struggles within and between authoritative and expert elites are key to determining whether the creative potentialities inherent in hybridization stand any realistic chance of being achieved. These struggles surround access to and control over the positional authority and expert practices through which institutional innovation, and organizational change within it, are to be realized and legitimated. Creative synthesis may be possible between the contradictory elements contained within the hybridization process. It may result in novel institutional configurations that are better equipped to deal with higher levels of complexity and the uncertainty it necessarily generates. How such configurations emerge depends ultimately on dynamic elite power struggles, and their longer-term impact on the governance regimes through which contrasting forms of elite domination are reproduced. Nevertheless, all organizational hybrids are potentially unstable. Polyarchic regimes internalize contradictory political demands and pressures that are likely to disrupt, eventually, whatever governance arrangements elites put in place to contain and manage them.

Two of Scott's (2008, p. 32) elite 'ideal-types' are differentiated according to the stratification mechanisms sustaining elite domination. Both types mainly 'derive their power from the discursive formation of signifying and legitimating' that implies who should control whom and why (rather than controlling allocative resources through coercion or inducements). Reed (2012a) suggests that *authoritative* elites are ruling minorities seeking monopoly control over the means and mechanisms of institutional *regulation*. They make and adjust rules that establish and maintain a socio-political order, and pre-empt or defend it against threats to its effectiveness or legitimacy. Authoritative elites are positioned at the strategic level, in the top administrative positions of bureaucratic hierarchies coordinating governmental activities to create and sustain viable regimes for institutional governance. They frame and service *command situations*, the stratified configuration of authoritative positions and their inter-relationships within and across the organizations constituting institutionalized governance regimes. The stability of command situations is inherently open to internal struggles between elite factions, and to external challenge from other elites.

Expert elites, administratively supporting authoritative elites at the strategic level or based at intermediate and local levels, possess specialized technical knowledge. It is typically organized into 'professional' structures and practices. They pursue monopoly control over the means of *acculturation*: the active shaping of beliefs, norms and values within a socio-political order. Expert elites predominate in professionally staffed organizations and associated institutional networks. The operational complexity of such organizations requires a 'double reflexivity', the capacity for self-monitoring and coordination, alongside reflective expert practice in their area of responsibility. The theoretical and technical knowledge involved is thus of a specialized nature. It is rationalized into various forms of 'expert systems' on which societies and organizations increasingly depend.

According to Scott (1996, 2008), relationships developing between authoritative and expert elites are fundamental to the social workings of power, constituting socially overlapping and institutionally interconnected networks of corporate agents. Together, these elites have the political and cultural capacity to mobilize 'moral vocabularies of discourse': means of seeking to legitimate their dominant structural positions and to organize governance regimes that most closely reflect their long-term material and social interests. Hierarchical power ('domination') and horizontal power ('influence') come together within these evolving complex relational networks. They comprise dynamic and shifting political alliances between authoritative and expert elites to form hybrid governance regimes and organizational technologies, capable of coping with the increased complexity and uncertainty inherent in modern economies and societies. As noted above, hybridized regimes and technologies will contain structural and ideological contradictions and tensions – embodying competing, yet overlapping, collective interests and values mobilized by their respective elite members and other, non-elite, stakeholder groups (Clegg et al., 2006). Nevertheless, they remain the essential organizational means of achieving some degree of socio-political stability and cultural continuity within contemporary socio-economic environments. They are increasingly characterized by systemic uncertainty and the escalating risk that it presents to the maintenance of social order.

Considered in these analytical terms, polyarchic governance systems have become increasingly influential since the 1990s as a distinct form of elite rule. They recombine selected elements of plutocracy (government by the wealthy), technocracy (government by technical experts) and oligarchy (government by the few) consistent with the power structures prevailing under 'democratic elitism' (Clegg et al., 2006; Dahl, 1958, 1971). Such structures empower citizens to express 'voice', though not necessarily to stimulate a response. Polyarchy is a form of elite rule that reconciles elite domination and pluralistic democratic participation, at least temporarily, under contingent political and economic conditions. It operates through the development of hybrid governance regimes and control technologies: means of operationalizing aspects of the neo-liberalist project. Together they create a workable – if inherently unstable – compromise between maintaining centralized strategic power and decentralized stakeholder involvement. The upshot is to preserve the outward symbolic appearance and institutional trappings of a competitive market democracy, while sustaining the political reality of elite domination through a judicious compromise between and co-optation of key oppositional groups and organizations into the policy-making process (Bottomore, 1993; Crouch, 2005, 2013; Smith, 2009). In this way, polyarchy sustains the dominant position of plutocratic, pro-business elites based on extreme concentrations of economic wealth and income (Piketty, 2014). But it is tempered with selected elements of technocratic expertise and oligarchic paternalism, in order to draw in various key stakeholder groups who need to be placated if a particular strategic policy narrative and its attendant 'discursive imaginary' are to be effectively legitimated and mobilized.

However, sustaining a polyarchic governance regime, as an institutional expression of the political ideology of 'democratic elitism in action', is pivotally dependent on the power relationship between authoritative and expert elites, who must develop and sustain a relatively stable modus vivendi between centralized policy formulation and delegated policy implementation. Elites based at strategic, intermediate and local levels are all implicated in *orchestrating* the operationalization of policy shifts. Orchestration entails coordinated activity expressed by a network of actors in senior formal positions, within constraining structural parameters, to instigate, organize, oversee and consolidate complex change across part or all of a multi-organizational system (Wallace, 2007). This delicate process implies the overt and unobtrusive promotion of a desired trajectory, within bounded scope for choice of action, alongside monitoring and contingent corrective action to maintain direction. Orchestration entails steering the brokering process, and mediating change as it interacts with ideologically framed discourses and institutionalized practices reflecting organizational and professional cultures.

Authoritative and expert elites seek to stabilize the complex governance regimes and control technologies through which their power-bases are maintained and reproduced. To do so they need sufficient confidence in their respective capacities to frame the policy narrative and orchestrate its operationalization through various kinds of 'initiatives' or 'programmes' and their accompanying promotional discourse. The ideological and institutional nexus between political authority and technical expertise has to be sustained in the face of inevitable challenges to its legitimacy and cogency if polyarchic regimes are to remain effective in 'stakeholderizing' disagreements and conflicts in ways that absorb and contain any threats to its continued viability. As Monbiot (2014) has noted, both private and public corporations that have developed polyarchic forms of governance try to 'stakeholderize every conflict ... they embrace their critics, involving them in a dialogue that is open in the sense that a lobster pot is open, breaking down critical distance and identity until no one knows who they are any more'. This process of co-optation and colonization entails a 'twin-track' strategy of 'outsourcing' and 'marginalization' in which authoritative and expert elites co-operate to ensure that conflicts are transferred to external agencies, of one sort or another, and then rendered-down and diluted in various ways, so that they become the responsibility of everybody and nobody (Newman, 2001, 2005, 2013).

Thus authoritative and expert elites have to translate neo-liberal policy narratives promoted by policy advisory groups, think-tanks and consulting agencies operating at a global and national level (Loveridge, 2014; Mirowski, 2013; Peck, 2010; Reed, 2014) into sustainable social practices – from 'marketizing' public services, through 'flexibilizing' employment relations, to 'financializing' international, national and household economies. Consequently, these elites meet with criticism and resistance that have to be contained if they are to maintain their ideological momentum and political impact. Insofar as innovative policy discourses and the programmes that flow from them derive from and promote new 'logics of legitimation' (Newman, 2005), they have to be translated, mediated and negotiated through complex hierarchies and networks of power relations. On the way, the terms and conditions under which they gain operational traction become modified in some degree (Fischer, 2003). Thus, neo-liberalism may be characterized as a congenitally 'failing forward' (Peck, 2010, p. 6) political doctrine and policy discourse when the radiant ideological heat that it generates as a pure discursive imaginary meets with the cold pragmatic air of the inherently messy programmes and initiatives to which it breathes life. But, however ideologically compromised through political and managerial practice, neo-liberalism has provided 'a multi-level, multi-phase, multi-sector approach to the building of the political capacity to incubate, critique and promulgate' (Mirowski, 2013, p. 54) policies and programmes that have reimagined and reconfigured the economic, social and political structures of contemporary capitalist societies.

Polyarchic governance regimes have provided the regulative mechanisms and organizational practices through which neo-liberal ideology has been mobilized: both to legitimate new policy discourses and narratives, and to translate them into operational programmes that can successfully accommodate the partially incompatible interests and concerns of diverse stakeholder groups. They provide a means whereby authoritative and expert elites can regularly come together, formally and informally. Their aim is to agree to the terms and conditions under which new policy initiatives can be mobilized in ways that are consistent with a neo-liberal state that holds hard to market competition, consumer sovereignty and possessive individualism as the ideological lodestars of policy-making and implementation.

At the same time, these ideological principles have to be supported through the expert design, construction and management of a pervasive accountability regime mandating core requirements and articulating priorities, policed through continuous surveillance of performance and punitive sanctions if behaviour falls short of normalized expectations (Miller & Rose, 2008; Rose, 2005). In this respect, the neo-liberal state and the polyarchic governance regimes that sustain it are both political hybrids. They selectively recombine elements of markets, hierarchies and networks to generate highly complex but sustainable structures and processes through which coalitions of authoritative and expert elites can continue to govern in the name of 'market democracy'. As Peck (2010, p. 7, emphasis added) argues, neo-liberalism's utopian ideological vision of a universalized and unchallengeable 'free market society' can never be realized. Consequently:

> ... in practice, neo-liberalism has never been about a once-and-for-all liberalization, an evacuation of the state. Instead, it has been associated with *rolling programmes of market-oriented reform*, a kind of permanent revolution which cannot simply be judged according to its own fantasies of free-market liberalization ... the concern here is with *neo-liberalization as an open-ended and contradictory process of regulatory restructuring*.

DISCURSIVE AND INSTITUTIONAL INNOVATION IN ENGLISH PUBLIC SERVICES

The provision and management of public services is a key institutional domain where the relationship between authoritative and expert elites underpins the fabrication of ideologically coherent and operationally viable, if potentially unstable, polyarchic governance regimes. Over recent decades, policy discourses and their operationalization within 'New Public Management' amongst Anglo-American and Antipodean welfare systems have variably reflected neo-liberal marketization and privatization strategies (Lane, 2000; Pollitt & Bouckaert, 2011). They aim to minimize the role of the state in providing such services through disengagement, as far as possible, from direct involvement in their funding and management (Leys & Player, 2011). Meanwhile, remote control mechanisms keep the fostered diversification of market activity within the bounds of acceptability to government elites, and the voters on whose future support such elites ultimately depend.

European welfare states with a strong corporatist tradition have tended to be circumspect about neo-liberal public service reform (Goldfinch & Wallis, 2010; McLaughlin, Osborne, & Ferlie, 2002; Pollitt & Bouckaert, 2011). But like-minded authoritative and expert elites in Anglo-American and Antipodean welfare systems have come together to form effective 'advocacy coalitions' (Sabatier & Jenkins-Smith, 1993). These powerful groups ideologically promote the neo-liberal agenda in public service reform through discursive initiatives, international 'policy borrowing' and institutional innovations. Such interventions generate 'contested hybrids' of organizational provision and governance where the formal role of the state is progressively minimized and that of non-state actors, such as private corporations, the voluntary sector or public-private partnerships, are increasingly emphasized (Newman, 2001, 2005). Elite approaches to promoting public service reform agendas combine three elements:

- Intent through *political projects* to realize governmental interests, as with the neo-liberal devolution of responsibility for service provision within a centralized surveillance and sanction regime;
- Persuasion through *discourse strategies*, such as the production of neo-liberal policy documents and media statements;
- Behavioural leverage through *control technologies*, ranging from 'hard power' mandates and sanctions, including the introduction of performance management, to 'soft power' culture management (Pollitt, 1993), as with the centralized leadership development initiatives that will mainly concern us here.

Elite advocacy coalitions in the United Kingdom and other Anglo-American and Antipodean welfare are increasingly relying on leadership discourse, overlaying an initial emphasis on public service organization management, as a soft policy lever for public service reform (OECD, 2001, 2010). The leadership lever has played a strategic role in ideologically crystallizing and culturally refracting a neo-liberal agenda embodying deep-seated structural contradictions and the political tensions that they inevitably generate − not least the accompanying accountability regimes delimiting the proclaimed 'freedom of action' within the public service marketplace. These contradictions and tensions require 'mediated management' at various levels of policy (authoritative) making and operational (expert) practice which have become lodged in the very 'contested hybrids' that leadership discourse has helped to create and sustain over the recent reform period.

The emergence of leaderism as an elite-sponsored discourse in the English public services relates to the demise of longstanding hierarchical 'command and control' governance regimes, hitherto orchestrated by elite top-level politicians and administrators across both central and local government characterizing 'club government' (Moran, 2007). Thus state-funded education had long been typified as 'a national service, locally administered', prompting the informed comment four decades ago that 'the English education system is decentralized, untidy and, compared with European [sic] systems, unique in its relative freedom from control by the central government' (Griffiths, 1971, p. 7).

But as DuGay (2000, 2005, 2008) has consistently argued, debates about the 'modernization' of central and local government institutions in the United Kingdom since the 1990s have revolved around a critique of the incapacity of such bureaucratic forms of directive public administration to generate innovative service provision and management. New ways of doing things are deemed necessary to facilitate the strategic direction and operational flexibility demanded in an increasingly competitive marketplace for public services. In turn, this critique has generated increasing interest in 'leadership' amongst elite politicians and administrators. It constitutes a powerful discursive narrative, providing a range of policy rhetorics and practices. They legitimate the customer-led innovations and performance-oriented reorganizations that public services must adopt to survive in the brave new neo-liberal world of market competition. 'Leadership' becomes the vital discursive conduit legitimating innovative organizational service provision and management practices that translate market mechanisms into operational realities. The potentially negative long-term impact of these reforms on professional autonomy, political neutrality and institutional memory has been counteracted by the political power that a discourse of 'leadership' provides. Within this discourse, markets and marketization are seen as the primary sources of legitimacy and efficiency in a novel neo-liberal environment, where 'market populism' (Frank, 2001) is the dominant ideological force.

'Market populism' is viewed as a powerful ideological weapon in the politics of institutional modernization and innovation. According to DuGay (2008, p. 98), it legitimates a policy narrative in which any institution that does not 'answer to the market' is not, by definition, 'answering to the people'. At one level, this ideology seems profoundly anti-elitist, undermining any claims to authority not based on market-determined criteria and the high levels of popular support 'naturally' associated with them. However, once discursively re-aligned with policies and practices supporting the new innovation-driving forms of 'leadership and leaders' that 'modernized public services' demand, then 'an elite of anti-elitists' emerges to drive subsequent phases of institutional and organizational change. It provides the leadership discourses, personnel and practices that will galvanize public services to transform themselves from 'bureaucratic dinosaurs' into 'flexible networks'. These networks will be closely attuned to the changing needs of market-empowered customers, and to their ever-increasing demands for more responsive and high-quality service 'delivery'. Leadership (reflecting, for us, the discourse of 'leaderism') provides the ideological framework and organizational practices that promote the marketization and modernization of UK public services. It does so in ways that are consistent with the changing material interests and symbolic values of elite politicians, administrators and professionals at the centre of public life. These shifting elite interests relate to their struggle to come to terms with 'market populism' and the process of 'creative destruction' that it has let loose on public services since the gradual break-up of the post-Second World War welfare settlement during the 1980s (Clarke, 2004; Clarke & Newman, 1997; Newman, 2001).

Moran's (2007) broader historical analysis of the British 'regulatory state' identifies an underlying process of 'hyper-innovation' between the 1970s and 1990s. It was generated by the conjuncture of an economic policy crisis and an institutional system crisis that undermined 'club government'. This process has been framed within a discursive narrative of modernization in which new forms of regulatory governance replace 'oligarchic, secretive rule with something more open and accountable' (Moran, 2007, p. 7). The discourse of modernization drives towards a new regulatory state in which quantification, marketization and democratization become the sine qua non for institutional reform and their realization through flexible forms of 'managed market competition'.

Yet this public service modernizing project meets with strong elite resistance from elite professionals in the welfare state and higher education system, and elite politicians located within the central and local state apparatus. They retain a commitment to older, less 'open' and 'contested' modes of decision-making. In particular, these recalcitrant elite factions take exception to the intrusive micro-management control technologies, such as central target-setting, that institutional hyper-innovation and modernization within the 'regulatory state' brings in its wake. Moran accepts that this form of state increasingly operates within globalized and through localized forms of 'network governance'. For public services it may entail the collective oversight, with representation from multiple stakeholder groups including users, of provision offered across a cluster of service organizations (Newman, 2001; Osborne, 2006). Each may be jurisdictionally autonomous, dictating horizontal, voluntarily negotiated inter-organizational relationships. Since the hierarchical line-management relationships characteristic of bureaucratic organizational forms are ruled out, networked forms replace 'command and control' with what Moran terms 'reflexive regulation', selectively recombining elements of centralized 'remote control' and decentralized 'delegated autonomy' (Reed, 2011a, 2011b). In this respect, successive central governments 'have strengthened central control but also strengthened sources of opposition to central control' (Moran, 2007, p. 192).

We contend that leaderism has influenced public service reform policy and practice in England since the mid-1990s. It constitutes a key component of a strategy designed by elite politicians and administrators within central government to co-opt recalcitrant elite professionals into supporting the modernizing project that Moran identifies. This strategy is necessarily subject to a complex process of mediation within dispersed public service networks. The more 'hybridized' forms of public service organization and delivery emerging from this process of discursive co-optation represent an unintended consequence of the compromises between centralized (direct or remote) control and decentralized forms of delegated autonomy that 'polyarchic governance regimes' embody (Clegg et al., 2006, pp. 336–339). A central oligarchy unobtrusively retains strategic control over local oligarchies by opening-up the hierarchically containable horizontal exercise of local power. First, by partly decentralizing governance, within 'rules of the game' that rule-out legitimate challenge to the centre. Second, by promoting participation and contestation amongst the local oligarchies, while encouraging multiple subgroups to pursue diverse sectional interests so that they remain fragmented – and therefore unlikely to threaten the established order. Thus ruling elites harness leaderism towards their search for a viable modus vivendi between selectively retained elements of oligarchic power and pluralistic stakeholder engagement. Consequently, they are likely to generate innovative regulatory regimes and control technologies. These innovations incrementally displace less adaptable and flexible governance systems that struggle to cope with the endemic structural contradictions and tensions intrinsic to the neo-liberal environment. The precarious sustainability of such polyarchic regimes rests on the delicate balance between decentralization through extending delegated autonomy and delimiting its scope to pre-empt any emergent threats to centralized control. Such a balancing act is inherently vulnerable to destabilization, should the pluralistic exercise of delegated autonomy proceed in directions of which ruling elites disapprove, or local groups coalesce around their shared interests to form uncontainable 'grass roots' counter-elites.

As Courpasson and Clegg (2012) have recently argued, the increasing salience of such polyarchic forms of organization and management in public services represent the outcome of a wider political strategy undertaken by ruling elites. It has been developed in response to growing stakeholder resistance at intermediate and local levels of the system-wide power structure. Within this political strategy, accommodation and discipline are recombined in ways that transform orthodox hierarchical bureaucracies into hybrid polyarchic governance regimes. Delimited stakeholder inclusiveness and participation become the necessary political price that ruling elites must pay for sustaining overall control. This is where we suggest leaderism has a crucial part to play as a pivotal ideological and discursive component of the shift towards polyarchic governance regimes in English public services. It legitimates a form of regulation and control where 'powerful internal professional groups are developed in the image that elites favour, not by imposing a single unitary loyalty and viewpoint but by maintaining conflicting loyalties and viewpoints in a state of tension ... they [polyarchic bureaucracies] build a plurality of constituencies while reinforcing the power of central managers' (Courpasson & Clegg, 2012, p. 74).

In the next section we explore further how leaderism has contributed towards the establishment of today's English public service polyarchy. Our account draws on the academic literature, several political biographies and our recent qualitative research into public service leadership development in school education, healthcare and higher education (Wallace et al., 2011). This substantial study involved a critical discourse analysis of 128 policy documents, and 218 interviews with 163 informants (55 informants were interviewed twice) from central government, national leadership development bodies (NLDBs) and service organizations.

We begin by outlining key contextual factors that have given government elites such extensive scope for manoeuvre. Next we consider the initiation of neo-liberal reforms during the period when the Conservative Party formed the central government from 1979 to 1997, highlighting the first national soft power initiative to bring school senior staff onside as 'managers'. We then draw on our own research to show how the succeeding Labour administrations of 1997–2010 continued this thrust, initiating the discourse of leaderism and enacting it through national leadership development initiatives for different public service sectors. We conclude the section by briefly noting how the present Conservative–Liberal Democrat coalition administration has redoubled the marketization effort. The ideologies and political values to which the authoritative elites forming each central government administration subscribe are inflected in the mix of marketization and accountability policies. Yet all three, since the appointment of Margaret Thatcher as Prime Minister in 1979, have consistently pursued versions of the neo-liberal political project. With rare exceptions (as in 1997 when the incoming Labour government reversed a Conservative policy to enable schools to 'opt out' of local government control), they have progressively extended marketization. The relevant policies, in turn, have generated new 'creative space' encouraging the diversification of provision, including greater involvement of the private sector. Alongside, all three have also introduced and serially readjusted accountability mechanisms to delimit the diversification of practices that ensue as expert elites at intermediate and, especially, local levels seek to colonize this space.

AUTHORITATIVE ELITE OPENING-UP AND EXPERT ELITE COLONIZATION OF INSTITUTIONAL 'CREATIVE SPACE'

The National Context for an 'Extreme Case'

The almost unequalled intensity and longevity of neo-liberal public service reform in England has been possible because central governments have greater scope for intervention than their counterparts in most other countries. Pollitt (2007, p. 534) contrasts the high degree of unilateral authority and relative freedom from constitutional and legal constraints that senior government politicians enjoy with those faced in other western nations, noting that 'the British system simultaneously maximizes the temptation to re-organize and minimizes the political penalties for so doing'.

But an unintended consequence has been an accretion of disruptive policy U-turns, revisions and ameliorative policies, because intervention itself reflects intractable dilemmas. Action directed towards one pole tends to generate undesired consequences, increasing pressure towards corrective action directed towards the opposite pole, which generates new undesired consequences ... (Ogawa, Crowson, & Goldring, 1999; Wallace & Hoyle, 2012). As implied earlier a core dilemma for neo-liberal marketization concerns both the pole of decentralization (promoting entrepreneurial innovation that addresses local concerns) and the opposite pole of centralization (keeping the ensuing diversity within bounds acceptable to government elites). Hence the perennial dialectic between marketization interventions and pre-emptive or responsive regulation – which, for local elites in service organizations, can mean no more than 'freedom to do what you're told' (Hoque, Davis, & Humphreys, 2004). This dialectic is most dramatically exemplified by the sporadic eruption of 'scandals' and their aftermath.

Illustratively, a scandal at the time of writing concerns the alleged leaking of documents written by Muslim activists to local newspapers, describing their 'trojan horse' tactics for forcing headteachers to resign and installing their supporters as school governors. The supposed goal is to ensure that a school is run according to Islamic principles (*Daily Mail*, 2014). The schools in question cater for a high proportion of Muslim pupils, and are 'academies', freed from local government oversight under central government marketization reforms. If true, the absence of local government involvement made the alleged 'plot' possible. In response, central government elites have ordered intensive surveillance by its inspection agency, have heavily sanctioned several allegedly targeted schools and will continue to monitor them through repeated inspections. Here a consequence of decentralization has brought unanticipated pressure on central government elites to employ – and even increase – its centralized control, to delimit the scope for any recurrence.

Another factor that Pollitt (2007) identifies as contributing towards sustained central government elite-driven reform in England is their proliferating employment of 'change management experts', especially in roles as consultants or special advisers. Pollitt notes the vested interest of such experts in promoting politically feasible forms of change that reflect their management knowledge. In essence, they possess a restricted repertoire of 'solutions in search of a problem' (Cohen, March, & Olsen, 1972) that they advise ministers to apply to public services. Often these solutions are derived from business settings. An early example is school site-based budgeting. Government elite politicians informed the development of policy by commissioning Coopers and Lybrand (1988), a private sector-based consultant, to produce an expert report. It claimed that the concepts underlying private-sector budgeting were 'just as applicable to the public sector as they are to the private sector' – in the absence of any evidence, since the practice had yet to be tried in schools.

Just how extreme the case of a 'permanent revolution' (Peck, 2010) in English public services has been since the 1970s can be gauged from many sources in the public domain: from historical overviews (2020 Public Services Trust, 2009), through policy document archives (for education see Gillard, 2014) and academic accounts of particular services (for healthcare see Paton, 2014; Rivett, 2014), to international comparative studies (see Pollitt & Bouckaert, 2011). We confine our attention to selected interventions that illustrate the unfolding of government elite-driven neo-liberal 'managed market' reform, and the emergence and enactment of leaderism within it.

Precursor to Leaderism: The Impact of Managerialism in the Era of Hyper-Innovation

By the 1970s the term 'management' had transferred from its private sector origins into public service discourse. But the compass of this discursive imaginary was largely confined to the coordination required for ongoing provision. The radical Conservative government elected in 1979, with a large majority, launched the political project of reform that has never ceased since. Full use was made of the 'creative space' the British majoritarian political system afforded to experiment with a raft of neo-liberal policies. Their implementation would itself constitute significant innovation in the institutions providing public services. The authoritative elites included senior politicians who subscribed to the managerialist operational ideology that 'business knows best', and sought to apply it to the reform of public services. A key figure was Sir Keith Joseph, with private sector business experience as the son of the Bovis building company's founder. His commitment to neo-liberalism was shared with Prime Minister Margaret Thatcher, for whom he acted as a close adviser (Denham & Garnett, 2001). He also had the rueful experience of attempting to improve the National Health Service (NHS), when responsible for healthcare in a previous administration, by reforming its management structure. But his efforts had merely increased expenditure without discernibly enhancing provision.

From the outset, central government elites orchestrated a twin-track approach, promoting the marketization of public services while delimiting the diversification of practice through the beginnings of a 'remote control' accountability regime. In both school and higher education marketization was pursued indirectly through regulation, to create more favourable conditions for entrepreneurial innovation by local elites in senior positions within service organizations. Its aim was radically to reduce control exercised by local government authoritative elites over provision. The elected majority in many local councils belonged to political parties in opposition to the Conservatives forming central government. They did not support neo-liberalism. Consequently, the 'local management of schools' initiative forced local government to devolve the operating budget to individual schools; in turn, this gave them greater scope over staffing and other resources. Similarly, local government-controlled higher education institutions were liberated and entitled to rebrand themselves as universities. Marketization of schooling was more directly promoted through other reforms. One move towards 'market populism' was to increase parental scope to express a preference for the local school their child might attend. It included providing information to facilitate such judgements, as with the required publication of periodic inspection reports and examination results. An early experiment in diversifying the range of schools, while bringing in the private sector, was to create 'city technology colleges': government-funded independent schools for which ministers (unsuccessfully) sought private sector sponsorship. It was augmented by regulation enabling schools to 'opt out' of local government control and become funded directly through a national government agency. Delimiting accountability measures included a centrally specified national curriculum, national tests for younger pupils (with a populist twist through the mandatory publication of results) and strengthened surveillance through a new inspection regime, conducted in part by contracted private agencies.

Within healthcare, central government elites orchestrated a parallel twin-track approach to establishing a 'regulated market'. It was similarly informed by external advice, but not only from the private sector. An influential private sector adviser was Sir Roy Griffiths, a director of the Sainsbury supermarket chain, commissioned to report on NHS management (Department of Health and Social Security [DHSS], 1983). His advice reflected the operational ideology of managerialism. Stimulating the introduction of general management, replacing traditional consensus decision-making by multidisciplinary teams of chief officers. Business practices for these general managers included short-term contracts, performance review and performance-related pay (Pollitt, Harrison, Hunter, & Marnoch, 1991). Influential advice also came from an American academic economist (Enthoven, 1985). His report on establishing an internal market in the NHS was passed to senior politicians, rather than being commissioned by them (Paton, 2014). Policies to create favourable conditions for marketization focused internally. A 'split' was established between 'providers' such as hospitals and 'purchasers' – principally doctors in general practice and administrative health authorities – now responsible for commissioning services from the providers. Hospitals were accorded 'trust' status, with a management board and significant budgetary discretion, now 'selling' their hospital services to the 'purchasers'. Moves to bring in accountability measures started with the introduction of performance indicators, and extended to targets for reducing non-emergency surgery waiting times, and reducing the proportion of deaths from specific diseases.

During this period, any training provided for such 'managers' remained internal to NHS organizations. Yet the first soft power foray by central government elites into large-scale co-optation of senior service organization staff as managers was undertaken in 1983 by Sir Keith Joseph, when in charge of the Department for Education and Science. (It constituted a precedent on which the successor Labour administration was to build in enacting leaderism.) The initiative targeted school headteachers and deputy heads. The National Development Centre for School Management Training (NDC) amounted to a control technology of very modest scope, in the form of a collaborative project between one university education department and another university business school. Its remit was to support government-funded training courses offered by approved higher education institutions (Bolam, 1986). Here intermediate-level academic expert elites moderately mediated the initiative – ironically by fulfilling its brief to learn from private sector practices. The NDC adopted the broader notion of 'management development' as a framework for developing guidance for local government and individual schools. Management development encompassed the construction of a policy and programme for developing staff with management responsibilities, treating training courses as only one way of meeting identified development needs. But the primacy accorded to local-level elites in local government and schools did not square well with the central elite concern to implement a centralized approach to training. Once the NDC's contract finished, regional provision of management training and related developmental initiatives, such as a national pilot scheme for mentoring new headteachers remained (Bolam, 1997). But the NDC guidance for local government rapidly became redundant as policies mentioned above, to reduce local government involvement in schooling, took hold.

The Rise of Leaderism and Leadership Development in the Era of Redisorganization

The successor Labour administration also enjoyed great scope for unilateral manoeuvre, combining a moderately more social democratic approach towards enacting neo-liberalism with a similar allegiance to managerialism for its operationalization. The Prime Minister, Tony Blair (2010, p. 284), immediately 'began to look for ways, all ways, of getting business ideas into public service practice'.

In the build-up to the general election he had worked behind-the scenes with other elite politicians and activists in the Labour Party to formulate the public service reform policies which were subsequently launched in the post-election period. A key education adviser had been the academic Michael Barber, who was immediately appointed to a top civil service post, where he assisted with implementing regulative policies to improve the achievement of literacy and numeracy standards in schools. Initially, greater central government elite emphasis was placed on strengthening accountability regimes than on opening-up markets (indeed, 'opted-out' schools were returned to local government control). A period of 'targets and terror' (Bevan & Hood, 2006) saw the imposition of multiple service priorities in school education, healthcare and other services, 'tough targets' for raising their achievement, surveillance arrangements for their regular measurement, and sanctions if they were not achieved – in the case of schools including the 'naming and shaming' of those judged through inspection to be failing. Barber (1996, pp. 55–60) had previously coined the term 'free-market Stalinism' to ridicule Conservative government imposition of marketization policies. With deep irony, after a few years within central government he had invented 'deliverology' (Barber, 2007) in his subsequent 'enforcer' role: driving through the implementation of public service reforms by measuring service 'delivery' performance and challenging local-level elites in service organizations to justify any shortfall against centrally imposed targets.

The push for accountability was soon complemented by a renewed push for marketization, whose emphasis gradually shifted from establishing a market amongst individual service providers towards more collective, networked local provision (Strategy Unit, 2008), opening-up creative space for a multiplicity of local arrangements. Indirect marketization policies to create favourable conditions included 'local strategic partnerships' between multiple services, some entailing 'co-production with user groups'. Direct marketization policies included expanding the diversity of service organizations to extend 'customer' choice of provider. Combined with the accountability measures, they proved as repeatedly disruptive in both school education and healthcare as during the earlier period of 'hyper-innovation', prompting the pejorative epithet 'redisorganization' (Pollitt, 2007; Smith, Walshe, & Hunter, 2001). Some new marketization policies remodelled arrangements of the previous Conservative administration. For example, a raft of new local 'primary care trusts' was serially introduced and reconfigured to adjust the internal 'purchasing' of healthcare services. Others augmented them. Thus having returned 'opted out' schools to local government control, central government elites promptly created 'academies', a new form of semi-privatized school. The academies programme was informed by the previous administration's city technology colleges initiative. This programme was also an example of adaptive international 'policy borrowing', informed by the Charter Schools movement in the United States. Charter Schools are publicly funded but operationally autonomous, many run by private sector organizations (Murphy & Shiffman, 2002). Academy schools remain state-funded but are owned and operated by sponsors, many from the private sector. Higher education institutions also faced neo-liberal policies bringing new 'consumer' pressure. Student tuition fees replaced payment through grants funded by taxation, coupled with government regulatory pressure to expand provision.

The articulation and enactment of leaderism from the late 1990s became a signature use of soft power by Labour central government elites. They rapidly overlaid the previous administration's soft power promotion of service organization 'management', through a more concerted discourse strategy promoting culturally oriented forms of leadership to generate momentum for further public service reform. While its origins are uncertain, they appear to combine a long-institutionalized political discourse, where politicians have traditionally construed themselves as 'leaders', with the more recent translation of highly normative academic ideas about visionary political leadership put forward by Burns (1978) in the United States and widely propagated in the business literature (e.g. Bennis & Nanus, 1985). The discursive imaginary of 'leaderism' constituted a conceptual hybrid combining elite hierarchical and horizontal network elements.

The main conception of leadership was implicitly 'transformational', where leaders and followers together identify and work towards a collective moral purpose for the common good (Burns, 1978), then 'distributed', embracing the formal influencing activity of those occupying a hierarchy of managerial roles and the informal activity of any organization member, as in teams (Bolden, Petrov, & Gosling, 2008). Characteristics of leaderism identified in our research from documents and informants are:

> a belief in elite systemic direction-setting through a hierarchically distributed pattern of persuasive influence, nurturing cultural change necessary for dissolving incompatible interests by fostering the collective pursuit of goals to realize a vision for improvement that becomes accepted as in the interests of all, so subordinating any sectional interests-at-hand that are incompatible with this vision.

The manipulative nature of leaderism is reflected in the eliding of sectional interests with the supposed universally shared collective interest that 'leaders' are legitimated to define and harness 'followers' to pursue. Central government policy documents (e.g. OPSR, 2002) implied a two-tier hierarchy of leaders: the government acts as the collective *leader of systemic reform*; *leaders within the system being reformed* in service organizations and agencies are to make reforms work within their domain, on behalf of the leaders of systemic reform. The political promotion of leaderism was subtle. Leadership was articulated as a generic influencing activity on the one hand, while targeted towards acculturating local-level expert elites and their associates – senior service organization staff – as committed leaders of marketization reform within the accountability regime, and subsequently of marketized services, on the other. The government's discourse strategy, built round this dual leadership role imaginary and part-linked to reforms, explicitly exhorted leaders 'to deliver joined up services through networks and loose coalitions (Performance and Innovation Unit [PIU], 2001, p. 16). Conditions were to be created for the balance between the hierarchical and horizontal power relationships in which leaders were embedded to lean further towards the horizontal, as they colonized the creative space the reforms would create for local innovation in service provision.

To mobilize the development of leaders within public service reform, government departments established a national 'leadership development' body (NLDB) for each sector. Their intermediate-level expert elite senior staff were generally recruited from public service professionals in the sector with management roles. Our research suggested that these new forms of national change agency organization offered sufficient creative space for expert elite senior NLDB staff to colonize through constrained innovation.

The National College for School Leadership (NCSL) and the NHS Institute for Innovation and Improvement (NHSIII) amounted to government control technologies for mobilizing reform through the acculturational impact of leadership development provision. Their documentation reflected the authoritative elite expectation that they would build sectoral capacity for leading the implementation of reforms and reformed services. However, scope for innovation lay in the absence of any specification that provision must be directed *exclusively* towards reform. Consequently, the NCSL and NHSIII brief left scope over how far to create leadership development programmes that were reform-related, or more generically associated with any change agenda. The Leadership Foundation for Higher Education (LFHE) constituted a more 'remote-control' technology within this hybrid public-private sector. Managerialism was reflected in the construction of a 'business case' prepared by professional associations representing senior university staff (Universities UK/Standing Conference of Principals [UUK/SCOP], 2003). The LFHE was funded primarily by universities, but also part-dependent on central government funding. Consistent with the marketization reforms in other sectors, the business case implicitly underlined the capacity for colonizing the creative space being opened-up for universities, as 'autonomous businesses', to 'drive' change through partnership with their 'clients'. LFHE documentation represented senior university staff as independent of government. But its provision addressed current reforms, nevertheless.

Our research interviews with NLDB expert elites suggested that they had colonized the modest creative space left to them. The programmes they provided or commissioned focused on more generic 'hierarchically distributed transformational leadership'. Training and other developmental activities acknowledged reforms as an important – but not dominant – aspect of participants' change agendas. These intermediate-level expert elites aimed to acculturate senior service organization staff as leaders, but not necessarily as co-reformers, so moderately mediating the authoritative elite endeavour to mobilize the implementation of reform by this means.

Similarly, local expert elites in receipt of NLDB provision appear also to have colonized such creative space as they could. Senior service organization staff reported that its main impact was to inform their thinking about their practice, rather than acculturating them as reformers (see Wallace et al., 2011). But they almost unanimously perceived themselves as leaders, whether or not they had received training from NLDBs or other providers. Most appeared to have inculcated 'hierarchically distributed transformational leadership' discourse. Their acculturation as leaders legitimated their efforts to maximize the scope of their agency as innovators, guided by the strong allegiance they retained to their service professional values. Most claimed to have mediated reforms by implementing them within their organizational jurisdiction as much adaptively as faithfully, while proactively pursuing independent agendas. However, most also implied that 'harder' accountability regime delimited their power to mediate. Leadership development and the spread of culturally oriented leadership discourse helped to create fertile conditions for local-level expert elites to innovate, although they were not acculturated as government change agents. But institutionalized authoritative elite regulatory mechanisms circumscribed its scope, especially in the school and healthcare sectors.

The near-universal identification of our informants with being leaders, driving change within their jurisdiction, confirms how versatile a change 'lubricant' leaderism is, easing the path for innovative colonization of the institutional creative space generated by marketization. An emerging institutional logic within public service organizations is that they are comprehensively *led*: expert elites use vision-building and other cultural means to foster support for unified direction-setting, in the face of the proliferating sectional interests that marketization empowers different stakeholder groups to pursue, and that leaderism elides. Speculatively, it is the *cultural* orientation of leaderism that renders it so attractive to authoritative and expert elites alike, encouraging both to use this form of soft power to win support from those on whom they ultimately depend to realize their interests. For while senior service organization staff may not have been fully acculturated as reformers, exposure to leadership discourse or leadership development programmes had acculturated them as leaders, making increasingly marketized services work.

Despite the conditions of financial austerity that surrounded the advent of the present Conservative and Liberal Democrat coalition government, there has been no let-up in the attempt to turn public services into a neoliberal 'regulated market', no respite from 're-disorganization', and an increased investment in co-optative leadership development. Indicatively, large numbers of schools have faced pressure from central government elites to become academies; the 'purchaser' side of the healthcare internal market has been radically reconfigured (again); and higher education institutions have been allowed to set higher tuition fees, resulting in greater student debt and increased 'consumer' pressure from them to receive 'value for money'. The NLDB for school education has had its remit extended to cover teacher training; a new dedicated NHS Leadership Academy has been launched, with increased funding, and the more autonomous LFHE for higher education has maintained its level of provision. Leadership development appears to have outlasted its potential vulnerability as a fad or fashion, proving, so far, to be of more lasting value for very different reasons to all the elite groups involved.

DISCUSSION AND CONCLUSIONS

The analysis provided above portrays how deeply neo-liberalism has become embedded in English public service policy, and how a combination of hard and soft power has become an enduring hallmark of elite approaches towards its enactment. Our research highlights the strategic role played by authoritative and expert elite leadership discourses in facilitating, while also bounding, the scope for institutional innovation within the education and health sectors of one Anglo-American public service setting. It located this analysis within a wider understanding of the major shifts in regulative orders occurring in public services since the 1980s. They have emerged from the ideological and political dominance of neo-liberalism and the ways in which it has been promoted by authoritative and expert elites operating within the hybridized, polyarchic governance regimes which have become more evident over this period. But since the discourse of leaderism is not intrinsically wedded to any specific economic ideology it could, in principle, be harnessed towards the pursuit of other goals. Thus it seems likely that leaderism is here to stay as a soft power resource for elites with potential to further a diversity of change agendas in other settings.

The design of our change process-focused study stopped short of exploring the content and outcome of changes that most senior service organization staff reported leading. But the reforms of the day did focus on developing new collaborative and co-productive service practices. We do know from other research and evaluations that there has been widespread engagement with innovations in different public service sectors that entail shared leadership (e.g. Bolden et al., 2008; Buchanan, Addicott, Fitzgerald, Ferlie, & Baeza, 2007; Ferlie, Fitzgerald, McGivern, Dopson, & Bennett, 2013; Martin, Currie, & Finn, 2009; Moore & Rutherford, 2012). Such studies suggest that institutional innovation is indeed precipitating further hybridization of organizational forms in English public services.

The account also suggests that leaderism may play an important facilitative role, even in less extreme national contexts, by underpinning leadership development as a soft, co-optative policy lever. In our case it nurtured (though not entirely successfully) the acculturation of local-level elites responsible for service organizations as leaders, acting both as conduits for reform and colonizers of institutional creative space in the resultant reformed services. The emergent 'command situation' that leaderism served here was clearly polyarchic. There was expanded scope for local-level elite 'leaders within the system' to develop innovatory provision based on cross-jurisdictional, horizontal power relationships. Yet it was delimited, as our informants attested, by the expanded strategic-level elite technologies of hierarchical 'remote control' that legitimated them, as 'leaders of the system', sustaining their dominant position as market regulators. But for how long? The stability of this polyarchy rests on remote control that keeps the range of innovatory provision within bounds acceptable to authoritative elites. Yet their 'administrative reach' is limited by their dependence, both on local-level expert elites to 'lead' the operation of local service markets, and on service users and other voters to continue approving of the authoritative elites responsible for establishing the regulated service marketplace. The way has been opened here for unpredictable institutional innovation, and possible challenging consequences for the strategic-level elites driving reform.

Complementary work could valuably reach beyond our study in exploring how local-level expert elites orchestrate institutional innovation and its consolidation within the expanding array of governance arrangements being created by marketization, with an eye to its contribution to the further hybridization of organizational forms. In turn, improved understanding of 'how the hybrid is made to happen' through the dynamic interplay between authoritative and expert elite power should put us in a better position to explain the complex political and cultural processes through which institutional innovation in contemporary public services emerges as a sustainable, if contested, socio-material reality.

Improved understanding of the complex dynamic interplay between inter-elite agency, institutional innovation and organizational hybridization in public services seems most likely to emerge from further research on the strategic role that 'advocacy coalitions' of authoritative and expert elites play in generating new 'moral vocabularies of discourse', such as 'leaderism'. This role may embrace the mobilization of field or sector-level institutional logics legitimating hybridized organizational forms that, in turn, recombine contrasting – and often competing – control technologies and practices. Inter-elite advocacy coalitions will, necessarily, carry and contain structural contradictions and ideological tensions. They will have to be 'worked through', at least in some minimally sustainable way, in order to make possible discursive and behavioural interventions that are consistent with the institutional innovations and organizational reforms they are striving to legitimate and implement. In this respect, the 'internal conversations' that advocacy coalitions will have with themselves, as corporate agents with the potential powers and mechanisms to generate contextual and operational change for and within public services, will be of strategic significance for subsequent phases of institutional innovation and organizational reform. The result will be to recombine, in novel and unpredictable ways, logics and practices that simply didn't seem to belong together – until now!

The study discussed here heralds the sort of research that we suggest is needed to get at the 'underside' of the discursive mechanisms and cultural processes at work in generating new institutional logics and organizational technologies for legitimating and delivering contemporary modes of public service provision. It will be important to track how far they attempt to break radically with previously established modes while retaining significant 'leftovers' from 'what went before'. Focusing on the highly complex interplay between inter-elite agency, institutional innovation and organizational hybridization is likely to prove of considerable worth to researchers as we strive to unpack the power relations and dynamics that continue to shape public service reform.

ACKNOWLEDGMENT

The research reported here was supported by the Economic and Social Research Council under grant number RES-000-23-1136. The views expressed are those of the authors and do not represent the views of the ESRC.

REFERENCES

Archer, M. (2003). *Structure, agency and the internal conversation*. Cambridge: Cambridge University Press.
Barber, M. (1996). *The learning game*. London: Gollancz.
Barber, M. (2007). *Instruction to deliver*. London: Politico's.
Bennis, W. G., & Nanus, B. (1985). *Leaders: The strategies for taking charge*. New York, NY: Harper & Row.

Bevan, G., & Hood, C. (2006). What's measured is what matters: Targets and gaming in the English public healthcare system. *Public Administration, 84*(3), 517–538.
Blair, T. (2010). *A journey*. London: Hutchinson.
Bolam, R. (1986). The national development centre for school management training. In E. Hoyle & A. McMahon (Eds.), *The management of schools (world yearbook of education)* (pp. 252–271). London: Kogan Page.
Bolam, R. (1997). Management development for headteachers: Retrospect and prospect. *Educational Management and Administration, 25*, 265–283.
Bolden, R., Petrov, G., & Gosling, J. (2008). *Developing collective leadership in higher education. Final report*. London: Leadership Foundation for Higher Education.
Bottomore, T. (1993). *Elites and classes*. London: Allen Lane.
Brunetto, Y. (2001). Mediating change for public-sector professionals. *International Journal of Public Sector Management, 14*(6), 465–481.
Buchanan, D., Addicott, R., Fitzgerald, L., Ferlie, E., & Baeza, J. (2007). Nobody in charge: Distributed agency in healthcare. *Human Relations, 60*(7), 1065–1090.
Burns, J. (1978). *Leadership*. New York, NY: Harper & Row.
Clarke, J. (2004). *Changing welfare, changing states: New directions in social policy*. London: Sage.
Clarke, J., & Newman, J. (1997). *The managerial state: Power, politics and ideology in the remaking of social welfare*. London: Sage.
Clarke, J., Newman, J., Smith, N., Vidler, E., & Westmarland, L. (2007). *Creating citizen-consumers: Changing publics and changing public services*. London: Sage.
Clegg, S., Courpasson, D., & Phillips, N. (2006). *Power and organizations*. London: Sage.
Cohen, M. D., March, J. G., & Olsen, J. P. (1972). A garbage can model of organizational choice. *Administrative Science Quarterly, 17*(1), 1–25.
Coopers and Lybrand. (1988). *Local management of schools*. London: Her Majesty's Stationery Office.
Courpasson, D., & Clegg, S. (2012). The polyarchic bureaucracy: Co-operative resistance in the workplace and the construction of a new political structure of organizations. In D. Courpasson, D. Golsorkhi, & J. Sallaz (Eds.), *Rethinking power in organizations, institutions, and markets* (Vol. 34, pp. 55–80). Research in the Sociology of Organizations. Bingley, UK: Emerald Group Publishing Limited.
Crouch, C. (2005). *Capitalist diversity and change: Recombinant governance and institutional entrepreneurship*. Oxford: Oxford University Press.
Crouch, C. (2013). *Making capitalism fit for society*. Cambridge: Polity Press.
Dahl, R. (1958). A critique of the ruling elite model. *American Political Science Review, 52*(June), 563–569.
Dahl, R. (1971). *Polyarchy: Participation and opposition*. New Haven, CT: Yale University Press.
Daily Mail. (2014). Revealed: Islamist plot dubbed 'Trojan Horse' to replace teachers in Birmingham with radicals. *Daily Mail*, 7 March. Retrieved from http://www.dailymail.co.uk/news/article-2575759/Revealed-Islamist-plot-dubbed-Trojan-Horse-string-schools-Birmingham-self-styled-Jihad.html. Accessed on June 11, 2014.
Denham, A., & Garnett, M. (2001). *Keith Joseph*. Durham, NC: Acumen.
Department of Health and Social Security. (1983). *NHS management inquiry (the Griffiths report)*. London: DHSS.
DuGay, P. (2000). *In praise of bureaucracy*. London: Sage.
DuGay, P. (2005). Bureaucracy and liberty. In P. DuGay (Ed.), *The values of bureaucracy* (pp. 41–62). Oxford: Oxford University Press.

DuGay, P. (2008). Keyser Suze elites: Market populism and the politics of institutional change. In M. Savage & K. Williams (Eds.), *Remembering elites* (pp. 80–102). Oxford: Blackwell.
Enthoven, A. C. (1985). Reflections on the management of the National Health Service. Occasional Paper No. 5. Nuffield Provincial Hospitals Trust, London.
Fairclough, N. (2010). *Analysing discourse: The critical study of language* (2nd ed.). London: Routledge.
Ferlie, E., Fitzgerald, L., McGivern, G., Dopson, S., & Bennett, C. (2013). *Making wicked problems governable? The case of managed networks in healthcare.* Oxford: Oxford University Press.
Ferlie, E., Fitzgerald, L., Wood, M., & Hawkins, C. (2005). The (non) spread of innovations: The mediating role of professionals. *Academy of Management Journal*, 48(1), 117–134.
Fischer, F. (2003). *Reframing public policy: Discursive politics and deliberative practices.* Oxford: Oxford University Press.
Frank, T. (2001). *One market under god: Extreme capitalism, market populism and the end of economic democracy.* London: Secker and Warburg.
Gamble, A. (2009). *The spectre at the feast: Capitalist crisis and the politics of recession.* Basingstoke: Palgrave Macmillan.
Gillard, D. (2014). *Education in England: The history of our schools.* Retrieved from http://www.educationengland.org.uk/. Accessed on June 11, 2014.
Goldfinch, S., & Wallis, J. (2010). Two myths of convergence in public management reform. *Public Administration*, 88(4), 1099–1115.
Griffiths, A. (1971). *Secondary school reorganisation in England and Wales.* London: Routledge & Kegan Paul.
Harvey, D. (2005). *A brief history of neo-liberalism.* Oxford: Oxford University Press.
Harvey, D. (2011). *The enigma of capitalism and the crises of capitalism.* London: Profile Books.
Hoque, K., Davis, S., & Humphreys, M. (2004). Freedom to do what you are told: Senior management team autonomy in an NHS acute trust. *Public Administration*, 82(2), 355–375.
Jamieson, I. (1996). Education and business: Converging models. In J. Pole & R. Chawla-Duggan (Eds.), *Reshaping education in the 1990s: Perspectives on secondary schooling* (pp. 26–39). London: Falmer.
Lane, J.-E. (2000). *New public management: An introduction.* London: Routledge.
Leys, C., & Player, S. (2011). *The plot against the NHS.* Pontypool: Merlin Press.
Loveridge, R. (2014). Designing legitimacy: The rise of global advocacy coalitions and the emergence of the proselytizing think-tank.
Martin, G., Currie, G., & Finn, R. (2009). Leadership, service reform, and public-service networks: The case of cancer-genetics pilots in the English NHS. *Journal of Public Administration Research and Theory*, 19, 769–794.
McLaughlin, K., Osborne, S., & Ferlie, E. (Eds.). (2002). *New public management: Current trends and future prospects.* London: Routledge.
Miller, P., & Rose, N. (2008). *Governing the present.* Cambridge: Polity.
Mills, C. W. (1956). *The power elite.* New York, NY: Oxford University Press.
Mirowski, P. (2013). *Never let a serious crisis go to waste: How neo-liberalism survived the financial meltdown.* London: Verso.

Monbiot, G. (2014). How have these corporations colonized our public life? *The Guardian*, 8 April.
Moore, T., & Rutherford, D. (2012). Primary strategy learning networks: A local study of a national initiative. *Educational Management Administration and Leadership*, *40*(1), 69–83.
Moran, M. (2007). *The British regulatory state: High modernism and hyper-innovation*. Oxford: Oxford University Press.
Murphy, J., & Shiffman, C. D. (2002). *Understanding and assessing the charter school movement*. New York, NY: Teachers College Press.
Newman, J. (2001). *Modernizing governance: New labour, policy and society*. London: Sage.
Newman, J. (2005). Enter the transformational leader: Network governance and the micro-politics of modernization. *Sociology*, *39*(4), 717–734.
Newman, J. (2013). Professionals, power and the reform of public services. In M. Noordegraaf & B. Steijn (Eds.), *Professionals under pressure; The reconfiguration of professional work in changing public services* (pp. 41–54). Amsterdam: Amsterdam University Press.
Nye, J. (2004). *Soft power: The means to success in world politics*. New York, NY: Public Affairs.
OECD. (2001). *Public service leadership for the 21st century*. Paris: Organization for Economic Co-operation and Development.
OECD. (2010). *Making reform happen: Lessons from OECD countries*. Paris: Organization for Economic Co-operation and Development.
Ogawa, R., Crowson, R., & Goldring, E. (1999). Enduring dilemmas of school organization. In J. Murphy & K. S. Louis (Eds.), *Handbook of research on educational administration* (pp. 277–295). San Francisco, CA: Jossey-Bass.
OPSR. (2002). *Reforming our public services: Principles into practice*. London: Office of Public Services Reform.
O'Reilly, D., & Reed, M. (2010). Leaderism: An evolution of managerialism in UK public services reform. *Public Administration*, *88*(4), 960–978.
O'Reilly, D., & Reed, M. (2011). The grit in the oyster: Professionalism, managerialism and leaderism as discourses of public services modernization. *Organization Studies*, *32*(8), 1079–1101.
Osborne, S. (2006). *The constructions of neo-liberal reason*. Oxford: Oxford University Press.
Paton, C. (2014). Garbage-can policy-making meets neo-liberal ideology: Twenty five years of redundant reform of the English National Health Service. *Social Policy and Administration*, *48*(3), 319–342.
Peck, J. (2010). *Constructions of neoliberal reason*. Oxford: Oxford University Press.
Performance and Innovation Unit. (2001). *Strengthening leadership in the public sector*. London: The Stationery Office.
Piketty, T. (2014). *Capital in the twenty first century*. Cambridge, MA: Harvard University Press.
Pollitt, C. (1993). *Managerialism and the public services* (2nd ed.). Oxford: Blackwell.
Pollitt, C. (2007). New labour's re-disorganization: Hyper-modernism and the costs of reform – A cautionary tale. *Public Management Review*, *9*(4), 529–543.
Pollitt, C., & Bouckaert, G. (2011). *Public management reform: A comparative analysis* (3rd ed.). Oxford: Oxford University Press.

Pollitt, C., Harrison, S., Hunter, D. J., & Marnoch, G. (1991). General management in the NHS: The initial impact 1983–88. *Public Administration*, *69*(Spring), 61–83.
Public Services Trust. (2009). *A brief history of public services reform*. London: Public Services Trust.
Reed, M. (2011a). Control in contemporary work organizations. In P. Blyton, E. Heery, & P. Turnbullm (Eds.), *Reassessing the employment relationship* (pp. 41–70). Basingstoke: Palgrave.
Reed, M. (2011b). The post-bureaucratic organization and the control revolution. In S. Clegg, M. Harris, & H. Hopfl (Eds.), *Managing modernity: Beyond bureaucracy?* (pp. 230–256). Oxford: Oxford University Press.
Reed, M. (2012a). Masters of the universe: Power and elites in organization studies. *Organization Studies*, *33*(1), 203–222.
Reed, M. (2012b). Theorizing power/domination and studying organizational elites: A critical realist perspective. In D. Courpasson, D. Golsorkhi, & G. Sallaz (Eds.), *Rethinking power in organizations, institutions and markets* (Vol. 34, pp. 21–54). Research in the Sociology of Organizations. Bingley, UK: Emerald Group Publishing Limited.
Reed, M. (2014). *Leviathan eviserated? The decay of sovereign power and the hegemony of neo-liberalism*. Unpublished manuscript.
Richards, D., & Smith, M. J. (2004). The 'hybrid state': Labour's response to the challenge of governance. In S. Ludlam & M. J. Smith (Eds.), *Governing as new labour* (pp. 106–125). Basingstoke: Palgrave Macmillan.
Rivett, G. C. (2014). *National Health Service history*. Retrieved from http://www.nhshistory.net/. Accessed on June 12, 2014.
Rose, N. (2005). *Governing the soul*. London: Routledge.
Sabatier, P., & Jenkins-Smith, H. (Eds.). (1993). *Policy change and learning: An advocacy coalition approach*. Boulder, CO: Westview Press.
Savage, M., & Williams, K. (Eds.). (2008). *Remembering elites*. Oxford: Blackwell.
Scott, J. (1996). *Stratification and power: Structures of class, status and command*. Cambridge: Cambridge University Press.
Scott, J. (2001). *Power*. Cambridge: Polity.
Scott, J. (2008). Modes of power and the reconceptualization of elites. In Savage and Williams, op cit., pp. 27–45.
Selznick, P. (1966). *The TVA and the grass roots* (2nd ed.). New York, NY: Harper.
Smith, J., Walshe, K., & Hunter, D. (2001). The 'redisorganisation' of the NHS. *British Medical Journal*, *323*(7324), 1262–1263.
Smith, M. J. (2009). *Power and the state*. Basingstoke: Palgrave Macmillan.
Spours, K., Coffield, F., & Gregson, M. (2007). Mediation, translation and local ecologies: Understanding the impact of policy levers on FE colleges. *Journal of Vocational Education and Training*, *59*(2), 193–212.
Strategy Unit. (2008). *Realizing Britain's potential: Future strategic challenges for Britain*. London: Cabinet Office.
Universities UK/Standing Conference of Principals. (2003). Business case for the leadership foundation for higher education. Mimeo. UUK/SCOP, London.
Wallace, M. (1998). A counter-policy to subvert education reform? Collaboration among schools and colleges in a competitive climate. *British Educational Research Journal*, *24*(2), 195–215.

Wallace, M. (2007). Coping with complex and programmatic public service change. In M. Wallace, M. Fertig, & E. Schneller (Eds.), *Managing change in the public services* (pp. 13–35). Oxford: Blackwell.

Wallace, M., & Hoyle, E. (2012). The dynamics of irony in organizational change: Coping with a school merger. *Public Administration, 90*(4), 974–999.

Wallace, M., O'Reilly, D., Morris, J., & Deem, R. (2011). Public service leaders as change agents – For whom? *Public Management Review, 13*, 65–93.

Weber, M. (1978). *Economy and society.* Berkeley, CA: University of California Press.

Zald, M., & Lounsbury, M. (2010). The wizards of Oz: Towards an institutional approach to elites, expertise and command posts. *Organization Studies, 31,* 963–996.

ELITES AND THE POLITICS OF CRISIS

BUSINESS ELITES AND UNDEMOCRACY IN BRITAIN: A WORK IN PROGRESS

Andrew Bowman, Julie Froud, Sukhdev Johal, Michael Moran and Karel Williams

ABSTRACT

This exploratory paper discusses the undemocratic agenda setting of elites in Britain and how it has changed politics within a form of capitalism where much is left undisclosed in terms of mechanism and methods. It argues for a more radical exploratory strategy using C. Wright Mills' understanding that what is left undisclosed is crucially important to elite existence and power, while recognising the limits on democratic accountability when debate, decision and action in complex capitalist societies can be frustrated or hijacked by small groups. Have British business elites, through their relation with political elites, used their power to constrain democratic citizenship? Our hypothesis is that the power of business elites is most likely conjuncturally specific and geographically bounded with distinct national differences. In the United Kingdom, the outcomes are often contingent and unstable as business elites try to manage democracy; moreover, the composition and organisation of business elites have changed through successive conjunctures.

Keywords: Business elites; C. Wright Mills; elite power; finance; UK industry; railways

> Wherever possible, substitute construction out of known entities for inferences to unknown entities. (Bertrand Russell, *Logical Atomism*, 1924, p. 363)

> In so far as the structural clue to the power elite today lies in the political order, that clue is the decline of politics as genuine and public debate of alternative decisions. (C. Wright Mills, *The Power Elite*, 1956, p. 274)

This paper is work in progress in a double sense: the undemocratic agenda setting of elites in Britain and elsewhere is changing political work in progress, just as the social scientific understanding of elites is developing intellectual work in progress. In both cases, powerful elites and smart intellectuals find mastery of the world or the argument is frustratingly elusive. The shared dilemma of business elites and academics who study them is that they both live in a capitalism where much is undisclosed, so that unacknowledged and unmanaged realities irregularly intrude in a disruptive way. This has implications for our knowledge heuristic because we have a choice, laid out in the two opening quotations from Bertrand Russell and C. Wright Mills, of two alternative, conservative and radical exploratory principles.

Few social scientists will be familiar with the opening quotation from Bertrand Russell which gives us his version of Occam's razor. In Russell's version, the explanatory principle of simplicity and parsimony via fewer assumptions becomes the injunction to work with known entities. Yet, the practice of most social scientists does fit with Russell's heuristic: social scientists typically adopt a conservative exploratory strategy and make new empirical investigations using established apparatus with concepts and methods substantially carried over so that their work involves construction out of known entities. Much sociological discussion of stratification, for example, proceeds on this basis insofar as it supposes that 'class' can be read off the occupational hierarchy or takes a more cultural Bourdieusian line. There are many good reasons for doing this. If science is a craft involving an epistemic community, the conservative strategy ensures internal debate and the progress of what Kuhn long ago termed normal science.

But, when it comes to understanding elites, we argue for the different and more radical exploratory strategy which is implicit in the second quotation from C. Wright Mills. His quite different starting point is that the undisclosed is crucially important to elite existence and power, which is often technically obscured or politically denied. They are technically obscured, because (as we argue in the next section) elite groups are on the margins of what is knowable for many social scientific conceptualisations and techniques, both in Mills' era and in our own. They are also politically obscured because, in parliamentary democracies, elites are anomalously undemocratic and therefore stand to gain from discretion which leaves their identities and effects blurred and shadowy. If we wish to understand elites under these conditions, we would argue that Russell's principle and standard social science practice should be suspended, as the radical exploratory strategy is more appropriate to the special case.

If knowledge is here a matter of inference to and from unknown entities, the process of knowing involves reading what Mills (1956) called 'structural clues'. This is what Mills is arguing in the second opening quotation, where the decline of 'genuine and public debate of alternative decisions' is read as an elite effect which is a clue to the existence of a power elite in the United States in the 1950s. This inference from the effect — or clue — to the elite — or hitherto unknown entity — is both a neat intellectual move and a reminder of why elite studies matter even though they often fit uneasily into the dominant knowledge practices of the social sciences. We focus on elites because, through them, we start to comprehend an important aspect of 'undemocracy' — the often undisclosed forces that obstruct the full realisation of democratic citizenship.

The universal franchise and the mass party were twentieth century democratic inventions which were for all kinds of reasons bound to disappoint. In a complex capitalist economy and society, the powers of debate, decision and action are both exercised hierarchically and also inevitably dispersed in ways that elude electoral command and control. The limits on democratic accountability and agenda setting are a recurring theme in social sciences, from Michels (1911) on oligarchical control in mass parties to Latour (2005) writing about the limits on democratic participation in an uncertain world of technical issues and expert knowledges. The powers of debate, decision and action in complex capitalist societies can be frustrated or hijacked by small groups with agendas which then frame executive action and electoral debate. One question arising is then about whether and how business elites have (partly through their relation with political elites) used their power to constrain democratic citizenship.

If the aim is to read clues to the existence and power of business elites, the reading is not made on the assumption that elite power is always and everywhere the same in its ends and means. Business elites in Britain, as in the United States, have to live with an imperfect but robust democratic order in a changing economic structure, so that their world is full of new opportunities and potential challenges to the exercise of elite power. In thinking about such differences, our hypothesis is that the power of business elites is most likely conjuncturally specific and geographically bounded. In the United States in the 2010s, for example, we would not expect to find a reproduction or transposition of the relations between elites and democratic politics identified by Mills in the 1950s; any sketch of British elites would have to take account of the differences between here and there, as well as between now and then.

If the task is to understand the often contingent and unstable ways in which business elites try to manage democracy in the United Kingdom, we need to analyse how the composition and organisation of business elites have been changing, and how their economic and political field of action has developed through successive conjunctures (and explain how and why all this has been occluded by mainstream social science). The essay which does this here is organised in four sections. The first explains how social science framings often marginalise elites and explains how we set up the problem rather differently from elite studies. The second section offers a brief prehistory about how economic deindustrialisation and political defenestration in the United Kingdom marginalised productionist elites in the 1980s. The third and fourth sections then present readings of elite power in two sectors (finance and railways).

FRAMING ELITES AND MAKING THEM (IN)VISIBLE

> The power elite is composed of men ... (who) are in positions to make decisions having major consequences. (C. Wright Mills, *The Power Elite*, pp. 3–4)

It will never be easy to identify elite groups (whose decisions have consequences) because capitalist circumstance and intellectual resources change. Thus, elite studies needs to be intellectually updated so that it is made relevant to the present conjuncture. The challenge now is to incorporate the constructivist insights of sociology about how knowledge formats the world, without losing the old historico-political insight of Mills about the trail of clues from undemocracy to elites at work. If it does not rise to this challenge, elite studies is at risk of becoming methods-bound through a commitment to network analysis which fixes it in a managerial capitalist world of corporate directors and chief executives, without recognising new intermediary groups like fund managers. As our response to this challenge, we criticise established framings and argue for a descriptive turn and a renewed concern with elite *effects*; this is coherent with Mills' exploratory strategy.

Sociology is increasingly concerned with performativity and how concepts of power and methods of analysis can format knowledge and thereby make entities like elites appear or disappear. From this point of view, Mills' writings on elites present an argument against the pluralism of Dahl and its founding assumption that sovereign power is subject to multiple social checks and balances that constrain the power of every social group. This is relevant because a pluralist view implies that elites cannot be an important object of knowledge for political science. More recently, as Savage and Burrows (2007) have argued, the rise of the sample survey in sociology in the 1960s and 1970s made elite groups disappear because such techniques required larger groups to study; equally, subsequent Foucauldian arguments about capillary power and governmentality distracted from older ideas about the exercise of sovereign power by agents (Savage & Williams, 2008, pp. 4–10).

But if these developments eclipsed elite studies, they did not abolish them; indeed, they were academically sustained by the parallel development of more sophisticated techniques of social network analysis and allied concepts of nodes and bridges, as well as by the availability of suitable empirical source material on the careers of senior executives and directors in large public corporations. Network methods can find interconnections between corporations manifest in exchange of high level personnel; they can also show that (despite the general decline of elite club governance) such personnel have elite career formations. Social network techniques can thus make small, untypical, interlocking, high level groups appear and these groups can then be called business elites. What makes members of such groups interesting is, by implication, the extent and character of connections with peers or members of other occupational or functional groups.

But it is altogether more difficult in the next stage of the argument to convince sceptics that such elite groups matter because their existence has consequences for decisions and outcomes. Hence in the 1990s we have the blunt 'so what' rejoinder of Pettigrew (1992) to research on company board linkages and Mizruchi's (1996) question, 'what do interlocks do?'. This was a constructive question because it opened up new lines of research about how, for example, networked companies behave differently in the political sphere (or, vice versa, about how outcomes are framed by networks). We have used this approach to show how the UK FTSE 100 and 250 are networked through the recycling of senior managers as non-executive directors; case evidence was then used to argue that such circulation enforces the shareholder value principle that companies should be auctioned to the highest bidders (Froud, Leaver, Tampubolon, & Williams, 2008).

But, if the limits of network knowledge techniques can be worked around, they cannot be completely transcended because interconnections and background can only be mapped where there are suitable databases, as for public corporations where there is data on shareholding owners, senior executives and company directors. Network analysis can find empirical novelty with each new research project, but the novelty is only within a field of known corporate managerial entities.

As we have pointed out (Folkman, Froud, Johal, & Williams, 2007), the rise of finance in the United States and the United Kingdom greatly increased the number and role of well-paid intermediaries, like investment bankers, private equity partners or hedge fund managers who play a major role through operating in a world of deregulated credit creation. They have until recently been more or less completely neglected by elite studies because they do not 'command bureaucracies' (Mills, 1956, p. 286); moreover, intermediary backgrounds and careers cannot be studied with the techniques used for corporate executives because the relevant disclosures and directories simply do not exist. In a subsequent interview-based study of the founders of British private equity, we were intrigued to see that some of these partners chose to make themselves visible as philanthropists or media pundits while others enjoyed anonymity because there were almost no public sources of information about them (Froud, Green, & Williams, 2012).

More subtly, the traditional preoccupation with corporate elites rests on the assumption that, by virtue of office, chief executive or directors have some power of command and control over a corporate hierarchy within the boundaries of one giant firm. But this is disputable in the case of many banking firms in the financial sector where the firm is arguably a hollow shell with intermediaries at desks and divisions working for themselves within and across the boundaries of the firm. The Libor scandal revealed that firm boundaries were permeable because rate fixing requests were routinely made by traders outside the firm that was misreporting the rate. In response to questioning by the UK's Parliamentary Banking Commission, the current chief executive and chairman of Barclays have publicly agreed (Thurso, 2013) with CRESC's description of their firm as 'a loose federation of money making franchises' (Bowman et al., 2012a, p. 3). The process of outsourcing in the public sector and in traditional 'productionist' firms is likely to have similar effects in blurring the boundaries of giant organisations as they morph into sectoral activity clusters organised around financial flows, contracts and political favours. In such contexts, the actors who are of interest may not be found in particular job roles or be visible outside their organisations.

So, we cannot assume that the business elites who matter are all or mostly within the purview of established techniques of network analysis; or that the boundaries of the giant firm have the same unproblematic significance as they had in earlier conjunctures. In response, our suggestion is that elite studies should take a more descriptive turn away from formalism about networks and towards a more open exploratory strategy which is both descriptive and analytic in that it involves reading elite effects. What does this approach imply?

As demonstrated in the next section, the descriptive starting point for this kind of elite studies would be the changing configuration and structure of (national) economy and polity, which creates a field of action that combines a distinctive and changing economic habitat and political ecology. This emphasis on the national field of action does not mean that we would deny the existence of regional or transnational business elites, described by authors like Sklair (2001) or Van der Pijl (1998). But changing national circumstance is the obvious starting point in Western Europe because there are marked differences between, say, the United Kingdom, Germany and France in terms of the national field of action. Two sets of differences are immediately relevant: firstly, there are important national differences in structural commitment to activities like manufacturing or finance, ownership of strategic economic activities and macroeconomic trajectory; secondly, there are marked national differences in taxation and market regulation partly related to the very variable progress of the 'neoliberal' structural reform project of marketisation and flexibilisation in different national domains.

A descriptive turn of this kind will quickly turn up putative new elite groups and differences, like the large number of financial intermediaries in the United States and the United Kingdom related to the presence of large international financial centres in New York and London. Such groups can then be resourcefully investigated from official sources like tax returns as well as by interview and ethnography. But as the new knowledge accumulates, so the old *so what* question returns: how do we know that financial intermediaries (or a subgroup of such, like private equity partners) are a power elite which makes a difference to decisions and outcomes?

Here we need to balance description with an analytic turn towards analysing elite effects on political agendas and accepted definitions of reality. This would conserve the political thrust of Mills' approach and honour him as a major figure of the 1960s whose exploratory strategy can be reworked in the updating of elite studies for the 2010s. As the opening quote indicates, for Mills, the absence of discussed alternatives or (as we would now say) agenda control, was the structural clue that indicated the presence of a power elite in 1950s America. And we should look for similar clues and agenda control indicators of elite effect in present day capitalism.

At the same time, we should not assume that the clues will disclose a unitary power elite of the Millsian kind, that is one dominant national elite of executives at the apex of the key hierarchies which, for Mills, were political, military and industrial. Our understanding of Mills has been coarsened by the reductionist remembering of this one big idea. For better or worse, there is much more to *The Power Elite:* it included, for example, a Weberian insistence that the absence of a neutral bureaucracy underpinned the unchallenged power of the US power elite; as well as an historical argument about the manipulative role of the media in mass society which had made Jeffersonian democracy obsolete. It is also worth remembering that Mills included such diverse arguments because *The Power Elite* is not presenting a generalising theory of elite power but a conjunctural analysis that invokes elite effects so as to explain a specific, historical problem: how the United States was committed to the cold war without democratic consent through the imposition of military definitions of reality.

On this reading of Mills, it is acceptable to bracket his big conclusion about a unitary elite as specific to the 1960s; and also to accept that parts of his argument (e.g. about the role of media in mass society) are completely unacceptable to present day social scientists because times change and so does our episteme. But, the durable, reusable aspect of Mills is the exploratory strategy which involves the reading of elite effect clues to produce a political and social analysis of power that is conjunctural and specific. From this point of view, Mills is also both respectfully invoked and rather misunderstood by authors like Wade and Veneroso (1998) or Bhagwati (1998), who transpose and update his 1950s analysis of the 'military industrial complex'. For Wade and Veneroso or Bhagwati, this becomes a 'Wall Street–Treasury complex' with much emphasis on mechanisms like the revolving door in the United States between the corner office in investment banking and executive office in public roles like that of Treasury Secretary.

We do not, of course, deny the importance in the United States of figures like Robert Rubin and Hank Paulson, who both passed through this revolving door. The problem is with crediting these individuals or a small group with a distinctive elite effect that produces different and undemocratic outcomes. As we have argued in *After the Great Complacence* (Engelen et al., 2011), senior central bankers, regulators, politicians, economic experts and media right across the high income Western world accepted the same rhetoric about the benefits of financial innovation and limited regulation; just as their juniors in finance departments or journalism did not question this doxa. In this conjuncture of near universal complacency, it did not matter who was in charge or how many times the doors revolved. Hence, the British got outcomes and results in terms of unregulated banking irresponsibility which were as bad or worse although they operated with much stronger partitions between elite compartments and a Bank of England largely staffed by life-time employees.

If we are concerned with the classic Millsian power to control agendas and impose definitions of reality, it may now be much more revealing to consider elite effects at a sectoral level within one country, especially in the changing conjuncture since 2000. The 'neoliberal' project can be understood (and criticised) as a generic project which introduces the same structural reforms of privatisation, marketisation and flexibilisation, regardless of time and place. But, except when national crisis empowers broad front change, the modus operandi of structural reform is usually more like house-breaking, in that it targets one sector in one country at a time. And whatever the sequence and scale of structural reform, the result is not a once-and-for-all transformation because the legacy of reform is a set of privatised, outsourced and flexibilised activities that need business friendly, and usually sector-specific, rules. Furthermore, if we consider a sector like banking and finance after 2008, this result is in no way guaranteed because, in this case, the sector has to resist demands for radical reform after suffering massive reputational damage and public hostility after it socialised its losses.

While the key Millsian structural clue to be found within sectors such as banking is the absence of genuine debate of alternatives for radical reform, the effective exercise of elite power depends on appearances being quite the opposite. Pressure for genuine reform is stymied only when there is a simulacrum of debate about alternatives. Just as the daily rounds of cross party bickering creates an impression of genuine democratic choice while frontbench mindsets remains jammed in the post-political centre-ground, so on a sectoral level various forms of political theatre enable a partially convincing performance of alternatives that confuses reformist impulses.

This simulacrum takes three forms. Firstly, there is the performance of fierce intra-elite rivalry, in which companies vie against one another for dominance of consumer markets and victory in competitive tendering processes. These contests generate an easy flow of colourful stories for business journalists and bolster narratives around private sector meritocracies and the successes of structural reforms in empowering consumers. However, when sectors remain structurally unchanged, with limited net growth and a relatively homogenous product to deliver, this remains in essence a fauxpluralism: alternatives to an unsatisfying state of affairs are always lying close at hand in the form of companies deemed more or less innovative, trustworthy, or customer-focused; problems within a sector are instantly resolvable by shaming and punishing the bad and rewarding the virtuous (positions which can in time be swapped).

Thus in the recent horsemeat scandal which hit supermarket retail in the United Kingdom, fundamental structural problems with complex and adversarial food supply chains (see Bowman et al., 2012b) are submerged under a flow of stories about individual supermarket chains and specific products. Supermarkets can devote more energy to differentiation via ethics policy statements, and consumers can buy their groceries somewhere else, but business models and structural conditions remain outside the scope of alternatives. Likewise, accumulating scandals around poor delivery on the part of companies awarded major government outsourcing contracts led to the creation of an informal blacklist of a few 'high risk' companies to be excluded from future tendering exercises (*Financial Times*, 2012). It did not, however, provide grounds for debate about alternatives to outsourcing, where competitive tendering processes necessitate bidding companies inflating the limits of what they can deliver.

A second form of the simulacrum is the theatre of 'strict regulation' and political censure, in which misbehaving companies and dysfunctional sectors receive verbal dressing-downs from politicians and slaps on the wrist from regulators as a substitute for reform. These create the impression of something being done, but without intrusions into the core problems where easy solutions do not present themselves. In recent scandals around tax evasion in the United Kingdom, for example, angry denouncement from frontbench politicians and the Parliamentary Public Accounts Committee have become a substitute for reform for parties wary of alienating the business community. Domestic energy supply and telecoms, for example, are mature, sheltered markets cleaved out of former state monopolies, in which winning market share becomes a zero-sum game played with confusion marketing: accusations of 'bad value for money' — for instance at gas companies which have continued to raise bills in contrast to falling wholesale energy prices, healthy profit margins and directors pay packages — or misbehaviour such as mis-selling, lead to regulators producing strong words and modest fines, with the promise of minor reforms such as price simplification in tow. This is because in the case of most sectors in the foundational economy, regulators are independent of direct democratic control and based around constitutions which limit them to reinforcing marketisation (Bowman et al., 2014).

Finally, the simulacrum works to preclude debate of genuine alternatives via the individualisation of economic problems: in times of crisis, visible elites are isolated and punished, with the removal of senior executives taken as a proxy for company or sectoral transformation. Individualisation also stymies the debate of alternatives in a more subtle way by placing the analysis of sectoral problems onto the level of morality rather than political or economic tangibles, so that vague promises of 'cultural change' in organisations can absorb anger and stall more meaningful reforms.

The argument so far has been general and analytic. The purpose of the following sections is to use illustrations to show how this alternative intellectual strategy can, in practice, be realised. The next section provides a historical description of the economic and political undermining of productionist business elites in the United Kingdom in the 1980s as part of a longer term rebalancing towards new sectors. The two subsequent sections read elite effects in two sectors, UK finance and privatised rail, by demonstrating the capacity of elites to control the reform agenda.

HISTORY: UK DEINDUSTRIALISATION AND THE 1980S DEFENESTRATION OF PRODUCTIONIST ELITES

History is the shank of social study. (Mills, 1959, *The Sociological Imagination*, p. 143)

If Wright Mills was correct about the need for history, the question is what kind of history would help our understanding of British business elites? In line with our previous argument, this section presents a history of the changing economic and political space available to British business elites. It focuses on the undermining of productionist elites based in tradable goods sectors through parallel processes of economic deindustrialisation and political defenestration in the 1980s; it also highlights the longer term rebalancing towards deregulated finance and foundational service sectors franchised by privatisation and outsourcing. The object of description here is what we might call the economic habitat of business elites and the political ecology of their relation to other groups.

The *Oxford English Dictionary* defines habitat, in its natural history usage, as the kind of physical locality in which a plant or animal lives 'as the sea shore, rocky cliffs, chalk hills or the like', on the basis that different environments create different sets of ecological possibilities. The analogy with business has fairly obvious limits. The business habitat is not a given (like rich and fertile soil) but something which business can and will seek to modify through political action. Furthermore, firms are heterogeneous, from small workshops to large multinationals so that business occupies a multi-scalar space. But, if we are (in the Millsian way) searching for business elites with agenda setting capacity in a specific historic context, our starting point has to be the changing sectoral activity space available to different sections of national business elites and the political disposition of forces around organised business elites with specific activity bases.

The process of deindustrialisation in the United Kingdom is usually understood through the macro indicators as one of relative decline: manufacturing's share of GDP has been more or less halved towards 11% because there has been no sustained increase in the real value of output since the 1970s. As labour productivity was increasing, the outcome was disastrous for the workforce with numbers employed declining from around 7 million to just over 2.25 million by the late 2000s. As shareholder value was in the ascendant, the outcome was just as disastrous for large British manufacturing firms, especially the giant conglomerates which economically and politically led the tradable goods sector in the 1970s and the 1980s. And a new activity space opened by the 2000s for supermarkets, banks and outsourcers in what we call 'the foundational economy'; significantly, this space is sheltered and levered on the state (Bentham et al., 2013).

The dramatic start-to-finish changes in elite habitat are tracked in Tables 1 and 2, based on company report and accounts. These tables track the changing composition of the FTSE 100, the index of the 100 quoted companies with the largest market capitalisation on the London Stock Exchange. In Tables 1 and 2, we make the comparison between 1984 and 2007; the first date is the year when the FTSE index was first calculated,

Table 1. Large FTSE 100 Manufacturing Firms with More than 30,000 Employees in 1984.

Firm	Turnover (£Mill)	Total Employment	UK Employment
Assoc. British Foods	2,700	81,800	68,300
Allied Lyons	2,900	71,400	35,200
Brit. Am. Tobacco	10,100	212,800	50,800
BET	1,900	49,500	25,100
BOC	2,100	38,700	9,100
BAE	2,500	76,000	68,000
Cadbury	2,000	33,800	18,500
GEC	4,800	170,900	131,800
GKN	2,100	54,900	33,500
Hanson	1,600	67,000	30,000
Hawker Siddeley	1,500	41,500	27,300
ICI	9,900	115,600	58,600
Imperial Group	4,600	92,600	60,000
Pilkington	1,200	44,000	16,700
Racal	800	31,900	19,100
Rowntree	1,200	32,000	17,200
United Biscuits	1,700	41,100	29,800
Whitbread	1,200	39,700	39,700
BTR	3,500	60,300	Undisclosed
Courtaulds	2,000	70,000	Undisclosed
Plessey	1,300	38,900	Undisclosed
Unilever	5,900	140,000	Undisclosed
Thorn EMI	2,800	89,100	Undisclosed

Source: Company annual report and accounts.

just after the first Thatcher recession, and the second date comes right at the end of the long boom which ended in the financial crash. At the beginning of our period, the FTSE 100 was effectively a national index of large British firms and manufacturing was the dominant sector. By 2007, the position is more complicated because in a globalised world the FTSE 100 index includes international mining firms and brewing giants.

The first Thatcher recession of 1981–1983 had permanently reduced manufacturing output and capacity by some 20%, but the FTSE 100 of 1984 still included 39 large British manufacturing firms which accounted for nearly 40% of the sales and profits of all FTSE 100 companies. All 39 firms disclosed total employment and 25 of these manufacturing firms employed more than 30,000, which made them giants by British or European standards. The subtotal of UK employment is more difficult to calculate but some 17 of the 39 firms employed more than 15,000 in the

Table 2. Large FTSE 100 Manufacturing Firms with More than 30,000 Employees in 2007.

Firm	Turnover (£Mill)	Total Employment	UK Employment
Assoc. Brit. Foods.	6,800	84,600	29,100
AstraZeneca	7,400	67,400	11,800
Brit. Am. Tobacco	10,000	98,000	Undisclosed
BAE	14,300	88,000	34,000
Cadbury	8,000	71,700	14,000
GSK	22,700	103,000	Undisclosed

Source: Company annual report and accounts.

United Kingdom in 1984, if we add together the 12 firms which disclosed UK employment plus 5 others which we know had extensive British operations. The implication is that in 1984, the FTSE 100 was dominated by large firms which had the economic presence through scale and technology to anchor domestic supply chains; just as these large firms had the political clout to represent the interest of the tradable goods sector as central to national welfare.

By 2007, the position is very different. Even if we include the (international) brewer SAB Miller, there are no more than 15 large manufacturing firms in the FTSE 100 and these 15 firms by 2007 account for less than 10% of all FTSE sales; they are now very narrowly based in a few related sectors with 12 of the 15 firms operating in what might be called the 'oral consumable' sectors of food, drink, tobacco, pharma and hygiene. If the FTSE 100 of 2007 does include 15 large manufacturing firms, only 8 of these employ more than 30,000 in total worldwide and no more than 3 manufacturing firms (Associated British Foods, British Aerospace and Rolls Royce) disclose that they employed more than 15,000 in the United Kingdom, with two others having extensive British operations. Two of these firms are exceptions which owe their survival to government treatment of defence contracting and aero engines as special case sectors where strategic national interests require a national champion.

The British textiles, engineering and chemical conglomerates like Courtaulds, GEC and ICI were all closed down and/or broken up in the 1990s; while car assembly is now a patchwork of branch assembly plants largely adjunct to foreign owners so that the British car components sector has no firm like Lucas, which was once capable of supplying major systems and sub-assemblies. This sectoral shift against indigenous manufacturing was much sharper in the United Kingdom than in Germany where manufacturing remains the leading sector, or in France which struggles against German competition. Both these countries, for example, still sustain engineering conglomerates like Siemens or Alsthom, car assemblers like BMW or Renault or car component suppliers like Bosch and ZF or Michelin and Valeo. These companies still operate like their British predecessors of the 1970s and 1980s because they sell tradable goods into internationally competitive markets (with variable success) from a national base which is the centre of their mechanical or electrical engineering expertise and anchors a chain.

What replaced atrophied UK manufacturing? The two major developments were the brilliant success of the finance sector before the long boom turned into the present crisis and the ever growing importance of the 'foundational economy' which meets every day needs through retail chains including high street banks and supermarkets, privatised utilities and outsourcing (Bentham et al., 2013). The two developments were overlapping because the City of London was an international wholesale financial centre and base for mainly foreign firms in an era of unregulated credit creation inaugurated by big bang after 1986; but it fed off mass marketing of mortgages and pensions by high street banks. The foundational sectors had a common logic. With or without overseas operations, these firms all relied on oligopolistic positions in a sheltered UK market which gives them a lien on British household income subject to domestic competition.

At the same time the pattern of growth was different because the finance sector (wholesale and retail together increased their share of national gross value added (GVA) from 6.6% in 1992 to 8.0% in 2007). But the numbers employed in the finance sector did not exceed 1 million, of which no more than 300,000 were employed in and around wholesale finance; and, partly for this reason the huge growth of finance created only one FTSE 100 bank, Barclays, which had a substantial wholesale workforce. But privatisation, outsourcing and the advance of the supermarkets created many new giant firms, partly because the big corporates could grow through the transfer of state activity and the cannibalising of small scale retailing. The United Kingdom still has giant firms with large British operations as well as UK headquarters but they are now concentrated in these sectors, as Table 3 shows. In 2012, the FTSE 100 included 16 firms like Lloyds Bank, Marks and Spencer, Capita, Tesco and BT employing more than 15,000 in the United Kingdom and some 13 of these firms employ more than 30,000 in the United Kingdom.

This kind of double activity shift in the United Kingdom towards finance and the foundational intensified the dependence of corporate

Table 3. Large FTSE 100 Foundational Economy Firms in 2012 with More than 15,000 Employees in the United Kingdom.

Firm	Total Employees	UK Employees
Banking		
Barclays	139,200	55,300
HSBC	270,000	48,000
Lloyds Group	92,800	89,800
RBS	119,200	71,200
Retail and supermarkets		
Kingfisher	666,900	23,500
Marks and Spencer	81,200	74,800
ABF	106,200	37,500
Supermarkets		
Morrisons	94,100	94,100
Sainsbury's	101,900	101,900
Tesco	406,400	205,900
Utilities		
BT	89,000	73,800
Centrica	38,600	30,600
SSE	19,500	18,871
Outsourcing groups		
Capita	47,600	41,700
Compass Group	508,700	50,000
Serco	96,100	28,500

Source: Company annual report and accounts.

business on national politics. Business is a franchise to take turnover and make profit which often needs political sponsorship, and this is true whether it be manufacturing, big box retail or private equity. Hence the importance in all high income societies of detailed national regulations about corporate tax rates, investment allowances, urban planning and such like. The progress of structural reform like privatisation and outsourcing diminishes the directly state-controlled sector but increases the importance of political decisions because it creates formal franchises in regulated privatised utilities and an outsourced, para-state sector of private firms, such as the nurseries and care homes that depend on state funding. National politicians typically initiate structural reform and afterwards manage public opinion for or against business, which is most easily mobilised around national issues. This is especially so in the centralised United Kingdom with limits on federal devolution downwards and much hostility towards supra-national power.

If sectoral activity shift had political implications, everything was accelerated because the slow economic process of deindustrialisation in Britain over two decades since the 1980s has its political corollary in the speedy defenestration of productionist business elites under Thatcher, which took place in a couple of years from the early 1980s. Thatcher, who is mainly remembered for fighting union leaders, was equally resolute in marginalising what she regarded as failed corporatist business leaders. That defeat is the background to the famous (or notorious) threat in 1981 by Terry Beckett, who had moved from Ford to become Director General of the Confederation of British Industry (CBI), that the Confederation would have a 'bare knuckle' fight with a government which was pursuing policies so damaging to the manufacturing sector (Grant, 1993).

In Britain in the decade before 1979, (productionist) national business elites did not so much set the agenda as continuously partner successive national governments, in the effort to solve a series of acute problems: the United Kingdom's lack of competitive success in European manufacturing; internal issues about labour strife and industrial relations; and an unresolved relation with the Common Market. Thus Donald Stokes and Arnold Weinstock were government-favoured private sector managers in the state-sponsored private merger phase of the 1960s, which put them in charge of sectoral behemoths like British Leyland (BL) and General Electric Company (GEC). Equally, Paul Chambers from ICI and Terry Beckett from Ford led organised big business in the 1970s and early 1980s when the CBI was a 'a governing institution' (to use Middlemas, 1979 phrase) in Britain's primitive corporatist phase. The work of such elites involved continuous interaction with the political classes and organised labour on prices and incomes policy as well as more generally articulating the needs of big business. The CBI, for example, led a significant pro-Europe big business campaign in the 1975 referendum.

Then, in a remarkable shift, nationally based productionist elites who had a leading role in the 1970s were defenestrated in a few years in the first half of the 1980s as the British government moved quite explicitly to rebalance the economy towards services and finance, and symbolically embraced Japanese branch factories in manufacturing.

Manufacturing was permanently diminished by the monetarist experiment which induced the 1981–1983 recession, before the windfall gain of North Sea oil eased the balance of payments constraint so that poor export performance no longer produced recurrent payments crisis. Meanwhile, the government's turn against quasi-corporatism left giant manufacturing firms with nothing to negotiate and nobody to talk to. The rearguard action of British manufacturers in the 1985 Aldington House of Lords Select Committee Report predicted a terminal trade crisis; but this was discounted by a government which wanted 'to encourage enterprise to get the whole economy to perform better' (Lord Young, House of Lords, 3 December 1985). The government was at this point well advanced in negotiations with Nissan, which led to the 1986 opening of the Sunderland plant as part of a policy that put UK car manufacturing under new management and foreign ownership. At the same time, the government was sponsoring a new order private sector built on sheltered services, shareholder value and deregulated credit: the first two major privatisations were British Telecom (BT) in 1984 and British Gas in 1986; this was also the year of the 'Big Bang' that deregulated financial services.

This historical retrospective on the 1980s raises two questions. Firstly, do the new sectoral spaces of finance, privatised utilities and the para-state sustain agenda-setting business elites? Secondly, is the power of the new business elites more robust than that of their productionist predecessors? That is an open question because the defenestration of the 1980s demonstrates that established elite power can be fragile in adverse circumstances. In line with our earlier argument, we will consider elite power at sectoral level in two of the most interesting areas that grew out of post-1980s political change. Firstly, the next section considers deregulated UK finance which was through the City of London both the most successful new sector in generating profits for itself and then uniquely destructive in dumping liabilities onto the taxpayer. And secondly, the fourth section considers railways, which is interestingly quasi-paradigmatic of the para-state because rail was privatised but remained heavily dependent on state subsidy.

THE POWER OF FINANCE (BEFORE AND AFTER 2008)

> These men have replaced mind with platitude and the dogmas by which they are legitimated are so widely accepted that no counter balance of mind prevails against them.
> (C. Wright Mills, *The Power Elite*, p. 356)

Mills recognised the importance of elite-endorsed narrative in generating closure and blocking out alternative frames and agendas. Trade narratives about the social benefits of private activity acquired a new importance in post-1980s Britain after the renunciation of any kind of corporatist representation of employers and organised labour. In finance and other new sectors like pharmaceuticals or privatised utilities, trade associations developed local narratives about sector specific national contribution in the form of jobs created, tax revenue, trade balance and products that met social needs (with each sectoral story highlighting two or three of these elements as relevant). The sectoral narrative of national contribution then provides legitimating cover for trade association lobbying in Whitehall and Westminster. As we argue below, this is an important part of how finance controlled the regulatory agenda and secured a permissive light touch regulatory regime before 2008. It is also how finance has constrained the reform agenda since 2008 by (so far) successfully resisting wholesale structural reform to banking and finance. This latter point about limited and constrained reform, despite sustained public hostility to finance, is important in itself and because it is, in a Millsian frame, a very strong indicator of entrenched elite power.

The first precondition of financial power was the development of powerful and sophisticated lobbying networks that linked London finance with the apex of the core executive, especially in the Treasury. In the 1990s, the transformation of the social character of the City of London after the Big Bang (the increasing domination of markets by foreign firms, the integration of the City into global markets, the rise of the European Union (EU) as a significant regulatory actor and the wider spread of organised business lobbying) all combined to promote organised lobbying. The change in the character of the British Bankers' Association (BBA) is emblematic: it was rescued from a moribund condition in the 1980s to lobby for the banking industry in the EU; after 1997, under the leadership of Angela Knight, previously a Treasury Minister in the Conservative (Major) governments it was turned into a formidable voice defending the regulatory exceptionalism enjoyed by the City. By the new millennium an even more impressive City lobbyist had been reorganised: the City of London Corporation, historically a manager of City charities and City ceremonials, developed a significant intelligence and advocacy capacity.

An active system of professional lobbying worked partly through narrative which dignified self-interest in a way that was both platitudinous and never more than half true because the success of London finance was attributed to light touch regulation, while its contribution to the national economy through taxes paid was exaggerated, for example, by focusing on corporation tax not total taxes (Engelen et al., 2011, pp. 146–150). Two linked narratives predominated: they recurred repeatedly in speeches on quasi-ceremonial occasions like the Lord Mayor's banquet, and were more systematically propagated in City-commissioned reports. One narrative celebrated the deregulated, finance-led economy inaugurated by the Thatcher reforms as a new model of successful Anglo-Saxon capitalism which more regulated European economies would do well to emulate. The second celebrated the intelligence of lightly regulated financial markets in developing mechanisms and instruments for the management of risk. The platitudes carried conviction in the minds of market operators, regulators like central bankers, and elected politicians: hence the long litany of affirmations of the genius of City markets in the years leading up to the great crash of 2007–2008 (Engelen et al., 2011).

Trade lobbying plus narrative defence was backed up by the City's embrace of Murdochism. From the early 1990s, the City had no fixed attachment to the Conservatives as a centre right party of business. Instead, like newspaper proprietor Rupert Murdoch, the City switches political donations and ostentatious public support between centre left and right according to which party was most likely to win the next election and would afterwards gratefully remember its funders in a world where both major parties compete to represent themselves as business friendly. New Labour won City support through the 'prawn cocktail offensive' in the early 1990s, and retained it through Blair's three electoral victories until, under the Brown premiership, City money switched to the Conservatives. In 2005, when David Cameron became leader of the Conservative Party, the financial services industries were the source of just under a quarter of total cash donations to the party; by 2010 the figure had risen to just over 50% (Bureau of Investigative Journalism, 2011; Watt & Treanor, 2011). In 2010, 57 individuals from the financial services sector made donations of £50k and became a member of the 'Leader's Group', with an entitlement to meet 'David Cameron and other senior figures from the Conservative Party at dinners, post-PMQ lunches, drinks receptions, election result events and important campaign launches' (Conservative Party, 2011).

Organised lobbying plus a narrative defence backed by financial contributions were enough to completely neutralise the threat of closer regulation before 2008. In 1997 the passage of the Financial Services Act, and the creation of a single Financial Services Authority, seemed to signal that finance too was now being subjected to growing controls. The reality, as has now been widely documented, was very different. The creation of the new Authority began a period of celebrated 'light touch' regulation designed to maximise the freedom of markets to run their own affairs. Legitimation of this state of affairs by central bankers and by regulators involved familiar tropes borrowed from City PR narratives (Froud, Moran, Nilsson, & Williams, 2012). Accounts stressed the capacity of markets to anticipate and package risk and celebrated the success of light touch regulation in London in ensuring the City's continued international dominance, especially over more restrictively regulated centres elsewhere in the EU.

As we have documented elsewhere, after the catastrophic crisis of 2007−2008, the financial elite faced moments of great danger, as popular anger mounted at the growing evidence of widespread incompetence, recklessness and greed which had not been purged from the system (Engelen et al., 2011). Finance, after socialising its post-2008 losses at great cost to the taxpayer, is much more blameworthy than (merely) uncompetitive British manufacturing was in the 1980s. Yet, since 2008, financial elites have been able to avoid the defenestration inflicted on their productionist predecessors after 1983.

The British Social Attitudes survey periodically asks questions about public confidence in key business institutions. In 1983 it asked its sample of the population whether banks in Britain were well run. Ninety-per cent agreed that they were: the confidence expressed was higher than for any other institution surveyed. By 2009, when a similar question was asked, the figure had dropped to 19%. In reporting these figures, Curtice and Park remark that: 'This is probably the biggest change in public attitudes ever recorded by the *British Social Attitudes* series' (2011, p. 141). This collapse followed a series of disastrous appearances in public venues by leading bankers. In March 2009, for instance, there was the televised arraignment of several former heads of the stricken banks before the House of Commons Treasury Select Committee, which was accompanied by headlines in the tabloid press such as 'Scumbag millionaires', in *The Sun* on 11 February 2009. Subsequent appearances have been just as damaging to the reputation of the industry. The hostility after Bob Diamond disastrously gave evidence to the Treasury Select Committee in July 2012 about the Libor scandal (Watt & Treanor, 2012) precipitated a full scale crisis of morale in the bank as management claimed that they intended to fix the culture.

Yet in the UK case it proved strikingly easy for the financial elite to control the terms of the debate about reform, and to control the management of the stricken institutions. The Labour Government (in office until 2010) produced proposals for only the most marginal of reforms; through the Bischoff Report, New Labour continued to endorse the City narrative about the social benefits of finance for tax revenue, employment and trade

(Froud, Moran et al., 2012). There was a new rhetoric from all three main parties about the need to rebalance the economy but this was always to be done by growing manufacturing faster not shrinking banking and finance, even though the banks had assets and public liabilities equal to five times GDP. The successor coalition, in office from May 2010, set up a banking commission which was designed to shunt difficult issues about ownership and banking practices away from front line politics. This Independent Commission on Banking did not make radical proposals for structural reform by breaking up the big banks or disrupting oligopolistic competition on the high street by using state-owned RBS and Lloyds-HBOS for purposes other than shareholder value creation. Instead, the main national proposal for reform was for ring fencing retail from wholesale activities in a way that was bank-friendly (Independent Commission on Banking, 2011). Significantly this reform was endorsed by all three main political parties though much expert opinion was not convinced. Popular hostility in the United Kingdom to banks and bankers made no difference to this outcome which was negotiated between banking elites and politicians or civil servants who did not represent 'counterbalance of mind' to finance. And this compromise which protects banking is evidence of a powerful semi-visible elite in and around finance.

A key reason for the absence of genuine alternatives in this reform process has been not only the interconnections between banking and political elites, but also the successful simulacrum of alternatives which has operated in this instance through the isolation and punishment of individuals. Throughout the crisis, problems in the major banks have been laid at the feet of those in leadership positions, whose exit from the organisation or sector, or public shaming by regulator, provides the grounds for heralding cultural transformation which allows past mistakes to be laid to rest. This has involved, most notably, stripping the knighthoods from former Royal Bank of Scotland chief executive Fred Goodwin and former HBOS chief executive James Crosby after extended periods of criticism from the press and parliament. Former Barclays chief executive Bob Diamond resigned following the libel scandal in the face of public opprobrium and apparent behind the scenes encouragement from key regulators. On a lower level, large-scale institutional failures have been pinned on lower-ranking individuals who receive more meaningful punishments via the courts, notably UBS's rogue traders Kweku Adoboli and Thomas Hayes.

Scapegoating and the cult of leadership are of course nothing new, but in the case of banking the issue has been more complex as the anthropomorphisation of the sectors problems moved the debate about reform away from business models and towards individual morality. As earlier CRESC papers observed, this meant that in the wake of the Libor scandal, 'banking culture' – taken in the ideational sense of motives and values rather than as arising from material conditions – become the object of reform for elites rather than banking business models (Bowman et al., 2012a). The result is that the final report of the Parliamentary Commission for Banking Standards (2013), 'Changing banking for good' (set up after the Libor-fixing scandal of 2102), is centred around means by which the regulator can intervene on individual motives and values. The problem, the report says, is that 'Too many bankers, especially at the most senior levels, have operated in an environment with insufficient personal responsibility ... they then faced little realistic prospect of financial penalties or more serious sanctions commensurate with the severity of the failures with which they were associated' (Parliamentary Commission on Banking Standards, 2013). Naturally, the only major structural fix is, as in every sector, to encourage greater competition and choice to create better functioning markets. 'Making individual responsibility in banking a reality' by deferring bonuses, threatening jail terms and drawing up new codes of conduct does little to address underlying causes of the banking crisis or resolve remaining problems, but fits perfectly in the simulacrum in whereby the appearance of change is maintained in areas which causes little fundamental disruption.

And this compromise of limited reform plus the simulacrum which protects banking is evidence of a powerful, semi-visible elite in and around finance. This elite is clearly visible in the statistics on income inequality assembled by authors like Atkinson (2005) or Piketty and Saez (2003) who highlight the emergence of a new stratum of 'working rich' with high incomes, and whose leading representatives in the United Kingdom and the United States are those who work in and around investment banking in London and New York. The City of London is a machine for manufacturing millionaires (not least because of the 'comp ratio' system in investment banking and fat fees in fund management) (Folkman et al., 2007); the BBA and other more specialist trade groups like the British Private Equity and Venture Capital Association (BVCA) use narrative to make their special pleading look socially respectable; and political contributions close the circle so that it is very difficult for frontbench politicians to be unsympathetic.

If it is hard to deny the elite power in finance, many would nevertheless suppose it is a sectoral exception. This was a sector unlike any other because deregulated finance had a huge economic throw weight in the United Kingdom and its influence was unusually concentrated in one centre adjacent to political power. Furthermore, much discussion of finance and the real economy assumes that the productive economy has a different logic. It is, therefore, significant to find agenda control through similar means in other sectors, which also suggests elite presence.

ANOTHER SECTOR: UK RAILWAYS IN THE 2010S

> The elite cannot be truly thought of as men who are merely doing their duty. They are the ones who determine their duty, as well as the duties of those beneath them.
> (C. Wright Mills, *Power Elite*, p. 356)

This kind of agenda control is not confined to finance. In the United Kingdom, if we consider the privatised utilities and the para-state of privately owned, publicly funded activities (such as in health and social care), sectoral business elites also define the duty of politicians, civil servants and regulators. These business activities create widespread public suspicion and hostility, yet sectoral elites are able to control reform agendas and do so in very similar ways by producing trade narratives. Specifically, these narratives distract from complex and questionable funding and organisational arrangements so that official public discourse about the operation of the sector is about how best to give private interests what they want. The section below describes the rail sector which is untypical only in terms of the scale of the serial shambles and its cost in terms of huge accumulating public liabilities.

The dominant private players in rail are the train operating companies (TOCs) which have successfully bid for regional franchises to operate the trains; they lease trains from (for-profit) rolling stock operating companies (ROSCOs) and pay track access charges to (not-for-dividend) Network Rail which manages and invests in the track infrastructure. Over a decade or more, the result has been increasing dysfunction which has been well-documented by industry commentators like Wolmar (2005) and by independent academics like McCartney and Stittle (2011, 2012) or Shaoul (2004, 2006), as well as in our own *Great Train Robbery* Report (Bowman et al., 2013). Privatised rail remains a public problem because passenger revenues have never covered operating costs, leave alone generated a surplus for investment; the rail system therefore requires ongoing public subsidy. The scandal is that subsidy is offered without control of predatory private interests or regard for public consequences for the taxpayer.

The manifest failure to control the high profits made by the ROSCOs from train leasing indicates much larger problems centred on the role of Network Rail. This company has funded infrastructural investment by issuing £30bn of private debt guaranteed by the taxpayer. The Network Rail debt cannot be repaid out of revenue because track access charges have been lowered in a way that artificially boosts the profits of the TOCs; these are typically special purpose vehicles whose standard practice is to distribute what they earn as profits to corporate parents like Virgin or Stagecoach. As argued in Bowman et al. (2013), a train franchise represents a low investment, low risk option on profits, with an option to walk away with modest penalties if disappointing passenger numbers lead to expected losses. Successive transport ministers and Department for Transport (DfT) civil servants have failed to control the gaming of this system by franchise bidders who succeed by over-bidding with back-loaded premium payments to the state. Low premium payments in the early years allow profit taking with the option to walk away with minimal penalties and avoid high premium payments in the later years of the franchise.

The Association of Train Operating Companies (ATOC) tells a rather different story and makes very dubious claims about public benefits as it 'brings together all train companies to preserve and enhance the benefit for passengers' (ATOC, n.d.). Thus, ATOC asserts that 'privatisation has been accompanied by an injection of over £30bn in private sector investment, steady improvements in safety, and renewal of rolling stock, so that the fleet is now the youngest in Europe' (ATOC, 2009). Bowman et al. (2013, p. 75) show that private investment by the TOCs in stations, track and signalling is much less than the dividends they have paid out[1] and the average age of rolling stock is now higher than in the last years of British Rail. In ATOC's narrative, the TOCs claim credit for increased passenger numbers but this claim is doubtful. The secular rise in passenger numbers began 10 years before privatisation, is recently concentrated in the South East (Bowman et al., 2013, p. 112) and is driven by GDP growth. The TOCs effectively admitted this point when they lobbied to build GDP risk into franchise contracts. The same contradiction between narrative claim and lobbying objective recurs in ATOC's role as 'major player' in improving punctuality.

As in finance, the half-truths of the trade narrative about post-privatisation performance (and the demonising of British Rail) provide the frame through which policy makers deal kindly with the dominant sectoral players. The train operators have been able to control the reform agenda so that it becomes one of making the franchising system work better, rather than exploring alternatives as part of a wider review of the rail system. ATOC's claims and assumptions have been routinely copied out into official reports into the rail industry, such as the 2011 *Rail Value for Money Study*, chaired by Roy McNulty (DfT, 2011). The McNulty report's declared aim was to avoid structural change: 'as far as possible, to adapt existing structures rather than to sweep them away, and to focus the efforts of all concerned primarily on the areas where efficiency can be improved rather than on total reorganisation' (DfT, 2011, p. 46). The result was recommendations for improvement through longer franchises and new ways of risk sharing.

This consensus was not upset by the fiasco around the award of the West Coast Main Line (WCML) contract in 2012, when an initial award had to be withdrawn because of errors made by the department in the franchising process. Two reviews were commissioned by the DfT in response to the crisis: the Laidlaw report considered the mistakes of DfT civil servants in handling the WCML franchise (DfT, 2012a, p. 18); while the Brown review's remit was to 'consider the implications for the remainder of the rail franchising programme of the position reached on the InterCity West Coast competition' (DfT, 2012b). The letter from the Secretary of State to Richard Brown suggested the objective as 'how to get the other franchise competitions back on track as soon as possible' (DfT, 2012b). Brown recommended reforms which would strengthen the TOCs: 'I share the Government's view ... that the rail industry works, and that there is no credible case for major structural change ... It is very important that the franchising programme is restarted as soon as possible' (DfT, 2013). This is entirely consistent with the view of the chief executive of one of the TOCs, First Group, who opined 'the franchise system is not broken or needs no major overhaul' (*Financial Times*, 2012).

Here again the simulacrum of alternatives proved effective in confusing the issue. Virtuous Virgin Rail were able to claim responsibility for the transformation of the WCML, having received £2.5bn in direct state subsidy and a £10bn taxpayer-funded track upgrade, and present themselves as victims of duplicity on the part of First Group and incompetence on the part of the DfT: petitions demanding that Virgin keep the franchises succeeded in gathering over 150,000 signatures (Virgin Trains, 2012). The reward for Richard Branson's dubious claims that the success of the Virgin Trains franchise was down to management acumen, was support among the public and, following the failure to find a swift solution to the re-tendering process, a risk-free management contract running up to 2017.

The WCML as a franchise was a high value, high prestige operation which achieved high levels of customer satisfaction. Although a combination of state subsidy and the option to walk away means that no franchise represents any form of financial risk to prospective operators, lines which have been less fortunate in terms of state investment suffer from lower levels of passenger support. The beauty of rail franchising though, as with many other forms of state outsourcing, is that failure on the part of one provider leads not to pressure for reforms but for hope that another provider can do a better job next time around, endowing the system with a sort of perpetual motion driven by new logos and more outlandish promises. In the case of the East Coast Mainline, the financial failure of two franchises in quick succession between 2007 and 2009 led to the state taking over the service through its hastily assembled company, Directly Operated Rail (DOR) (McCartney & Stittle, 2011). Despite better than adequate performance by DOR, the DfT has pledged to return the ECML to a private franchise holder as soon as possible, promising that customer choice will play a greater role in the selection of winning companies in future.

The TOCs' unchallenged control of the reform agenda is quite remarkably maintained despite sustained popular hostility to the UK's privatised rail system whose public face is the TOCs. The TOCs can point to the official Passenger Focus survey evidence under 31 headings, which shows passengers are generally satisfied with quality of service (though not with fares, which are generally higher than in Europe). But this frames the problem very narrowly as a consumer issue and in doing so diverts attention from other important citizen issues about private ownership. The public cannot understand the obscure flow of public subsidy around the rail sector but it is suspicious and dissatisfied with private ownership. Indeed, opinion polls point to a high level of public support for renationalisation: 51% support in a 2009 *PoliticsHome* survey (with a further 18% favouring greater state involvement short of renationalisation) (*PoliticsHome*, 2012); two-thirds of respondents in an October 2012 poll carried out by Vision Critical for the *Sunday Express* (2012); and 70% of respondents in a GfK NOP poll carried out for Rail Media in September 2012 (*Rail*, 2012). Opinion poll evidence should be treated with caution but the succession of polls shows a dissatisfied citizenry whose preference for nationalisation indicates a consistent public demand for an integrated not-for-profit public railway and an alternative future, but which has had no influence whatsoever on policy makers.

The success of the TOCs in controlling the rail agenda raises the question of who the elites are and how they are organised. In finance, the elite beneficiaries and agenda fixers are either the same individuals, or the fixers are a representative subset of the much larger group of beneficiaries in investment banking and fund management. In railways, the beneficiaries and fixers are quite distinct groups. The major beneficiaries in privatised transport are those who had major ownership stakes in new opportunities, a group which would include not only Richard Branson but also humbler, provincial figures like Brian Souter of Stagecoach or Moir Lockhead, formerly of Grampian Regional Transport and then of First Group. The work of fixing and agenda alignment is done by well-paid managers who have built their careers at the interface of the public and the newly private rail sector. From this point of view, it is interesting to consider the careers of Sam Laidlaw and Richard Brown who were brought in to conduct 'independent' reviews after the West Coast franchise debacle to ensure both legitimacy and narrow debate.

Sam Laidlaw is a well-connected senior utility manager who is Whitehall house-trained as an insider who understands the politics of privatised, regulated industry and the need to keep things going. Currently Laidlaw is CEO of Centrica, the FTSE 100 company formed by the 1997 demerger of the privatised British Gas plc and he was already in place as the lead non-executive director on the board of the DfT at the time of the WCML fiasco. Richard Brown is the complete rail industry insider who is currently Chair (and formerly CEO) of Eurostar. He started in the industry with British Rail before privatisation where he progressed to divisional manager in Midland Mainline; he joined National Express Group when they were awarded that franchise after privatisation and progressed to become Commercial Director. As well as direct management experience in a variety of freight and passenger operations, Brown has operated at industry level as chair of ATOC; most recently, he has been appointed to the board of HS2.

The operating conditions for the privatised industry are politically set and authentication by elite intermediary fixers like Laidlaw and Brown has been sufficient to avoid radical change and to ensure agenda control survives as the DfT is scapegoated and TOCs are strengthened. The outcome of agenda control in other sectors needs to be researched but prima facie is broadly similar because we can think of no utility where private interests have been confronted rather than conciliated.

CONCLUSION: SO WHAT (DOES IT MEAN)?

Any concluding discussion of elite power should start with a caution about how it would be rash to draw large conclusions from two sectoral cases in one country. But, in the exploratory spirit of Wright Mills, finance and railways do provide clues to the existence of elites and the modalities of elite power in the present conjuncture.

In the United Kingdom, more than 30 years after the watershed of 1979, the Thatcher/Blair style of 'neoliberalism' through structural reform, privatisation and outsourcing is not so much a project of structural reform but a kind of permanent revolution: a revolution whose structural results are increasingly embedded in an economy that has been reconfigured by a complex process involving both politically sponsored structural reform and the (sustained) relative failure of manufacturing with the (short term) success of finance, measured either by shareholder value or market share in tradables. The implication of our argument is that, in finance and in a privatised sector like railways, these double processes have embedded operators and lobbyists who undemocratically set sectoral agendas that suit corporate private interests (regardless of public costs and the opinion of voters). The outcome in both sectors meets what might be called the Wright Mills test of elite presence: because in both sectors we have the promotion of definitions of reality and sectoral settlements which suit private financial interests and obstruct politics understood as 'the genuine and public debate of alterative decisions'.

More research is needed. But, if our results are confirmed for other sectors, it is hard to be optimistic about the immediate prospects of politically controlling these elites and reopening the democratic conversation. Whereas Wright Mills believed one unitary power elite made a difference in Cold War America, the prospect now is of dispersed, invasive, sectorally based power elites who are very difficult to challenge, not least because they are only semi-visible and their definitions of reality can only be unpicked by a kind of critical intellectualism which has few funders. This situation of capitulation to business is not without precedent because nineteenth-century British governments had to live with the parliamentary power of sectoral interests like industrial assurance, private railway companies and the coal owners who were all untouchable even when they had no electoral constituency. The Atlee government after 1945 did displace these politically over-mighty business elites but that displacement only became possible after two world wars, under pressure from an organised labour movement and with a mass social democratic party. If we consider present day business elites and their sectoral effects, the economic and political conditions for change are most likely absent and likely to remain so, as long as economic policy keeps things going for the majority of the citizenry. In the meantime, the pressures for change could be levered by providing more sectoral analysis of the political and economic effects of the different sectoral elites who altogether build a giant system of welfare for undeserving corporates.

NOTE

1. For instance, in 2011 the TOCs collectively invested £29m in stations, track and signalling and paid out £165m in dividends.

REFERENCES

Atkinson, A. B. (2005). Top incomes in the UK over the 20th century. *Journal of the Royal Statistical Society, 168*(2), 325−343.
ATOC. (n.d.). *About us*. Retrieved from http://www.atoc.org/about-atoc
ATOC. (2009). *ATOC, 'electrification − ATOC's view'*. Retrieved from http://www.aTOC.org/clientfiles/File/Policydocuments/IndustrystructurePrivatisation.pdf
Bentham, J., Bowman, A., de la Cuesta, M., Engelen, E., Ertürk, I., Froud, J., ... Williams, K. (2013). *Manifesto for the foundational economy*. CRESC Working Paper No. 131. University of Manchester/Open University, CRESC. Retrieved from http://www.cresc.ac.uk/publications/manifesto-for-the-foundational-economy
Bhagwati, J. (1998). The capital myth. The difference between trade in widgets and dollars. *Foreign Affairs, 77*(3), 7−12.
Bowman, A., Ertürk, I., Froud, J., Johal, S., Law, J., Leaver, A., ... Williams, K. (2012a, August). *The madness of banking: Culture and business models. CRESC submission to the Parliamentary Commission on Banking Standards*. Manchester/Milton Keynes: CRESC.
Bowman, A., Ertürk, I., Froud, J., Johal, S., Law, J., Leaver, A., ... Williams, K. (2014). *The end of the experiment*. Manchester: Manchester University Press.
Bowman, A., Folkman, P., Froud, J., Johal, S., Law, J., Leaver, A., ... Williams, K. (2013). *The great train robbery: Rail privatisation and after*. Manchester/Milton Keynes: CRESC. Retrieved from http://www.cresc.ac.uk/sites/default/files/GTR%20Report%20final%205%20June%202013.pdf
Bowman, A., Froud, J., Johal, S., Law, J., Leaver, A., & Williams, K. (2012b). *Bringing home the Bacon. From trader mentalities to industrial policy*. Manchester/Milton Keynes: CRESC. Retrieved from http://www.cresc.ac.uk/publications/bringing-home-the-bacon-from-trader-mentalities-to-industrial-policy
Bureau of Investigative Journalism. (2011). *City financing of the conservative party under Cameron*. Retrieved from http://thebureauinvestigates.com/2011/02/08/city-financing-of-the-conservative-party-doubles-under-cameron/. Accessed on April 27, 2011.
Conservative Party. (2011). *Donor clubs*. Retrieved from http://www.conservatives.com/Donate/Donor_Clubs.aspx. Accessed on April 28, 2011.

Curtice, J., & Park, A. (2011). A tale of two crises: Banks, MPs' expenses and public opinion. In A. Park, M. Phillips, E. Clery, & J. Curtice (Eds.), *British social attitudes survey 2010–2011. Exploring labour's legacy – The 27th report* (pp. 131–154). London: Sage.

Department for Transport (DfT). (2011). *Realising the potential of GB rail. Final independent report of the rail value for money study*. Department for Transport, London. Retrieved from https://www.gov.uk/government/publications/realising-the-potential-of-gb-rail

Department for Transport (DfT). (2012a). *Inquiry into the lessons learned for the Department for Transport from the InterCity West Coast Competition*. The Laidlaw inquiry: Initial findings report. Retrieved from https://www.gov.uk/government/publications/report-of-the-laidlaw-inquiry

Department for Transport (DfT). (2012b). *Text of letter from the Secretary of State to Richard Brown*. Retrieved from https://www.gov.uk/government/uploads/system/uploads/attachment_data/file/9197/letter-to-richard-brown.pdf. Accessed on October 15, 2012.

DfT. (2013). *The brown review of the rail franchising programme*. Cm 8526. London: The Stationery Office. Retrieved from https://www.gov.uk/government/uploads/system/uploads/attachment_data/file/49453/cm-8526.pdf

Engelen, E., Erturk, I., Froud, J., Johal, S., Leaver, A., Moran, M., ... Williams, K. (2011). *After the great complacence. Financial crisis and the politics of reform*. Oxford: Oxford University Press.

Financial Times. (2012). Firstgroup dividend pledge under threat. *Financial Times*, November 7. Retrieved from http://www.ft.com/cms/s/0/69ca39e0-28b9-11e2-9591-00144feabdc0.html

Folkman, P., Froud, J., Johal, S., & Williams, K. (2007). Working for themselves? Capital market intermediaries and present day capitalism. *Business History*, 49, 552–572.

Froud, J., Green, S., & Williams, K. (2012). Private equity and the concept of brittle trust. *Sociological Review*, 60(1), 1–24.

Froud, J., Leaver, A., Tampubolon, G., & Williams, K. (2008). Everything for sale: How non-executive directors make a difference. In M. Savage & K. Williams (Eds.), *Remembering elites* (pp. 162–186). Oxford: Blackwell Publishing.

Froud, J., Moran, M., Nilsson, A., & Williams, K. (2012). Stories and interests in finance: Agendas of governance before and after the financial crisis. *Governance*, 25(1), 35–59.

Grant, W. (1993). *Business and politics in Britain*. Basingstoke: Palgrave.

House of Lords. (1985). Select Committee on Overseas Trade, The Aldington Report. London: HMSO.

Independent Commission on Banking. (2011). *Final report recommendations*. Retrieved from http://www.hm-treasury.gov.uk/d/ICB-Final-Report.pdf

Latour, B. (2005). *Reassembling the social. An introduction to actor network theory*. Oxford: Oxford University Press.

McCartney, S., & Stittle, J. (2011). 'Carry on up the East Coast' – A case study in railway franchising. *Public Money and Management*, 31(2), 123–130.

McCartney, S., & Stittle, J. (2012). "Engines of extravagance": The privatised British railway rolling stock industry. *Critical Perspectives on Accounting*, 23, 153–167.

Michels, R. (1911). *Political parties*. New Brunswick, NJ: Transaction Publishers.

Middlemas, K. (1979). *Politics in industrial society: The experience of the British system since 1911*. London: Harper Collins.

Mills, C. W. (1956). *The power elite*. New York, NY: Oxford University Press.

Mills, C. W. (1959). *The sociological imagination*. New York, NY: Oxford University Press.

Mizruchi, M. (1996). What do interlocks do? An analysis, critique and assessment of research on interlocking directorates. *Annual Review of Sociology, 22*, 271–298.

Parliamentary Commission on Banking Standards. (2013). *Changing banking for good*. House of Lords/House of Commons Papers HL 27/HC 175. London: The Stationery Office.

Pettigrew, A. (1992). On studying managerial elites. *Strategic Management Journal, 13*, 163–182.

Piketty, T., & Saez, E. (2003). Income inequality in the United States, 1913–1998. *Quarterly Journal of Economics, 118*(1), 1–39.

PoliticsHome. (2012). Majority of public support full railway nationalisation. *PoliticsHome*, July 2. Retrieved from http://www.politicshome.com/uk/majority_of_public_support_full_railway_nationalisation.html

Rail. (2012). 70% want end to privatisation. *Rail*, September 13. Retrieved from http://www.rail.co/2012/09/13/70-want-end-to-rail-privatisation

Russell, B. (1924). Logical atomism. In *Contemporary British philosophy*. London: Peter Lang.

Savage, M., & Burrows, R. (2007). The coming crisis of empirical sociology. *Sociology, 41*(5), 885–889.

Savage, M., & Williams, K. (2008). *Remembering elites*. Oxford: Blackwell Publishing.

Shaoul, J. (2004). Railpolitik: The financial realities of operating Britain's national railways. *Public Money and Management, 24*(1), 27–63.

Shaoul, J. (2006). The cost of operating Britain's privatized railways. *Public Money and Management, 26*(3), 151–158.

Sklair, L. (2001). *The transnational capitalist class*. London: Blackwell.

Sunday Express. (2012). Poll demands railways must be renationalised. October 21, 2012.

Thurso, J. (2013). *Question to Antony Jenkins and David Walker, in oral evidence taken before the Parliamentary Commission on Banking Standards*, February 5, Q.3620. HC 606-xxxii. Retrieved from http://www.publications.parliament.uk/pa/jt201213/jtselect/jtpcbs/c606-xxxii/c60601.pdf

Van der Pijl, K. (1998). *Transnational classes and international relations*. London: Routledge.

Virgin Trains. (2012). *Virgin Trains e-petition reaches 100,000 target*. Retrieved from http://www.virgin.com/travel/virgin-train-e-petition-reaches-100000-target

Wade, R., & Veneroso, F. (1998). The Asian crisis. The high debt model versus the wall street-treasury-IMF complex. *New Left Review, 228*(March/April), 3–23.

Watt, N., & Treanor, J. (2011). Revealed: 50% of Tory funds come from the city. *The Guardian*, February 8. Retrieved from http://www.guardian.co.uk/politics/2011/feb/08/tory-funds-half-city-banks-financial-sector

Watt, N., & Treanor, J. (2012). Bob Diamond's evidence to MPs branded implausible. *The Guardian*, July 4. Retrieved from http://www.guardian.co.uk/business/2012/jul/04/libor-bob-diamond

Wolmar, C. (2005). *On the wrong line: How ideology and incompetence wrecked Britain's Railways*. London: Aurum Press Ltd.

FROM DESIGNERS TO DOCTRINAIRES: STAFF RESEARCH AND FISCAL POLICY CHANGE AT THE IMF

Cornel Ban

ABSTRACT

Soon after the Lehman crisis, the International Monetary Fund (IMF) surprised its critics with a reconsideration of its research and advice on fiscal policy. The paper traces the influence that the Fund's senior management and research elite has had on the recalibration of the IMF's doctrine on fiscal policy. The findings suggest that overall there has been some selective incorporation of unorthodox ideas in the Fund's fiscal doctrine, while the strong thesis that austerity has expansionary effects has been rejected. Indeed, the Fund's new orthodoxy is concerned with the recessionary effects of fiscal consolidation and, more recently, endorses calls for a more progressive adjustment of the costs of fiscal sustainability. These changes notwithstanding, the IMF's adaptive incremental transformation on fiscal policy issues falls short of a paradigm shift and is best conceived of as an important recalibration of the precrisis status quo.

Keywords: IMF; staff research; Keynesian; New Consensus Macroeconomics; austerity

FROM GREAT EXPECTATIONS TO MODEST RECALIBRATIONS

In 2008, many expected that the widespread outrage and economic hardship caused by the financial crisis would lead to the replacement of the neoliberal policy paradigm.

The rediscovery of Keynesian macroeconomics in 2008−2009 by the leaders of the G20 seemed to indicate that change was imminent. Indeed, mainstream macroeconomic and finance economics seemed on their way to a historical trial. For a while, decades of debates over the details of the best version of the efficient market hypothesis and the most refined dynamic general stochastic equilibrium models seemed out of place.

In the United States, mythical figures of mainstream macroeconomists were dragged in front of the Congress to explain themselves, their apathy for lawmakers' concerns about unemployment exposed in full view.[1] Allan Greenspan, the former chairman of the Fed and the guru of neoliberal practice offered a few public admissions of contrition over his beliefs. *Financial Times* editors called for the nationalization of large financial institutions and their transformation in public utilities. In Paris, Nicholas Sarkozy, a conservative president who campaigned on a neoliberal ticket the year before, allowed himself to be photographed leafing through a copy of Das Kapital. The world, it seemed, was ripe for a new economic model based on anything but more of the same neoliberal theory. If reality was of any empirical use, the case against mainstream economics was clear:

> [g]overning neoliberal ideas pretty much denied such a crisis could ever happen. So when it happened it was bound to open up some room for ideas that said such events were bound to happen if you left markets alone to regulate themselves, which is exactly the Keynesian point. Given this, it was hard to defend publicly the logic of self-correcting markets at a time when they were so obviously not self-correcting [...] Furthermore, as well as denying it could happen, neoclassical policy was entirely focused upon avoiding one problem, inflation, and providing one outcome, stable prices. As a result it seemed to have very little to say about a world where

deflation was now the worry and price stabilization meant raising, not lowering, inflation expectations. (Blyth, 2013)

But by late 2009, it turned out that the proponents of neoliberal theory had much to say and that they would go a long way to defend the theory's core. As a result, instead of drastic change, the following years brought a mere recalibration of neoliberal theory, testimony to its adaptability in the face of countervailing political and economic dynamics.

Scholars have showed that international economic organizations such as the International Monetary Fund (IMF) have been instrumental in crafting and disseminating neoliberalism. This paper continues this research agenda through an analysis of the "austerity debate" inside this established "lab" of applied orthodox macroeconomics. It departs from the observation that the IMF's reaction to the Great Recession has been to balance adherence to orthodoxy and the attempt to make fiscal neoliberalism more flexible. While the IMF's shifting views on fiscal policy have baffled its critics, the depth, significance, and causes of the shift remain unexplored. This paper addresses this gap by asking how deep the change has been and how has the Fund's research elite contributed to it. It suggests that the contribution of staff research to doctrinal change has been important but that far from being a Damascene road toward a new economic paradigm, so far this interregnum has spawned a fiscal policy hybrid that does not represent a dramatic departure from the core of neoliberal fiscal policy thinking.

WHAT IS FISCAL NEOLIBERALISM?

This paper defines fiscal neoliberalism as a set of economic theories about fiscal policy that play a prominent role because they speak to essential problems of distribution in society. Whether they are organized under the aegis of New Classical Macroeconomics, New Keynesian Economic, or the synthesis of the two, in the so-called "New Neoclassical Synthesis," neoliberal ideas on fiscal policy are tied together by skepticism about the expansionary effects of government spending and a penchant for spending cuts and regressive tax increases as a preferred fiscal adjustment strategy.

This reading of neoliberalism resists the tendency to see it as a revamped version of the universalistic aspirations of liberal political economy and neoclassical economics, or even as market fundamentalism (Somers & Block, 2014; Stiglitz, 2008). These popular characterizations have made it harder to grasp the ways in which actually existing neoliberalism has been both pro-market and pro-state.

Even the critics of austerity agree that the macroeconomics of neoliberalism has a considerable Keynesian layer (Arestis, 2012). Anti-market ideas and policies prop up the housing sector in the United Kingdom (Hay, 2011) and the United States acts as a developmental state when it comes to using government resources to spur industrial innovation (Mazzucato, 2013). Since 2008, both sides of the Atlantic nationalized large swathes of their financial sector and effectively guarantee the balance sheets of too big to fail (in the United States) and too big to bail institutions (in the EU) (Blyth, 2013).

I propose a definition of neoliberalism that factors in both market−society relations as well as the distribution relations within society. To this end, I see neoliberal ideas aimed not at destroying the state, but at transforming it. When put together, they remove social constraints on market freedoms, support the operation of the market, and mobilize state power to redistribute freedoms and privilege toward the top of the social pyramid. In the "big tent" represented by neoliberalism, economic ideas about fiscal policy are central because they define what is scientifically legitimate in terms of how the state should distribute resources. It is to this specific niche of the neoliberal ideational universe that this paper speaks to.

THE REFORM OF NEOLIBERAL MACROECONOMICS

Until 2008 the IMF upheld the so-called "Treasury view," according to which expansionary fiscal policy is generally a misguided attempt to stimulate an economy in recession. Instead, it is austerity that should be pursued (Gabor, 2010; Krueger, 1998; Mussa & Savastano, 2000). But three days before the tumultuous year 2008 came to a close, the IMF surprised its critics by endorsing the use of fiscal stimulus as a way to overcome the greatest crisis that capitalism had known since the Great Depression. Two years later, when European policymakers stated that austerity was not just necessary to lower debt but could even lead to growth, the IMF begged to differ. As one critic of the IMF put it, this revisionism was part of an "interregnum pregnant with development opportunities" (Grabel, 2011).

Specifically, in addition to allowing the stimulus option (for some) and discrediting the argument that austerity leads to growth, the Fund's research and general policy advice suggested that where fiscal consolidation is "inevitable," it should be introduced only gradually and by recalibrating its instruments so as to strengthen state investments and improve the economic status of those at the very bottom of the income distribution.

At the same time, rather than place mass unemployment as the main challenge of fiscal policy, the IMF's has not displaced financial market credibility through debt sustainability as the main goal of fiscal policy. By subordinating fiscal policy to the vote of financial markets, the Fund leaves the stimulus option open only to a dozen or so countries at any given time during the crisis. Moreover, ever for those cases, the Fund suggests that "entitlement reform" (cuts to social security and other programs) is a way of maintaining long-run credibility with the bond markets.

Given the intellectual path-dependency of credibility as the main goal of fiscal policy, it is not surprising that the staff either obscured or closed more heterodox paths to reducing debt and to creating fiscal space for stimulus. Moreover, its support for more redistributive taxation and spending options has been hamstrung by neoliberal skepticism toward universal social benefits and the value of sharply progressive taxation. This adaptive change appears a lot more modest than the transformative yet non-paradigmatic change uncovered by some scholars in the Fund's recent capital account policy (Chwieroth, 2013; Gallagher, 2014a, 2014b; Gallagher et al., 2012; Grabel, 2011).

Nevertheless, even an adaptive shift needs to be explained. To do so, the paper shows that beginning with 2008, the IMF's epistemic community experienced a rapid and important change in personnel that brought to the fore ideational entrepreneurs who built a revisionist network inside the Fund. To this end, they took advantage of the widening rift in academic macroeconomics between fiscal policy pessimists and optimists. To prevail in a professional environment constrained by orthodox thinking, these IMF economists refrained from battling the main goal of fiscal policy and framed their arguments in the lexicon of mainstream methods and models. In so doing, they won the debate inside the Fund at the cost of putting the brakes on a more systematic reconsideration of fiscal policy for hard times.

THEORETICAL FRAMEWORK

Political economists have begun to examine the internal sources of change in IMF's economic ideas and policies. In a constructivist vein, they argued that IMF staff's experience of a crisis is shaped by their interpretations of its causes and remedies (Broome & Seabrooke, 2012; Chwieroth, 2009, 2013; Clift & Tomlinson, 2012; Grabel, 2014; Lütz & Kranke, 2013; Momani, 2005; Moschella, 2011, 2012a, 2012b; Park & Vetterlein, 2010). The paper contributes to this emerging scholarship by drawing on the insights of three bodies of scholarship that had not been connected before: constructivist studies of international organizations, the sociology of the economic profession, and the sociology of science.

Constructivists argue that international economic institutions derive legitimacy from their exercise of epistemic authority over economic policy (Barnett & Finnemore, 2004; Broome & Seabrooke, 2007; Chwieroth, 2009, 2013; Seabrooke, 2012; Weaver, 2010). This legitimacy can be threatened by crises that challenge economic orthodoxy. Most of the time, however, such situations trigger changes that are less than paradigmatic shifts, with incrementally adaptive and transformative change emerging as the most likely outcomes (Chwieroth, 2009, 2013). Change, then, takes place at the level of policy instruments and settings, while policy goals survive.

Paradigmatic change occurs only when the goals of policy shift (Hall, 1993). In the context of this paper, the change from an orthodox to a heterodox (e.g., Keynesian) policy paradigm would entail a shift from the goal of fiscal sustainability through deficit cuts to full employment and the closing of the difference between actual and potential GDP via spending increases, sharply progressive taxation, and financial repression. In contrast, policy change is of a lesser order if only policy instruments and policy settings change. If the Fund's growth theory is reliance on public investments and income transfers more than they on tax cuts, the Fund engages in a change of instruments rather than goals. At the level of the settings of policy, if IMF economists plead for "backloading" (gradual introduction of) austerity, this does not show that the Fund has gone through a Keynesian paradigm shift, only that this sequencing is more likely to balance growth with debt sustainability.

Within this non-paradigmatic spectrum, changes are transformative if the new instruments and settings are derived predominantly from heterodox schools of thought and result in an incremental challenge to the main policy goals (the case of the Fund's endorsement of capital controls under certain conditions). In contrast, they are adaptive if they are drawn from a mixed bag of orthodox and heterodox theories and their cumulative effect is the reproduction of the orthodox policy goal.

To pursue this route, the paper maps out the revisions made by IMF researchers to the traditional content of fiscal policy. Then, to establish the extent to which staff research had an impact in the general policy advice of the Fund, the analysis turns to the general reports of two critical bureaucracies in the Fund: the departments of Research and Fiscal Affairs.

What explains adaptive change on fiscal policy? Some argue that shifts in the dominant economic ideas of the economic profession at large are eventually and incrementally reflected in how the IMF thinks (Chwieroth, 2009, 2013; Woods, 2006). This is because "the Fund recruits almost exclusively from the economics profession, which leaves it highly susceptible to developments within the academic community [...]" (Chwieroth, 2009). In other words the Fund and the economic profession are what Seabrooke and Tsingou (2009) called "linked ecologies." While there has been no scientific paradigm shift among academic economists before or during the crisis (Blyth, 2013), the internal diversity that some critics of mainstream macroeconomics (Arestis, 2012; Hein & Stockhammer, 2010) have uncovered within it should be taken more seriously. Given the "linked ecology," a widening rift during the crisis and the growing strength of the supporters of activist fiscal policy (fiscal optimists) could be an enabler of revisionism at the Fund.

Growing fiscal optimism in academia was a great opportunity for change at the Fund, but somebody had to grab that opportunity for it to have an impact. The paper hypothesizes that the second mechanism of ideational change is insider entrepreneurship carried via three sub-mechanisms: administrative intervention, conceptual editing, and methodological framing. While the first mechanism affects relations of power in the Fund's research infrastructure, editing and framing are needed to "sell" the revisionist message as long the orthodox in the Fund are not completely displaced.

RELAXING THE BOUNDARIES OF FISCAL ORTHODOXY

Contrary to conventional thinking, the crisis seems to have deepened the divisions between fiscal policy optimists and pessimists. When the Lehman crisis struck, mainstream macro was the intellectual universe of New Consensus Macroeconomics (NCM), a school of thought forged during the late 1990s from the convergence of New Classical economics and New Keynesianism (Arestis, 2012; Colander, 2011; Fontana, 2009; Mankiw, 2006). NCM was skeptical toward fiscal policy and somewhat optimistic toward monetary policy. Indeed, if there was any hope for countercyclical macroeconomic management in hard times, NCM economists limited its ambit to the policy action of the central banks.

NCM argued that the rational expectations of economic agents beat the Keynesian effects of fiscal policy. When the government tries to stimulate the economy, households and firms expect tax increases in the future and therefore cut spending and investment (Ricardian equivalence). Some New Consensus economists like Alberto Alesina at Harvard and Roberto Perotti at Bocconi University argued that because of this, both deficit spending and tax cuts will have low multipliers (i.e., output changes less than in proportion to the fiscal shock). Therefore, some argued that in order to improve expectations and kick-start growth, the government should frontload fiscal consolidation measures (expansionary austerity).[2] The New Keynesian faction inside NCM further consolidated this fiscal policy pessimism when they factored in Keynesian rigidities such as unionized wage bargaining. In the case of developing countries this fiscal policy skepticism was supplemented with remarks about their narrow automatic stabilizers and constrained access to capital markets (Hemming, Kell, & Mahfouz, 2002).

From outside the mainstream, neo-Keynesians and post-Keynesians critiqued the fiscal policy pessimism of NCM by showing that once you take out long time horizons, perfect foresight, perfect capital markets, and the absence of liquidity constraints, fiscal pessimism is no longer warranted.[3] But given the traditional proximity of the Fund to the mainstream, what truly shaped debates at the Fund were internal critiques coming from the NCM camp itself.[4]

As early as 2001, these critiques began to emerge after prominent NCM economists began to find positive and high fiscal multipliers (well above zero, but below 1.0),[5] thus implying that fiscal policy could have expansionary effects on economic output.[6] One of the champions of this revisionist position to NCM was Olivier Blanchard, an MIT economics professor and IMF consultant who went on to become the chief economist of the Fund after 2008.

To get more specific, I looked at debates on fiscal policy published during between 2008 and 2012 in elite economics journals such as *American Economics Review* and *Journal of Economic Literature*.

Already by 2009, revisionists from top academic departments began to calibrate DGSE models to approximate the conditions of the crisis (tight microeconomic fundamentals, zero lower bound interest rates) and found consistently high multipliers. Some of the most pivotal studies of this kind were authored by a group of economists from Berkeley (Alan Auerbach,

Brad deLong, Yuri Gorodnichenko) and Northwestern (Martin Eichenbaum, Larry Christiano, Sergio Rebelo). One of the DGSE papers finding a dramatic bang for the government spending buck at zero lower bound was Gauti Eggertson, an Icelandic economist from the Fed who had done his PhD with Paul Krugman and coauthored with leading NCM economist Michael Woodford.[7]

Some of the articles argue that fiscal policy activism is needed in the Great Recession and deplore the lack of attention from macroeconomists to fiscal policy design. Berkeley's Alan Auerbach and Harvard's Martin Feldstein make the case for stimulus from within the parameters of orthodoxy. After they bows to one of neoliberalism's foundational moments (the Lucas critique), they go on to argue that in very special circumstances (an environment with liquidity constraints, zero interest rates, a recession longer than 12 months, and credit market disruptions) fiscal policy interventions do have some benefits. With this tight specification in mind, Auerbach and Feldstein propose that such interventions should consist of tax refunds for corporations, lower corporate income tax, the indefinite postponement of higher tax rates on dividends, capital gains, and high-income individuals, and even the resuscitation of Reagan era tax schemes meant to incentivize corporate investment and household consumption.

Surprisingly, it is Martin Feldstein, the economist with a more conservative reputation of the two who makes the case that increased government spending along the lines proposed by the then President elect Barack Obama that should do the heavy-lifting through a stimulus designed to be "big, quick and targeted at increasing aggregate activity and employment" (Feldstein, 2009, p. 558). Should it fail, the response would be first even higher spending, followed by a combination between currency devaluation and retrenchment in substantial and permanent tax cuts on personal and corporate income.

Prior to the crisis there was a robust consensus that cuts have robust multiplier effects but if they are expected to be permanent and are targeted at low and medium income, indebted households have the highest multiplier. During the crisis elite economists suggested that same was true of the multiplier effects of welfare payments, unemployment insurance, and corporate investment incentives (review by Auerbach et al., 2010, pp. 146–150).

Moreover, a recalibrated NCM model with financial frictions finds that increases in government expenditure can be a more powerful stimulus in the short run than tax cuts (Fernandez-Villaverde, 2010). Below is a presentation of the affiliation of "revisionists" working on fiscal policy.

The revisionist drive continued as the sovereign debt crisis deepened in Europe. Using New Keynesian models, fiscal policy "mandarin" Michael Woodford further boosted the case for countercyclical government spending, arguing that with sticky prices and wages, fiscal multipliers can be larger than one and can lead to an increase in welfare (2010). Lawrence Christiano and Martin Eichenbaum's supported his findings with an article showing that when nominal interest rates are bound at zero, the fiscal multiplier is significantly larger than predicted under standard NCM models. To this end, they provided empirical evidence for a new pro-stimulus argument: multipliers are large because the rise in government spending increases output, marginal cost, and expected inflation. Since nominal rates are at zero, a rise in inflation causes a decrease in real interest rates, which leads to a rise in private spending. This initiates the process of rising output levels again, and the net result becomes a large increase in output.

THE ORTHODOX RESISTANCE

Since the multiplier debate did not consume so much of the energies of the profession until 2008, the defenders of the status quo did not mobilize against revisionism until the first few months of the crisis. What triggered this was that Berkeley professor Christina Romer who was then Obama's economic advisor coauthored a study whose "old" Keynesian model suggested multipliers around 1.5 that justified the need for fiscal policy stimulus in recessions triggered by credit crunches (Romer & Bernstein, 2009). This was a major turnaround considering that the Romers had previously bolstered the orthodox idea that monetary policy is useful in recessions while fiscal policy is not (Romer & Romer, 1994).

The orthodox charge against this position was spearheaded by a joint US−German research team who found very low and negative multipliers (Cogan, Cwik, Taylor, & Wieland, 2010). Critically, these economists rejected the Romer study for not using the NCM model (DGSE) that academic economists, central banks, and international organizations could find respectable.

As the crisis deepened, it became clear that even when after the Great Recession struck, not all mainstream economists rediscovered Keynes in their foxholes. Some argued that the debate over fiscal policy cannot be settled during to the indeterminacy of research on multipliers, thus suggesting that policy should err on the side of conservatism (Ramey, 2011).

Others showed that higher debt cancels the effects of higher multipliers (Uhlig, 2010) while others radicalized fiscal neoliberalism arguing that welfare should be turned into tradeable financial instruments, thus turning welfare recipients into entrepreneurs (Snower et al., 2009). Others still deepened the neoliberal tax regime by advocating for the further lowering taxes at the high end of the income distribution and the non-taxation of capital income (Mankiw, 2010) or for the replacement of progressive income taxation a flat tax consumption tax (Correia, 2011).

In contrast to the revisionists, Stanford's John Taylor (2011) resist the argument that discretionary fiscal policy is effective when the short-term interest rate reaches the lower bound of zero. Modern neo-Keynesian arguments such as those advanced by Summers, Krugman, or Romer are written off by Taylor with the argument that they don't use mainstream dynamic general stochastic equilibrium modeling (DGSE) and fail to include New Classical rational expectations.

An ECB study found new evidence for a foundational moment of neoliberalism: Robert Lucas' (1986) onslaught against the Keynesian Phillips curve. Others attacking the New Keynesian "sticky prices" theory by arguing that prices respond quickly to idiosyncratic shocks (like the Lehman Brothers) but only weakly and slowly to nominal shocks such as expansionary monetary policies.

An analysis of the EMU finds that it led to the fiscal profligacy, suggesting that tougher and more depoliticized fiscal constraints should be put in place (Beetsma & Giuliodori, 2010). In a preemptive strike against demands for increasing the tax burden at the top of the income distribution, some economists argued that the estate tax has little effect on the investment and saving decisions of small businesses but by distorting the decisions of larger firms it reduces aggregate output and savings (Cagetti & de Nardi, 2008).

Christopher Nekarda and Valerie Ramey took the battle further by investigating the effect of growth in government expenditure at the industry level. Their study found that the transmission mechanism that renders fiscal policy ineffective is the "old" neoclassical reasoning where increased labor hours result in lower real wages. This offsetting change causes markups to remain unchanged, and thus fiscal policy has failed to increase output. Similarly, Cohen, Coval, and Malloy (2010) attack the conventional Keynesian wisdom that government expenditure results in increased income in the economy by using an innovative instrumental variable to produce exogenous shocks in state level expenditure. Their article finds that the significant increase in federal funds to the home state of members of Congress lead to significant reduction in investment, employment, research and development, and payout decisions by firms. According to the paper, this occurs because of crowding out through the mechanisms of labor market and fixed industrial assets.

Five years into the crisis it is safe to say that the revisionists have an edge in the conversation but have not displaced the orthodox. Beyond the multiplier debate, however, the revisionists were much less inclined to rock the boat. At the end of the day, their work intimated that fiscal expansions should be carried out only if there is fiscal space and investor credibility, two variables whose measurements have been subject to a great deal of conservative calculations and market panics. Indeed, the entire debate has taken place in terms that do not challenge the political goal of not "scaring" the markets. Ultimately, the revisionist papers are either oblivious to or are casually dismissive of the use of sovereign debt restructuring or higher inflation as ways to create fiscal space for stimulating the economy. The Keynesian goal of full employment is nowhere to be seen.

How did academic orthodoxy and/or revisionism reach the Fund and with what consequences for its policy advice? It is to these transmission channels that the paper turns to next by focusing on the research cited by the IMF's official reports on fiscal policy doctrine: the World Economic Outlook and the Global Fiscal Monitor.

STAFF PAPERS AND THE FUND'S DOCTRINE

Editing entailed the introduction of ideas with Keynesian policy implications into select elements of NCM theoretical continuum. The outcome was a new perspective on the expansionary virtues of austerity, the utility of the fiscal stimulus, and the timing and composition of fiscal consolidation. This section will analyze these patterns by looking first at staff research authored by individual staff and then at general research reports containing the official view of the Fund's Research Department (RED) and Fiscal Affairs Department (FAD).

Against the strong neoclassical thesis that austerity can in fact lead to economic expansion, most IMF research suggests that in the specific conditions of the post-2008 crisis fiscal consolidation is in fact contractionary while fiscal stimulus packages are more likely to be expansionary (e.g., Ball, Leigh, & Loungani, 2011; Batini et al., 2012; Baum, Poplawski-Ribeiro, & Weber, 2012; Blanchard & Leigh, 2013; Cottarelli & Jaramillo, 2012; Eyraud & Weber, 2013; Guajardo, Leigh, & Pescatori, 2011; Spilimbergo,

Symansky, Blanchard, & Cottarelli, 2008; Spilimbergo, Symansky, & Schindler, 2009). Judging by its extensive citation, the December 29, 2008 joint staff position note by two Research and Fiscal Affairs departments was the defining moment of this doctrinal shift (Spilimbergo et al., 2008).

The paper was coauthored by RED and FAD directors and laid down the groundwork for macroeconomic policy during recessions: "a timely, large, lasting, diversified, and sustainable fiscal stimulus that is coordinated across countries with a commitment to do more if the crisis deepens" (p. 2). According to that paper, crisis economics had two policy priorities: stabilize the banking sector and increase aggregate demand through monetary and fiscal expansion. New Consensus skepticism about the need for fiscal policy activism in recessions was suspended. Moreover, a few of the IMF policy doxa (export-led recovery, activist monetary policy) were dismissed in the name of the transnational character of recession and the looming zero lower bound in interest rates. Concerns with low multipliers were brushed aside: all multipliers were declared uncertain and so policy diversification to stimulate aggregate demand was urgent. The orthodox objection that spending increases have long lags was declared irrelevant given the expected long recession. There were to be tax cuts for the most credit constrained, more spending on existing programs (mainly transfers to sub-national entities), increased provision of unemployment benefits, expansions of safety nets where these were limited. The Fund economists demanded support for those facing foreclosures, cash transfers to buy cars, government guarantees of new credit for firms in Chapter 11 type procedures and public works targeted at long-term growth potential. Higher taxes on high-income brackets were considered a sustainability mechanism. Hoover's America emerges as the poster case for how not to run a crisis.

Yet upon closer inspection the change looked more modest. Most importantly, the plea for fiscal expansion was limited to countries that did not face volatile capital flows, high public and foreign indebtedness, and large risk premia. Second, new entitlement programs were criticized for being hard to reverse and already creating long-term problems. Third, there remained orthodox skepticism about wage increases and sectoral subsidies, as they distort the uneven playing field toward MNCs. Finally, to make this stimulus sustainable, the Fund asked for anti-discretionary institutions: reversible measures with clear sunset clauses or certain economic conditions and independent fiscal councils.

This policy line was bolstered in future IMF staff papers. The most forceful case for expansion or at least neutral fiscal policy during recessions came from IMF staff working with a key methodological problem of the policy area under investigation here: fiscal multipliers. The orthodox studies on multipliers use models that did not allow them to vary between expansion and recession while failing to capture monetary policy. In 2012, the coalition of IMF and Berkeley academic economists took the initiative on this front as well. The Berkeley Auerbach and Gorodnichenko (2012) study and two IMF papers (Baum et al., 2012; Bettina et al., 2012) addressed these problems and found consistently high multipliers and particularly so in recessions. Using an innovative methodology, Batini et al. (2012) found that smooth and gradual consolidations are to be preferred to frontloaded or aggressive consolidations. Against conventional IMF studies, they found that this was especially the case for economies in recession facing high-risk premia on public debt, because sheltering growth is key to the success of fiscal consolidation in these cases. Consistent with the analytical framework embraced by this paper, this IMF study stresses layering when they argued that the estimates of the multipliers they estimate for both recessions and expansions are "broadly consistent with the theoretical arguments in both (old) Keynesian and (new) modern business cycle models" (Bettina & Alfred, 2012, p. 7). Similar points were made by Baum et al. (2012), whose study adds that when the output gap is negative at the time the fiscal shock is initially implemented, frontloading consolidation will have a larger short-term impact on output than a more gradual fiscal adjustment.

Other studies further enlarged the horizons opened by Spilimbergo et al. (2008). While some find new arguments against frontloading consolidation across national policy contexts, others demanded an enhanced role for public investments. One endorses expansions and stresses increased capital spending, with a bias for public sector investments due to their high multipliers (Muir & Weber, 2013). It argues that increased capital spending financed by higher indirect tax revenue collections through base broadening has sizeable growth effects over the medium and long term. Increasing spending by 2 percent of nominal GDP leads, in the long run, to a 30 percentage point increase in the stock of public infrastructure. This, in turn increases the productivity of factors of production in the economy, so that real GDP increases about 3 percent relative to its baseline value. Moreover, they argue that a permanent increase in government investment can be more effective than an increase in private investment, as government investment is typically on infrastructure such as roads, hospitals, public institutions, etc., which depreciate at a slower rate than the stock of machinery and equipment.

Cautionary notes about frontloading austerity stress not business expectations, as in the standard New Consensus framework, but workers' expectations. A study coauthored by the deputy director of the Research department (Ashoka Mody) found that despite the 2009 recovery, uncertainty of households remained and so did their steep increase in pro-saving behavior. The key explanation was the economy-wide unemployment rate. It was not future taxes, but catastrophic income loss via job loss that is positively correlated with the saving rate even after controlling for disposable income growth and the interest rate (Mody, Ohnsorge, & Sandri, 2012). Along the same lines, a study authored by two favorite IMF collaborators from Bocconi university questioned the New Consensus stress on the expectations of the financial sector when they showed that in recessions with sticky prices, the brunt of tax increases is more likely to be expansionary if it favors constrained borrowers rather than savers (Monacelli & Perotti, 2011).

A research paper coauthored by senior staff at RED demonstrated empirically the importance of expansionary credit policy in a recession triggered by a banking crisis (Claessens, Köse, & Terrones, 2008). Similar points were made for developing countries in position papers coauthored by a RED deputy director (Ghosh et al., 2009) and the director of the Western Hemisphere Department (Eyzaguirre, 2009).

In Keynesian fashion, these papers argued that given the collapse in private demand, states were supposed to ramp up both public investments and transfers to those who were more likely to spend (the unemployed and the poor households). Against the orthodox line, they stressed the role of public investments and downplayed the expansionary virtues of tax cuts with the Keynesian argument that they are more likely to be saved. They also dismissed once fashionable items of the IMF policy advice for recessions (export-led recovery, exclusive reliance on activist monetary policy) and spurned as irrelevant for a prolonged recession the orthodox objection that spending increases have long lags.

Yet this fiscal policy optimism was heavily qualified by orthodox concerns. Even if they agreed with the hypothesis that fiscal policy had high multipliers in the conditions of the crisis, virtually all these papers raised the issue of credibility with the markets. Indeed, the main goal of policy remained the reassurance of financial markets through "long-run debt sustainability." Revisionist studies (Baldacci, Gupta, & Mulas-Granados, 2012; Cottarelli & Jaramillo, 2012) joined orthodox ones (Baldacci & Kumar, 2010; Kumar & Woo, 2010) in highlighting the negative effects on growth of debt levels over 60 percent of GDP, a much more demanding threshold than the 90 percent threshold proposed by the subsequently discredited study of Reinhart and Rogoff (2010). Therefore, the stimulus was deemed appropriate only for countries with low levels of debt and deficits[8] and with strong fiscal institutions.[9] For the others, as the FAD director recently put it, "some adjustment is needed, but at a steady even pace, without frontloading, except in countries facing pressures from markets (and even in this case, there would be a speed limit to fiscal adjustment)" (Cottarelli, 2013). As a former deputy chief economist of the Fund recently noted, the Fund's main mission has been and continues to be reassurance of sovereign bond markets.[10]

Even where the IMF papers endorse stimulus, they demand neoliberal institutional reforms: the constitutionalization of fiscal policy-making (budget ceilings, fiscal councils, more power to central banks and finance ministries), long-term retrenchment and especially cuts in the future growth of "entitlement" programs like healthcare and pensions.[11] In the same vein, they stress the constraints of institutional depth in estimating the size of the fiscal space in developing countries, whose poorer tax collection capacity and volatile sovereign bond market conditions could only afford smaller (if any) stimulus opportunities.

Perhaps the most dramatic departure from the mainstream is represented by evidence for the (neo-)Keynesian argument advocated for some time by Paul Krugman, Brad deLong, and other "unreformed" Keynesians that fiscal consolidation can be self-defeating in countries that had problems with credibility. After 2011, several teams of IMF researchers — including some led by the RED and FAD directors — argued that the resulting fall in output can trigger a raise in public debt, and lead to potentially higher risk premia in sovereign debt markets (Batini et al., 2012; Baum et al., 2012; Blanchard & Leigh, 2013a; Cottarelli & Jaramillo, 2012; Eyraud & Weber, 2013). Moreover, one recent study went as far as demonstrating that the most consistent fiscal consolidators end up being punished by the markets because their efforts to get the debt ratio to converge to the official target leads to repeated rounds of tightening that in turn worsen the outcome even more (Eyraud & Weber, 2013).[12] Nevertheless, as the next section shows, these charges against the Fund's neoclassical orthodoxy have not traveled into the RED and FAD reports.

Another intriguing pattern is that research moved the debate on the content of fiscal consolidations in a direction that is more sensitive to issues of distribution. Contrary to conventional wisdom about the IMF's indifference to economic inequalities, poverty, and unemployment, distributional concerns articulated with unorthodox ideas began to loom large in IMF staff research (Baldacci et al., 2011, 2012; Bastagli, Coady, & Gupta, 2012; Berg & Ostry, 2011; Cottarelli & Viñals, 2009; Spilimbergo et al., 2008).

These papers advised tax cuts for the most credit constrained, increased spending on automatic stabilizers, and an expansion of the scope of the safety nets where these were too narrow.

There was support for public works likely to reduce unemployment and boost growth potential. A more progressive tax burden that included higher wealth taxes, externality correcting taxes (carbon tax), and financial sector taxes emerged as appropriate mechanisms to rekindle growth. Moreover, a paper coauthored by a deputy director at RED argued that what is missing from models that estimate future expectations is the specter of catastrophic income loss triggered by unemployment (Mody et al., 2012). Such pleas were part of IMF's concerns about the negative effects of austerity on productivity, competitiveness, debt sustainability, and financial stability, but one study also found a causal connection between high inequality and high debt (Kumhof, Laxton, Muir & Mursula, 2010).

Finally, there has been a great deal of editing in the Fund's view of the composition of fiscal policy. To the IMF's canned sermon on the importance of labor market deregulation, staff research added the imperative of blending centralized wage setting mechanisms with firm-level industrial relations (Blanchard & Leigh, 2013b). Critically, tax rises were preferred to expenditure cuts due to the fact the latter improve both private sector expectations and competitiveness (Baldacci et al., 2010; Corsetti et al., 2012; Cottarelli & Jaramillo, 2012; Guajardo et al., 2011; Spilimbergo et al., 2008). Several studies suggested that increases in public investments (capital outlays) and cuts in the VAT are critical for growth while income tax cuts are not (Arslanalp, Bornhorst, & Gupta, 2011; Baldacci et al., 2012). Some papers go as far as arguing that government investments should be prioritized because they create public goods that depreciate at a slower rate than the private sector's stock (Baldacci et al., 2012; Muir & Weber, 2013).

As for the defense of the old status quo, the studies upholding the expansionary austerity line on fiscal policy rely on country studies done by regional desks (Berkmen, 2011; Purfield & Rosenberg, 2010) and that few choose direct confrontation with the revisionist studies presented above. For example, one study that found much less fiscal space in the countries regarded by fiscal policy optimists as eligible for fiscal expansion and suggested they should frontload consolidation as well (Velculescu, 2010). Another study shows that under some conditions, lenders have neoclassical rather than Keynesian expectations about the future and therefore can help trigger the expansion of corporate credit (Agca & Igan, 2013). Other studies strengthened the orthodox line when they showed that households move from non-Ricardian to Ricardian behavior at government debt levels that exceeds 60 percent of GDP (Bhattacharya & Mukherjee, 2010; Kumar & Woo, 2010).

To assess the extent to which this IMF research traveled into its policy recommendations, the analysis now turns to the content of the general reports put forth by RED (World Economic Outlook) and FAD (Global Fiscal Monitor). Unlike the staff papers, these reports represent the official views of these departments. They are important for another reason: they function as "epistemic courts" (Toulmin, 1969) that adjudicate and enforce what constitutes consensus about the Fund's economists shared problems, methods, and ideas about how the economy works.

DOCTRINAL CHANGES

While they generally integrated the research findings reviewed above, some of the more transformative policy ideas from staff research have not shaped the policy line of the reports.

Certainly, some of the more extreme views on austerity were rejected. Citing staff papers, the reports rejected both the expansionary austerity thesis as well as the frontloading of austerity everywhere for the sake of credibility. In contrast, the researchers' hostility toward unorthodox debt reduction is emphasized throughout.

On other aspects of the fiscal policy debate, the integration of innovative IMF research is more uneven. The defense of inequality and unemployment-reducing social services, progressive tax reforms, and job programs has become part and parcel of the reports and cohabits with the Fund's old neoliberal answer to unemployment (labor market deregulation, lower corporate taxes, tightening eligibility for social benefits, including disability pensions; reducing the duration and level of social benefits when "too high," etc.). But the arguments made in some IMF studies that progressive tax increases are less contractionary that expenditure cuts has not.

An even more complex pattern emerged with regard to the content of the credibility thesis. Stimulus remains an option not only for the handful of "advanced" countries that faced contractions with stronger fiscal positions and lower public debt, but also for low- and middle-income states that met these conditions.

But reassuring the bond markets via debt reduction remains the main goal and there is only a very limited incorporation of staff research highlighting the self-defeating nature of fiscal consolidation with regard to debt reduction. While the IMF endorsed an expansion of the social safety net in low- and middle-income states where it was too thin, it demanded its extensive retrenchment in high-income states where embedded liberalism had left behind generous social services.

The extent to which orthodoxy was thus edited varied over time. There was a great deal of fiscal policy optimism in 2008 and 2009, when reports suggest that where fiscal space, credible institutions, and credibility were available, stimulus measures should continue as long as exit strategies are announced for the medium term. By 2010 the tone changes slightly in favor of an earlier, sharper, and institutionally bound exit from stimulus. Yet contra the enthusiasm for "growth-friendly fiscal consolidation" prevailing in the G20 meeting of the same year, the reports caution against an "abrupt withdrawal" (a cut in the deficit greater than 1 percent a year). The 2010 WEO sounded Keynesian when it argued that when the rest of the world is tightening at the same time, the output cost of a 1 percent of GDP fiscal consolidation can double to 2 percent for a small open economy where the interest rate is at the zero lower bound. The door to stimulus remained open when the report noted that if growth threatened to slow appreciably more than expected, advanced economies with fiscal room, good fiscal institutions, and safe haven status should let the fiscal stabilizers operate and slow the pace of adjustment.

In 2011 the reports took a more conservative stance, praising Europe's strong frontloading of austerity and making optimistic projections of its effects on credibility. Moreover, based on a FAD study showing that bond yields in emerging markets are very sensitive to global risk aversion, they counseled low- and middle-income economies to rebuild fiscal buffers and cut spending despite the fact that they were facing less market pressure than developed countries. Nevertheless, the report contains an unambiguous denunciation of the expansionary austerity thesis.

Subsequent reports qualify this retrenchment. The 2012 Monitor stresses that "in the current recessionary context, the negative impact of fiscal adjustment on activity can be expected to be large, as confirmed by new work on the size of fiscal multipliers during periods of weak economic activity" (p. ix). This idea is taken to its logical conclusion in the October 2012 WEO, which incorporates IMF research from 2011–2012 showing that multipliers were much higher than the Fund had thought. The 2012 Monitor also finds the 2008–2009 output shock was in fact greater than anything in IMF datasets and therefore that growth would arrive later than expected. Nevertheless, despite such acknowledgments of revisionist research, debt reduction remained the main policy goal and therefore deficit reduction remained the main policy instrument.

By 2012, following the acceptance of revisionist research on multipliers, both RED and FAD reports demanded a slower adjustment in the countries with low credibility and stressed the importance of expansion in the countries with credibility. The reports of both departments now have a more poignant critique of the excessively harsh budget cuts in the United States and Europe based on the argument that such excessive austerity is likely to worsen the downturn and investors' expectations through government's focus on nominal rather than structural deficit targets.

Suggestively, the October 2012 WEO report reflected the fact that staff that had made the case for higher multipliers in recessions were winning the internal debate. At the beginning of the crisis, an IMF study (Spilimbergo et al., 2009) found that government consumption multipliers are 0.5 or less in small open economies, with smaller values for revenue and transfers and slightly larger ones for investment. But as the crisis advanced, other staff put forth papers suggesting that multipliers are significantly larger in recessions (Batini et al., 2012; Baum et al., 2012). In practice, the IMF used forecasting models using average multipliers of 0.5 to measure the impacts of fiscal consolidation on growth prospects. In contrast, the October 2012 WEO found that in fact they ranged between .9 and 1.7 (the Eurozone periphery is closer to the higher end of the range), an error that explained the IMF's extremely optimistic growth projections for countries who frontloaded fiscal consolidation. Assuming the multiplier was 1.5, a fiscal adjustment of 3 percent of GDP – as much as Spain has to do next year – would lead to a GDP contraction of 4.5 percent. It was momentous finding and those who had been skeptical of the virtues of austerity felt vindicated.[13]

Olivier Blanchard's role was critical in this regard. His research used higher values for multipliers as early as 2001 and his appointment as the Fund's chief economist in September 2008 relaxed the traditional fiscal policy skepticism of the institution. This relaxation was also facilitated by the appointment of Carlo Cottarelli, a skeptic of expansionary austerity as head of the influential Fiscal Affairs Department of the IMF. From this position, he was responsible for the development and publication of the Fiscal Monitor, one of the three IMF flagship publications. With these new appointments, New Keynesian fiscal policy optimism had a better chance to prevail in the Fund.

As early as December 2008, Blanchard coauthored a paper that made the frontloading of fiscal stimulus measures a centerpiece of crisis economics, at least for certain countries. This entailed tweaking balanced budget rules to prevent cuts in existing programs, increasing the state's share in public–private partnerships, increases in public sector employment, more transfers for those at the bottom end of the income distribution (the minimum wage workers, the unemployed, the foreclosed). Where the social safety net was narrow, the state had to step in to expand it. While it cautioned against industrial policies targeted at domestic firms, the paper urged governments to offer guarantees on new credit for firms whose fate was threatened by the credit crunch. This was hardly the bad cop material associated with the IMF medicine in the past decades.

But there was an important caveat to all this: fiscal activism was legitimate only as long as financial markets deemed it sustainable. At the time, it seemed that the entire Eurozone still benefited from "safe haven" status for bond investors so the IMF agreed to fiscal expansions there. But countries that faced pressures in the bond markets (Hungary, Latvia, and Romania in 2008−2009) had to engage in fiscal consolidation in order to rebuild confidence. The same applied to Southern Europe and Ireland after 2010. As a result, the Fund was in agreement with the European policy line on the "periphery" − including by marshaling models with low multipliers − but disagreed with them on the need for austerity in the Eurozone's "core." The last WEO changes a lot of things, but not the IMF's prescription of austerity where it hurts the most.

At any rate, at least at the doctrinal level, there was a resolute turn against frontloaded austerity in the 2012 WEO. There are warnings about the risk of deflation (Decressin & Laxton, 2009) but what is particularly striking is that two new lines of attack appear. The most important is the finding that since 2008 the economic slack was so large, the interest rates so low, and fiscal adjustment so synchronized that fiscal multipliers were constantly well over 1. This finding implies that the IMF underestimated the negative effects of austerity output because it assumed values of the fiscal multiplier that were too low (Batini et al., 2012). This concern is echoed in IMF studies cited in the year's GFM (Baum et al., 2012). Second, even as another cited study encouraged spending cuts in health, pensions, and public employment in wealthy countries like Italy, its findings also stressed that fiscal consolidation had been ultimately self-defeating in the past because it increased public debt levels (Ball et al., 2011). The same finding is echoed in studies cited in GFM that argue that fiscal consolidation when the multiplier is high erodes some of the gains in market credibility as a result of a higher debt ratio and lower short-term growth, which causes an increase in borrowing costs (Cottarelli & Jaramillo, 2012).

IMF research cited in the 2013 reports makes similar points but breaks precedent by emphasizing raising more revenue via increased taxation of the wealthy. In WEO, deflation warnings from a 2002 paper are sounded yet again (Decressin & Laxton, 2009) and the need for stimulus in countries that enjoy fiscal space is reaffirmed (Blanchard & Leigh, 2013a; Kang et al., 2013; Ostry et al., 2010; Spilimbergo et al., 2008). These ideas share space in the report with warnings about the growth-depleting effects of high debt (Kumar & Woo, 2010). The GFM struggles to achieve a similar balance. It cites studies that establish the ineffectiveness of default (Borensztein & Panizza, 2009; Das, Papaioannou, Gregorian, & Maziad, 2012) and inflation (Akitoby, Komatsuzaki, & Blinder, 2013) as debt reduction strategies while stressing the importance of reducing debt.

At the same time, the GFM cites studies that seem to represent the emergence of a new taxation philosophy at the Fund. They continue to endorse a few old recipes (the reduction of income taxes while increasing consumption, the scrapping of loopholes in personal and corporate income tax, the elimination of differential VAT rates, resistance to high marginal income tax, reduced employers' social contributions) yet also advocate greater reliance on taxes targeted at the wealthy: property taxes targeted at the top 1 percent (a measure estimated to raise between 2 and 3 percent of the global GDP in new tax revenue), financial transactions tax, and a coordinated taxation of offshore incomes (Acosta & Yoo, 2012; Norregaard, 2013; Torres, 2013).

Skeptics of fiscal consolidation also tend to be more concerned with the distribution of the costs of fiscal consolidation. However, they frame measures against inequality not as a normative imperative but as consistent with the IMF's concerns with the political sustainability of consolidation and with low productivity challenges (Berg & Ostry, 2011). Indeed, contrary to the Fund's previous agnosticism to inequality, a discussion paper authored by a research team involving no less than the Fund's deputy director Sanjeev Gupta sees fiscal consolidation as an opportunity to reverse the shrinking of social benefits and the progressiveness of income taxes. They suggested that equality-friendly fiscal consolidation should include reducing opportunities for tax evasion and avoidance, increasing the progressivity of income taxes over higher income brackets, cutting unproductive expenditures, and expanding means-tested programs. To make this argument they suggested that enhancing the distributive impact of fiscal policy in developing economies will require improving their capacity to raise tax revenues and to spend those resources more efficiently and equitably. Resource mobilization should focus on broadening income and consumption tax bases and expanding corporate and personal income taxes by reducing tax exemptions and improving compliance. Expenditure reforms should focus on reducing universal price subsidies, improving the capacity to implement better-targeted transfers, and gradually expanding social insurance systems (Bastagli et al., 2012; Berg & Ostry, 2011).

If one looks outside the range of cited IMF papers, one generally finds a similar range of views, although the orthodox voices are more widely represented. One study found much less fiscal space in the countries regarded as eligible for expansion and suggested they should frontload consolidation as well (Velculescu, 2010). Working with firm-level data, a joint GWU–IMF study showed that under come conditions (stable government, lax monetary policy, devaluations), if fiscal consolidations are large and focused on VAT and entitlement cuts, lenders have neoclassical rather than Keynesian expectations about the future and therefore can help trigger expansion of corporate credit (Agca & Igan, 2013). Other studies showed that households move from non-Ricardian to Ricardian behavior at government debt that exceeds 60 percent of GDP (Bhattacharya & Mukherjee, 2010). Others praise Latvia's orthodox austerity program and even contend that not using devaluation was appropriate (Purfield & Rosenberg, 2010) while a case study of several African countries and Japan respectively stresses both the growth-inducing and credibility-enhancing effects of fiscal consolidation (Berkmen, 2011).

From Doctrine to Practice

Empirical studies show that the way in which the IMF communicated its doctrine to governments via article IV consultations has been broadly in line with the skepticism of IMF researchers about expansionary austerity or the frontloading of fiscal consolidation in all countries. Surprisingly, these studies avoid the developed capitalist core, a gap that this paper attempts to address.[14]

With regard to low-income countries (LICs), Waeyenberge, Bargawi and McKinley (2011) have found more flexibility in the Fund's approach: in 13 of them, the IMF played the orthodox card but in 6 of them more expansionary policies were employed. At the same time, the Fund remained passive on boosting LIC potential for mobilizing additional domestic revenue, or for creating greater fiscal space with additional debt relief initiatives or further grant assistance. And even where expansion was allowed, the focus was on current expenditures rather than on capital investment, a chronic source of weakness for LICs' long-term development prospects. Yet additional studies conducted by the ILO (Ramos & Roy, 2012) found a clearer pro-frontloading bias when the sample was expanded to include middle-income countries. For example, in 48 out of 50 cases analyzed the Fund's standard recommendation was fiscal discipline irrespective of the cycle. Nevertheless, the Fund showed skepticism toward the New Classical arguments that consolidation is best done via spending cuts. The study found that the IMF had a clear preference for additional revenue mobilization (42 out of 50 countries), with expenditure restraint being advised only in 24 countries. These findings confirm the mainstream view among IMF researchers that the confidence effects of fiscal consolidation in low- and middle-income countries should take precedence over concerns with their short-term contractionary effects on output. The findings of some IMF research showing that frontloaded fiscal consolidation is bad for confidence have yet to travel in IMF advice to the global periphery.

These studies only code the early crisis years and do not look across the Global North−Global South frontier. To address this gap, this study did a content analysis of article IV consultations conducted with low-, middle-, and high-income states between October 2011 and October 2012. This analysis is then supplemented with a close reading of all article IV reports published since the October 2012 WEO in order to identify potential echoes of the high-level endorsement of high multipliers at the IMF's "grassroots" level. The content analysis reviewed 20 IMF article IV consultations and the coding unit was the policy recommendation. This was understood to be any recommendation that either (a) confirmed a policy adopted or planned to be adopted by the government under review or (b) went beyond policies being implemented or that are planned to be implemented.

All coded reports do not give any indication on the growth effects of fiscal consolidation. On the contrary, they see this policy as a contractionary policy option, but one that is imposed on some countries by concerns with debt sustainability. For LICs' fiscal measures the analysis revealed a preference for neutral fiscal policy (in three out of five). In addition to standard IMF policy measures, these fiscal packages reflected the Fund's new enthusiasm for increased social security and infrastructure spending (Angola, Bolivia, Guatemala, Nepal). Of particular interest was the Fund's praise for Bolivia's poverty and inequality-reducing programs.

In contrast, a preference for consolidation is clear in the case of the middle-income sample of countries. However, the Fund demanded backloaded consolidation where bond market and deficit constraints were weak (Brazil, South Africa) and frontloaded fiscal consolidation where such constraints were strong (Hungary, Lebanon). The menu of fiscal measures from outside of the usual menu but reflecting of IMF research findings included higher public capital investment (Brazil, South Africa), more investment in public infrastructure (Pakistan), more progressive tax system (Hungary), higher social spending (Lebanon, Pakistan), the introduction of universal health coverage (South Africa), and higher taxes on capital gains and property (Lebanon, Pakistan).

Article IV reports on high-income countries are also in line with IMF staff research: expansions for fiscally virtuous countries facing recessionary dynamics (Sweden, Germany), frontloaded fiscal consolidation where deficits and bond market vulnerability is high (Ireland, Spain). Interestingly, a slower and more gradual fiscal consolidation (although no backloading) is suggested both where the government (a) has still high deficits but faces no sovereign bond market problems (Britain) and where the deficit is high but the contraction is so big that it risks undermining credibility with bond markets (Spain). In terms of specific measures, one finds consistent advise for reducing reliance on expenditure cuts and increasing revenue measures (Ireland, Spain), higher property taxes on the wealthy (Britain, Ireland), strengthening the safety net for the most vulnerable (Ireland, Spain).

How much has the WEO 2012 report changed article IV reports? My analysis suggests that three patterns of fiscal crisis economics have emerged: putting austerity on hold for the fiscally virtuous, further expenditure cuts and tax increases in the countries with fiscal imbalances, higher and more progressive taxes in countries that used fiscal consolidation to orchestrate libertarian attacks against the state. The dominant pattern has been the reassertion of orthodoxy. In Bulgaria, Romania, Hungary, Portugal, Lithuania, and Estonia the Fund praised the frontloading of consolidation and urged its continuation irrespective of the cycle to this policy option in conjunction with privatizations and structural reforms whenever its staff noted flagging commitment going forward. Advice for privatizations centered around the use of privatization revenues for cutting debt and/or building buffers for future shocks. Throughout the Fund stresses poor tax collection capacity, yet not all revenue-maximizing measures are applauded. Indeed, the Fund makes some clear choices on this front that reflect the endurance of supply-side economics and conservative social policy. Revenue-boosting measures not certified by the IMF that forced largely multinationals to share the burden of adjustment (the Hungarian sectoral taxes on banks, privatized energy companies, and retailers) are criticized by the Fund as distortionary. Similarly, the Fund remains cold on higher taxes in high-income states. Thus, the Portugal report stresses that Portugal's level of taxation is high enough and that consequently further cuts in social transfers and public sector wages are advisable instead.

Second, the October 2012 WEO did produce some limited effects. In two cases the Fund was more at ease with suggesting/endorsing the backloading of fiscal consolidation as a countercyclical policy. Puzzlingly, this was the case not only in the IMF advice to a country that has traditionally enjoyed safe haven credibility and a reputation for fiscal rigor (the Netherlands). The IMF also applauded short-term expansionary policy in a middle-income country whose economy imploded in 2008 (Estonia) and in low-income economy whose state nearly collapsed a decade ago (Albania). What the first two have in common are sustainable debt levels and an impeccable record with budgetary discipline during the crisis. Moreover, in the eyes of the IMF Estonia validated its theory that recoveries can be obtained through internal devaluation. Once budgetary discipline was achieved, the Fund endorsed projected increases in public capital spending. social spending, unemployment benefits, means-tested child allowances, the wage bill (following a 3-year wage bill freeze), and an increase in public investment associated with EU structural funds. This was a qualified endorsement. First, in Estonia such measures were accepted only so long as they were offset by reductions in current spending and were, as a result, budget neutral. Second, to forestall future deviations from orthodoxy, the Fund's blessing of expansionary measures came together with praising the adoption of multiyear expenditure ceilings (already applied in Holland) and suggesting them where they were not in the books (Estonia).

The third pattern is the Fund thinks that fiscal consolidation measures have been too anti-state and anti-poor in some countries. This is clearly the case in Lithuania, where the IMF critiques a revenue-to-GDP ratio that is the lowest in the EU, capital taxation levels well below the EU average, and where excessive reliance on (regressive) indirect taxes is matched by very low taxation of wealth, notably real estate and motor vehicles. Similar remarks have been made in the case of Romania. Consequently, the Fund advises a bigger and more progressive government in terms of taxation for this exemplar of libertarian political economy (Blyth, 2013; Bohle & Greskovits, 2012). The report on Lithuania also provides an insight on what the IMF has to say about high unemployment when the country under review has already deregulated the labor market. In such cases the IMF's last bullets are education reforms aimed at reducing skill mismatches and boosting capital formation by reducing administrative burdens and streamlining territorial planning procedures would help raise investment.

CONCLUSIONS

This paper makes two related claims. First, the crash of 2008 has not led to a Berlin Wall moment for neoliberalism. Although there has been greater acceptance of fiscal stimulus and gradual, rather than frontloaded austerity – where the Fund deemed that the stimulus was unaffordable – overall the emphasis on states' credibility with the financial markets has remained the primary goal of the Fund's fiscal policy paradigm. In this way, the expansion of the policy space has taken place in parallel with the further entrenchment of the market-disciplinary modes of governance associated with neoliberalism. As such, the Fund's revisions of its traditional fiscal policy thinking may be seen as part of an effort to reprogram the instruments and settings of neoliberalism for the political and economic characteristics of the Great Recession.

Second, the explanation of this cannot be complete without examining the way in which IMF staff interpreted the fiscal policy dilemmas brought by a depression in developed economies that was triggered by the financial sector. The paper shows that given the tight epistemic interconnectedness between IMF researchers and mainstream academic economics, the long-run debate in mainstream economics over the value of fiscal multipliers was eventually internalized in the Fund, carving space for "revisionist" ideas that eventually filtered into the IMF's official doctrine.

At a more general level, this paper suggests that the observed hybridity, coexistence with incongruous intellectual formations, incompleteness, and even temporary breakdowns should not be equated with imminent paradigmatic changes. It also intimates that one should not dismiss the possibility that the adaptive incremental transformation noted in fiscal policy will morph into a transformative one or, more ambitiously, into a paradigm shift. Alternatively, some of the evidence presented here can be read in a more skeptical register. The Fund' fiscal revisionism could be construed as an opportunistic, experimental, and perhaps reversible intellectual contradiction. Far from being the symptom of a metastatic development, a skeptical eye might see this policy hybrid as a necessary instrument in any job of tinkering with paradigms in order to ensure their survival in a challenging environment.

NOTES

1. When asked why mainstream macroeconomic models have little to say about real-world unemployment, V. V. Chari, a luminary of modern macroeconomics said that "providing unemployment benefits does tend to discourage people from looking as intensively for jobs (...) it tends to make them more unwilling to accept jobs when they do come up" (U.S. House of Representatives "Building a Science of Economics for the Real World" Hearing before the Subcommittee on Investigations and Oversight," serial no. 111−106, Washington, July 20, 2010, p. 51).
2. For an in-depth overview and in-depth critique of expansionary austerity see Blyth (2013).
3. For an overview of external critiques see Arestis (2012).
4. Author interview with European Department economist, January 2012.
5. The fiscal multiplier is the ratio of change that government spending produce in national income. A positive multiplier means that fiscal expansions increase growth. As far as mainstream economics is concerned, this is an uncontroversial calculative device.
6. This means that if the multiplier is higher than one, the economy grows more than the amount spent on the fiscal stimulus.
7. For an overview of this debate see Batini, Callegari, and Melina (2012).
8. IMF research shows that debt levels significantly reduce growth when they exceed the 90 percent threshold (Baum, Checherita, & Rother, 2012; Kumar & Woo, 2010). Other studies, endorsed by Fiscal Affairs (Cottarelli & Viñals, 2009), operated with a more demanding 60 percent threshold (Horton, Kumar, & Mauro, 2009).
9. A subsequent IMF study found that Australia, New Zealand, Korea, Sweden, and Denmark fit these conditions with a high degree of confidence (Ostry et al., 2010).
10. Speech by Michael Dooley, Boston University, April 6, 2013.
11. http://www.imf.org/external/pubs/ft/fandd/2009/09/blanchardindex.htm; http://www.imf.org/external/pubs/ft/fandd/2009/03/cottarelli.htm
12. Recent statements against austerity by the biggest buyer of sovereign bonds (PIMCO) suggest that they continued to inhabit a world that chief economist Olivier Blanchard saw as positively "schizophrenic" (http://blog-imfdirect.imf.org/2011/12/21/2011-in-review-four-hard-truths/)
13. http://krugman.blogs.nytimes.com/2012/10/13/times-like-this-are-different/; http://notthetreasuryview.blogspot.co.uk/2012/10/more-on-multipliers-why-does-it-matter.html; http://mainlymacro.blogspot.co.uk/2012/10/multipliers-using-theory-and-evidence.html
14. The exception is the Weisbrot and Jorgensen (2013) study of article IV reports in the EU, but its content analysis is flawed as it does not distinguish between frontloaded and backloaded fiscal consolidation.

REFERENCES

Acosta-Ormaechea, S., & Yoo, J. (2012). *Tax composition and economic growth*. IMF Working Paper 12/257.
Agca, S., & Igan, D. (2013). *Fiscal consolidation and the cost of credit: Evidence from syndicated loans*. IMF Working Paper No. 13/36. International Monetary Fund.
Akitoby, B., Komatsuzaki, T., & Blinder, A. (2013). *Inflation and debt reduction in advanced economies*. IMF Working Paper.
Arestis, P. (2012). Fiscal policy: A strong macroeconomic role. *Review of Keynesian Economics*, (1), 93–108.
Arslanalp, S., Bornhorst, F., & Gupta, S. (2011). Investing in growth. SSRN 1886487.
Auerbach, A., & Gorodnichenko, Y. (2012). *Fiscal multipliers in recession and expansion*. Retrieved from http://www.nber.org/chapters/c12634.pdf
Auerbach, A. J., Gale, W. G., & Harris, B. H. (2010). Activist fiscal policy. *The Journal of Economic Perspectives*, 141–163.
Baldacci, E., & Kumar, M. (2010). *Fiscal deficits, public debt, and sovereign bond yields*. IMF Working Papers (pp. 1–28).
Baldacci, E., Gupta, S., & Mulas-Granados, C. (2012). Reassessing the fiscal mix for successful debt reduction. *Economic Policy*, *27*(71), 365–406.
Ball, L., Leigh, D., & Loungani, P. (2011). *Painful medicine*. IMF Fiscal Consolidation.
Barnett, M., & Finnemore, M. (2004). *Rules for the world: International organizations in global politics*. Ithaca, NY: Cornell University Press.
Bastagli, F., Coady, D., & Gupta, S. (2012). *Income inequality and fiscal policy*. Retrieved from http://ideas.repec.org/p/imf/imfsdn/12-08r.html
Batini, N., Callegari, G., & Melina, G. (2012). *Successful austerity in the United States, Europe and Japan*. Retrieved from http://papers.ssrn.com/sol3/papers.cfm?abstract_id=2169736
Baum, A., Checherita-Westphal, C., & Rother, P. (2012). The impact of high government debt on economic growth and its channels: An empirical investigation for the euro area. *European Economic Review*, *56*(7), 1392–1405.
Baum, A., Poplawski-Ribeiro, M., & Weber, A. (2012). *Fiscal multipliers and the state of the economy*. Retrieved from http://papers.ssrn.com/sol3/papers.cfm?abstract_id=2202637
Beetsma, R. M. W. J., & Giuliodori, M. (2010). *Discretionary fiscal policy: Review and estimates for the EU* No. 2948. CESifo Group Munich.
Berg, A., & Ostry, J. (2011). Equality and efficiency. *Finance & Development*, *48*(3), 12–15.
Berkmen, P. (2011). *The impact of fiscal consolidation and structural reforms on growth in Japan*. IMF Working Papers (pp. 1–21).
Bhattacharya, R., & Mukherjee, S. (2010). *Private sector consumption and government consumption and debt in advanced economies: An empirical study*. IMF Working Papers (pp. 1–27).
Blanchard, O., & Leigh, D. (2013a). *Fiscal consolidation: At what speed?* VoxEU. Accessed on June 17.
Blanchard, O. J., & Leigh, D. (2013b). *Growth forecast errors and fiscal multipliers*. Retrieved from http://www.nber.org/papers/w18779
Blyth, M. (2013). *Austerity: The history of a dangerous idea*. New York, NY: Oxford University Press.

Bohle, D., & Greskovits, B. (2012). *Capitalist diversity on Europe's periphery*. Ithaca, NY: Cornell University Press.

Borensztein, E., & Panizza, U. (2009). The costs of sovereign default. *IMF Staff Papers, 56*(4), 683–741.

Broome, A., & Seabrooke, L. (2007). Seeing like the IMF: Institutional change in small open economies. *Review of International Political Economy, 14*(4), 576–601.

Broome, A., & Seabrooke, L. (2012). Seeing like an international organisation. *New Political Economy, 17*(1), 1–16.

Cagetti, M., & De Nardi, M. C. (2008). Wealth inequality: Data and models. *Macroeconomic Dynamics, 12*(S2), 285–313.

Chwieroth, J. M. (2009). *Capital ideas: The IMF and the rise of financial liberalization*. Princeton, NJ: Princeton University Press.

Chwieroth, J. M. (2013). 'The Silent Revolution': How the staff exercise informal governance over IMF lending. *The Review of International Organizations, 8*(2), 256–290.

Claessens, S., Köse, M. A., & Terrones, M. E. (2008). Financial stress and economic activity. *Journal of BRSA Banking and Financial Markets, 2*(2), 11–24.

Clift, B., & Tomlinson, J. (2012). When rules started to rule: The IMF, neo-liberal economic ideas and economic policy change in Britain. *Review of International Political Economy, 19*(3), 477–500.

Cogan, J. F., Cwik, T., Taylor, J. B., & Wieland, V. (2010). New Keynesian versus old Keynesian government spending multipliers. *Journal of Economic Dynamics and Control, 34*(3), 281–295. IMF.

Cohen, L., Coval, J. D., & Malloy, C. (2010). *Do powerful politicians cause corporate downsizing?* National Bureau of Economic Research Working Paper No. 15839.

Colander, D. (2011). Is the fundamental science of macroeconomics sound? *Review of Radical Political Economics, 43*(3), 302–309.

Correia, I., et al. (2011). *Unconventional fiscal policy at the zero bound*. No. w16758. National Bureau of Economic Research.

Corsetti, G., et al. (2012, January). *Sovereign risk, fiscal policy and macroeconomic stability*. IMF Working Paper No. 12/33.

Cottarelli, C., & Jaramillo, L. (2012). *Walking hand in hand: Fiscal policy and growth in advanced economies*. Retrieved from http://papers.ssrn.com/sol3/papers.cfm?abstract_id=2127031

Cottarelli, C., & Viñals, J. (2009). A strategy for renormalizing fiscal and monetary policies in advanced economies. IMF.

Cottarelli, C. (2013). The austerity debate. In *Public debt, global governance and economic dynamism* (pp. 301–308). Milan: Springer.

Das, U. S., Papaioannou, M. G., Gregorian, D. A., & Maziad, S. (2012). *A survey of experiences with emerging market sovereign debt restructurings*. IMF Working Paper.

Decressin, J., & Laxton, D. (2009). Gauging Risks for Deflation. IMF Staff Position Note 09/01.

Eyraud, L., & Weber, A. (2013). *The challenge of debt reduction during fiscal consolidation*. IMF staff papers.

Eyzaguirre, N. (2009). *Latin America and the Caribbean: Finding space for countercyclical fiscal policy*. Posted by iMFdirect.

Feldstein, M. S. (2009). *Rethinking the role of fiscal policy*. No. w14684. National Bureau of Economic Research.

Fernández-Villaverde, J. (2010). Fiscal policy in a model with financial frictions. *The American Economic Review*, 35–40.

Fincke, B., & Greiner, A. (2012). How to assess debt sustainability? Some theory and empirical evidence for selected euro area countries. *Applied Economics*, *44*(28), 3717–3724.

Fontana, G. (2009). *Whither new consensus macroeconomics? The role of government and fiscal policy in modern macroeconomics*. Working Paper No. 563. Levy Economics Institute.

Gabor, D. (2010). The International Monetary Fund and its new economics. *Development and Change*, *41*(5), 805–830.

Gallagher, K. P. (2014a). Countervailing monetary power: Re-regulating capital flows in Brazil and South Korea. *Review of International Political Economy*, 1–26 (ahead-of-print).

Gallagher, K. P. (2014b). *Ruling capital: Emerging markets and the reregulation of cross-border finance*. Cornell University Press.

Gallagher, K. P., et al. (2012, March). *Regulating global capital flows for long-run development*. Pardee Centre Task Force Report. Boston University, Boston, MA.

Ghosh, A. R., Chamon, M., Crowe, C., Kim, J. I., & Ostry, J. D. (2009, April 23). Coping with the crisis. IMF Staff Position Note, SPN/09/08.

Grabel, I. (2011). Not your grandfather's IMF: Global crisis, 'productive incoherence' and developmental policy space. *Cambridge Journal of Economics*, *35*(5), 805–830.

Grabel, I. (2014). The rebranding of capital controls in an era of productive incoherence. *Review of International Political Economy*, 1–37 (ahead-of-print).

Guajardo, J., Leigh, D., & Pescatori, A. (2011). *Expansionary austerity: New international evidence*. IMF staff paper.

Hall, P. A. (1993). Policy paradigms, social learning, and the state: The case of economic policymaking in Britain. *Comparative Politics*, *25*(3), 275–296.

Hay, C. (2011). Pathology without crisis? The strange demise of the Anglo-liberal growth model. *Government and Opposition*, *46*(1), 1–31.

Hein, E., & Stockhammer, E. (2010). Macroeconomic policy mix, employment and inflation in a post-Keynesian alternative to the new consensus model. *Review of Political Economy*, *22*(3), 317–354.

Hemming, R., Kell, M., & Mahfouz, S. (2002). *The effectiveness of fiscal policy in stimulating economic activity – A review of the literature*. IMF Working Paper No. 02/208.

Horton, M. A., Kumar, M. S., & Mauro, P. (2009). *The state of public finances: A cross-country fiscal monitor*. Washington, DC: International Monetary Fund.

Kang, J. S., Shambaugh, J., Tressel, T., & Wang, S. (2013). *Rebalancing and growth in the euro area*. IMF Staff Discussion Note.

Krueger, A. O. (1998). Whither the World Bank and the IMF? *Journal of Economic Literature*, *36*(4), 1983–2020.

Kumhof, M., Laxton, D., Muir, D., & Mursula, S. (2010). *The Global Integrated Monetary and Fiscal Model (GIMF) – Theoretical structure*. International Monetary Fund.

Lütz, S., & Kranke, M. (2013). The European rescue of the Washington consensus? EU and IMF lending to central and Eastern European countries. *Review of International Political Economy*, *21*(2), 310–338.

Lucas, R. E., Jr. (1986). Principles of fiscal and monetary policy. *Journal of Monetary Economics*, *17*(1), 117–134.

Mankiw, N. G. (2006). *The macroeconomist as scientist and engineer* (No. w12349). National Bureau of Economic Research.

Mankiw, N. G. (2010). Questions about fiscal policy: Implications from the financial crisis of 2008−2009. *Federal Reserve Bank of St. Louis Review, 92*(May−June).

Mazzucato, M. (2013). *The entrepreneurial state: Debunking public vs. private sector myths.* New York, NY: Anthem Press.

Mody, A., Ohnsorge, F., & Sandri, D. (2012). Precautionary savings in the great recession. *IMF Economic Review, 60*(1), 114−138.

Momani, B. (2005). Limits on streamlining fund conditionality: The International Monetary Fund's organizational culture. *Journal of International Relations and Development, 8*(2), 142−163.

Monacelli, T., & Perotti, R. (2011). Redistribution and the Multiplier. *IMF Economic Review, 59*(4), 630−651.

Moschella, M. (2011). The global financial crisis and the reforms to IMF lending. *St Antony's International Review, 7*(1), 48−60.

Moschella, M. (2012a). *Governing risk: The IMF and global financial crises.* London: Palgrave Macmillan.

Moschella, M. (2012b). Seeing like the IMF on capital account liberalisation. *New Political Economy, 17*(1), 59−76.

Muir, D., & Weber, A. (2013). Fiscal multipliers in Bulgaria: Low but still relevant.

Mussa, M., & Savastano, M. (2000). The IMF approach to economic stabilization. In *NBER macroeconomics annual 1999* (Vol. 14, pp. 79−128). Cambridge, MA: MIT.

Norregaard, J. (2013). *Taxing immovable property: Revenue potential and implementation challenges.* IMF Working Paper 13/129.

Ostry, J. D., et al. (2010). *Fiscal space, IMF staff position note.* SPN/10/11, Washington, DC.

Park, S., & Vetterlein, A. (2010). *Owning development: Creating policy norms in the IMF and the World Bank.* Cambridge, UK: Cambridge University Press.

Purfield, C., & Rosenberg, C. (2011). *Adjustment under a currency peg: Estonia, Latvia and Lithuania during the global financial crisis 2008-09.* International Monetary Fund.

Ramey, V. A. (2011). Can government purchases stimulate the economy? *Journal of Economic Literature, 49*(3), 673−685.

Ramos, R. A., & Roy, R. (2012). *Has IMF Advice Changed After the Crisis?* No. 134. International Policy Centre for Inclusive Growth.

Romer, C., & Bernstein, J. (2009). The job impact of the American recovery and reinvestment plan. Retrieved from http://www.illinoisworknet.com/NR/ rdonlyres/6A8FF039-BEA1-47DC- A509-A781D1215B65/0/ 2BidenReportARRAJobImpact.pdf

Romer, C. D., & Romer, D. H. (1994). What ends recessions? In *NBER Macroeconomics Annual 1994* (Vol. 9, pp. 13−80). MIT Press. Retrieved from http://www.nber.org/chapters/c11007.pdf

Seabrooke, L., & Tsingou, E. (2009). Power elites and everyday politics in international financial reform. *International Political Sociology, 3*(4), 457−461.

Seabrooke, L. (2012). Pragmatic numbers: The IMF, financial reform, and policy learning in least likely environments. *Journal of International Relations and Development, 15*(4), 486−505.

Snower, D. J., Brown, A. J. G., & Merkl, C. (2009). Globalization and the welfare state: A review of Hans-Werner Sinn's "Can Germany be saved?". *Journal of Economic Literature*, 136−158.

Somers, M., & Block, F. (2014). The return of Karl Polanyi. *Dissent, 61*(2), 30–33.
Spilimbergo, A., Symansky, S., Blanchard, O., & Cottarelli, C. (2008). *Fiscal policy for the crisis.* IMF Staff Position Note, December 29.
Spilimbergo, A., Symansky, S., & Schindler, M. (2009). *Fiscal multipliers.* IMF Staff Position Note No. 9/11.
Stiglitz, J. (2008). The end of neo-liberalism? *Project Syndicate,* July 7.
Torres, J. L. (2013). *Revenue and expenditure gaps in fiscal consolidation: A cross country analysis.* IMF Working Paper.
Toulmin, S. (1969). *The uses of argument* (2nd ed.). Cambridge University Press.
Uhlig, H. (2010). Some fiscal calculus. *The American Economic Review,* 30–34.
Van Waeyenberge, E., Bargawi, H., & McKinley, T. (2011). *Standing in the way of development? A critical survey of the IMF's crisis response in low-income countries.* Third World Network.
Velculescu, D. (2010). *Some uncomfortable arithmetic regarding Europe's public finances.* IMF Working Papers (pp. 1–32).
Weaver, C. (2010). *Hypocrisy trap: The World Bank and the poverty of reform.* Princeton, NJ: Princeton University Press.
Weisbrot, M., & Jorgensen, H. (2013). *Macroeconomic policy advice and the Article IV consultations: A European union case study.* No. 2013-03. Center for Economic and Policy Research (CEPR).
Woo, J., & Kumar, M. S. (2010). *Public debt and growth.* International Monetary Fund.
Woodford, M. (2010). *Simple analytics of the government expenditure multiplier.* No. w15714. National Bureau of Economic Research.
Woods, N. (2006). *The globalizers: The IMF, the World Bank, and their borrowers.* Ithaca, NY: Cornell University Press.

FIGHTING THE FINANCIAL CRISIS: THE SOCIAL CONSTRUCTION AND DECONSTRUCTION OF THE FINANCIAL CRISIS IN DENMARK

Peer Hull Kristensen

ABSTRACT

This paper is concerned to show how the Danish political elite interpreted and responded to the consequences of the 2008 financial crisis for the Danish economy. In particular, the paper describes how this interpretive construction focused primarily on three features of the Danish context to the exclusion of other perspectives; the first was an emphasis on the problems of the financial sector, of interest rates and state finances; the second was that Danish productivity increases were falling behind other comparable countries and part of the solution required new strategies towards labour and unemployment benefits; thirdly, the adverse effects of the crisis were causing an increase in government expenditure and a decline in government revenues which was rapidly becoming unsustainable. As a consequence, the Danish elite fell into the broader interpretation of the crisis embedded in the dominant view within the EU institutions as well as among the international financial institutions such as the IMF and the World Bank, that a period of austerity and fiscal consolidation was the required remedy, even though this was likely to be pro-cyclical in its effects. However, the paper shows that alternative data which is more reflective of Denmark's position in the global economy and the trajectory and form of its growth over the last decade reveals that the interpretation of the Danish elite has been too narrow and neglects the distinctive roots of Denmark's competitive strengths. Indeed, by responding in the way which they have, the Danish elite is in danger of undermining the very conditions of Denmark's competitiveness.

Keywords: Financial crisis; Denmark; austerity; alternative paths to growth

INTRODUCTION

This paper is concerned to show how the Danish political elite interpreted and responded to the consequences of the 2008 financial crisis for the Danish economy. In particular, the paper describes how this interpretive construction focused primarily on three features of the Danish context to the exclusion of other perspectives; the first was an emphasis on the problems of the financial sector, of interest rates and state finances; the political consensus among the elite was that interest rates had to be kept low in order to ensure that those individuals who had borrowed heavily in the earlier part of the decade to move on or up the housing ladder as house prices were booming would not be left with unsustainable repayments; the second was that Danish productivity increases were falling behind other comparable countries and part of the solution required new strategies towards labour and unemployment benefits; thirdly, the adverse effects of the crisis were causing an increase in government expenditure and a decline in government revenues which was rapidly becoming unsustainable. As a consequence, the Danish elite fell into the broader interpretation of the crisis embedded in the dominant view within the EU institutions as well as among the international financial institutions such as the IMF and the World Bank, that a period of austerity and fiscal consolidation was the required remedy, even though this was likely to be pro-cyclical in its effects. Thus, politicians focused on all the signs that could be collected to help sustain this image of the crisis, that is stagnation or negative growth in Gross National Product (GNP) and productivity, wage increases and loss of competitive position, falling house prices, loss of private sector employment. However, the paper shows that alternative data which is more reflective of Denmark's position in the global economy and the trajectory and form of its growth over the last decade reveals that the interpretation of the Danish elite has been too narrow and neglects the distinctive roots of Denmark's competitive strengths. Indeed, by responding in the way which they have, the Danish elite is in danger of undermining the very conditions of Denmark's competitiveness. In order to develop this argument, the paper firstly presents a 'prelude' describing how finance, credit and a housing bubble created high levels of debt in Denmark in the years immediately preceding the 2008 crisis and in turn generated a particular form of vulnerability to the crash. It then describes how the crisis was constructed by Danish politicians while simultaneously throwing doubt on this construction by presenting alternative data and interpretations of Denmark's position post-crisis. The following section provides a summary of the argument that Denmark had created a distinctive growth regime in the 1990s but that politicians failed to understand this, preferring to apply their own familiar models as policy guidelines during the 2000s. The 2008 crisis, rather than being an opportunity to reimagine and reconsider their models, became an opportunity to apply them with increased severity, potentially at the expense of undermining the real engines of growth in the Danish economy. The final section of the paper considers whether this reflects a deliberate turn towards neo-liberal thinking among the Danish political elite (both Liberal-Conservative and Social-Democrat).

PRELUDE: PREPARING DENMARK FOR THE 2008 STORM

Up until the outbreak of the 2008 financial crisis, Danish industry was characterised by extremely low unemployment – in some regions well below 1 per cent; beyond capacity utilisation, shortage of time for making continuous improvements; and stagnating productivity. Overheating generated negative growth. Visited factories in early 2008 had difficulties recruiting cleaners and specialised workers and it was impossible to find craftsmen. They were relying on workers without the normally required skills and had no time for training them. The work organisation so carefully constructed during the 1990s and onwards based on highly skilled workers, working in autonomous teams and continuous improvement cross-teams, continuously upgrading skills through an extensive collaboration with technical schools and AMU centres, was being undermined. Factories were running behind schedule, and productivity was declining as frequent rushed orders necessitated constant resetting. Contracts on continuous cost-reduction were abandoned as surplus-demand totally undermined capacity to carry out continuous improvement in productivity, quality and on all other benchmarks. They needed a break to reset the system and come back on track.

In many ways the noughties stood in stark contrast to the 1990s where in Denmark rapid globalisation – in terms of foreign trade, an increase in in- and outbound foreign direct investment (FDI); up-scaling of skills, transformation to high-performance organisations and new business models – went hand-in-hand so that a new growth and development regime, based on new generic forms of enterprises and capacitating welfare state institutions seemed to be emerging (Kristensen & Lilja, 2011). These transformations had provided the foundation for Denmark to take advantage so successfully of the economic upturn of the noughties, but now the overheating undermined this very foundation.

So while Denmark was celebrating with the other Nordic countries their rise to very high positions in nearly any international comparative benchmarking on economic and social performance (*ibid.*, chap. 1), they were undermining their causes. With unemployment brought down from 12 per cent in 1993 to 2 per cent in 2008, with surpluses on current accounts in balance of payments and public finances, there seemed, however, to be very good reasons for being optimistic – for households, firms and the state. This optimism found in particular its expression in a sudden and explosive housing boom. In itself, drops in unemployment in an egalitarian economy will trigger improvements in the economic situation of households, which triggers a housing bubble (Mortensen and Seabrooke, 2008).

Econometric analysis estimated income increases (corrected by rising housing supply) and low-interest rates for 30-year bonds to account for about 20 per cent of the housing price increase between late1999 and early 2007 (Dam, Hvolbøl, Pedersen, Sørensen, & Thamsborg, 2011, p. 57). Everything else being equal, Denmark would have experienced a small housing bubble as did many other countries (*ibid.*, p. 50). But by freezing housing taxes and financial liberalisation, the Liberal-Conservative government constructed an explosive bubble. Liberalisation triggered new ways of financing houses with the issue of short-term loans with variable interest rates with up to 10 years of delayed repayments, and together with freezing of housing taxes the estimated increase in housing prices became instead 71 per cent over the period. Copenhagen led the game by an increase above 100 per cent, with the remaining part of the country lagging behind, especially outside larger towns (*ibid.*, p. 48). The transition from the traditional fixed-termed loans with a duration of 30 years and gradually increasing repayments based on bonds issued by building societies towards variable short-term loans and delayed repayments is estimated to account for 40 out of the 71 per cent increase (*ibid.*, p. 51). Whereas fixed-term and variable loans with repayments dominated the market as late as 2003, by 2007 loans without repayments on variable short terms had taken prominence together with bank loans, a development that was reinforced after the financial crisis (*ibid.*, p. 49).

On top of this, the general tax freeze under the Liberal-Conservative government during the noughties meant a halt to increasing housing taxes in proportion to housing price increases. Dam et al. (2011, p. 55) estimates this factor to have contributed by 5–9 per cent to the average price increase. This factor played a particular role where price increases were high. In Copenhagen households typically saved DKK 20–25,000 annually by 2007, while in peripheral localities households would only save around DKK 5,000 annually, thus contributing to redistribution of wealth.

According to alternative estimates, from 2000 to 2007 house prices 'rose nationally by 85 per cent for single family houses and 105 per cent for owner-occupied flats' (Erhvervs- og Vækstministeriet, 2013), but even these higher estimates are modest compared with the more serious price bubble for commercial real estate, 'with prices rising by approximately 200 per cent, and on the market for commercial properties for mixed residential and commercial properties, which rose by about 150 per cent' (*ibid.*, p. 7).

Behind these figures hide substantial behavioural changes among households and property developers. Young families rushed into the housing market using a new calculation rule based on the boom: if house prices were increasing by say €133,000 annually, they could refinance the property and borrow more than €100,000 annually within the 80 per cent limit of building society financing, which would both finance their mortgages and make it possible to install new kitchens, bathrooms, make it affordable to have an extra car and buy plenty of luxury products.[1] But the young families acted in good faith as Danish macro-economic-indicators on trade, balance of payments, public debt, innovation and economic sustainability looked very, very promising. If there was a problem, it would emerge around 2020 when a decline of 8,000 people in the labour force was predicted. But this was also a promise of continuous low unemployment and therefore of continuous prosperity for young wage earners not being faced with a dual labour market, increasing inequality and the prospect of joining the ranks of the working poor, as in other countries.[2]

Optimism also marked commercial real estate as bank and building societies were willingly lending speculators money, expecting continuous price increases. Later, it was revealed that speculators created circles in which they sold, bought and resold real estate to each other at still increasing prices, simply to accumulate capital by taking out more loans. Even before the financial crisis, the typical end-game for such circles was to let the final corporate owner go bust and allow financial institutions to carry the losses.

Danish agriculture constitutes a special case of taking on debt, both in a Danish and comparative perspective. As in most other European countries, both land prices and the proportion of debt-financing increased, but this happened in Denmark much more than in any other comparable country – even Holland and Ireland (Pedersen & Brandt, 2013, p. 71ff). This extreme development seduced farmers into engaging in SWAP contracts, which they hardly understood and which were badly regulated OTC products, often sold without making the possible consequences obvious to the borrower. As farmers facing falling earnings by 2007 would SWAP to loans in Swiss Francs to save on interest rates, they prepared themselves for insolvency when the Swiss Franc was revalued against the Euro after the crisis.

Private debt thus increased exponentially just before the financial crisis and turned Danes into the most indebted population within the OECD. Danish finance ministers, however, focused attention on the gross public debt, which was crucial if Denmark was to apply for full membership of the European Economic and Monetary Union. Denmark's EMU debt had peaked in 1993 at 68 per cent of GNP. Then successive governments systematically brought it down to 27.5 per cent by 2007 by incurring a surplus annually on current public accounts. And yet the Liberal-Conservative government after 2000 practised pro-cyclical spending, adding fuel to the overheating economy.

THE CRISIS COMES TO DENMARK: REDISCOVERING ECONOMIC VOLATILITY

For Denmark's small open economy, the international crisis in 2009 implied an immediate decline in exports of 20 per cent, which triggered rising unemployment leading to a drastic drop in household optimism and demand. Within a short period the private sector lost 200,000 jobs. Unemployment quickly increased from a historical low of less than 2 per cent to 4, and later approximately 7 per cent. In an active welfare state, rising unemployment has a comparatively high negative effect on public finances, which further suffered from reduced VAT returns with falling private consumption. This drop was caused by a total reversal of the spending behaviour of households. Thus Danish private Keynesianism, instead of being contra, was procyclical, destabilising the economy this time towards negative growth.

Market forces would have counteracted private debt during the bonanza years had international finance not been liberalised. First of all, international finance became 'an underlying prerequisite for Danish banks' ability to finance the mounting deficit on deposits' (Erhvervs- og Vækstministeriet, 2013, p. 7), and for building societies to refinance short-term mortgages by arranging international bond-auctions. Until 2003 deposits and lending had been in surplus or balance, but then the deficit lending in banks increased to a full DKK 600 billion by 2008 (ibid., p. 187). Prospects were worrying as the drop in international liquidity with the financial crisis risked causing a total collapse of the Danish economy.

When the Lehman Brothers collapsed, the largest Danish bank, 'Den Danske Bank', believed its losses would be limited. It had been unable to assess the risks of the financial derivatives.[3] But losses were indeed large, not least because it had engaged in globalisation, in particular through takeovers of banks in Ireland, where the collapse went very deep and risked drawing it and many smaller Danish banks into collapse. Though the immediate financial crisis in Denmark was thus partly imported, the dependence on international liquidity was so extreme that cumulative effects could have become enormous.

The Central Bank intervened by increasing interest rates to defend the currency's fixed rate to the Euro, but thereby also speeding up the drop in housing prices, which fell by 25–30 per cent within a few years. The state stepped in with the first of a series of banking packages that secured the liquidity of the banks and later structured the process of liquidating or merging failing banks (Carstensen, 2013; Wolf, 2014). Loans to building constructors, commercial housing speculators and young farmers caused losses to and insolvency of a range of small- and medium-sized banks. Building societies, having only financed up to 80 per cent of the value of a house were only marginally affected, while banks had financed the mortgage deed of the remaining 20 per cent. Obviously, if the housing market fell even further, it could cause very big trouble and steep increases in interest rates on the bonds building societies annually auctioned to refinance private houses. It was easy to imagine a very dramatic vicious circle in which increasing interest rates would cause major problems for young families in particular, big losses for building societies and more collapses among even the largest banks. Denmark became very dependent on managing the entire economy according to how it could keep interest rates low so that such a vicious circle could be avoided.

So in dealing with the crisis, governments tiptoed around to please a sector that had itself caused major problems, while at the same time trying to solve the forecasted shortage of labour supply by reducing the period on unemployment benefits from 4 to 2 years and rolling the rights for and timing of early retirement back (we will return to this later). Instead of compensating for the steep drop in private demand by higher growth in public spending, the government, in accordance with the EU financial pact, introduced a system of tough fines on municipalities which spent beyond agreed budgets. To aggravate the situation and put itself under pressure, marginal income taxes were reduced. Thus, while the public sector experienced considerable annual growth during the bubble, it was now being forced to stagnate and decline during the crisis – and even before the statistical arguments for public austerity had been constructed. So instead of stimulating the economy, the public sector added to unemployment by laying off public service workers, which further stimulated the propensity for household savings. By a dramatic drop in bank lending and an increase in deposits, gross deposits and loans were back in balance by 2012 (*ibid.*, 2013, p. 187).

THE POLITICAL CONSTRUCTION OF CRISIS AND ITS FACTUAL DECONSTRUCTION

The following story illustrates how Danish politicians managed the crisis.

In 2009, when a *prognosis* on public debt on current accounts for the first time in many years predicted a collision with the 3 per cent annual deficit limit of the EMU convergence criteria, a journalist phoned the EU Commission to learn whether Denmark now risked becoming the subject of EU critique. The immediate response was 'No'. On the contrary, the civil servant assured the journalist that the Nordic countries, including Denmark, were seen as 'boy scouts', allowed to let expansionary fiscal policies balance austerity enforced on other EU countries. In the afternoon, however, the civil servant called back and told the journalist that he had been wrong. Denmark was considered to be in the danger zone and would be kept under surveillance. The journalist guessed that the Danish Ministry

Fighting the Financial Crisis in Denmark 379

of Finance had been in contact with the Commission between the two responses and had convinced the EU to speak (at least in public) with a new voice about the Danish situation. Since then the EMU convergence criteria have been held as a basic argument for following a restrictive financial policy in Denmark, also during the later Social-Democratic-Centre government. From then onwards, Danish economic ministries predicted that the annual public deficits for the years 2010, 2011 and 2012 would move beyond 3 per cent of the GNP limit. Though the deficit proved repeatedly to be lower, it was always used in next year's prediction and served as a main argument for austerity by dominant government circles. A look at the official EMU debt numbers is indeed worrying and supports these arguments. Recall that Denmark reached a historical low of accumulated gross government debt by 2007 at 27.5 per cent of GNP; 2007−2011 deficits soared by DKK 364 billion to reach DKK 831 billion, that is 46.6 per cent of GNP.

Deconstructing these figures proves interesting. Only DKK 64 billion, that is 17.6 per cent of the increase, comes from accumulated deficits on public current accounts over the 5 years. EMU calculates gross and not net debt, thus neglecting the fact that some debts are also assets. The largest increases came from the state building up a fortune in its Central Bank account (DKK 135 billion, i.e. 37.7 per cent of the increase and 16 per cent of the total gross debt); from having re-lent money to a set of state-owned companies (8.8 per cent of the increase), as the state would pay lower interest rates on state bonds than if the companies themselves were borrowing; from financing 'Bank packages' (16.8 per cent of the increase), to be paid back by banks, probably with a net gain for the state, etc. According to Frederik I. Pedersen, the Danish state could restructure its balance and bring down its official EMU debt to approximately 16 per cent of GNP, reaching one of the lowest levels in Europe. The debt would only have increased by 2.2 per cent of GNP compared to the official 19.1 per cent over the 5-year period. Using such alternative calculations, Danish net debt had only accumulated by 3.3 per cent of GNP in 2011 or close to what is accepted annually by the EMU convergence criteria.[4]

Despite the fact that gross public debts could be deconstructed in this way, the gross figures were used together with alarming annual budgeted deficits to impose strong limits on government and municipal spending. They were simultaneously used to search for cuts in transfer-payments and terms for unemployment benefits and social insurance. In this way, even long after the Social-Democratic-Centre coalition came to power, the Danish government looked very 'responsible' both to the EU and to the financial community.

With this intervention, during the European debt crisis, Denmark came to be seen as one of the very safe havens to place money – whether in government or building society bonds. After a short period the country therefore benefitted from very, very low-interest rates. Seen from the Danish state perspective, it has been a clever policy to take up loans and lend them on to 'independent' state-owned companies, etc., and to accumulate a large account in the Central Bank. Such a re-lender role can in itself generate an additional income for the state – as in the case of the loans given through the 'Bank packages'.

One state-owned company that was supported in this way by the state is 'Dong', an energy company that is gradually specialising in constructing off-shore windmill farms internationally and which has recently announced plans to engage in a larger second-generation bio-ethanol project in Brazil. Thus Dong is not only offering a very active implementation of a pathway to sustainable energy, it is doing this on a global scale by benefitting from a very sophisticated Danish knowledge base, and using sophisticated financial products and procedures to attract financial resources from pension funds. Without the financial crisis, the state would probably have privatised this company by selling off its majority shareholdings. Now the state has secured its successful international expansion, but at the same time used it in its argument for austerity.

It is no enigma that the Leftist constituency behind the Social-Democratic-led government is confused. Austerity for the unemployed, welfare-dependent and pensioners, while at the same time generous liquidity for banks, tacit subsidies to home-owners and globally offensive state-owned enterprises. What kind of policy is that?

QUESTIONING THE ROLE OF DEBT FIGURES IN MACRO-ECONOMIC NAVIGATION

If the Danish case concerning the huge difference between gross and net debt is the least illustrative for the situation among a number of well-off countries in the EU, it indicates that the EMU convergence criteria are restrictive for developing Social Europe. With the financial pact, this self-limiting governance has been further institutionally consolidated at a time when there is an obvious need for reforms in the opposite direction. Denmark has, rather than protesting against these foundations for EU policies, followed Angela Merkel in imposing them more strongly. In this way Danish Social-Democrats participated in the game by which 'an elite hijacked a continent' (Fazi, 2014).

The Danish state – assisted by annual advice and reports from the EU Commission – argues that it has to be extraordinary careful because of the extreme high private debt. And indeed, figures are at first sight worrying. According to the Wikipedia 'List of countries by external debt' (including both private and public debt owed to non-residents), Denmark (together with the other Nordic countries) scores quite highly at the level of 180 per cent of GNP compared to the United States (105 per cent) and the EU average (85 per cent). But this is also the case for other successful countries such as Switzerland, the Netherlands and, to an extreme extent, Luxembourg.

But these figures ignore what foreigners owe to Denmark. Measured by 'Net international investment position', the NIIP (the difference between a country's external financial assets and liabilities) in Denmark has a solid surplus of 6 per cent of GNP, whereas the United States has a deficit of 16.9 per cent and the Euro zone of 11.4 per cent. Instead, this data indicates that Denmark is interwoven financially in the international economy in a very balanced way – that there is neither capital flight nor unbalanced takeovers. However, the high level of integration also indicates that Denmark is highly dependent on flows of international financial assets and that it will be highly influenced by the volatility of international finance. Thus there may be good reasons for tip-toeing around when managing the international economy. And perfecting the art may bring great advantages. Ironically, up to this point, the Euro crisis and the economic risks of lending to a number of South European countries have served Denmark well by bringing down her interest rates to very low levels.

Effected by these financially driven considerations, the Social-Democratic-Centre government has since 2010 implemented the plans of the former Liberal-Conservative government and especially through the new rules of budget-discipline for municipalities brought down public employment by almost 25,000 (from 2010 to 2012), quite a high proportion of the approximately 170,000 that are currently unemployed.[5]

Though Denmark has not introduced the Euro, it has signed the recent EU financial pact and agreed to operate according to its austerity principles of *Balance* (public budgets shall be in surplus or balance over a certain period), *Correction mechanisms* (if out of balance, spell out how to deal with the problems in coming years) and *Implementation by national laws*. This is implemented through a budget law that obliges the state, the regions and municipalities to save on budgets within a very narrow frame; if not observed, they will be fined with extraordinary budgetary constraints in coming years. Municipalities will be forced to reduce budgets for daycare for children, schools and care for the elderly and handicapped. In many ways this type of policy has almost been prepared for by subsequent reductions in marginal income taxes (at the level of 40 billion DKK in 2011 – close to the public deficit on current accounts that year).[6]

QUESTIONING THE CRISIS IN PRODUCTIVITY AND COMPETITIVENESS

Danish politicians do not simply explain their politics of austerity with reference to the EMU convergence criteria, the EU financial pact and the housing market, but also argue that Denmark must regain lost private jobs by lowering the costs of production and increasing productivity; and to achieve this, it is necessary to save on and increase the efficiency of public sector services, and to reduce taxes to allow space for comparatively lower wage increases, all in all to create a stimulus for making it attractive to invest in Denmark.

Denmark is said to have lost its former high positions on the international WEF competitiveness index (demoted from one of the best five to 12th position in 2013), due to comparatively high wages and stagnating productivity. Whereas high wages have primarily been discussed with reference to Germany and Sweden, the productivity issue constitutes such an enigma that a commission has been formed to search for explanations.

Indexes on competitiveness are indeed strange. Is it really beyond discussion that high wages weigh on the negative side when measuring competitiveness? Is a business sector not the more competitive the better it can pay its workers? But countries have been competing for bringing down their wage costs in exports. After the financial crisis, some countries – for example Sweden and the United Kingdom – lowered their wage costs by devaluating their currencies. Some East European countries effected the same outcome by directly lowering wages by state decree. Germany has done it more incrementally and systematically over a decade, during which their salaries dropped from the highest to a comparatively much lower level – so low that a large proportion of German full-time workers are today among the working poor. Within the Euro zone, individual countries cannot devalue in a normal way, but American economists have argued that devaluation effects can be tricked by simultaneously lowering income taxes (to give space for lower wages) and increasing consumption taxes (VAT). This was what Germany did in 2006, thereby adding problems for other countries within the Euro zone and beyond (Farhi, Gopinath, & Itskhoki, 2011).

Centre-Left politicians and employer organisations argue jointly that Denmark must improve competitiveness by bringing down income taxes and duties to change the cost structure for industry. This can only be done, they argue, by saving on public services, reducing unemployment benefits, social insurance and stipends for students. The difference between unemployment benefits and wages must be enlarged to make it 'attractive' for the unemployed to actively search for employment, and the period on unemployment benefit has already been reduced from 4 to 2 years to induce a faster return to work. Obviously, the political system is very focused on making the 'reserve army' be effective on the level of wages in both the private and public sectors. The Danish welfare state, internationally known for its generosity, is today administered towards its clients with a deliberate pettiness. Across the political spectrum it is as if politicians see civilians as a bunch of opportunists, free-riders and shirkers who only work if economic inducements are high enough. Transaction cost economics and principal-agent theories have certainly entered into the minds of the administrative system.

In any case, this type of elite-autopoiesis neglects a number of essential facts about the Danish economy. Despite high wages and taxes and probably some of the world's highest duties on energy, water and pollution, Danish exports – after a drop of 20 per cent in 2009 – very quickly came back to the pre-crisis level, and since then the Danish trade balance (goods and services) has been positive at the level of 100 billion DKK annually and preliminary topping DKK 120 billion in 2013. Some have seen the current surplus on the balance of payments as the largest since the Viking ages.[7] One would guess that such a situation would speak for itself, and ought to cause cautious self-evaluation as to how Danish exports flourish (together with exports from other high-wage countries such as Switzerland, Norway and the Netherlands). Part of the explanation of the high surplus is, of course, that Danish imports have been declining. The number of employed in Denmark has dropped to the level of 2001–2006; only when compared to the high level reached in 2007–2008 when the economy overheated is it a drop.

Christensen Sørensen[8] has suggested that a country has problems with its competitiveness if it has a substantial deficit on balance of payments (relative to its GNP) simultaneously with a high unemployment rate. The gap between the two has systematically narrowed since 1984 (while it was widening from 1972 to 1984). To him, the major problem is that private spending has never regained the pre-crisis level and by 2012 private savings surpassed private investments by 175 billion DKK (23 billion Euro) annually. Similar arguments have been made by Bjarke Refslund,[9] who consequently groups Denmark together with Germany, the Netherlands, Sweden, Norway and Switzerland in terms of ability to regain strengths in exports. For instance, the increase in exports since 2008 has been similar in Denmark and Sweden despite Sweden devaluating its currency against the Euro, while Denmark did not. Though Denmark's primary export locations are in Europe, its exports to the BRIC countries have doubled since 2005. He also argues against the widely held view that industrial jobs have been reallocated towards the BRICs. While the loss of such jobs was at the level of 6,300 annually from 2001 to 2006, it was 5,000 annually from 2009 to 2011.

However, it has been argued that between 2003 and 2012 Denmark experienced a drop in comparative competitiveness, caused by a relative fall in productivity during the 2007—2008 peak that simultaneously led to a relative decline in wage competitiveness, combined with an increase in the relative value of the Danish currency from 2009 to 2011. But this situation has been reversed since then.[10]

But the question still remains as to whether the productivity problem is more of a structural kind. The productivity enigma emerged as figures showed that the level of productivity gains from 1995 to 2010 were much less than they had been in the previous period from 1975 to 1995. Even if focus alone is on productivity in sectors where goods and services are exchanged through the market, the two periods show very different productivity increases. In the years 1975—1995 the average annual increase in hourly labour productivity of the market economy was 3.2 per cent, while it was only 0.7 per cent during 1995—2010 (Andersen & Spange, 2012, p. 43). Compared with the best and similar types of countries, Denmark is clearly lacking behind on numerous aspects (Graversen, Napier, & Rosted, 2011). There are no easy explanations as it seems as if Denmark has done most to improve (Andersen & Spange, 2012; McGowan & Jamet, 2012) and there is a tendency for various analysts to diagnose the problem according to ideological positions: low national competition (Andersen & Spange, 2012; McGowan & Jamet, 2012) or low functional capabilities and collaborative relations of the national innovation system (Graversen, Napier, & Rosted, 2011). A closer look reveals that the problem is very heterogeneous and unevenly distributed across branches and among different company sizes (*ibid.*; DI's Produktivitetspanel, 2013).

It has been quite natural to take for granted that the public sector contributed to the problems of productivity improvements, but as this sector's productivity measures were based on cost calculations (the input-method), the situation and development was very difficult to assess. Recent calculations based on the output method, however, show that whereas the former method for the period 2003–2009 showed an annual drop of 0.1 per cent in productivity, the new one shows an increase of 0.4 per cent annually for public sector services.[11] This productivity increase is especially intense from 2006 to 2008 – the years when unemployment went from low to extremely low. But more children per nursery teacher, more students per teacher in public schools, vocational schools and universities, more patients per doctor and nurse in hospitals, more clients per social worker, etc., do not lead automatically to improved services in terms of child development, learning, curing of illnesses, re-socialisation and activation of people with complicated problems in private lives and occupations. Actually, the measurements that were introduced to control public employees seem to have had more focus on how many people the public services were able to handle and not how well they handled their clients and helped solve their problems.

A parallel problem has recently been discussed in relation to the measures of productivity in the exporting industries and services (Nielsen & Pedersen, 2013, p. 6ff). The decline in Danish productivity is significant if measured in fixed prices over time. What is then measured is how labour and capital inputs relate to volume of products. Normally, it is taken for granted that productivity increases mean that more goods can be exported for lower prices. But Danish export goods are characterised by enabling increasing prices internationally, especially compared to Sweden and Finland, where firms such as Ericsson and Nokia have been able to increase exports by lowering prices. It could be that what Denmark exports can be sold for increasing prices exactly because it is considered to be of increasing value to importers. Is it – as we would suggest – because Danish goods are continually improved, so that the same item is different? Then productivity should not be based on output measured in fixed prices as is currently the case.

QUESTIONING GNP STAGNATION AS A SIGN OF CRISIS

In the general crisis debate in Denmark, it has also caused alarm that the country recently (2010) dropped to be only the 15th richest country measured in GNP per capita (correlated for real purchasing power in fixed prices). Also here the picture changes very much if calculations are made in PPP in current prices, where Denmark then holds number 10 position (Nielsen & Pedersen, 2013, p. 5) behind Luxembourg, Norway, the United States, Switzerland, the Netherlands, Ireland, Austria and Sweden. But the picture changes again if the measure is in Gross National Incomes (GNI) instead of GNP. Measured in GNI per capita, Denmark holds position no. 7, and since the early 1970s it has made frequent swings between being no. 6 and no. 12 in this last ranking.[12] Thus, if Danish wealth is measured in fixed prices GNP PPP the country lost five positions in the international ranking of countries between 2003 and 2010, whereas measured in terms of current prices GNI PPP it gained eight positions in these rankings.

In Danish discourses the stagnation or decline in GNP since 2007 has caused concern. This discourse ignores the fact that from 1999 and onwards Denmark went through a dramatic shift in its level of international integration (in terms of in- and outbound FDI) and therefore a considerable part of Danish labour and investments primarily affected the GNP growth of other countries. The national effect of globalisation should therefore result in growth in Danish GNI that in addition to GNP also includes income from labour and capital operating abroad (minus similar incomes that foreigners have taken out of Denmark). In terms of GNI per capita, Denmark had a growth rate of 10.4 per cent from 2007 through to 2011. Around 2000 it had a net foreign debt of around DKK 300 billion (measured in 2013 prices) on which it paid interest at the level 30–50 billion DKK annually. By 2012 the Danish net foreign fortune was around DKK 700 billion, generating an income beyond DKK 60 billion annually (Nielsen & Pedersen, 2013, p. 6).

So is the Danish economic crisis a fact or a fiction? It might be said that the political elite has been very effective in using dubious facts to create an imagined crisis that by leading to restricted public spending, fairly high unemployment and low household spending have caused a demand and investment crisis that in itself caused a GNP but not a GNI growth crisis.

Low-interest rates, at times lower than German, help sustain this difference, as in principle but not in practice they have elevated national activity. Reports on people wanting in vain to take a loan to buy a house and SMEs unable to raise loans for promising projects are manifold, while citizens' savings and large corporations' hoarding of liquid financial assets are massive as they see no promising business projects outside their current domain. The latter increased from DKK 24 billion in 2007 to DKK 165 billion in 2011. This suggests that the financial system is not performing its societal function of relocating financial means. Instead, it hangs like a shadow over everybody's head. Today, Danes benefit from low-interest rates on flexible loans, but these rates are only safe in the short term. Next year they may have to be exchanged with loans at a much higher interest rate.

Under the shadow of a financial regime that could drastically change the framework conditions of an economy, it is really difficult to assess how the 'real' economy is functioning: consumers seem to assess it negative, while the financial institutions consider it increasingly robust.[13]

IMAGINING ALTERNATIVES AND THE CURRENT POLITICAL CONSTRUCTION OF ROUTES TO PROSPERITY

We have previously argued (Kristensen, 2006, p. 315) that by creating an active labour market policy during the early 1990s, the Social-Democratic-Centre government had unintentionally created a new supply-oriented automatic economic stabiliser: when unemployment rates increase and industry is running below full capacity utilisation, workers and the unemployed would engage in massive skill-upgrading, motivated by personal aspirations for and mutual competition over skills, stimulated by firms that served their future interest in enlarging their skill base, and enabled by welfare provision and publicly financed training institutions. In this way Denmark would not only make use of recessions in a creative way, it would also prepare firms and employees to take better advantage of a coming boom.

This would underpin companies that had decentralised competency and responsibilities to shifting combinations of operative, continuous improvement and ad hoc innovative teams to engage in combinations of sophisticated product and service development that helped customer firms or public institutions carry out continuous improvement (Kristensen & Lilja, 2011). At the same time this evolutionary path and business model would engage the firms in increasingly advanced innovative networks, making it possible constantly to search for new comparative advantages. For this kind of business model, an active, capacitating and enabling use of welfare and educational institutions (Sabel, Saxenian, Miettinen, Kristensen, & Häutimäki, 2011) would be an advantage and make a highly developed public sector an asset rather than a cost.

With the drastic drop in demand for goods and the need for capacity reduction that followed in the aftermath of the financial crisis in the autumn of 2008, numerous employers and the unions argued in favour of following Germany and prolonging the formal period during which employees could work on short time work-schemes, being supplied with partial welfare compensation (Andersen, forthcoming). In this way, employers argued, companies would be able to hold on to their highly needed skilled workers, place them on continuous training schemes and prepare them and firms for a return to normal times. Thus a number of individual employers had intuitively understood the unintended secrets of the novel automatic stabilisers.

But they were speaking to deaf ears. The Liberal-Conservative government, overwhelmed by the over-employment of the previous period and the forecasts of the future shortage of labour power, focused entirely on how they could use institutional measures to make the unemployed search for new jobs as actively and as quickly as possible. The government had also during their reign since 2000 reduced support for continuous training, counselling of the unemployed wishing to improve their long-term chances, etc. − in short undermined much of what was elegant in the Danish activation policies of the 1990s (Jørgensen, 2009). Their vision was that anybody should be forced to take on any job, no matter how little it reflected their existing skills, future career aspirations or the coming needs of industry.

As argued elsewhere (Kristensen & Lilja, 2011; Kristensen & Morgan, 2012; Sabel et al., 2011), during the last half of the 1990s and specifically in relation to the active labour market policy, Denmark made a major step towards more experimental forms of organisations (both in the private and public sectors) and more individualised service provision by the public sector. This happened by a number of reforms that decentralised responsibilities from central to county and municipal levels and by granting higher autonomy to employees and teams at the bottom of organisations (both public and private) supported by an enhanced level of further training. There are strong indications that this unleashed a strong ability to carry out much more innovation and continuous improvement at the level of individual jobs and workplaces. However, compared to centralised and hierarchical forms of lean production, it happened without simultaneously creating a system, so that what was achieved in one space could be brought to use in others. Learning became local instead of organisational and systematic. In other words, Denmark had developed firms, public organisations and institutions that were experimentalist but had not developed experimentalist governance. This would at least demand a common system for spotting functional deficiencies, diagnosing problems, describing solutions and cures for problems based on experimental evidence, ways of systematically diffusing best practices, and reflective bodies to improve the entire system. There is hardly any doubt that such a system of experimental governance in both the private and public sectors would be able to deal much more effectively with the productivity challenges that Denmark has experienced recently, and more importantly, it was in principle pointing in the direction of a new growth and development regime.

But this way of seeing things was never a part of the Social-Democratic or the Liberal perspective. Rather, a paradigm of 'structural unemployment' came to constitute a core for the political discourse between the two main opponents from the beginning of the 1980s (Larsen & Andersen, 2009) and would be later reinforced by a constant fear of labour shortage, based on demographic predictions that by 2020 the economic active population would drop by 8,000 and then quickly become worse, so that a fast decreasing number of economically active people would have to support a fast increasing number of old-age pensioners, creating an enormous long-term deficit on public current accounts.

Whether such a thing as structural unemployment does in fact exist is highly questionable (*ibid.*), but the idea of its existence would in many ways encircle the understanding of the economy and lead to similar conclusions, as would more pronounced neo-liberal ideas. From the beginning of the 1980s, a certain level of 'structural unemployment' (at approximately 8 per cent) was consensually seen as being necessary to hold back on wage increases and inflation according to the shape of the Danish Phillips curve. But gradually it became clear during the 1980s that in the wake of unemployment, the phenomenon of *hysteresis* (Blanchard & Summers, 1986) would follow with the destruction of human capital, especially as youth unemployment increased. As those in employment became heavily engaged in further training and reskilling in relation to new technologies and changes in work organisation (Kristensen & Høpner, 1994) during the same years, structural unemployment became increasingly related to the widening skill gap between the unemployed and the skills needed in industry. The unemployed, so to speak, neither served as an effective reserve army nor as a reservoir for growth. Up to 1993 the Conservative-Liberal government tried to solve this problem by a mixture of forced activation of long-term unemployed youth and by preparing the ground for a dual labour market in which the unemployed could enter service occupations at low wages. Generous unemployment benefits and social insurance were a barrier to this solution, and therefore they wanted to reduce benefits. However, in an economy mounting towards a figure of 12 per cent unemployed, there was political resistance to solving the problem in this way and hysteresis accumulated towards 1993, when a Social-Democratic-Centre government came into power.

Based on a number of successful local experiments, the new government wanted to close the skill gap and make people employable at the general wage levels that existed in Denmark by giving the unemployed a right to activate through a combination of further training, job-practices and welfare services according to the needs of each individual and formulated in an individual activation plan. In exchange, the unemployed would be obliged to follow this plan to have the right to receive unemployment benefits, the duration of which was reduced from 7 to 4 years. These schemes became locally integrated in highly interesting ways with further training activities initiated to enable changes in work organisation of firms under the guidance of Regional Labour Market Councils (Kristensen & Lilja, 2011, chap. 3). But the Social-Democratic lesson was primarily understood in terms of its macro-economic effect, by which the shape of the Phillips curve could be changed and the level of 'structural unemployment' brought down. Probably very few saw the deeper and micro-based processes by which labour markets were changed in tandem with the organisation of firms and the emergence of new business models. Some saw it as a change from a social insurance to a more active welfare state providing capacitating individualised social services (Sabel et al., 2011; Torfing, 2004). The outcome was immense and unemployment dropped very considerably to one of the lowest levels in Europe during the 1990s and the Danish model of *flexicurity* gradually became prominent and worth copying within the framework of a Social Europe.

The return of a Liberal-Conservative government and generally low unemployment in the noughties saw a farewell to the focus on further training in general and in particular for those still unemployed. Instead, active labour market policies came to mean schemes that forced the jobless to actively search for work and would punish inactivity in that respect. These attitudes also involved people on social insurance, and the idea was that a general mobilisation of all citizens for work − no matter how bad their conditions were − was needed. Thus in the period before the financial crisis, the general attitude was that all who wanted a job could get one, and the problem for society was not only an immediate but also a long-term shortage of labour power.

These generally held prospects meant that during the financial crisis, governments of shifting colours have been very fiercely constructing labour market reforms that could increase the proportion of the active against the economically non-active population. By reforming both early retirement schemes, the formal retirement age (from 65 years of age today to 71 in 2050) and reducing the duration of unemployment benefits to 2 years instead of 4, the prospects are now stagnation until 2015 and then fast expansion towards 2050, by which time there will be 350,000 more people belonging to the economically active population than today.[14] Instead of the previously predicted drop of 8,000 in the economic active age group by 2020, forecasts now are an increase of 14,000, primarily due to immigration from foreign countries. And as the economic models in Denmark (the DREAM model) see the supply of labour as the primary cause of growth, while neglecting the factors that determine the demand for labour, the dominant politicians and the state seem to think that these reforms have solved the basic long-term problems of the economy. So the prospects of creating a large and active reserve army competing for jobs looks pretty favourable or terrible – depending on the observation of the observer.

COMPARING MAINSTREAM PROSPECTS: DENMARK AGAINST EUROPE

With these reforms carried out simultaneously with an aggressive policy of austerity, especially designed to punish municipalities if they overspend, Denmark seems to have overcome most of the problems that economists predicted for both the short and long term and these economists now foresee Denmark as one of the most robust economies of the whole OECD club if the course on public spending is followed strictly in the future.[15] The idea shared by most politicians is that the number of jobs should increase in the private sector, while being cut back or held stagnant in the public. In this respect the visions of Danish Liberals and Social-Democrats seem very similar to both neo- and ordo-liberalists (Blyth, 2013; Foucault, 2004), but for very different reasons than in most other EU countries.[16]

To a lot of European countries the coming boom in the proportion of elderly people constitutes a major challenge in terms of public sector budgets, one that understood within a general neo-liberalist understanding of the economy becomes very serious, if not frightening, depending on how the respective pensions systems of different countries are construed.

Before current reforms Denmark had already one of the most adequate and sustainable pensions systems in the world (according to several OECD reviews), but since the new reforms the Melbourne Mercer Global Pension Index by 2012 has assessed the Danish system as the only one worthy of an

A-grade and ranking it higher than the Netherlands, Australia, Sweden, Switzerland and Canada, the closest competitors. And because Denmark in the past had numerous pensions schemes where savings would lead to tax reductions, large groups of pensioners will use these savings to generate considerable tax revenues for the state,[17] thereby reducing the coming pressure on public finances.

Denmark has fewer reasons than most EU countries to have imposed a very tough version of the financial pact and labour market reforms on itself. And, indeed, in a Europe captured by austeria-hysteria (Blyth, 2013), Denmark seems to be more balanced, as it combines automatic stabilisers and active finance policy in a way that adds up to the most expansive finance policy among the EU countries in 2009–2013.[18] To no surprise Ireland, Spain, Italy and Portugal have quite high automatic stabilisers, but have combined these with negative, that is contractive, active finance policies. Most surprising, however, is that a number of well-off countries, for example Germany and Austria, combine low automatic stabilisers with neutral activist policies. France, Great Britain and the United States combine fairly low automatic stabilisers with contracting finance political actions in this comparison.

Thus, though it seems from within our country as if Denmark is pursuing a pro-cyclical contractual policy, trying to reduce public budgets, comparatively speaking this is much less the case than in most other European countries and the United States. Sweden, Germany, Austria, the Netherlands and Finland could do a lot more demand stimulation without becoming more exposed to financial volatility than Denmark. But these countries make use of the EMU convergence principles and the recent financial pact to impose a stronger than needed austerity.

While this is being written, the Social-Democratic-Centre government is preparing two new reforms, one for employment policy and another for vocational training, and these could, judging by current rumours, contain some of the elements that made the labour market policy of the 1990s so promising. But again, this will have to take place within the limitations of the EU financial pact and a generally stagnant public spending. So experimentalist vigour might be limited.

Current global governance, EMU convergence criteria and the international financial market seem to combine in such a way that countries are following a similar route as during the crisis of the 1920–1930. Thus, is it possible that countries that pursue a successful globalisation strategy supported by activist state actions wind up being punished by financial institutions so that their further global activities are limited, while the room of manoeuvre shrinks nationally, forcing states to down-size personnel and budgets – as happened for multinational corporations (Kristensen & Zeitlin, 2005)? If that is the case, the crisis is more than about the financial crisis and reaches into the very core of global governance. Is Europe pursuing a policy of deliberate self-limitation imposed by fear of a volatile financial system?

And the question is whether Europe and Denmark, by measuring their respective successes in GNP rather than GNI, imposes on itself a restrictive governance that does not reflect the way they globalise. In fact very few European countries faced a drop in GNI per capita in the period that is currently seen as the most severe crisis since the 1930s. Everything else being equal, it gives a more wrong assessment of a country's creditworthiness if one relates its debt to GNP rather than GNI per capita in an age of globalisation, and if the general situation of the EU is that there is a stagnation of GNP but considerable growth in GNI per capita, then the EU-convergence criteria by this source of flaws alone tend to become falsely restrictive for state economic action. In the way that the EMU convergence criteria currently functions as governance it punishes countries with progressive globalisation strategies by limiting the room of manoeuvre for progressive and activist national development strategies pursued by the state. Denmark is a good example of exactly this, but comparatively spoken not a typical example, unfortunately.

AUSTERITY AND THE IDEATIONAL FOUNDATIONS OF THE DANISH ELITE

When the Social-Democratic-Centre government came into power in 2010, several observers would have expected that they would have been in opposition to existing EU coalitions in favour of austerity. Instead, they continued the position of the former Liberal-Conservative government, the economic policy of which they had agreed to continue in the agreement that the three constitutive parties signed when the new government was formed.

It is not easy to see this outcome as a deliberative turn to neo- or ordo-liberal thinking by the Social-Democratic party, which during election campaign had confronted the Liberal party by saying that Denmark would have to choose between an improved welfare state or tax reductions, as both were not possible, and they would favour the first alternative. In this respect they were against one of their coming coalition partners,

De Radikale (a social liberal party), which has a tradition for being progressive in issues of education, while being more reluctant concerning social insurance aspects of the welfare state.

The result is that there has been a high continuity in following a policy that tries to avoid the welfare state in itself helping create structural unemployment or reducing the supply of labour, whereas parties on the right and left agree to protect what are now considered core welfare state obligations such as child-care, effective health-care and education. This means that reductions in income taxes, rolling back early retirement schemes and delaying pension age are all seen as necessary for calibrating the welfare state for global competition (the Social-Democratic vision), whereas it is a project on its own for the more ultraliberal of the political landscape.

The voice of neo-liberalism has no doubt grown louder over the last couple of decades in Denmark. CEPOS is an influential think-tank that has received contributions and memberships from the Liberal party, circles around employers' associations and university economists. Teaching at universities for economists has become dominated by neo-classical and liberal orientations to the neglect of Keynesianism. Economic models have become supply- rather than demand-oriented so that the discourse on growth and economic development has become more dominated by the logics of market dynamics. Young generations of economists, political science candidates and those who have been elected to parliament are clearly dominated by this way of thinking and understand much better the complicated relations within the state and towards its citizens in terms of principal-agent schemes.

Employers' associations, liberal and conservative parties, CEPOS, etc., always speak in favour of lowering marginal taxes to sustain job creation inside the borders of Denmark. However, there is no indication that Denmark has an elite or elite-faction that is centrally placed within the network that constitutes the current neo-liberal hegemony (Plehwe & Walpen, 2005). The current members of government are very young with a considerable influence of women who can hardly be seen as belonging to a self-reproductive elite, and the so-called business elite seems very open to new entrants and only to a very limited extent a space for inter-generational reproduction (Munk et al., 2013). Furthermore, only very few from the Danish business elite hold membership in such networks as the Bilderberg Group, the Trilateral Commission or the European Round Table of Industrialists that have a more direct influence on EU politics and the current dominance of neo-liberalist thought.[19]

The Danish political elite has been very reluctant in putting boundaries on, taxing and regulating the financial elite and its institutions, and one can say that on the whole this elite has recaptured its space because it provided the means for rescuing the young urban middle-class from going bust with their over-priced houses. The marginalised, low income, badly educated working classes have paid the bill through wage-restraints, and reduced social and unemployment benefits.

But what seems to be lacking is an alternative way of seeing the new functions of the welfare state in relation to business strategies and models under globalisation, and if such a vision took hold it could constitute a new ideational foundation for forming a more offensive political course. There have been several signs of moving towards such a view, in particular from the left, emphasising up-skilling instead of meaningless activation of the unemployed, from the more visionary circles of unions, and from Social-Democratic mayors who have visions of transforming local versions of welfare states in more promising directions for creating more advanced private firms. There is tacit experimentation among vocational schools, firms and other labour market institutions that may be related to the ongoing experimental search for novel ways of organising work, but currently these experiments are too fragmented and too bounded in scope by austerity to break free and become visible rehearsals of practising more prosperous futures. There seems, however, currently to be no space where partial steps can be taken to help foster an integrative understanding of how to navigate in an alternative way. Compared to this polyphony of voices, the voices of the neo-liberal vision seem much more coherent and loud, although its tune is much more pragmatic and less loud than in other parts of Europe.

NOTES

1. In retrospect the comparative level of overspending in Denmark has become clear. Between 2001 and 2010 Danes on average had a net saving rate of −1.0 per cent, while it was −0.3 per cent for Great Britain, +3.7 per cent for the United States, +5.3 per cent for Norway, +6.4 per cent for Spain, +6.8 per cent for Holland, +7.0 per cent for Sweden, +10.7 per cent for Germany and +11.9 per cent for France. Debt in housing rose from a level of DKK 600 billion in 2000 to DKK 1,750 billion in 2011 (*Politiken*, 13 March 2013, p. 11).

2. Therefore it need not be such an anomaly as suggested by Crouch (2012) that private Keynesianism could also be observed in Denmark, though it mainly characterised liberal market economies, where the low-skilled and middle classes

used the rising housing prices to finance traditional consumption levels by taking on more debt.

3. *Politiken*, Økonomi, 23 January 2013, p. 2.

4. *Berlingske Business*, 7 November 2012, p. 11, and from private e-mail exchange with Frederik I. Pedersen from AER. To make the proportion of the Danish 'public debt crisis' even more insignificant, it is ironic to observe that since the state in 2005 took over the task from municipalities of collecting citizens' arrears to the public sector, these have increased dramatically to a level of 80 billion DKK in 2012. Probably the accumulated debt on current accounts and the arrears in 2011 were pretty much at the same level.

5. *Politiken*, 12 January, p. 11.

6. SEnyt, 21 April 2012: Henrik Herløv Lund: Budgetlov AmputererØkonomisk Handlerum.

7. *Politiken*, 13 February 2013, Kultur, p. 8: Henning Jørgensen og Kelvin Baadsgaard: Myter om Dansk Økonomi. In 2011 the surplus on balance of payments amounted to 5.6 per cent of GNP. Some see this surplus as mainly reflecting the fact that Denmark is investing less than it saves (*Politiken*, Økonomi, 13 March 2013, p. 10: Torben M. Andersen: Stort plus på betalingerne, men ...).

8. *Politiken*, 7 February 2013, Kultur, p. 8: Christen Sørensen: Konkurrenceevne bedre end sit rygte.

9. *Politiken*, 2 January 2013, Kultur, p. 8: Bjarke Refslund: Dansk Økonomi er slet ikke så svag.

10. *Politiken*, Økonomi, 30 January 2013: Thomas Flensburg: Vi flytter Produktion til Ungarn Alligevel.

11. *Mandag Morgen*, 26 November 2012: De Offentlige Ansatte fører i Produktivitetsræset.

12. *Politiken*, 16 December 2012, p. 17: Peter G.H. Madsen: Danmark er stadig et af verdens rigeste lande.

13. In March 2013 it nearly evoked a national celebration that Denmark was ranked among the eight best triple A countries in the world (also including the other Nordic countries, Switzerland and Canada (but not Germany)) by rating agencies. And the government took this as a proof of the soundness of its economic policy.

14. *Politiken*, 17 December 2012, p. 10: Thomas Flensburg: Om 40 år er der 350.000 flere på arbejdsmarkedet end i dag.

15. Jens Reiermann (2014): Reformer har trimmet Danmark til Verdensklasse. *Mandag Morgen*, 3 February.

16. As I am writing this, it is now two months since the annual auditing by the EU Commission on the situation of the member states in terms of financial and budgetary criteria. In this report, Denmark, Luxembourg and Malta were the only countries that received no orders or suggestions for further action. Up to now no politician or economist has commented in public on this seemingly crucial fact that could break with the carefully constructed image of a crisis.

17. These coming incomes for the state are not taken into consideration when assessing Denmark's accumulated debt according to the EMU convergence criteria.

18. *Politiken*, Økonomi, 23 January 2013: Torben M. Andersen: Forstærker finanspolitikken krisen.

19. Marianne Kristensen (2014): Danske topchefer står uden for de magtfulde erhvervsnetværk. *Mandag Morgen*, 14 February. According to Jürgen Roth it is exactly in such associations and networks that neo-liberal ideas are nurtured, while obviously they are held in a much more structured way by Central banks and financial institutions under the strong leadership of Mario Draghi of the European Central Bank (Interview, *Politiken*, Økonomi, 30 April 2014, p. 6).

REFERENCES

Andersen, A. L., & Spange, M. (2012). Produktivitetsudviklingen i Danmark. *Nationalbanken, Kvartalsoversigt, 1. Kvartal, 1*, 41–56.
Andersen, S. K. (forthcoming). Making sense of changing employment policies. In S. Boras & L. Seabrooke (Eds.), *Sense-making and institutional change*. Oxford: Oxford University Press.
Blanchard, O. J., & Summers, L. H. (1986). Hysteresis and the European unemployment problem. In S. Fischer (Ed.). *NBER macroeconomics annual* (Vol. 1, pp. 15–78). Cambridge, MA: MIT Press.
Blyth, M. (2013). *Austerity. The history of a dangerous idea*. New York, NY: Oxford University Press.
Carstensen, M. B. (2013). Projecting from a fiction: The case of Denmark and the financial crisis. *New Political Economy, 18*(4), 555–578.
Crouch, C. (2012). Employment, consumption, debt, and European industrial relations systems. *Industrial Relations, 51(S1)*, 389–412.
Dam, N. A., Hvolbøl, T. S., Pedersen, E. H., Sørensen, P. B., & Thamsborg, S. H. (2011). Boligboblen der bristede: Kan boligpriserne forklares? Og kan deres udsving dæmpes? *Kvartalsoversigt, 1* (del 1, pp. 47–69). Copenhagen: Danmarks Nationalbank.
DI's Produktivitetspanel. (2013, January 9). *Erhvervslivets Produktivitetsudvikling*. DI's Produktivitetspanel. Danmark op i gear, Copenhagen.
Erhvervs- og Vækstministeriet. (2013). *Den Finansielle Krise I Danmark – årsager, konsekvenser og læring*. Copenhagen: Ministry of Business and Growth.
Farhi, E., Gopinath, G., & Itskhoki, G. (2011). *Fiscal devaluations*. NBER Working Paper No. 17662. Retrieved from http://www.nber.org/papers/w17662
Fazi, T. (2014). *The battle for Europe. How an elite hijacked a continent and how we can take it back*. London: Pluto Press.
Foucault, M. (2004). *The birth of biopolitics*. New York, NY: Picador.
Graversen, A. B., Napier, G., & Rosted, J. (2011). *Produktivitet i Danmark. Den danske vækstudfordring*. Copenhagen: FORA.
Jørgensen, H. (2009). From a beautiful swan to an ugly duckling: Changes in Danish activation policies since 2003. Paper for the ASPEN/ETUI activation conference, Brno, 20–21 March.
Kristensen, P. H. (2006). Business systems in the age of the "new economy": Denmark facing the challenge. In J. L. Campbell, J. A. Hall, & O. K. Pedersen (Eds.), *National identity and the varieties of capitalism. The Danish experience*. Montreal: McGill-Queen's University Press.

Kristensen, P. H., & Høpner, J. (1994). Fleksibilitetens Strukturform. Efteruddannelse, Virksomhedsorganisation, Arbejdskarriere i Danmark. Copenhagen: Nyt fra Samfundsvidenskaberne.
Kristensen, P. H., & Lilja, K. (Eds.). (2011). *Nordic capitalism and globalization. New forms of economic organization and welfare institutions*. Oxford: Oxford University Press.
Kristensen, P. H., & Morgan, G. (2012). From institutional change to experimentalist institutions. *Industrial Relations, 51(S1)*, 413–437.
Kristensen, P. H., & Zeitlin, J. (2005). *Local players in global games. The strategic constitution of a multinational firm*. Oxford: Oxford University Press.
Larsen, C. A., & Andersen, J. G. (2009). How economic ideas changed the Danish welfare state. *Governance, 22(2)*, 239–261.
McGowan, M. A., & Jamet, S. (2012). *Sluggish productivity growth in Denmark: The usual suspects*. Working Papers No. 975. OECD Economics Department, Paris.
Mortensen, J. L., & Seabrooke, L. (2008). Housing as social right or means to wealth? The politics of property booms in Australia and Denmark. *Comparative European Politics*, 6(3), 305–324.
Munk, M. D., Ellersgaard, C., & Larsen, A. G. (2013). A very economical elite – The case of Danish top CEOs. *Sociology, 47(6)*, 1051–1071.
Nielsen, A. P., & Pedersen, F. I. (2013). Myte at dansk velstand rasler ned. Notat 19. December. Arbejderbevægelsens Erhvervsråd, Copenhagen. Retrieved from www.ae.dk
Pedersen, R. M., & Brandt, J. (2013). *Indtjening og gæld i dansk landbrug*. Speciale fra Institut for Finansiering og Regnskab. Copenhagen: Copenhagen Business School.
Plehwe, D., & Walpen, B. (2005). Between network and complex organization: The making of neoliberal knowledge and hegemony. In D. Plehwe, B. Walpen, & G. Neuenhofer (Eds.). *Neoliberal hegemony: A global critique*. New York. NY: Routledge.
Sabel, C. F., Saxenian, A.-L., Miettinen, R., Kristensen, P. H., & Häutimäki, J. (2011). *Individualized service provision in the new welfare state*. Helsinki: Sitra Studies 62.
Torfing, J. (2004). *Det Stille Sporskifte i Velfærdsstaten*. Aarhus: Aarhus Universitetsforlag.
Wolf, C. (2014). *The power of inaction. Bank bailouts in comparison*. Ithaca, NY: Cornell University Press.

FROM CLASSWIDE COHERENCE TO COMPANY-FOCUSED MANAGEMENT AND DIRECTOR ENGAGEMENT

Michael Useem

ABSTRACT

Defining features of the American corporate apex have evolved in recent decades from a modest classwide coherence to a more dispersed amalgam of company-focused management and then to greater director engagement in company leadership. The rise of institutional investing had moved executives and directors to focus more on the specific interests of their own firms and less on their common concerns. More recently, the nation's borders that have long defined its business elite have been giving way to an elite-ness transcending those boundaries. While the classwide sinews of the American business elite are diminishing within the United States, we find evidence that they have at the same time been strengthening with other national business elites to create a transnational informal network with a modicum of global coherence.

Keywords: Business elite; classwide coherence; company ownership; institutional investors; corporate directors

A country's elites — whether the wealthy, the prominent, or the powerful — are an enduring source of both fascination and consternation. On the alluring side, celebrity CEOs at American companies like Apple, Berkshire Hathaway, and Facebook attract incessant media attention, and the "great and the good" in the United Kingdom invite notice there. On the critical side, observers have repeatedly skewered the banking elites in the United States and the United Kingdom for bringing about the 2008−2009 financial crisis, and Occupy Wall Street added to the public scorn with its targeting of the "1 percent" (Khurana, 2004; Sorkin, 2011; Tett, 2009).

Study and criticism of national elites have a long academic heritage as well, as the papers in this volume and elsewhere well attest (e.g., Conyon, Judge, & Useem, 2011; Lounsbury & Hirsch, 2010). Like research on the dynamics on social inequality, study of the top tier can offer special insight into a country's social character, a kind of X-ray into the otherwise hidden principles that shape a nation's evolving foundations. This is evident, for instance, in the paper by Ergur, Yamak, and Özbilgin (2015) that draws upon the experience of Turkish company executives with their government to better appreciate the power of the state over private business, and in the paper by Murphy and Willmott (2015) that uses the Occupy movement and a counter-ideology as a window into income inequality and the forces deepening it.

We have chosen to focus on the U.S. business elite here, and arguably at its center are the major owners, top executives, and board directors of the nation's largest corporations. Drawing on the papers of this books and prior research, we suggest that the defining features of the American corporate apex have evolved in recent decades from a modest classwide coherence to a more dispersed amalgam of company-focused management and then to director engagement. We also suggest that the nation's borders that have long helped define the American business elite are giving way to an elite-ness transcending those boundaries. Our focus is in keeping with the paper in this volume by Morgan (2015) that urges greater attention on how elites change in concert with changing company dynamics.

CLASSWIDE COHERENCE

Three distinct company developments came together, we believe, to give the American business elite a modest degree of classwide coherence during the latter half of the twentieth century. By company developments we refer to commercial forces that transform the goals, organization, and operating principles of large business firms. By classwide coherence we reference a common network and shared willingness of company executives and directors to take stands that transcend single company goals to achieve broader business objectives. No one of these company developments by itself would have made the difference, but in combination they helped generate a period of common purpose and collective endeavor within the upper tier of the American business elite.

The first company development was the well-chronicled managerial revolution of the early part of the twentieth century that moved owner-founders out of company management and then even out of company ownership, exemplified by such firms as General Electric, General Motors, and Procter & Gamble. A product of decisions by controlling families to raise capital through stock offerings to the public, the unintended effect was to move professional managers into the company apex. Technocrats increasingly came to dominate those commanding heights, seemingly answerable to no one as they decided on company strategies, investment decisions, and employment practices. Driving their decisions were the several goals of professional management, self-preservation, and even "soulful" service (Berle & Means, 1932; Kaysen, 1996; Marchand, 1998; Mason, 1959).

The second company development was what Charles Perrow has termed the "organizational society," the congealing of resources and management more in the hands of larger organizations and less in the grasp of smaller groups, family networks, or informal aggregates. In an era increasingly defined by organizations, elites came to be marked more by their high place in a hierarchy and less by their family wealth or professional stature. And since major corporations came to dwarf other private organizations in their capital and human assets, this second development had the effect of placing senior managers of large firms at the center of the most influential echelon of the American business elite. By contrast, their owners and corporate directors moved to the periphery, the first too small in holdings to exercise much influence on the firm and the second too much the "pawns" of management to have much influence either (Lorsch & MacIver, 1989; Perrow, 1991).

Corporations and their managers came to comprise a diverse array of thousands of structurally similar entities little connected by personal familiarity, mutual obligation, or business purpose. This is where a third company development came to generate professional coherence and collective identity within the American business elite, though one that would later prove transitory. Market regulators had required that publicly traded firms establish independent boards of directors, and companies sought outsiders for their boards who would bring expertise, legitimacy, and resources to the boardroom and the company. And since outsiders who best represented those qualities tended to serve as executives or directors of other large firms, the result was the formation of an informal national network of directors and executives who served across one another's governing boards and executive suites, an "interlocking directorate" (Mizruchi, 1982; Pennings, 1980; Vion, Dudouet, & Grémont, 2015).

The product of these three company developments was the emergence of a degree of classwide coherence rooted in that trans-corporate network of executives and directors. They came to know and work with their counterparties from other firms, they established associations to advance their joint interests, and they offered business counsel through a host of public and nonprofit advisory bodies and governing boards.

The rise of professional managers, their separation from company ownership, the growing primacy of organizations, and the resulting formation of an influential trans-corporate network together had the effect of moving executives and directors to take actions that on occasion transcended their own company interests. In traveling the byways of this largely invisible network, executives and directors came to constitute a kind of inner circle rooted in the nation's largest companies, an elite within an elite that shared a commitment to promote the concerns of big business, not just their own enterprises. They found common ground in charitable giving and through associations like the Business Roundtable (Clemens, 2015; Useem, 1982, 1984).

COMPANY-FOCUSED MANAGEMENT

If the dispersed ownership holdings of large corporations had served as a platform for the emergence of modest classwide coherence in the middle part of the twentieth century, that ownership dispersion became far less so in the years that followed — and as a consequence so also had the inner circle's classwide coherence. The forces behind the reconcentration of ownership are many, including a seemingly inexorable rise of managed retirement accounts, pension funds such as the California Public Employees' Retirement System and TIAA-CREF, and investment companies such as Fidelity Investments and Vanguard Group (Davis, 2008, 2009; Useem, 1996, 1998).

Whatever the drivers of the owner reconcentration, equity holdings in large American firms flowed from millions of individual holders into the hands of a just several thousand professionals. In 1950, 6 percent of the equity in publicly traded firms was held by institutional investors, but by the end of the century that fraction had grown tenfold. Among the largest companies that define the upper tier of the American business elite, the ownership reconcentration was even greater. Of the 1,000 biggest publicly traded U.S. firms by market value, institutional investors held 46 percent of the shares in 1987 but 73 percent in 2009, as seen in Fig. 1.

With company ownership more concentrated among a smaller set of money managers, the professionals learned from experience that they could influence companies to strengthen performance through proxy fights, takeover threats, and media campaigns. This rise of institutional investing and the accompanying articulation of a shareholder-rights ideology moved directors and executives to focus more on the specific interests of their own firms and less on their classwide concerns. The earlier model of a "soulful" corporation, driven by the transcendent business concerns of those freed from ownership oversight, yielded to a very different model of executives driven by their owners to optimize the total shareholder return − dividends and share price increases − of only their own firm (Mason, 1959).

This trend is evident in many metrics of what one groups of researchers has termed the rise of shareholder "democracy" in place of managerial "dictatorship" (Gompers, Ishii, & Metrick, 2003). Governing boards became more shareholder friendly and less management cozy, as shown in Table 1.

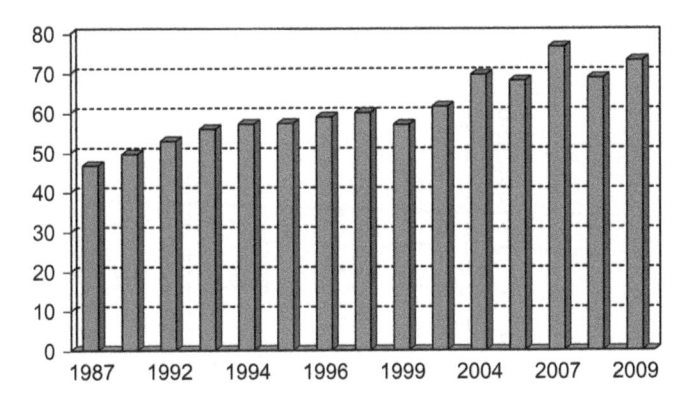

Fig. 1. Percentage of Shares of Largest 1,000 U.S. Companies Held by Institutional Investors, 1987−2009. *Source*: Conference Board (2009).

Table 1. Percentage of S&P 500 Companies with Shareholder Monitoring Device, 1998–2012.

Monitoring Device	1998	1999	2001	2002	2003	2004	2005	2006	2007	2008	2009	2010	2011	2012	% Δ
CEO is the only nonindependent director	23	21	27	31	35	39	30	39	43	44	50	53	57	59	36
CEO is not chair of the board	16	20	26	25	23	26	29	33	35	39	37	40	39	43	27
Board with lead or presiding director	n/a	n/a	n/a	n/a	36	85	94	96	94	95	95	92	92	92	n/a
Independent governance or nominations committee	67	69	70	75	91	98	100	99	100	100	100	99	100	100	33
Directors receive equity in addition to retainer	38	46	42	42	47	50	60	64	72	74	79	79	77	76	38

Source: SpencerStuart (2012) and earlier years.

We see that the proportion of governing boards of Standard and Poor's (S&P) 500 boards that

- have a single nonindependent director increased from 23 percent in 1998 to 59 percent by 2012;
- separated the role of chief executive from the position of board chair climbed from 16 to 43 percent;
- appointed an independent "lead" or "presiding" director rose from 36 percent in 2003 (the first year for which data are available) to 92 percent;
- had no insiders on the governance committee grew from 67 to 100 percent; and
- paid directors in equity rose from 38 to 76 percent.

These trends are paralleled by analogous declines in the prevalence of anti-takeover devices, generally deemed to shield company executives from investor influence. Among the S&P 500 over the same period, as seen in Table 2,

- poison-pills dropped from 59 percent in 1998 to 8 percent in 2012;
- classified-boards (those with two- or three-year terms for directors) declined from 61 to 17 percent over the same 14 years.

With data from 2002 to 2012, we also see a drop among the S&P 500 in

- limiting director removal only "for cause" from 52 to 34 percent;
- prevention of shareholders from calling a "special meeting" from 59 to 47 percent;
- requiring a supermajority vote for mergers from 31 to 21 percent; and
- requiring a supermajority vote to remove directors from 33 to 23 percent.

As one indicator of the growing influence of institutional investors on company practices, we consider an instructive metric, the compensation of company executives. Professional company managers would presumably prefer to see their annual compensation assured, regardless of their yearly performance, while professional money managers would by contrast rather see the executives' compensation contingent on what the executives produced for shareholders. Accordingly, as investor influence increased over the past several decades, we should anticipate that companies paid less in salary-and-benefit compensation and more in equity-based compensation. We indeed see this trend in the remuneration of the seven most senior managers of 45 large U.S. manufacturing firms from 1982 to 2012.

Table 2. Percentage of S&P 500 Companies with Anti-Shareholder Devices, 1998–2012.

Anti-shareholder Device	1998	1999	2000	2001	2002	2003	2004	2005	2006	2007	2008	2009	2010	2011	2012	% Δ
Poison pill	58.8	57.2	59.8	60.2	60.0	57.0	53.2	45.4	34.2	28.8	21.4	16.8	13.2	10.2	7.6	−51.2
Classified board	60.6	60.6	60.0	58.8	61.2	57.2	53.3	47.4	41.5	36.1	34.2	32.5	28.9	24.4	16.9	−43.7

Percentage of S&P 500 Companies with Anti-Shareholder Devices, 2002–2012

Anti-shareholder Device	2002	2003	2004	2005	2006	2007	2008	2009	2010	2011	2012	% Δ
Directors removed only for cause	52.2	51.8	48.8	45.0	42.5	39.6	39.6	38.8	37.5	35.5	33.6	−18.6
Shareholders cannot call special meetings	59.1	59.0	59.6	58.1	57.7	56.9	55.1	52.9	51.1	49.7	46.8	−12.3
Supermajority vote for mergers	31.0	29.3	29.9	29.0	28.1	26.0	24.4	24.0	23.4	22.0	20.9	−10.1
Supermajority vote to remove directors	32.9	32.8	32.4	31.0	30.0	28.7	28.5	28.1	25.5	23.6	23.4	−9.5

Source: FactSet Research Systems Inc. (2012) and earlier years.

As displayed in Fig. 2, companies shifted executive pay packages from primarily fixed to predominantly variable, with virtually all of the later compensation based on stock options and other share-based devices. Executives going to the office on the first workday of 1982 could expect to receive 63 percent of their total pay, regardless of their performance on behalf of shareholders. In 2012, by contrast, executives would receive only 20 percent of their salary and benefits for showing up, the remainder contingent on how they performed for the owners. More generally, studies have repeatedly confirmed that institutional investor pressures on executives have generally led them to improve their company's delivery of total shareholder return (Bebchuk & Weisbach, 2010; Brown & Caylor, 2009; Cronqvist & Fahlenbrach, 2009; Finegold, Benson, & Hecht, 2007; Gillan, 2006; Gillan & Starks, 2007; Kang & Zardkoohi, 2005; Larcker & Tayan, 2011).

As institutional investors pressed executives to stick to their own knitting, less to service other firms or to assist the public or nonprofit sphere, the informal trans-corporate network of directorships that had served as a backbone for classwide coherence also contracted, as seen in Table 3. Here we see among the S&P 500 that from 1998 to 2012,

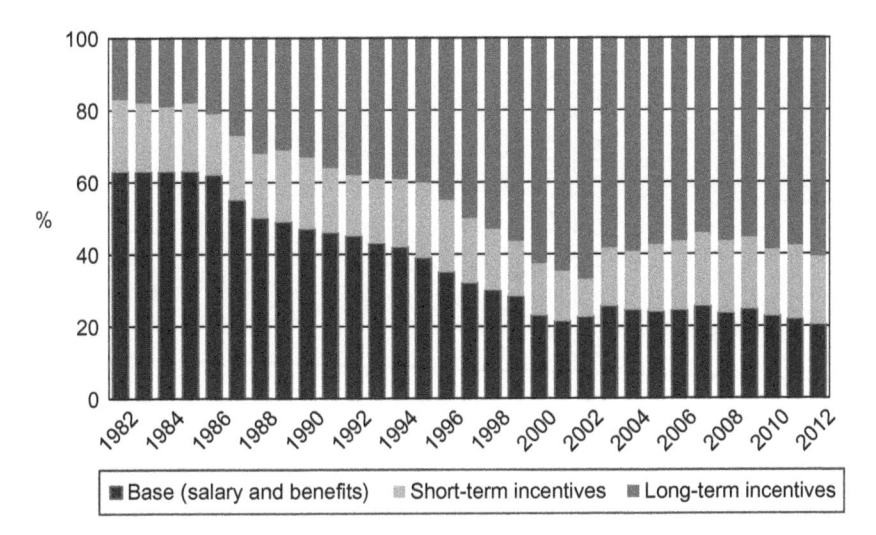

Fig. 2. Compensation of Top Seven Executives of 45 Large U.S. Manufacturing Firms, 1982–2012. *Source*: Hewitt Associates, personal communication (2012) and earlier years.

Table 3. Average Number of Other Directorships Held by CEO among S&P 500 Companies, 1998–2012.

CEO	1998	1999	2000	2001	2002	2003	2004	2005	2006	2007	2008	2009	2010	2011	2012	% Δ
Average no. of directorships	2.0	1.6	1.4	1.2	1.2	1.1	0.9	0.9	0.8	0.8	0.7	0.7	0.6	0.6	0.6	−1.4

Percentage of S&P 500 Companies that Limit Outside Directorships, 2005–2012

Limit Outside Directorships	2005	2006	2007	2008	2009	2010	2011	2012	% Δ
By CEO	50	51	58	56	67	62	67	58	8
By directors	n/a	27	55	56	67	71	74	74	47

Source: SpencerStuart (2012) and earlier years.

- company CEOs had reduced their outside directorships on average from 2.0 to 0.6;

And from 2005 to 2012,

- companies that set limits on the number of outside directorships held by their CEO rose from 50 to 58 percent; and
- companies that set limits on the number of other directorship held by directors rose from 27 percent (in 2006) to 74 percent.

The impact of the contraction of the inner circle's network of shared directorships has been documented by Mark Mizruchi in his aptly titled work, *The Fracturing of the American Corporate Elite* (2013). He found executives and directors of large companies in recent years to be retreating from a shared sense of civic responsibility and toward greater focus on optimizing their own stock price and dividends. In turning to greater focus on the total shareholder return of their own company, executives and directors moved away from classwide coherence and toward the company-focused goals of a century earlier.

DIRECTOR ENGAGEMENT

As institutional investors pressed directors and executives of large companies to limit their attention to their own firm's shareholder value, they also set the stage for a third change in the American business elite. Directors became more influential on business decisions and more ascendant in the business elite, though not in ways intended.

Government regulators, equity investors, and governance raters pressed for more independent and better organized boards. The Sarbanes–Oxley Act of 2002, the New York Stock Exchange rules of 2003, and the Dodd–Frank Act of 2010 offered specific measures intended to empower directors as monitors of management on behalf of shareholder value. Institutional holders such as public pensions and hedge funds urged more independent and more empowered directors. Governance raters such as Institutional Shareholder Services urged board separation of chair and CEO and the end of multiyear terms for directors.

The Sarbanes–Oxley Act, for instance, requires that boards meet separately from executives and nonindependent directors, and that a "lead" director chair such meetings. Dodd–Frank instructs the U.S. Securities and Exchange Commission to create procedures to make it easier for shareholders to propose and elect their own nominees to a board, strengthening director oversight of managers on behalf of owners. The New York Stock Exchange requires that all members of the board's audit committee be "financially literate" and "independent," and that their duties include "oversight" of the "integrity of the company's financial statements," again intended to strengthen the influence of owners on executives.

One of the most fateful of the new rules was the requirement of a lead director, defined as an independent nonexecutive director who takes responsibility for the board's operations and decisions when the chief executive and board chair are one in the same (Penbera, 2009). As we have seen in Table 1, virtually all boards of S&P 500 companies now have a lead director, up from none a decade earlier.

In requiring the new role of lead director, regulators also in effect helped boards strengthen their influence on executives not only as monitors of management but also as decision partners with management. The monitoring was intended, but the partnership was serendipitous. The designated board leader could now aggregate and articulate the directors' voice, facilitating their engagement in company decisions ranging from business strategy and risk tolerance to talent development and cultural tenor. With 10 nonexecutive directors in the room, most bringing extensive experience in corporate management, the board leader was in a position to organize them not only to offer shareholder oversight but also informed counsel (Charan, Carey, & Useem, 2014).

Evidence of this development can be seen in an annual survey of corporate secretaries and general counsels of S&P 500 firms beginning in 2008. They reported that company strategy had come to be a central boardroom preoccupation, even more so than the traditional focus on shareholder value. In 2008, company strategy and shareholder concerns ran neck and neck in reported attention, but by 2009 strategy had emerged as the number-one concern, and it outdistanced shareholder attention by more than two-to-one in the three years that followed (Fig. 3).

A second development that has led executives to actively seek counsel from their directors, not just passively waiting for counsel from them, is the growing complexity of company decisions. The telecommunications industry, to draw on just one example, has seen a handful of service plans at the original ATT explode to more than half a million plans among dozens of carriers now. Another illustrative contributor has been the movement of sales and operations of S&P 500 company abroad. In 2001, for example, foreign markets accounted for 32 percent of total sales of the S&P 500 companies, but a decade later, 46 percent have come from abroad (Table 4).

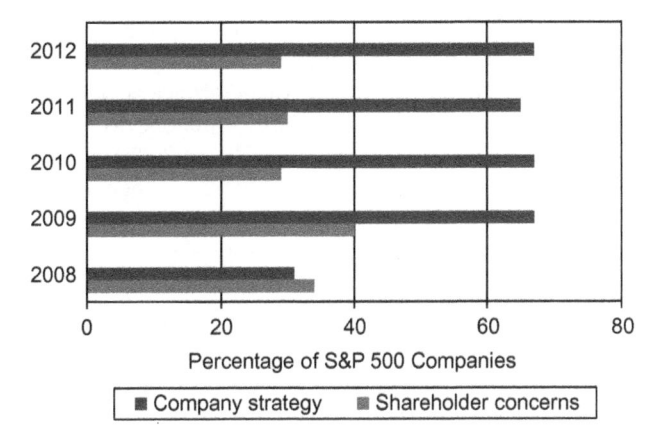

Fig. 3. Governance Topics Requiring Greatest Attention by S&P 500 Boards of Directors, 2008–2012. *Source*: SpencerStuart (2012) and earlier years; survey of corporate secretaries and general counsels of S&P 500 companies ($N = 101$ in 2012; 102 in 2011; 92 in 2010; 123 in 2009; 127 in 2008).

Table 4. Percentage of Sales Outside the United States by S&P 500 Companies, 2001–2010.

	2001	2003	2004	2005	2006	2007	2008	2009	2010	2011	% Δ
Foreign sales as % of total sales	32.3	41.8	43.8	43.3	43.6	45.8	47.9	46.6	46.3	46.1	12.8

Source: Standard and Poor's, various years.

Across many industries, complexity has emerged as a primary management concern. A periodic survey asked executives at a range of companies in the United States and abroad to identify their greatest challenge, and in the surveys of 2004 and 2006, managers reported that their top concern was coping with change. By 2010, however, "complexity" had replaced change as the dominant concern (IBM, 2010, 2012).

With increasing complexity in how markets operate, greater premium is placed on managing complexity, and here directors can offer expert counsel since so many have served or are serving as executives or directors of other large companies with their own complexity issues. Directors can thus provide executives with a kind of prepaid substantive guidance on a host of management issues to better inform their decisions since directors are experienced in management, informed about management, and sworn by their fiduciary duties to help management. Executives consequently are increasingly turning to directors for counsel, and many directors are embracing the request. Supportive evidence for this embrace is beyond our scope here but is reported elsewhere (Charan, Carey, and Useem, 2014; Pettigrew & McNulty, 1995; Useem, 2012a; Useem & Zelleke, 2006).

Taken together, these developments have strengthened the hand of directors, giving them more influence not only over executive decisions that directly impact shareholder value but also more say on company strategy and other issues that are less directly related to shareholder value. Since the ascendance of director influence is a relatively recent phenomenon, its foundation, contours, and implications are yet to be mapped, but we believe that this development will significantly reshape the defining qualities and goals of the American business elite during the coming decade. It is likely,

Table 5. Company Developments, Elite Goals, and the Inner Circle of the American Business Elite.

Period	Company Developments	Business Elite Inner Circle	Elite Inner-Circle Goals
1900–1950	Separation of ownership and control; rise of organizations; boards coming to be dominated by executives and director of other large companies	Large-company executives and directors who also serve on the governing boards of other large firms	Professional management, self-preservation, and classwide coherence on public policies affecting business
1950–2000	Concentration of ownership among institutional investors and their creation of methods for pressing executives to focus on their own firm, not others	Major stockholders and company executives of large firms	Optimization of total shareholder return by focal company
2000–present	Rising complexity in company decisions; strengthening of governing boards to serve as substantive partners in those decision with company executives	Major stockholders, company executives, and independent directors	Professional management and total shareholder return of focal company

for instance, to return a greater balance between the sometimes competing goals of professional management shareholder value.

The decline of the business elite's classwide coherence, the rise of company-focused management, and the ascendance of director influence lead to several implications that are worthy of attention. First, the criteria for director recruitment are likely to shift toward greater emphasis on business background and less on monitoring experience. Second, government regulators, governance raters, and academic researchers are wise to look beyond the outward features of government such as the separation of CEO and chair, and focus instead on how boards are organized and how directors work in the boardroom with executives. And third, company performance is likely to be increasingly driven by the business experience that directors bring to the board and how they are organized to render their counsel once in the boardroom. The principal-agent tensions between owners and executives are giving way, we believe, to a three-way alliance of investors, directors, and executives focused on company performance. These developments are summarized in Table 5.

BUSINESS ELITE WITHOUT BOUNDARIES

While the classwide sinews of the American business elite are diminishing within the United States, we believe that they have at the same time been strengthening with other national business elites to create a transnational informal network with a modicum of global coherence, as other have argued as well (Carroll, 2010; Rothkopf, 2008; Sklair, 2000). Exploring this fourth development exceeds the space available here, but we single-out one indicator that points in this direction: large-company executive and director engagement in the World Economic Forum.

Founded in 1987 as a vehicle for European business executives to learn from their American counterparts, the World Economic Forum has grown into an association of major companies from a host of countries. The forum's annual meeting in Davos, Switzerland attracts some 2,500 participants, primarily executives and directors of the world's largest corporations. The forum's stated mission is to strengthen a shared commitment "to improving the state of the world" – not just the state of participating firms, though of course much time is devoted to the latter as well in Davos.

The World Economic Forum and its leadership have long pressed participating executives and directors for actions that broadly benefit business and beyond. One of the 2007 meeting co-chairs, for instance, Coca-Cola chief executive E. Neville Isdell, used his stage time to urge common cause rather than soda sales: The Davos gathering, he said, should not be seen as the "epicenter of ego" but rather as the "epicenter of commitment." In closing the 2007 meeting, WEF founder and executive chairman Klaus Schwab urged the same: "We invite back those who are concerned about the world and will do something about it" (Useem, 2012b, 2013; World Economic Forum, 2009).

To appreciate the glimmerings of an emergent global inner circle — an elite within an elite whose commitments transcend their own firm — we focus here on companies whose executives and directors participated in the 2008 annual meeting of the World Economic Forum. As a baseline for comparison, we draw upon on the world's 5,000 largest publicly traded companies by market capitalization.

The American inner circle of an earlier period was skewed toward executives and directors of the nation's largest firms, and this is evident here as well. A good predictor of whether one of the 5,000 large publicly traded global firms sent an executive or director to Davos was the size of the enterprise. The correlation of a company's executive or director engagement in Davos with the company's market value was 0.292, and with the firm's gross income 0.276, net income 0.246, sales 0.276, and number of employees 0.197.

Three additional company predictors of Davos engagement point to the emergence of at least the rudiments of classwide cohesion within the inner circle of the global business elite. As a first indicator, companies that are more international in operations are more likely to send their executives and directors to Davos. The correlation of engagement with foreign sales is 0.270, foreign sales as a percent of total sales is 0.114, foreign assets is 0.168, and foreign assets as a percent of total assets is 0.128.

As a second indicator, companies that are more engaged in leadership development are also more likely to dispatch their executives and directors to Davos. Since the metrics here are less self-evident, we offer brief description of data compiled by human-resources consulting firm Hewitt Associates. Beginning in 2001, Hewitt conducted biannual surveys of company leadership development practices in the United States, adding other regions and refining its methods in subsequent years. Hewitt mailed a request in 2007 to human-resource executives of major companies in North America, Europe, Asia-Pacific, and Latin America. It sent the survey to the *Fortune* list of the 1,000 largest U.S. companies ranked by revenue, and to similar lists of the largest firms in the other regions (Khurana & Useem, 2015).

As an incentive to respond, Hewitt explained that the "value for participating is gaining clear insights and facts on how organizations use leadership practices to drive business," with an opportunity to benchmark one's own company practices against those of the other responding firms. Hewitt received fully completed responses from 528 companies, and most were relatively large: 69.5 percent earned at least $500 million in revenue in 2006; the mean employment total stood at 28,140; and 29.0 percent were among Standard and Poor's roster of the 1,200 largest global corporations. Among the better known companies in the United States were American Express and General Electric; in India, ICICI Bank and Infosys; and in China, China Mobile and China Vanke. Given the nature of the survey, it is probable that the responding companies viewed leadership development as more strategic and had instituted a larger number of leadership development practices than those not responding.

We focus on the 20 companies that a review panel identified as the "top companies for leaders" based on the survey data and financial performance of the companies. The list includes General Electric, GlaxoSmithKline, Nokia, and Infosys. A comparison of 19 of the top 20 companies for leaders with all large firms on whether they had sent at least one executive or director to Davos in 2008 is displayed in Table 6 (one company on the top company list, McKinsey, was not among the largest publicly listed firms). We see that the likelihood of a "top company for leaders" sending an executive to Davos was more than four times greater than among other large companies.

And as a third indicator for the emergence of classwide cohesion transcending individual company self-interest, we draw upon the United

Table 6. Top Companies for Leaders in 2007 and the Likelihood that They Sent Executives and Directors to the 2008 Annual Meeting of the World Economic Forum.

Top Companies for Leaders	Executives and Directors *not* in Davos (%)	Executive and Directors in Davos (%)	Number of Companies
Yes	57.9	42.1	19
No	92.8	7.2	4732

Note: $p \leq .001$.

National Global Compact, a roster of some 5,000 firms that have pledged to implement 10 principles in support of U.N. goals. To join the compact, a company must be "serious about its commitment to work toward implementation of the Global Compact principles throughout its operations and sphere of influence, and to communicate on its progress." The principles include advancing human rights, labor standards, environmental protection, and anti-corruption measures, and we see in Table 7 that companies that have signed the compact are significantly more likely to send their executives and directors to Davos (United Nations, 2013). It should be noted, however, that some company commitments may be as much in the pursuit of self-interested legitimation strategies as any transcendent commitment to the general advancement of business interests, as suggested by the paper in this volume by Helfen, Schüßler, and Botzem (2015).

Since several company factors help send executives and directors to Davos, we examine the distinctive impact of a company's signing of the U.N. Global Compact net of other potentially confounding factors. The results of a binary logistic regression of company engagement in Davos confirm that the Global Compact factor remains a significant driver. Though these are only several indicators of the emergence of an informal global network of large-company executive and directors, they do point toward a new transnational inner circle, an elite within the global business elite that is more committed to building company leadership and more concerned with issues that transcend narrowly defined company self-interest.

The sheer number of large companies based in the United States that are represented in Davos could suggest that the U.S. is at the center of the global inner circle, but companies incorporated in other countries also send large numbers of executive and directors to Davos, and proportionally some dispatch more executives and directors than American companies,

Table 7. Companies that have Signed the U.N. Global Compact and the Likelihood that They Sent Executives and Directors to the 2008 Annual Meeting of the World Economic Forum.

Company has Pledged Support of U.N. Global Compact	Executives and Directors *not* in Davos (%)	Executive and Directors in Davos (%)	Number of Companies
Yes	76.2	23.8	361
No	94.4	5.6	4639

Note: $p \leq .001$.

including Germany, India, and the United Kingdom. It would appear on brief study that the emergent transnational inner circle is without a dominant national center.

CONCLUSION

We have argued that a defining feature of the American business elite has evolved from one of classwide coherence to company-focused management and then to director engagement. Developments behind the first include the separation of management from control, growth in the importance of organizations, and the stocking of boards of large publicly traded companies with executives and directors from other large publicly traded companies. Developments behind the second include the concentration of company ownership among institutional investors and the latter's creation of a host of devices for pressing company executives and directors to focus more on their own firm's total shareholder return and less on classwide concerns. Developments behind the third include a strengthening of governing boards to serve as substantive partners with company executives and the rising complexity of company decisions.

National elites have long attracted critical attention, stretching back to early works by Vilfredo Pareto and Gaetano Mosca and more recent works including C. Wright Mills' (2000) *The Power Elite* and G. William Domhoff's (2009) *Who Rules America*? The specific form of their business elites depends, however, on the company developments that may vary greatly over time, and the most recent company developments have elevated American owners and directors to a more influential place alongside American executives. Still other development have also moved the upper tier of the American business elite into a network that cuts across the upper ranks of the business elites rooted in world's major economies.

These national developments may at the same time be accompanied by distinct or even contrary developments within specific market sectors or geographic regions (Campbell, Hollingsworth, & Lindberg, 1991). While the American business elite has become less coherent in recent years, executives, directors, and investors among high-technology firms based in California's Silicon Valley, for instance, may have become more coherent as their intensified concerns over public education, stock options, and foreign talent have stimulated shared action among them (Kenney, 2000; Saxenian, 1996). Similarly, companies headquartered in the same metropolitan region are often particularly well connected and given to shared outlook (Galaskiewicz & Wasserman, 1989).

One implication of these developments is for the owners, executives, and directors of the upper tier of the American business elite to be less socially active at home and more so abroad. With diminished classwide coherence but greater company-focused management and director engagement, business leaders are likely to rivet on professional management and total shareholder return of their own company — rather than issues of classwide concern to many companies. Owners, executives, and directors as a result may opt to retreat from social involvement in the community and their country. Those business leaders who are personally called to social engagement may opt to do so more with their own wealth than company assets, as Microsoft's Bill Gates and Berkshire Hathaway's Warren Buffet have done so in the United States. At the same time, the emergence of a global inner circle may lead them toward greater social commitment to entities like the U.N. Global Compact and the World Economic Forum.

Finally, it would appear that these developments are not unique to the American business elite: A comparison of the executives and directors of large Swiss firms in 1980, 2000, and 2010 by Davoine, Ginalski, Mach, and Ravasi (2015) in this volume finds much the same kind of contraction of shared directorships among Swiss firms and their expansion across Swiss boundaries. If studies of the upper tier of business elites in other countries reveal similar developments, as some already have (e.g., Kentor & Jang, 2004), it would imply that the transformation of the American business elite outlined here is paralleled by analogous developments in other major economies.

REFERENCES

Bebchuk, L. A., & Weisbach, M. S. (2010). The state of corporate governance research. *Review of Financial Studies*, 23, 939—961.

Berle, A. A., & Means, G. C. (1991[1932]). *The modern corporation and private property*. Piscataway, NJ: Transaction Publishers.

Brown, L. D., & Caylor, M. L. (2009). Corporate governance and firm operating performance. *Review of Quantitative Finance & Accounting*, 32, 129—144.

Campbell, J. L., Hollingsworth, J. R., & Lindberg, L. N. (1991). *Governance of the American economy*. New York, NY: Cambridge University Press.

Carroll, W. K. (2010). *The making of a transnational capitalist class: Corporate power in the 21st century*. London: Zed Books.

Charan, R., Carey, D., & Useem, M. (2014). *Boards that lead*. Boston, MA: Harvard Business Review Press.

Clemens, E. (2015). The democratic dilemma: Aligning fields of elite influence and political equality. In G. Morgan, P. Hirsch, & S. Quack (Eds.), *Elites on trial* (Vol. 43). Research in the Sociology of Organizations. Bingley, UK: Emerald Group Publishing Limited.

Conference Board. (2009). *Institutional investor report*. New York, NY: Conference Board.

Conyon, M., Judge, W. Q., & Useem, M. (2011). Corporate governance and the 2008−09 financial crisis. *Corporate Governance: An International Review, 19*(September), 399−404.

Cronqvist, H., & Fahlenbrach, R. (2009). Large shareholders and corporate policies. *Review of Financial Studies, 22*, 3941−3976.

Davis, G. F. (2008). A new finance capitalism? Mutual funds and ownership re-concentration in the United States. *European Management Review, 5*, 11−21.

Davis, G. F. (2009). *Managed by the markets: How finance re-shaped America*. New York, NY: Oxford University Press.

Davoine, E., Ginalski, S., Mach, A., & Ravasi, C. (2015). Impacts of globalization processes on the Swiss national business elite community: A diachronic analysis of Swiss large corporations (1980−2010). In G. Morgan, P. Hirsch, & S. Quack (Eds.), *Elites on trial* (Vol. 43). Research in the Sociology of Organizations. Bingley, UK: Emerald Group Publishing Limited.

Domhoff, G. W. (2009). *Who rules America?* (6th ed.). New York, NY: McGraw-Hill.

Ergur, A., Yamak, S., & Özbilgin, M. (2015). Understanding the changing nature of the relationship between the state and business elites. In G. Morgan, P. Hirsch, & S. Quack (Eds.), *Elites on trial* (Vol. 43). Research in the Sociology of Organizations. Bingley, UK: Emerald Group Publishing Limited.

FactSet Research Systems Inc. (2012). *And earlier years*. Retrieved from http://www.factset.com/data

Finegold, D., Benson, G. S., & Hecht, D. (2007). Corporate boards and company performance: Review of research in light of recent reforms. *Corporate Governance: An International Review, 15*, 865−878.

Galaskiewicz, J., & Wasserman, S. (1989). Mimetic processes within an interorganizational field: An empirical test. *Administrative Science Quarterly, 34*, 454−479.

Gillan, S. L. (2006). Recent developments in corporate governance: An overview. *Journal of Corporate Finance, 12*, 381−402.

Gillan, S. L., & Starks, L. T. (2007). The evolution of shareholder activism in the United States. *Journal of Applied Corporate Finance, 19*, 55−73.

Gompers, P., Ishii, J., & Metrick, A. (2003). Corporate governance and equity prices. *Quarterly Journal of Economics, 118*, 107−156.

Helfen, M., Schüßler, E., & Botzem, S. (2015). Legitimation strategies of corporate elites in the field of labor regulation: Changing responses to global framework agreements. In G. Morgan, P. Hirsch, & S. Quack (Eds.), *Elites on trial* (Vol. 43). Research in the Sociology of Organizations. Bingley, UK: Emerald Group Publishing Limited.

IBM. (2010). *Capitalizing on complexity: Insights from the global chief executive officer study*. Armonk, NY: IBM.

IBM. (2012). *Leading through connections: Insights from the global chief executive officer study*. Armonk, NY: IBM.

Kang, E., & Zardkoohi, A. (2005). Board leadership structure and firm performance. *Corporate Governance: An International Review, 13*, 785–799.
Kaysen, C. (Ed.). (1996). *The American corporation today.* New York, NY: Oxford University Press.
Kenney, M. (2000). *Understanding silicon valley: The anatomy of an entrepreneurial region.* Redwood City, CA: Stanford Business Books.
Kentor, J., & Jang, Y. S. (2004). Yes, there is a (growing) transnational business community: A study of global interlocking directorates 1983–98. *International Sociology, 19*, 355–368.
Khurana, R. (2004). *Searching for a corporate savior: The irrational quest for charismatic CEOs.* Princeton University Press.
Khurana, R., & Useem, M. (2015). *Emergent business leadership in a borderless era.* Unpublished paper, Wharton School, University of Pennsylvania, Philadelphia, PA.
Larcker, D., & Tayan, B. (2011). *Corporate governance matters: A closer look at organizational choices and their consequences.* Upper Saddle River, NJ: Pearson Prentice Hall.
Lorsch, J. W. with MacIver, E. (1989). *Pawns or potentates: The reality of America's corporate boards.* Boston, MA: Harvard Business School Press.
Lounsbury, M., & Hirsch, P. M. (Eds.). (2010). *Markets on trial: The economic sociology of the U.S. financial crisis*: Part A (Vol. 30A). Research in the Sociology of Organizations. Bingley, UK: Emerald Group Publishing Limited.
Marchand, R. (1998). *Creating the corporate soul: The rise of public relations and corporate imagery in American big business.* Oakland, CA: University of California Press.
Mason, E. S. (Ed.). (1959). *The corporation in modern society.* Boston, MA: Harvard University Press.
Mills, C. W. (2000). *The power elite.* New York, NY: Oxford University Press.
Mizruchi, M. S. (1982). *The American corporate network 1904–1974.* Thousands Oaks, CA: Sage Publications.
Mizruchi, M. S. (2013). *The fracturing of the American corporate elite.* Boston, MA: Harvard University Press.
Morgan, G. (2015). Elites, varieties of capitalism and the crisis of neo-liberalism. In G. Morgan, P. Hirsch, & S. Quack (Eds.), *Elites on trial* (Vol. 43). Research in the Sociology of Organizations. Bingley, UK: Emerald Group Publishing Limited.
Murphy, J., & Willmott, H. (2015). The rise of the 1%: An organizational explanation. In G. Morgan, P. Hirsch, & S. Quack (Eds.), *Elites on trial* (Vol. 43). Research in the Sociology of Organizations. Bingley, UK: Emerald Group Publishing Limited.
Penbera, J. J. (2009). What lead directors do. *MIT Sloan Management Review, 50*, 20–24.
Pennings, J. M. (1980). *Interlocking directorates: Origins and consequences of connections among organizations' boards of directors.* San Francisco, CA: Jossey-Bass.
Perrow, C. (1991). A society of organizations. *Theory and Society, 20*, 725–762.
Pettigrew, A., & McNulty, T. (1995). Power and influence in and around the boardroom. *Human Relations, 48*, 845–873.
Rothkopf, D. (2008). *Superclass: The global power elite and the world they are making.* New York, NY: Farrar, Straus and Giroux.
Saxenian, A. L. (1996). *Regional advantage: Culture and competition in Silicon Valley and route 128.* Boston, MA: Harvard University Press.
Sklair, L. (2000). *The transnational capitalist class.* Hoboken, NJ: Wiley-Blackwell.

Sorkin, A. R. (2011). *Too big to fail: The inside story of how Wall Street and Washington fought to save the financial system − And themselves.* New York, NY: Penguin Books.

SpencerStuart. (2012 and earlier years). *Spencer Stuart Board Index.* Chicago, CHI: SpencerStuart.

Tett, G. (2009). *Fool's gold: How unrestrained greed corrupted a dream, shattered global markets, and unleashed a catastrophe.* New York, NY: Simon & Schuster.

United Nations. (2013). *Global compact.* Retrieved from http://www.unglobalcompact.org/AboutTheGC/TheTenPrinciples/index.html

Useem, M. (1982). Classwide rationality in the politics of managers and directors of large corporations in the United States and Great Britain. *Administrative Science Quarterly, 27,* 199−226.

Useem, M. (1984). *The inner circle: Large corporations and the rise of business political activity in the U.S. and U.K.* New York, NY: Oxford University Press.

Useem, M. (1996). *Investor capitalism: How money managers are changing the face of corporate America.* New York, NY: Basic Books.

Useem, M. (1998). Corporate leadership in a globalizing equity market. *Academy of Management Executive, 12,* 43−59.

Useem, M. (2012a). The ascent of shareholder monitoring and strategic partnering: The dual functions of the corporate board. In T. Clarke & D. Branson (Eds.), *The Sage handbook on corporate governance.* Sage.

Useem, M. (2012b). Davos 2012: Joblessness and its discontents. *European Business Review,* (March/April), 4−6.

Useem, M. (2013). A 'sigh of relief' at Davos: Confidence and caution shared center stage. *European Business Review,* (March/April), 3−5.

Useem, M., & Zelleke, A. (2006). Oversight and delegation in corporate governance: Deciding what the board should decide. *Corporate Governance: An International Review, 14,* 2−12.

Vion, A., Dudouet, F.-X., & Grémont, E. (2015). Euro zone corporate elites at the cliff edge (2005−2008): A new approach of transnational interlocking. In G. Morgan, P. Hirsch, & S. Quack (Eds.), *Elites on trial* (Vol. 43). Research in the Sociology of Organizations. Bingley, UK: Emerald Group Publishing Limited.

World Economic Forum. (2009). *World Economic Forum: A partner in shaping history, the first 40 years, 1971−2000.* Geneva, Switzerland: World Economic Forum.

ABOUT THE AUTHORS

Cornel Ban is Assistant Professor of International Relations at Boston University. He holds a BA/JD from Babes-Bolyai University in Rumania and a PhD from the University of Maryland. He is Co-director of The Global Economic Governance Initiative at the Frederick S. Pardee Center at Boston University. He was previously a postdoctoral fellow at the Watson Institute for International Studies at Brown University. He is currently completing a book manuscript on the political economy of crises, with a focus on the role of economic ideas and the interaction between international and domestic actors.

Sebastian Botzem is Professor for International Political Economy at the Institute of Intercultural and International Studies, University of Bremen, and heads the research group 'Transnational political ordering in global finance'. His research interests centre around cross-border standardization, transnational governance and the regulation of global finance. He is the author of *The Politics of Accounting Regulation* (Edward Elgar, 2012).

Andrew Bowman is a postdoctoral Research Associate at the Economic and Social Research Council funded Centre for Research on Socio-Cultural Change (CRESC) at the University of Manchester. Prior to this he wrote his PhD thesis at the University of Manchester's Centre for the History of Science, Technology and Medicine. His research with CRESC has focused on issues surrounding modern industrial policy, financialization and public utilities.

Elisabeth Clemens is Professor and Chair of Sociology at the University of Chicago. Her research explores processes of organizational and institutional change in the context of American political development, particularly the arrangement of governance through configurations of public agencies and private entities, including firms, voluntary associations, and non-profit organizations.

Eric Davoine is Professor of HRM and Cross-Cultural Management at the University of Fribourg in Switzerland. His current areas of research include French-German Cross-cultural Management, internationalization of

European top management profiles, as well as HRM and international mobility within Multinational Companies.

François-Xavier Dudouet is CNRS Researcher at the IRISSO, University of Paris Dauphine, Paris. He works on corporate and elite network analysis, socio-historic studies of drugs control, and socio-economic processes of standardization. He co-edited with Eric Grémont, *Les grands patrons français. Du capitalisme d'Etat à la financiarisation* (Lignes de Repères, 2010), and, was co-author of the paper 'Retour sur le champ du pouvoir économique en France. L'espace social des dirigeants du CAC 40', in the *Revue Française de Socio-Economie*, 13 June 2014 (with Eric Grémont, Hervé Joly and Antoine Vion). His previous studies of Euro Zone elites appeared in *Financial Elites and Transnational Business: Who Rules the World?* (edited by John Scott and Georgina Murray: Edward Elgar, 2012), and *The field of Eurocracy: Mapping EU Actors and Professionals* (edited by Didier Georgakakis and Jay Rowell: Palgrave Macmillan, 2013).

Ali Ergur has an undergraduate degree in public administration (1989) and a master's degree (1992) in sociology from Marmara University, Istanbul, and a PhD in sociology from Middle East Technical University, Ankara (1997). Ali Ergur is currently Professor of Sociology at Galatasaray University, Istanbul. His research areas are technologies of information and communication, consumption, surveillance and post-industrial society.

Julie Froud is a Professor at Manchester Business School in the United Kingdom. Her current research interests have grown out of earlier work on shareholder value and the corporation to include elites in financialized capitalism and the reframing of the economy to emphasize foundational or mundane economic activities often neglected by policy makers. Recent joint books include *After the Great Complacence* (OUP, 2011) and *The End of the Experiment* (Manchester University Press, 2014).

Stéphanie Ginalski is Lecturer at the Institute of Economic and Social History, Lausanne University, and at the Swiss Federal Institute of Technology Lausanne. Her main research interests focus on corporate governance, business elites, corporate networks and more generally the transformations of capitalism during the 20th century.

Eric Grémont is the Chair of the Observatoire Politico-Economique des Structures du Capitalisme, Paris, a non-profit organization dedicated to studying elites and corporate change in Europe. He develops corporate and elite network analysis, financial appraisal of firms and studies of oil industries. On French elites, he co-edited with François-Xavier Dudouet, *Les grands patrons français. Du capitalisme d'Etat à la financiarisation* (Lignes de Repères, 2010), and, published among other papers, 'Retour sur le champ du pouvoir économique en France. L'espace social des dirigeants du CAC 40', in the *Revue Française de Socio-Economie*, 13 June 2014 (with François-Xavier Dudouet, Hervé Joly and Antoine Vion). Previous studies of Euro Zone elites appeared in *Financial Elites and Transnational Business: Who Rules the World?* (edited by John Scott and Georgina Murray: Edward Elgar, 2012), and *The field of Eurocracy: Mapping EU Actors and Professionals* (edited by Didier Georgakakis and Jay Rowell: Palgrave Macmillan, 2013).

Charles Harvey is Professor of Business History and Strategic Management at Newcastle University. He has a PhD from the University of Bristol. His research focuses upon the historical processes that inform contemporary business practice and the exercise of power by elite groups in society.

Markus Helfen is a Senior Research Fellow at the Management Department at Freie Universität Berlin. His current research focuses on collective action in interorganizational networks including applications to transnational industrial relations and service multinationals. Recent work has been published in Human Relations, Organization Studies, the British Journal of Industrial Relations and Industrielle Beziehungen.

Paul Hirsch is the James L. Allen Professor of Strategy and Organizations at the Kellogg School of Management at Northwestern University. In 2009, he was elected President of the Western Academy of Management, and earlier served as co-editor of its *Journal of Management Inquiry*. Professor Hirsch has written extensively about careers and organizational change; his articles have appeared in a wide variety of scholarly journals – most recently *Strategic Organization* and *American Sociological Review*. He was among the first to anticipate and write on widespread changes in the employment relationship stemming from corporate mergers and continuing on through the present. Hirsch's recent work has also focused on policy and ethical issues raised by the mortgage meltdown. He has published articles and organized conferences about it, and is co-editor of Markets on Trial, a volume of original essays exploring the meltdown's origins and consequences.

Sukhdev Johal is a Professor at Queen Mary University of London. His current research interests include critical research on UK finance and understanding employment and wealth changes in the United Kingdom.

He has a longstanding interest in financialization and its impact on business models and is an established collaborator with the CRESC research team. As well as co-authored books he has produced public interest reports on issues such as UK rail privatization, an alternative report on UK banking reform and regional growth disparities.

Shamus Rahman Khan teaches in the sociology department at Columbia University. He writes on culture, elites, inequality and research methodology. His most recent book is *Privilege: The Making of an Adolescent Elite at St. Paul's School* (Princeton University Press, 2012).

Gerhard Kling is Professor of International Business and Management in the School of Oriental and African Studies, University of London. He received his PhD in Economics from the University of Tuebingen. His current research focuses on corporate governance, statistical and mathematical modelling and corporate finance.

Peer Hull Kristensen is Professor in the Sociology of Firms and Organization at the Department of Business and Politics, Copenhagen Business School. His research focuses on multinationals, relations between firms, work-organization and institutions. Most recent book is *Nordic Capitalisms and Globalization: New Forms of Economic Organization and Welfare Institutions* (edited with K. Lilja: Oxford University Press, 2012).

André Mach is Senior Lecturer (Maitre d'enseignement et de recherche) in comparative political economy and Swiss politics at the Institute of International and Political Studies (University of Lausanne). His areas of specialization include Swiss politics, organized interests, Swiss elites, Swiss corporate governance, industrial relations, competition policy and more generally the impact of globalization on national policies.

Mairi Maclean is Professor of International Management and Organisation Studies at Newcastle University Business School. She received her PhD from the University of St Andrews. Her research interests include elite power from a Bourdieusian perspective, history and organization studies, and entrepreneurial philanthropy.

Michael Moran is Emeritus Professor of Government at the University of Manchester Business School. His most recent publications report collaborative work in CRESC at the University of Manchester, notably *After the Great Complacence: Financial Crisis and the Politics of Reform* (Oxford University Press, 2011) and *The End of the Experiment: From Competition to the Foundational Economy* (Manchester University Press, 2014).

Glenn Morgan is Professor of International Management at Cardiff Business School and Visiting Professor at the Department of Business and Politics, Copenhagen Business School. Recent book publications include *New Spirits of Capitalism? Crises, Justifications and Dynamics* (edited by Paul DuGay and Glenn Morgan: Oxford University Press, 2013), *Capitalisms and Capitalism in the Twenty-First Century* (by Glenn Morgan and Richard Whitley: Oxford University Press, 2012). *The Oxford Handbook of Comparative Institutional Analysis* (edited by Glenn Morgan et al.: Oxford University Press, 2010).

Jonathan Murphy balances his academic career with engagement in international democratic development. He has a permanent appointment at Cardiff Business School in Wales in international management. His research interests are varied and include the role of critical management thinking in promoting societal change. He is presently on academic leave, working with the United Nations for whom he leads a large project of technical support to the Tunisian democratic transition.

Mustafa Özbilgin is an Organizational Sociologist who studies equality and diversity at work from comparative perspectives. He holds professorships at Brunel Business School in London, Université Paris-Dauphine and Koç University in Istanbul.

Sigrid Quack is Professor of Sociology at the University of Duisburg-Essen and Associated Head of the Research Group on Institution Building across Borders at the Max Planck Institute for the Study of Societies. Book publications include *Governance across Borders – Transnational Fields and Transversal Themes* (edited by Leonhard Dobusch, Philip Mader and Sigrid Quack: Berlin, Epubl, 2013), *Transnational Communities. Shaping Global Economic Governance* (Marie-Laure Djelic and Sigrid Quack (Hrsg.): Cambridge, Cambridge University Press, 2010), *Globalization and Institutions. Redefining the Rules of the Economic Game* (by Marie-Laure Djelic and Sigrid Quack: Cheltenham, Edward Elgar, 2003).

Claudio Ravasi is teaching and research Doctoral Assistant at the University of Fribourg in Switzerland and PhD candidate at the University Paris Ouest Nanterre La Défense and ESCP Europe. His primary research interests include international HRM, expatriate management and top management careers and profiles.

Mike Reed is Emeritus Professor of Organizational Analysis at Cardiff Business School, Cardiff University, Wales, UK. His research interests are currently focused on the role that elites play in shaping the power structures through which work organizations are generated, reproduced and transformed. He is a founding editor of the journal *Organization*.

Elke Schüßler is Assistant Professor of Organization Theory at the Management Department at Freie Universität Berlin. Her research focuses on changing forms of value creation, transnational organizational governance and the role of field-configuring events for institutional innovation. Her work is published in journals such as the *Academy of Management Journal*, *Industrial and Corporate Change*, *Industry & Innovation*, *Organization Studies* and *Economic and Industrial Democracy*.

Michael Useem is Professor of Management and Director of the Center for Leadership and Change Management at the Wharton School of the University of Pennsylvania. His university teaching includes courses on leadership and change, and he offers programmes on leadership and governance in the United States, Asia, Europe and Latin America. He works on leadership development with companies and organizations in the private, public and non-profit sectors. He is author of *The Inner Circle*, *The Leadership Moment*, *Executive Defense*, *Investor Capitalism* and co-author of *Boards That Lead*.

Antoine Vion is Senior Lecturer at the Aix-Marseille University, and a member of the LEST/LabexMed, Aix-en-Provence. He co-edited with Ariel Mendez and Robert Tchobanian *Travail et compétences dans la mondialisation* (Armand Colin, 2012), prefaced by Michael Piore and, among other papers, 'Retour sur le champ du pouvoir économique en France. L'espace social des dirigeants du CAC 40', in the *Revue Française de Socio-Economie*, 13 June 2014 (with François-Xavier Dudouet, Eric Grémont and Hervé Joly). Previous studies of Euro Zone elites appeared in *Financial Elites and Transnational Business: Who Rules the World?* (edited by John Scott and Georgina Murray: Edward Elgar, 2012), and *The Field of Eurocracy: Mapping EU Actors and Professionals* (edited by Didier Georgakakis and Jay Rowell: Palgrave Macmillan, 2013).

Mike Wallace is Professor of Public Management at Cardiff Business School, UK. He researches the process of managing public service change, recently investigating the role of leadership development initiatives to facilitate politically driven reform. He has a special interest in understanding the ambiguities and ironies that such change generates, and strategies for coping with them.

Karel Williams is Professor at Manchester Business School and Director of the ESRC-funded Centre for Research in Socio Cultural Change (CRESC) where he has led the remaking capitalism work programme. As well collaborative work on financialization, he has jointly edited *Remembering Elites* (Wiley, 2008) with Mike Savage. His current interests include the development of the foundational economy programme of work, involving local authority and other partners.

Hugh Willmott is Research Professor in Organization Studies, Cardiff Business School, and previously held professorial appointments at the UMIST (now Manchester Business School) and the Judge Business School, Cambridge. He co-founded the International Labour Process Conference and the International Critical Management Studies Conference. He currently serves on the board of Organization Studies and Journal of Management Studies, and he is an Associate Editor of Academy of Management Review. Full details can be found on his homepage: https://sites.google.com/site/hughwillmottshomepage

Sibel Yamak is Professor of Management at Galatasaray University. She has a doctorate degree in Organization Theory from Bogaziçi University, Istanbul. Her publications which focus on business elites, top management teams, governance and corporate social performance have been published in peer-reviewed journals such as *British Journal of Management, Group and Organization Management* and *Strategic Management Journal*. She is the associate editor of European Management Review and vice president of European Academy of Management.